The Making of
the Arab–Israeli Conflict,
1947–51

THE MAKING
OF THE
ARAB–ISRAELI
CONFLICT
1947–51

Ilan Pappé

I.B.Tauris & Co Ltd
Publishers
London ● New York

Published in 1992 by
I.B.Tauris & Co Ltd
45 Bloomsbury Square
London WC1A 2HY

175 Fifth Avenue
New York
NY 10010

In the United States of America
and Canada distributed by
St Martin's Press
175 Fifth Avenue
New York
NY 10010

A CIP record for this book is available from the British Library

Library of Congress catalog card number available
A full CIP record is available from the Library of Congress

ISBN 1–85043–357–7

Printed and bound in Great Britain by
WBC Limited, Bridgend, Mid Glamorgan.

Acknowledgements

Anna Enayat, Albert Hourani, Roger Louis, Roger Owen and Avi Shlaim read extensive parts of the book and without their constructive criticism and moral support it would have been impossible to produce this book. Dick Bruggeman, Judy Mabro and Revital Sel'a have assisted in editing and stylizing the text and bringing it to its present form. To all of them and to all the Palestinian and Israeli friends who have patiently listened to my long monologues and loud pondering about the book, and who were willing to share with me their opinions and thoughts, I dedicate this work.

Contents

Preface

The declassification of new archival material in and outside the Middle East has unleashed a spate of scholarly works about the formative years of the Arab–Israeli conflict. The periodization and timing of this historiographical development is determined by the 'Thirty Years' secrecy act common to Britain and Israel which allows historians to update their accounts periodically. This has meant, *inter alia*, that by 1978 historians of the conflict were in a position to scrutinize new material concerning the war of 1948. Once this fresh evidence had been gathered, together with new historical data made available in other parts of the world, a revised history of the war began to emerge.

The new historians benefit first and foremost from the declassification of relevant documents in the British Public Record Office and the Israeli State Archives. Some have also tried to complete the historical puzzle by considering the British and Israeli evidence along with similar material in the American and French archives. Although these two countries have different regulations for declassification, most of their available material on the subject has been released since 1978. Moreover, in the late 1970s and early 1980s Arab scholars, and in particular Palestinian historians, have begun publishing their accounts of, and views on, the war of 1948. Based mainly on Arab material, such as diaries, letters and memoranda of all kinds, their works also contribute to the new historical picture of the war. Finally, various Palestinian documentation centres in the West Bank and Lebanon contain material which adds to our knowledge and understanding.

Considering the richness and originality of the material, it is obvious why the historiographical portrait of the war required drastic change. The transformation of our views has also been

aided by the passage of time; since the Arab–Israeli conflict is an
on-going process, our knowledge and understanding of its origins
and direction benefit from this new perspective.

The aim of this book is first to present the reader with a new
history of the war of 1948. Since in the process of this war a local
dispute between Arabs and Jews in Palestine turned into the
regional Arab–Israeli conflict, my intention is to provide a
historically accurate account of the formative years of that conflict
(1948 to 1949), by integrating new archival material with the
findings of the most recent scholarly works on the subject as well as
valuable accounts of the war written before the opening of the
archives.

The newly available material has served to demolish many
myths and misconceptions – to the extent that one scholar
considered it sufficient for his account of the war simply to
enumerate one shattered myth after another.[1] Wherever necessary
I shall refer to these myths and misconceptions, although my
purpose is a different one. Assisted by hindsight, I shall suggest
that the historian of the war should pay less attention to its
military development and instead address the political aspects.
There are two good reasons for adopting this approach. First, it
now seems clear that the fate of the war was decided by the
politicians on both sides prior to the actual confrontation on the
battlefield. Secondly, the failure of the parties to reach a
comprehensive peace in Palestine immediately after the war is the
main reason for the present Arab–Israeli conflict. While I do not
wish to underrate the importance of certain military campaigns, it
is my contention that most of them belong to the microhistory of
the war and that the outcome of each of the major confrontations
can be explained – some would even argue better explained – by
the success or failure of the political negotiations preceding the
war.

There is an additional reason, and a most important one, for
focusing on the political and diplomatic aspects of those formative
years of the conflict. From the work of those who have dealt with
the history of the war it is clear that it is more than just a sequence
of events: it is often a source of inspiration, particularly for the
historian who is living through the processes of the history he or
she is writing. It may be helpful here to recall the dictum which
E.H. Carr derived from the Italian philosopher of history, Bendetto
Croce, that history 'consists essentially in seeing the past in the

eyes of the present and in the light of its problems, and that the main work of the historian is not to record, but to evaluate'.[2] I shall therefore record the events of the war as accurately as possible but I shall also, when necessary, comment upon their relevance for the conflict today. The relevance for the present of past events will dictate selection from the vast sea of facts which constitute the history of 1948 and 1949. It follows that the book makes no claim to present a definitive and complete history of the war, but attempts to cover all the major political processes involved, and to trace their implication for the development of the Arab–Israeli conflict.

Finally, a note on the choice of an adequate name for the first Arab–Israeli war. Arabs and Jews describe the same event in contradictory ways. For the Arabs – and in particular the Palestinians – the events of 1948 are the *Nakba* or *Karitha*, terms that both signify in one way or another catastrophe, trauma and disaster. For the Jews – and in particular the Israelis – the war was a war of independence and 1948 is for them a year of miraculous and glorious events, the most notable being the creation of the state of Israel. I have chosen to call the war by its calendar name – the war of 1948.

The names given by Jews and Arabs point to two different historical approaches, both somewhat narrow but none the less legitimate. They clearly indicate that a proper historical treatment of the war of 1948 is a difficult task. When writing this account I have often thought of Lord Acton's instructions to the contributors to the 1906 edition of the Cambridge Modern History: 'Our Waterloo must be one that satisfies French and English.'[3] It seems inevitable that a scholarly, that is historically accurate, account of the war of 1948 will please neither of the adversaries and displease both.

Introduction

The Jewish National Movement and the Arab National Movement made their appearance on the historical stage simultaneously in the middle of the nineteenth century. With the arrival of the first Zionists in Palestine in the second half of the 1880s, the two movements were for the first time brought into direct confrontation. At this time Palestine was still part of the vast Ottoman Empire and the success or failure of the early Jewish settlers depended to a large extent on Istanbul's policy. Arab reaction in Palestine or elsewhere in the Middle East had only a marginal, if any, effect on Ottoman policy. From the onset of the Jewish attempt to settle in Palestine, the Ottoman government and Sultan Abd al-Hamid II (1875–1908), who was to be the last effective ruler of the Ottoman dynasty, had adopted a negative attitude towards Zionism. When the Young Turks came to power (in the Ottoman Empire) in 1908 they continued the same policy, fearing – like the Sultan before them – that Zionism was yet another vehicle for European ambitions in the Middle East and another way of undermining Istanbul's position there. In addition, the Zionist settlers were mainly from Russia and were perceived by the Turks as potential allies of the Russian Empire – whose ambitions in the Balkans and in the northern regions of Anatolia constituted one of the major external threats to the Ottoman Empire.

However, the last phase of Ottoman rule was marked by political instability and by the central government's inability to impose its will on the various districts of Ottoman Palestine. By means of bribery and other forms of persuasion the energetic heads of the embryonic Zionist movement succeeded in circumventing the categorical opposition of the Ottoman government to the settlement of Jews in Palestine. Thus, it was in the late Ottoman period and despite the official policy of Sultan Abd al-Hamid II that the foundations for the Jewish homeland were laid.

If the Ottomans appeared indifferent to the Palestinian position, the Zionist leaders totally ignored it. Theodor Herzl the leader and founder of Zionism, is often quoted as having stated that Palestine 'is a land without a people for a people without a land'.[1] It was in fact not Herzl but Israel Zangwill, one of the forefathers of the Zionist movement, who had said this in 1901.[2] Nevertheless, it is quite clear that, like other Zionists, Herzl was unaware of or gave little thought to the indigenous Palestinian population. When the first Jewish settlers tried to purchase land and settle they were immediately made very much aware of the presence of Palestinians in the 'Promised Land'. The first group of settlers to arrive in Palestine were young Russian intellectuals, called the 'Billuim. They had faced Arab indignation and hostility, since their arrival in 1883, and attributed this to the xenophobic attitude of Arabs everywhere. Nevertheless, we also possess ample historical evidence of a hospitable and generous Arab reception given to many of the new immigrant settlers.[3] It was only towards the end of the 1880s that reports emerged of increasing communal friction over questions of water exploitation, pastoral territory, harvesting, and so on. The first notable violent clash between indigenous Arab and Jewish settlers occurred on 29 March 1886, in the coastal strip. Arab villagers from Yahudiya attacked Petach Tikva, the oldest Jewish settlement (founded in 1878). This set the stage for attacks in other parts of Palestine and led to the first organized Palestinian protests against Jewish settlement efforts.

In 1893, Tahir al-Husayni, the Mufti of Jerusalem and one of the leaders of the Muslim community of Palestine – more than 75 per cent of Palestinians were Muslims – began to campaign against Jewish settlement and immigration. He regarded the attempts of the Jews to buy land and enlarge their numbers in Palestine as a direct threat to the Arab community there, a perception which has since been shared by many other members of the Husayni family. Tahir's son Hajj Amin al-Husayni, who became the Mufti of Jerusalem in 1920, succeeded not only to the post but also to the ideology of his father and continued the campaign against Zionism on a national basis.

Thus almost from the beginning the focus was on the land. Each purchase by the Jews was seen by many Palestinians as another step towards the realization of the Zionist dream – a dream whose fulfilment in their eyes could only bring harm to the Palestinians. Around 1910–11, intellectuals and journalists in Palestine and the Arab world at large began writing about the national conflict, and focused predominantly on the question of land.[4] Jewish activists in Palestine expressed themselves in similar terms on the conflict. In 1911 the dispute was aggravated by the struggle over employment. 'Hebrew Work' (*'Avoda 'Ivrit*) became the Zionist slogan of the day and Jews consciously competed with local Arabs for the few jobs available in the towns. While in 1910 this was no more than an attempt – and not a very successful one – at replacing Arab agricultural workers in Jewish farms and settlements with new Jewish immigrants, the problem would become more acute in the 1920s.

We have stressed these particular problems because as the Jewish presence in Palestine expanded, so the Zionist demands for land increased and exacerbated the struggle for work. In the 1930s, increased Jewish immigration into Palestine as a result of the rise of Nazism and Fascism in Europe engendered a growing sense of fear and indignation among the Palestinians, which culminated in the Arab Revolt of 1936–39.

Palestine came under British rule at the end of 1918. General Allenby, commander of the Egyptian Expeditionary Force, occupied the former Ottoman provinces of Palestine following a severe and bloody battle against Gamal Pasha, commanding the Fourth Turkish Army. Four hundred years of Ottoman rule and nearly a millennium of Muslim domination thus came to an end. The British established a military administration in Palestine as they had done elsewhere in the areas of the Arab Middle East occupied by the allies after the First World War. According to an understanding the British had reached with the French during the war, the Sykes–Picot agreement of May 1916, Palestine was to become an international enclave and the rest of the Arab Middle East was divided into either British or French spheres of influence. Yet, when in September 1919 the prime ministers of Britain and France, David Lloyd George and Georges Clemenceau, concurred on the revision of the Sykes–Picot accord, Palestine fell into Britain's orbit. In the course of their meeting in Deauville, France, Clemenceau, unwillingly and according to some accounts angrily, ceded Palestine and the Vilayet of Mosul to Britain.[5] The idea of Palestine becoming an international region was given up and

Mosul passed from French into British hands. In return, the British reiterated their support for French control over Syria and Lebanon as specified in the Sykes–Picot agreement. While the French seemed to have gained very little from the revision of the agreement, there were two strong arguments for giving in to British pressure. First, there were as yet hardly any French troops stationed in the Arab territories and, secondly, Clemenceau could not afford to lose Britain's goodwill in the discussion at the peace conference over the fate of Germany and Europe. Thus, when the last session of the peace conference convened in San Remo in April 1920, Britain was granted a mandate over Palestine and the military administration was duly replaced by a mandatory government later that year.

The Palestine mandate's charter included both the Balfour Declaration, which had been signed on 2 November 1917 and contained a vague British undertaking concerning the establishment of a Jewish home in Palestine; and the twenty-second clause of the League of Nations' Covenant, which bestowed upon Britain the 'sacred trust of civilization' to help Palestine achieve full independence. According to this clause the purpose of the mandate system was to assist the former Ottoman provinces of the Middle East to become independent states. It was to this end that the League appointed France and Britain, the victorious allies on the Middle East front, as the mandatory powers under whose guidance and supervision the newly-formed states were to progress towards full independence.[6] The United States had also been entitled to a mandatory role, but its withdrawal from world politics in 1920 – owing to increasing isolationist trends in Congress – left the arena to the two colonial European powers.

The borders of mandatory Palestine, first drawn up in the Sykes–Picot agreement, were given their definitive shape during lengthy and tedious negotiatons by British and French officials between 1919 and 1922. The two main problems were the northern and eastern borders – the southern border was an 'internal' British matter, as Egypt was under British influence, and the boundary which had been agreed upon in 1907, during the Ottoman period, remained intact. In the north, questions of water resources, strategic routes, and economic considerations determined the final delineation of the border. Since these borders have been of such fundamental importance throughout the Arab–Israeli conflict, it is worth remembering that in October 1919 the British envisaged the area that is today southern Lebanon and most of southern Syria as being part of British mandatory Palestine. Considerations of a wider colonial nature led the British to give this up and it was the officials of the Colonial Office and the Foreign Office Middle East Committee who in the end determined the territorial framework of Palestine.[7]

In the east, matters were more complicated. The difficulties arose from the debate about the future of Transjordan. This land, much of it barren and uninhabited, was part of the Ottoman province of Damascus which in the Sykes–Picot agreement had been allocated to the French. However, Sharif Husayn, the head of the Hashemite family of the Hijaz and Britain's ally in the war against the Turks, had been led to believe by London that Syria, or at least part of it, could become an independent Arab state after the war. This British pledge was included in a secret correspondence between Husayn and MacMahon, the British High Commissioner of Egypt, which had preceded the Sykes–Picot accord. As a dynasty, the Hashemites were to play an important role in the war of 1948 and the subsequent peace negotiations.

Originally from the Hijaz, the Hashemites were a noble clan, descendants of the Prophet Muhammad, who had been granted by the Ottomans the privilege of guarding the two holiest places for Islam, Mecca and Medina. In return for their assistance in the war against the Turks, they had been promised by the British a share in the control over some of the Arab areas previously controlled by the Ottomans. This was the gist of the Husayn–MacMahon correspondence – a vague, unclear agreement (in the eyes of most historians unintentionally so) which in fact contradicted the British understanding with the French about the future of the Arab Middle East.[8]

The British government was divided in its attitude towards the Hashemites. Eli Kedourie has claimed that the pro-Hashemite school in the British government caused Britain to commit one mistake after another in its Middle East policy, mistakes which would prove to be tantamount to voluntary suicide. That is, Britain, in spite of its ability at the time to impose any settlement it wished, had allowed local Arab leaders to gain control in areas which were vital to the British Empire.[9] After their occupation of Damascus in December 1918, the British allowed one of Husayn's sons, Faysal, to establish himself as the *de facto* ruler of Syria, later known as 'Greater Syria', which included Syria, Lebanon and

Transjordan. Though Faysal aspired to Palestine as well, it formed no part of Greater Syria. Thus, during this short-lived kingdom Palestine's eastern border was basically the river Jordan. However, the British Foreign Office, which at the time had no particular pro-Hashemite inclination, ruled in favour of a French Syria, thereby facilitating the conclusion of the Deauville agreement. Palestine's border was once more shifted into the Syrian desert and Britain's mandate was extended to include Transjordan (roughly today's Jordan excluding the West Bank).

The British army withdrew from Damascus at the end of 1919 and Faysal's Syrian army was left to confront the French forces which meanwhile had moved from the coast of Lebanon towards Syria. After the battle of Maysalun in July 1920, the kingdom of 'Greater Syria' became a French mandate within a matter of hours. Having fled to Haifa, Faysal was presented by the British with the offer of becoming king of Iraq instead of Syria – although, the former Arab officers in the Ottoman army promised the throne of Iraq to Faysul's brother, Abdullah. However, the British were the masters of the game and could move the Hashemites around like pawns on a chessboard. For the time being, the decision makers preferred to keep Abdullah a king without a kingdom and to secure the vacancy in Baghdad for his younger brother Faysal. Abdullah was relegated to the position of foreign secretary in his father's court in the Hijaz – which had been recognized as an independent state after the war.

Naturally, Abdullah was not content for long with this reduction in his position and, according to the latest biography, he also felt that the Hijaz was not a safe place for the Hashemites, being threatened by its neighbours on the south (the Idris of Asir) and its enemies in the east (the Saudis of Najd).[10] Abdullah was particularly aware of the Saudi threat, as he himself was responsible for the Hashemites' defeat in the battle against Ibn Saud in Turaba in May 1919. At the end of 1920 he recruited about 1,000 men and together with their families embarked on a long journey from the Hijaz into Transjordan, declaring his intention of redeeming Damascus from the French.[11]

There have been various historiographical attempts to explain Abdullah's decision to set out on this military expedition. Some believe that he did indeed intend to retrieve Syria, while others see him as a shrewd politician who had decided on this drastic step in order to gain a solid foothold (and possibly a kingdom), as far as possible from the political quicksands of Arabia. It does seem that the experienced Hashemite prince believed for a while that he could fare better than his brother in a military confrontation with the French.

Whatever the case, Abdullah made his way to Damascus in the winter of 1920–21 and the British authorities allowed him and his followers to stay in Transjordan for fear of complicating the Anglo–French relationship and because, even if they had wanted to do so, they lacked the forces to expel him. British officials ultimately succeeded in convincing the secretary of state for the colonies, Winston Churchill, that Hashemite rule in Transjordan would on the whole benefit Britain. Not only was it the cheapest way of controlling this relatively unimportant area, it could also serve as a form of compensation to the Hashemites for the loss of Damascus.[12]

Over time, the British came increasingly to depend on the Hashemites to keep things calm along the potentially troubling border of Palestine – settling Abdullah in Transjordan was as much a British interest as a Hashemite one. For the Zionists, the Hashemite presence in Transjordan signalled a very clear limitation on the area of Jewish settlement in Palestine – given that the Balfour Declaration which encouraged Jews to settle in 'Palestine', did not define its territorial boundaries.

For these reasons, Churchill decided to gather his Middle East experts in Cairo in March 1921 in order to discuss and set down British policy towards the area. Among other things, it was decided to allow Abdullah a trial period of six months as ruler of Transjordan. He must have passed the test because he never relinquished his kingdom until his death in 1951 by assassination.

The resolution of Hashemite ambitions in Transjordan raised the problem of a British promise previously made to the Jewish National Movement, Zionism. The Balfour Declaration of 2 November 1917, albeit in vague terms, granted the Jews the right to build their homeland in Palestine. Accordingly, when Palestine had become British, the Zionists expected Britain to set up a mandatory regime which would have as its immediate purpose the implementation of the declaration. Most Zionists at that time regarded Transjordan as part of biblical Palestine. However, with a Jewish community in Palestine constituting only one–tenth of the general population, most members of the Zionist leadership, which was both Anglophile and pragmatic, did not object to the creation

of a Hashemite entity in Transjordan. Because of this acquiescence, Vladimir Jabotinski, heading a group of more extreme
Zionists, seceded from the main stream of Zionism – thus creating
a rift which affects Israeli politics to this very day.

The Zionist acceptance of the new arrangement allowed
Churchill to proceed with the plans he had worked out in Cairo. It
should be noted that his decision to let Abdullah stay in
Transjordan stemmed from a disinclination to confront him
directly in Amman, as well as from his belief that the Hashemite
presence in Transjordan would facilitate British control over the
various Bedouin tribes in the region who traditionally rejected any
form of central government. It is also possible that he saw it as a
means of satisfying some of the Hashemite demands and of refuting
their allegation that Britain had betrayed its promises.[13]

The separation of Transjordan from Palestine in September 1922
did not alter the course or the development of the Arab–Jewish
conflict in western Palestine. Since the proclamation of the
mandate in July 1922 the crux of the matter was the contradiction
between the theory and reasoning of the mandate system on the
one hand, and the existing reality in Palestine on the other.
According to the mandate, Britain was responsible for the advance
of the country towards independence, but this also included the
Balfour Declaration with its vague commitment to a future Jewish
home in Palestine. Over time, these two aims were to prove
irreconcilable. There was not only the demographic situation,
namely the fact that the Jews in Palestine constituted only one-
tenth of the entire population, but also, and more importantly, the
emergence of an Arab Palestinian National Movement which
demanded independence for Palestine as contained in the charter.
During the first ten years of the mandate, the British government
still hoped that despite their conflicting interests the two
communities would be influenced by British power and authority
and would accept coexistence.

In 1926 the Jewish leadership, following a new wave of
immigration from Poland in the wake of pogroms there in 1924,
began to purchase considerable tracts of land in Palestine. As had
happened in the 1890s, the extraordinary increase in immigration
and land purchase alerted the Palestinians; and as in the early
years of the century, the Jewish slogan 'Hebrew labour' was again
perceived as a direct threat to Arab livelihood in Palestine.

The eruption of violence between Arabs and Jews in 1929

brought home to the British that Palestine might be more of a burden than a strategic asset. From 1930 onwards the British made a series of attempts to resolve the conflict, ranging from the partitioning of the country to its cantonization. Since the Arab Palestinian leadership hoped that Arab involvement and a basically pro-Arab Foreign Office would lead Britain to repudiate the Balfour Declaration and to consent to the establishment of a unitary Arab state in Palestine, they rejected most of the schemes. The Jews in Palestine, under Ben Gurion's leadership, accepted most of the plans, as in one way or another they all included a recognition of the right of the Jews to a state of their own.

The Jewish edifice in Palestine meanwhile was growing both in numbers and scope, and Palestinians became increasingly aware of the threats described by Hajj Amin al-Husayni. Bolder and less restricted than in the 1920s, the Jewish immigration and purchase of land reached record levels in the 1930s. With Hitler in Germany now openly advocating the expulsion of the Jewish people and Mussolini in Italy following suit, the Arab position on the necessity for a solution paled in importance when juxtaposed with the immediate need to save Jews from the onslaught in Europe and build a safe haven for them. By the mid-1930s the Jews formed one-third of the population in Palestine, a formidable minority which still enjoyed the blessing of the Balfour Declaration.

Despair at British policy pushed the Arab leaders in 1936 into a direct revolt against the Palestine government, which lasted for three years. Initially this involved regular strikes but it soon became guerrilla warfare directed against British installations in Palestine and involving Arab volunteers from Syria and Iraq as well as a supportive, at times coerced, rural Palestinian periphery (the urban population was the more nationalist and thus the more active in the revolt). Through the mediation of three Arabs rulers, Ibn Saud of Saudi Arabia, Faruq of Egypt and Abdullah of Transjordan, Britain consented in 1939 to a change in its policy in Palestine.

This new policy was embodied in the White Paper of 1939. Notorious in the eyes of many Jewish and Israeli historians, it promised the repudiation of the Balfour Declaration and severe restrictions on Jewish immigration and purchase of land. By that time, however, Britain was fully preoccupied by the war in Europe, and the Jewish organization in Palestine launched illegal immigration and settlement operations.

While in the early years of the war the Palestinians deluded themselves that Rommel's advance in North Africa heralded a new era in the Middle East which would be favourable to the Arabs, the Jews sided with the Allies, without even temporarily abandoning their political aspirations in Palestine. In this the Zionist leaders were attempting the impossible: co-operating with the British against the Nazis while at the same time preparing themselves for a possible conflict with Britain in the post-war period. Even before Germany was fully defeated an open confrontation between the Jewish underground and the British army had erupted at the end of 1944. It was the new Labour government in Britain, which had won the general election in July 1945, that had to face this confrontational Jewish policy.

The task of determining Britain's Palestine policy after 1945 was entrusted to the new foreign secretary, Ernest Bevin. In his first news conference, Bevin displayed considerable optimism about the chances of solving the conflict. His party had presented a pro-Zionist viewpoint during the election campaign and the Zionists therefore expected that Britain would now adopt a less hostile attitude towards them. Although a prominent Labour politician, Bevin was a most conservative foreign secretary who in his attitude both towards the Eastern bloc and the former British Empire hardly deviated from traditional British interests. He maintained a similar policy to that of the previous government – trying to appease the Arab world's apprehensions by limiting both Jewish immigration into Palestine and the purchase of land. Like his predecessors, Bevin proposed a number of solutions which this time were rejected not only by the Palestinians but also by the Zionists.

The first and most important effort to solve the conflict during Bevin's time was made by the Anglo–American committee which took up the question of Palestine at the end of 1945 and during 1946. On 31 August 1945, moved by the plight of the Jewish Holocaust survivors, the American president, Harry S. Truman, had pressured the British government to allow the immediate immigration of 100,000 Jews from Europe into Palestine. The British foreign secretary responded by suggesting the establishment of a joint Anglo–American committee of inquiry, which was to search for a solution to the situation of the Jewish survivors and at the same time to comment on a settlement of the Arab–Jewish conflict in Palestine.

Bevin's initially favourable response to the American initiative stemmed from his desire to involve the United States more actively in the question of Palestine. After the Second World War, the American isolationist policy had been replaced by a drive to defend and further the Western bloc's interests *vis-à-vis* the Soviet Union. This led to the creation of the famous Anglo–American alliance, of which Bevin was undoubtedly one of the main architects. For obvious reasons, he tried to take advantage of this new transatlantic common purpose in order to advance the chances of a solution in Palestine. Moreover, he believed that such an alliance would mitigate the influence of American Jewry on the White House, which he saw as the primary cause for the lack of unity in the two powers' policy towards Palestine. While most historians would claim that Bevin overrated the importance of the American Zionists both in the United States itself and in Palestine, he did correctly calculate the effect of the American administration on Zionist policy.[14] The Americans were critical of Bevin's attitude to Zionist aspirations but they themselves failed to offer an alternative course of action; in fact they were unwilling to share the burden of solving the problem.

In any case, six 'non-official citizens' of each country participated in the Anglo–American committee which set out for Palestine and Europe at the beginning of 1946.[15] The proceedings of this committee and its conclusions belong in some way to the account of the 1948 war, for they mark the beginning of the diplomatic struggle between the Palestinians and the Zionists over the sympathy and understanding of world public opinion. Not a mere abstract term, world public opinion had its forum and its institution: the United Nations, a supra-national body created in 1945 by the victorious Allies in order to solve international problems and precisely such regional conflicts as the Palestine question. Since the success of the Zionists at this early stage was to give them an important advantage in the next phases of the diplomatic battle, it will be described here in some detail.

The committee began its inquiry by touring the displaced persons camps in Europe and only then moved to Palestine. The main reason for the Zionist success was the impact of the Holocaust on the committee's members. Delegates from the Jewish community in Palestine persuaded many of the camps' dwellers to adopt a pro-Zionist view. The Jewish survivors all spoke about their wish to emigrate to Palestine: 'Most of the DPs who did not initially wish to go to Palestine were persuaded quite easily that for the sake of the majority they should present a united Jewish front to the committee.'[16]

When the committee arrived in Palestine it was warmly welcomed by the Jews and boycotted by the Arab Higher Committee. This tilted the committee to the Jewish side and it was also impressed by the military strength of the Jews and their achievements in expanding their settlements.[17] After the visit to Palestine most committee members agreed with the Zionists that the demographic situation of the Jews in Europe had to be linked with that of the Jewish settlement in Palestine.[18] In fact, the committee accepted the Zionist contention that one should take into account not only the size of the Jewish and Arab communities in Palestine itself but also the possibility of an imminent Jewish mass immigration to the country.

This point of view was taken by the American members of the committee to Washington. Historians differ in their explanations of the American refusal to co-operate with the British. Some assert that the Zionist movement benefited from frictions between the USA and Britain on various global matters, which pushed the American administration into a more pro-Zionist attitude.[19] Others emphasize that Truman's sincere concern for the plight of European Jewry played an important role in the pro-Zionist policy of his administration. Michael Cohen points out that 'Truman also had other, more mundane reasons for airing his sympathies for the Jewish victims. As a non-elected president eager to succeed in his own right, and indeed, as a highly unpopular president during his first term, Truman could hardly have failed to be less than hypersensitive' to this question.[20] Moreover, as shown by recent research, even the non-Zionist Jewish organizations in the USA – notably the American Jewish Congress – gave the committee and the administration the impression that, on practical grounds, they would support the idea of the establishment of a Jewish state.[21]

The association that had been forged in the minds of the committee's members between the fate of the displaced persons in Europe and that of the Jews in Palestine, is a vital factor in the understanding of the role played by the Holocaust in the creation of the state of Israel. Israeli historians today do not deny this link: 'There is much to be said for this thesis. Compassion for the victims of Nazism and the survivors languishing in the DP camps undoubtedly played an integral, albeit intangible role in the psyches of postwar politicians.'[22]

On 30 April 1946 the Anglo–American committee concluded its work. Its first recommendation to the two governments was to allow the admission into Palestine of 100,000 Jews from the DP camps in Europe. The second recommendation could only have pleased a marginal Jewish faction called 'Brit Shalom'; the committee suggested the establishment of a binational state under a UN trusteeship and offering equal rights to both communities. By the time the recommendations were made public both the Jews and the Arabs in Palestine had moved on to far more ambitious aspirations. The committee's proposals were subsequently rejected by the British government. Yet, the first recommendation certainly indicated a significant shift in Western public opinion and must have pleased the Zionist leaders.

This was the state of affairs when the two powers decided to rethink the failed recommendations of the Anglo–American committee by appointing two representatives, Britain's Herbert Morrison and the American diplomat Henry F. Grady, to yet another committee of inquiry. The Morrison–Grady committee suggested the division of Palestine into four provinces under international auspices and the British government invited both sides to participate in a joint conference to discuss the new scheme. Dividing the apple into four, however, was as unappealing to the Palestinians and the Jews as dividing it into two, and only the Arab states sent their representatives to take part in negotiations with the British. Without the participation of the directly interested parties, the conference remained a futile diplomatic overture.

Bevin's obvious dissatisfaction with the Anglo–American committee's conclusion and his disappointment at the parties' attitude towards the Morrison–Grady proposal led to one last British attempt to solve the conflict.[23] This was Bevin's own brain-child, and formed a compromise between the tendency of his Foreign Office to support the Arab demand for a unitary state and the determination of the new secretary for the colonies, Arthur Creech-Jones, to back the idea of partition. The Foreign Office based its stance on the 76th clause of the UN Charter which supported the right of independence for any nation which desired it. Independence would be implemented according to democratic principles, such as majority rule. In 1947 the Arabs constituted more than 65 per cent of the population of Palestine and had therefore won

Foreign Office support. Creech-Jones, on the other hand, while accepting the adherence to democratic values, claimed that not one Zionist, however moderate, would accept such a solution. He also stressed the British, and in particular the Labour Party's commitment to the Zionist movement. Bevin had to navigate between these two contradictory opinions and his compromise solution, introduced at the beginning of 1947, consisted of provincial autonomy in Palestine – that is, he suggested the cantonization of Palestine under British trusteeship. He accepted the plea to admit 100,000 Jews, but favoured doing so in stages – 4000 Jews every month over a period of two years.[24]

Bevin's plan was presented to a conference in London, attended by both Zionists and Arab Palestinians, but neither side accepted the proposals. It was not possible to bridge the gap as the Jewish leadership in Palestine 'would consider no solution other than partition' while the Arab leadership 'would settle for nothing less than immediate independence in the whole of Palestine'. Therefore, 'No amount of British pleading or British pressure could bridge the gap between the two sides.'[25]

The inability to find an acceptable solution, the increase in Jewish operations against British personnel and installations in Palestine, a particularly cold winter in the British Isles coupled with shortages of coal and bread, an economic crisis brought about by the American demand for a return with high interest of the funds transferred to Britain as financial assistance during the Second World War – all these developments contributed to the realization that the Palestine problem was insoluble, and led the British cabinet to submit it into other hands.

Strategic considerations played the most important part in this decision. For Prime Minister Clement Attlee, Palestine had become 'an economic and military liability,' as had been India and therefore, 'in the aftermath of the transfer of power in India, he began more and more to apply the same formula to Palestine.'[26] In India, the British succeeded in fixing a date for the evacuation and secured a prior inter-communal agreement. The Indian solution thus played a prominent part in the evolution of the thought of the prime minister.

Other historiographical explanations are also possible. Whereas there are Israeli and Arab historians who suspect that London did not wish to withdraw completely from Palestine but contemplated returning there with the help of the UN and the USA, British historians assert that Bevin was a competent statesman, who decided at the right moment to channel his energy and efforts to the emerging cold war in Europe and abandon minor concerns such as Palestine.[27] There are also those who trace the origin of the British decision back to the early 1940s.[28]

One might add the version of the official historians of right-wing Israeli political movements, who feel that their pre-state underground organizations had played a decisive role in forcing the British out of Palestine. As a partial explanation it can certainly be supported academically. British policy was undoubtedly affected by underground terrorism. The Jewish extremists' killing of British soldiers had created an unbearable atmosphere for a continued British presence in the country. However, it is doubtful whether this in itself would have persuaded Britain to abandon Palestine.[29]

Nevertheless, by February 1947 all concerned realized that the British mandate was at an end. As to who would rule Palestine after the British withdrawal, this question was left to the United Nations. The UN Charter included a pledge by the independent nations of the world to support the right of self-determination. The Charter also expressed the hope for peace on the part of a tired and wounded world. This was particularly difficult to achieve in regions where two national movements clashed over the same area of land.

1

The Diplomatic Battle: UN Discussions, February 1947–May 1948

UNSCOP

In February 1947 the question of Palestine was entrusted to the United Nations. The organization was then two years old and had as yet very little experience in the solving of regional conflicts. The major issue at the time, the fate of Germany, was discussed by the four big powers of the day, the USSR, the USA, Britain and France. The UN took no part in these negotiations, though it had been established precisely for this purpose: the preamble to the Charter of the UN begins with the declaration that the organization was determined to 'save succeeding generations from the scourge of war,' and its first article states the duty of maintaining international peace and security, a task to be achieved by solving international conflicts. Since the Second World War had ended with more than one regional conflict in its wake, from its inception the organization was called upon to fulfil the promises included in the Charter. Its first mission, which it accomplished successfully, was to secure the withdrawal of Soviet troops from Iran. Palestine was to be its first major challenge.

The machinery for solving regional conflicts was there in theory, but a period of trial and error was required before the realization that it was of little use without the force of sanction. In its early days the UN was also hampered by the fact that it had almost instantly become a battleground for the two superpowers (each with its camp of followers), and the chance of a successful UN intervention depended upon the degree of agreement between the two. In order to precipitate a solution to some of the problems arising from this bipolar international system, it was agreed to assign the task of maintaining international peace and security to the members of the Security Council – which consisted of five permanent members, representing the five big powers, and six non-permanent members, representing, in turn, different geographical areas of the world.

Thus, in February 1947, the Security Council was asked to investigate the question of Palestine. Following the British example but not learning from its shortcomings, the Council decided to send an inquiry commission to Palestine, and on 2 April 1947. Britain asked the UN Secretary-General to summon a special session of the General Assembly for the creation of a commission to study the Palestine situation and to submit a report on it to the organization.[1] Trygve Lie, the Secretary-General, objected to the convention of a full session of the Assembly and instead transferred the issue to the Political Committee of the UN, an *ad hoc* committee representing the various regions and alliances in the organization. It was agreed that the inquiry commission to be established should complete its work by September 1947 and prepare a final report for the General Assembly session scheduled for that month.[2]

The special session of the Political Committee lasted two weeks, from 29 April to 15 May 1947, and was entirely devoted to the question of the composition of the inquiry commission – there was obviously a need for a fair representation of Soviet and American interests, as well as those of Britain as the ex-mandatory power.

At the end of the two weeks, the Political Committee decided on the establishment of the United Nations Special Committee on Palestine (UNSCOP) which was to have eleven members. The chairman was Judge Emil Sandström from Sweden, who thereby opened a long history of Swedish mediation in the Arab–Israeli conflict which was to end only with Gunnar Jarring's mission to the area in the late 1960s. The secretary was a young American, Ralph Bunche, who will feature prominently in the chapters on the armistice negotiations. The other members came from Australia and Canada, representing the British Commonwealth; Holland, which jointly with Sweden represented Western Europe; Czechoslovakia and Yugoslavia from Eastern Europe; India and Iran from Asia, the latter representing the Muslim world; and Uruguay, Guatemala and Peru from Latin America representing the interests of the Holy See. The fact that ultimately none of the permanent members of the Council were included in the committee can be explained in two ways. According to the Czech delegate to the United Nations this was 'a direct result of the Great Powers' desire to withdraw from responsiblity on this very important question.'[3] A second and more plausible explanation, supported by American and British archives, was given by the Guatemalan delegate, Jorge Gracia-Granados, who said it was the result of an American design to prevent the Soviet bloc from playing a decisive role in this important part of the world.[4] The Russian suggestion that all five permanent members of the Security Council should participate in the committee was ruled out by the Americans simply because it would have meant direct Soviet involvement in determining the future of Palestine. As they enjoyed the support of a majority of pro-Western members in the organization, the Americans could secure rejection of the Russian proposal. In addition, the Holy See feared any intervention of Communism in the Holy Land and therefore guided most of the Catholic countries to support the American stance.[5]

Hence at the beginning the initiative in the UN was with the Americans. There is some irony in the fact that when the inquiry committee presented its final conclusions it was the Russians who showed the greater zeal and wholeheartedly supported the UNSCOP report. Despite the American efforts, therefore, they did have a say in shaping the UN view on the conflict. A further result of American policy was that the question of Palestine was left to inexperienced members from all parts of the world who had very little prior knowledge, if any, of the regional situation. As one of them admitted: 'It was no special knowledge on my part that led my colleagues to think of me as a member of the investigating committee. I knew very little about Palestine.'[6] This member, who in fact was totally ignorant about the region, was confident that he was chosen because of his reputation as a truth-seeker and fighter for justice. It would seem, however, that most members were chosen in order to serve the interests of one or other of the superpowers. Their ignorance about the situation in Palestine, or for that matter of the Middle East in general, became glaringly evident when the committee presented its final conclusions, in which, for example, they suggested the establishment of a Jewish state where half the population would be Arab.[7] For the small member states who otherwise had very little say in world politics, UNSCOP was a brief moment of glory, for its recommendations were accepted by the permanent members of the Security Council who, after careful scrutiny and revision, gave the final touch to the text of the subsequent UN decision.

Just before their official appointment, the committee members received their first lesson on the 'Question of Palestine'. On 28 April 1947 the UN invited spokesmen of the warring parties in Palestine to New York to appear before a special session of the Political Committee and to present the Jewish and Arab points of view. These were Abba Hillel Silver, the head of the Jewish Agency's office in New York, and Henry Cattan, a lawyer from Jerusalem and a member of the Arab Higher Committee, both highly capable advocates for their causes. Hillel insisted on the linkage between the problems of world Jewry and those of the Jewish community in Palestine, stressed the Jewish contribution to humanity and civilization and called upon the committee to acknowledge Palestine as the home of all Jews: 'Surely, the Jewish people is no less deserving than other peoples whose national freedom and independence have been established and whose representatives are now seated here.'[8] For his part, Cattan spoke of a chain of injustices, beginning with the Balfour Declaration, which the Arabs had suffered. He called for the creation of an independent and democratic Arab Palestine.[9] Cattan tried to persuade the members of the committee that their main mission was to 'enquire into the legality, validity and ethics' of the Balfour Declaration. Immediately after these representations, which already showed an almost unbridgeable gap, UNSCOP was officially established and its members left for Palestine where they intended to hear and collect the opinions of leaders on the spot.

The special session of the Political Committee ended with an unexpected speech, on 14 May 1947, by the Russian representative, Andrei Gromyko. Gromyko, who was then deputy foreign minister, declared that should the concept of a federated state prove impracticable, his government was in favour of partition as the most suitable solution for the Palestine problem.[10]

This sudden twist in Russian foreign policy came as a surprise to all involved. It is important to recall that in the political jargon of those days backing the proposal for the partition of Palestine meant favouring the establishment of a Jewish state. Those supporting partition, therefore, were considered to be pro-Zionist. This apparent shift in the hitherto anti-Zionist Russian policy, was considered by the British to be a *démarche* to seek ways of becoming involved in a possible future trusteeship settlement. The Americans, on the other hand, believed it to be part of the Russian tactic of leaving all options open and all warring parties satisfied before the situation had cleared and before having to make a final decision.[11] In view of the special relationship betwen the Zionists and the USSR in those days, the shift in Soviet policy may also have been part of their campaign to get the British expelled from the Middle East; partition may have seemed the safest and fastest way of achieving this objective.[12] Furthermore, the Anglo-Egyptian negotiations being held at the time had reached a deadlock, as a result of which Britain had to consider the possible transfer of its headquarters in the Middle East from Egypt to Palestine and this also may have postponed its decision on the evacuation of the Holy Land.[13]

While these reasons for the Russian position are interesting and important, historically speaking they pale in significance when compared with the final outcome of this shift in Soviet attitude: it effectively paved the way for Jewish independence in Palestine.[14] Recognition that the role played by the Russians was crucial in the creation of the Jewish state has important implications for the debate in Israel between 'old' and 'new' historians.[15] The previous generation of Israeli historians of the war regarded the creation of the state of Israel as a miraculous event, whose nature it was beyond the ability of an 'ordinary' historian to explain. The 'new' historians try to refute this somewhat mystical approach by pointing out historical connections and offering explanations for the events that led to the Jewish success in Palestine. One such explanation is the propitious global situation and feelings towards the Jews engendered by the Holocaust. Another is the sway of superpower interests and considerations. The USSR decision to co-operate with the Western members of the UN on the question of Palestine in 1947 was an opportunity which Jewish diplomats of the time deftly exploited and which resulted in a UN resolution regarded as favourable by the Jews and quite unacceptable by the Palestinians.[16]

Thus, aware of a pro-Zionist, American attitude and an equally benevolent policy towards the Jews by the Russians, UNSCOP's members left for Palestine in June 1947 with more than a faint idea of what the two superpowers' consensus would consider to be a desirable solution.[17]

Palestine was a country torn by war, not so much between Jews and Arabs – from 1939 after the Arab revolt had subsided, until the UN decision on Palestine in November 1947, the level of violence between the two communities remained low – but between the Jews and the mandatory authorities.[18] The main battle then being fought concerned the illegal immigration of Jewish survivors from Europe to Palestine, and this conflict was heightened by the activities of the members of two extreme Jewish underground movements. One was the National Military Organization, better known as the Irgun – 'the organization' (IZL). A paramilitary organization established in 1936, the Irgun aspired to gain Jewish control over all of Palestine and Transjordan. It called for persistent armed struggle against both the British and the Arabs and was dissatisfied with the relatively low key operations of the Hagana (the main military underground). The Irgun was particularly active between 1945 and 1947. The other group was LEHI, the Hebrew acronym for 'Israel Freedom Fighters', but better known as the 'Stern Gang' after its leader Abraham Stern. The LEHI activists seceded from the Irgun during the Second World War, when the latter, like the Hagana, decided to cease anti-British activities as long as the Allies were fighting the Nazis in Europe and North Africa. Subsequent severe retaliation against LEHI led these otherwise divided Jewish underground organizations to unite against the British, which made it possible for the Jewish Agency to continue successfully circumventing British anti-immigration measures. The British attempted to prevent Jewish immigration into Palestine until the very last day of the mandate, seeing this as the only way to maintain law and order; continued immigration would have caused, so they thought, extreme and violent reactions not only from the Palestinians but also from the Arab world at large.[19] This position was later to secure for them, and in particular for Ernest Bevin, a most unfavourable place in Israeli mythology and historiography.[20]

The British hoped that before UNSCOP reached the shores of Palestine the American government would ease the complexity of the problem by allowing more Jewish immigration into the United States from the displaced persons camps in Europe. They were encouraged in this by the initiative taken in April 1947 by Congressman William Stratton to pass legislation in the Congress that would allow a one-off immigration of 400,000 Jews to the USA. The State Department, however, and other sections in the American administration – although not the president himself – delayed this process and succeeded in blocking Jewish immigration. When the legislative process in the House was completed in

June 1948, it granted permission for immigration to non-Jewish rather than Jewish refugees.[21] To their dismay the British learned that not only was the United States pushing the Jews to Palestine, it was also doing very little to check the purchase of ships and recruitment of funds on American soil for illegal immigration; even a direct and public appeal by Prime Minister Attlee did not help to alleviate British worries.[22]

This was the political atmosphere in which UNSCOP, in July 1947, began meeting Jews and Arabs in Palestine. As we shall see, this somewhat delusive reality was to affect decisively UNSCOP's final recommendations – questions of Jewish immigration occupied an important part in their discussions and overshadowed problems relating to the ideological nature of the Palestinian–Jewish conflict.

The inquiry continued until November. Of the five intensive months UNSCOP devoted to discussing the fate of post-mandatory Palestine, only five weeks were spent in Palestine itself. Most of the discussions took place in Europe and the United States. The final outcome was the recommendation of a solution accepted by the General Assembly but rejected by the Arabs which would, in a way, lead to the war itself. However, it is important to remember that both camps had been preparing for the struggle over Palestine long before they knew about UNSCOP and its recommendations. Jews and Arabs alike regarded UNSCOP not as an arbitrating tribunal whose recommendations, in the form of UN resolutions, were to be respected and obeyed, but rather as a battleground for world public opinion. Historians concentrating on the reasons for UNSCOP's failure have often misconceived its historical function. The affair should be seen as one more stage in the diplomatic battle between the warring sides which began in 1946 with the Anglo-American Committee and ended in an impressive Jewish success.

As with the Anglo-American Committee, the visible horrors of the Holocaust would do much to reduce UNSCOP's choice when it came to decide on the question of Palestine. Also, it was not only the Jewish tragedy in Europe which directed UNSCOP along its pro-Zionist path, but also the behaviour of those Palestinians they met in Palestine itself. When UNSCOP was confronted by the Arab Higher Committee, one of its members, Jorge Gracia-Granados, described it as a 'political hierarchy ruled by a former Nazi collaborator'.[23] Granados referred here to the alliance concluded during the Second World War between the Mufti of

Jerusalem, Hajj Amin al-Husayni, and Nazi Germany's Adolf Hitler. Such prejudices against the Palestinian leaders were deepened by their decision not to co-operate with UNSCOP. The Arab Higher Committee may have sensed that the Palestinians were already facing an impossible task, and upon its arrival UNSCOP was notified of the committee's refusal to testify before it. Matters did not improve when the Arab Higher Committee staged a fifteen-hour protest strike in the country by way of reception for the committee.[24]

Ultimately, there was hardly any contact between UNSCOP and the Palestinian leadership. Palestinian historians have provided some form of explanation for the Arab Higher Committee's lack of participation in the international effort. They claim that there was no point in meeting UNSCOP's members when it was clear that the creation of an independent Arab Palestine was not the committee's objective.[25] It may seem curious that the Arab Higher Committee at the time thought it knew in advance what the recommendations of the committee would be, but the previous inquiry committees of 1946 and 1947 had taught the Palestinian leaders that their fate was to be directly affected by that of the Holocaust survivors in Europe. Even pro-Palestinians around the world could not deny that a tragedy had occurred in Europe which generated a moral imperative to allow the survivors to emigrate. The Anglo-American Committee in 1946 had hinted that Palestine should be the destination of these Jewish immigrants. The Palestinian leadership, however, lacked the pragmatism and ability to seize the historical opportunity and failed to realize that instead of rejecting it out of hand, it was better to be a party to a settlement, even a minimal one.

Aided by the official mandatory broadcasting corporation, UNSCOP toured the country in a quest for Palestinians who would be willing to represent the Arab case in Palestine.[26] When the visit to Palestine was coming to an end and no official Palestinian testimony had been heard, the committee decided after some hestiation to approach the Arab diplomatic representatives in Jerusalem in order to hear, at least for the record, the Arab point of view. While the general claims and aspirations of the Palestinians were of course known to the members, a testimony was needed to keep up the semblance of balance. After all, some members of the committee had remained unbiased and wished to consider the legal and political basis of the claims presented to them.

The committee was impressed, on the other hand, by the co-operation of the Jewish Agency and by its pragmatism. UNSCOP's members were pleasantly surprised by the Agency's apparent desire for compromise and by the willingness of most of the Zionist leaders to depart from the Biltmore programme which was then still the official policy of the Jewish Agency and included a Zionist claim to all of mandatory Palestine. The internal memoranda of the Jewish Agency, however, indicate that there was a growing consensus among the Zionist leaders about the desirability of partition.[27] David Ben Gurion appeared before the committee on 4 July 1947, and told the members that the Jews would be content with part of Palestine. His words were echoed by Chaim Weizmann who even suggested the revival of the partition suggested by the Peel Committee of 1937. The principle of partition was therefore, in a way, reintroduced to UNSCOP by the Jewish Agency in July 1947.[28] In fact, according to British reports at the time, the majority of UNSCOP members were in favour of partition at the beginning of their visit to Palestine, that is before they had even met any of the Arab representatives.[29] If this was not enough to create a favourable atmosphere for the Jews, the *Exodus* affair tipped the balance.

The *Exodus* was a Jewish refugee ship which had sailed from France to Palestine in the summer of 1947 and tried to break through the British blockade to bring its passengers ashore. The ship's arrival coincided with UNSCOP's visit. There could not have been a better demonstration of the ineluctable link between the fate of European Jewry and that of the Jewish community in Palestine. The linkage had already been acknowledged by the Anglo-American Committee in 1946, but its report had been shelved and its recommendations never followed up. Accepting the Zionist notion that Palestine was the haven and shelter for Jewish communities worldwide meant regarding the minority of Jews in Palestine as a temporary fact and expecting it to grow into a majority in due course. The British decision to capture the *Exodus* and turn it back to Germany helped UNSCOP to resolve this question. As the British historian Christopher Sykes comments: 'The clever thing to do was to allow the refugees to land as an exceptional concession made in exceptional circumstances, a procedure which the presence of UNSCOP could make perfectly natural and acceptable.'[30] In the event, the insensitive British decision prompted UNSCOP to discuss the fate of the Jewish survivors instead of the Arab demand to determine the future of Palestine according to the demographic reality of 1947. The outcome was that the committee decided to accept the link between the fate of European Jewry and that of Palestine.[31] It has been shown that American aloofness in the *Exodus* affair contributed to Britain's decision – despite Washington's interest in allowing these and other Jewish refugees to land in Palestine rather than have them queuing up on America's doorstep.[32]

This affair might have damaged Arab interests even more, had it not been for the hanging in the very same week of two British sergeants at the hands of the Irgun – the culmination of its operations against the British.[33] In February 1947 the Irgun had moved from isolated attacks on the British to large-scale operations against the 'foreign occupation of Palestine,' following LEHI's strategy. In April a British officers' club in Jerusalem had been blown up without warning – causing the death of a dozen officers. The British countered by imposing a severe curfew on central Palestine and seven Irgun activists who had been captured were executed; others were flogged and sentenced to life imprisonment. The two sergeants were kidnapped and hanged by the Irgun in retaliation. The action failed to win the sympathy of more than a small part of the Jewish community in Palestine and the Hagana condemned it as another proof that the Irgun had no moral or human inhibitions, and lacked political wisdom or responsibility for the defence of the Jewish community.

The American secretary of state, George Marshall, was more impressed by the hanging of the two British soldiers than by the *Exodus* affair, but his attitude was quite unique.[34] In the United Nations the British, and not the Jews, were seen as the villains. The tragedy of the *Exodus* and the overall British behaviour in Palestine resulted in UNSCOP moving another step towards a pro-Zionist position.

At this crucial moment in their history the Palestinians themselves were unable to unite and present a coherent stance. Moreover, the Palestinian leadership in the country had left the political initiative in the hands of the Arab League, which had its seat in Cairo, and allowed the Arab world to represent its case. This was not a new phenomenon. Since the days of the Arab revolt in the 1930s, the Palestinian cause had been fought and argued by the leaders of the Arab world. From 1945 this task had been assigned to the Political Committee of the Arab League (a body consisting of most of the Arab heads of state), which in the initial stages of UNSCOP's inquiry had ignored the Palestinian leadership's decision to boycott the committee. Such differences between the attitudes of the local and regional Arab leadership would become more apparent when the actual fighting began, but at this point a discrepancy already showed. Moreover, both in and outside the diplomatic arena the struggle was fought between the Arab world and the Jewish community, rather than between the Palestinians and the Jews. Not only before but also during the war and certainly after the fighting had stopped, the Palestinians themselves played only a very marginal role.[35]

None the less, representatives of Iraq, Saudi Arabia, Syria, Lebanon, Egypt and Yemen met UNSCOP in the Palace of the Lebanese Foreign Office on 22 July 1947.[36] These Arab representatives soon found that apart from the Indian delegate, Sir Abdul Rahman, not one member of UNSCOP could be seriously considered as pro-Arab.[37] Naturally, despair caused by the obviously biased opinions of the committee frustrated a dialogue between UNSCOP and the Arab League. However, it is doubtful whether even Sir Abdur Rahman wholeheartedly accepted the position that the Arab politicians presented in Beirut. It included a total rejection of any form of political representation for the Jews in Palestine, a refusal to allow any further Jewish immigration or purchase of land, and the creation of an independent Arab state.[38] Moreover, it is also doubtful to what extent the Arab politicians whom UNSCOP met were committed on the question of Palestine. As the diary of the then foreign minister of Syria, Adil Arslan, shows, the predominant occupation of the Arab politicians who came to Beirut was not the fate of Palestine but inter-Arab rivalries and disputes.[39]

The dry tone of the UN documents upon which we rely provide little evidence of the atmosphere in UNSCOP's meeting with the Arab leaders. However, Granados' pro-Zionist memoirs and Arslan's pro-Palestinian diary do not differ much in their account of the meeting. Both agree that, apart from the Indian delegate, the other ten members left Lebanon unconvinced by the sincerity of Arab concern for the fate of Palestine.

Before departing for Europe, UNSCOP visited Abdullah, who became king of Transjordan in May 1946, in Amman. Abdullah had refused to participate in the Beirut meeting on the grounds that his country was not a member of the UN. But as everyone in the Arab world and in UNSCOP suspected, and as the Jewish Agency already knew, the king's reluctance stemmed from his decision, reached towards the end of 1946, to go it alone on the Palestine question. Abdullah sought a separate understanding with the Jews over the fate of Palestine.[40] This obvious lack of unity among the Arab leaders inevitably left an unfavourable impression on UNSCOP as to the strength of the Arab commitment.

The visit to Amman concluded UNSCOP's tour of the Middle East. The next stop was to be the wretched displaced persons camps where the Holocaust survivors had been gathered. UNSCOP members spent considerable time in the camps, which held 118,000 Jews while about 350,000 more lived outside the camps. When the Anglo-American committee visited the camps it had been doubtful in its estimate of the number of refugees who actually wished to settle in Palestine, but the members of UNSCOP had a somewhat easier task in reaching a conclusion. There was by now virtually no other possible destination for these refugees – resettlement in their home countries, i.e., in Germany or Central Europe, was out of the question. Because of its recent immigration policy the United States was also closed to them. Thus, only Palestine remained a feasible solution.

Whether these refugees were all ardent Zionists or whether the lack of alternatives forced them to decide on Palestine as their destination we shall never know. According to General Lucius Clay, the American Military Governor of Germany, in an address to UNSCOP: 'I think there is an overwhelming desire in the camp for immigration to Palestine. Of course, I do not know how this would stand up against the opening up of other countries for immigration. I am quite sure it is a real desire. I only want to say I do not know how strong it would be were other opportunities open to them.'[41] We do know, however, that the Jewish Agency had sent two special envoys to co-ordinate the testimony of the refugees before the committee. This was necessary primarily because of the lack of political unity among the camp members, who were divided according to the various Zionist organizations and parties. The two delegates reported their success in preventing the appearance of 'undesirable' witnesses before the committee, that is those who would express a desire either to stay in Europe or to emigrate to the USA. Although the committee itself chose forty-two refugees for interview at random, these chance candidates seemed to be well rehearsed in Zionist terminology and propaganda.[42]

The committee also knew and took into consideration that most of the people in the camps would not be allowed by the Americans to settle in the USA. Jewish immigration history shows that the United States, for obvious reasons, was usually the favoured destination, but legislation had locked the gates to the displaced persons.

After its visit to the DP camps the committee retired to Geneva where it convened in the Palais des Nations. As if events were not already dramatic enough, UNSCOP concluded its work on the last hour of the last day of August 1947, five minutes before its term of office expired. Their report was presented to the United Nations General Assembly's session of 1 September 1947.[43]

At this point we should reiterate that we have very scattered and meagre evidence about the early stages of UNSCOP's work and process of decision making and thus rely mainly on the notes Granados kept and later published, or the reports of the British official who accompanied the commission in Palestine and Geneva.[44] It does seem that those members who at the beginning of the inquiry had been quite neutral became pro-Zionist after their visit to the camps.[45] Some of the atmosphere in which the committee's report was written may be gleaned from Granados' words: 'Back from the camps, sobered with what we had seen . . . I settled down with my colleagues to work out the solution we must bring to Lake Success by September 1.'[46] Whatever their opinions at the beginning of the mission, it appears that by the time they arrived in Geneva the majority of the members of UNSCOP were sympathetic to Zionist aspirations and antagonistic to Palestinian demands.

UNSCOP was almost unanimous on two points. First, most of the members called for an end to the British mandate. With the exception of the Australian member, they all felt that the mandate had been both unworkable and unsuitable for Palestine. The Australian member took a more cautious approach and suggested considering the continuation of the mandate. Granados thought at the time that in voicing this position the Australian was representing what he thought was the British point of view. If this was the case, then he possibly misunderstood British policy, for rather than staying in Palestine Britain was seeking ways of leaving the region. It seems likely that the Australian member was concerned about Britain's image and wanted at least to place on record a more favourable and positive summary of the mandate.[47]

The Diplomatic Battle

29

The second point of agreement was the future of Jerusalem as the holy city. The divergence of opinions in the committee revolved around the degree, not the principle, of internationalization. The compromise ultimately struck was a decision to call for the establishment of Jerusalem as an international enclave with autonomous rights for both communities. But there ended the consensus. The committee members were divided on the implications of the first recommendation, that is to whom the land was to belong. The debate was largely legal and to some extent moral – in that the committee tried to weigh the legal and moral foundations of each of the parties' political claims. Judge Sandström, the chairman of UNSCOP, looked at the problem from a legal point of view and, referring to the inclusion in the mandate of the Balfour Declaration, claimed that the promises which had been made to the Jews were sanctioned by the League of Nations whereas those given to the Arabs were not.[48] We must remember that Sandström, like Cleavland Rand from Canada and Sir Abdul Rahman from India, was a Supreme Court Judge and thus had a propensity towards legal argumentation. In fact, the Zionist strategy towards UNSCOP was based on the knowledge that many of its members were jurists, some even practising law.[49] The Jews presented the committee with many legal documents pertaining to the Balfour Declaration, and although the committee was not entirely blind to the fact that the nature of the problem was political and not legal, some of the members were most impressed by this Zionist approach.[50]

Other members resorted to moralistic justifications. For example, Professor Enrique Rodriguez Fabregat of Uruguay felt that his Christian duty was to rectify to the best of his ability the abuse inflicted upon the Jews by generations of his fellow believers.[51] Judge Cleavland Rand, who was a Protestant, also claimed that weighty moral issues were involved in the question of Palestine, though he was more inclined to see it as a struggle between the forces of progress and democracy on the one hand (the Jews) and backward societies on the other (the Palestinians). While the greatest impact on many of the members of the committee was that left by the *Exodus* affair and the unco-operative Palestinian attitude, this was particularly true of Rand who seemed to be extremely annoyed by the approach of the Arab Higher Committee and its refusal to participate in the committee's proceedings in Palestine.[52]

Against these claims, the three members from Iran, Yugoslavia and India formed a minority in the committee by arguing that there was no legal justification for demanding from the Palestinians documents that proved their link to or possession of the land in Palestine. Even these three members, however, could not envisage a solution which would allow Arab domination over the Jews, and advocated a binational state, an idea unacceptable to the Arabs and popular only among a marginal Jewish group in Palestine, Brit Shalom (the Alliance of Peace).[53] Only Sir Abdur Rahman came close to adopting the Arab position by calling for proportional representation as a principle guiding the binational state, since he claimed that the Jews were not a nation but an ethnic community in Palestine.[54]

However, the majority of the members of UNSCOP (as the Anglo-American Committee before it) perceived the Jewish community as a dynamic factor and their main argument against binationalism was consequently based upon the Jewish demographic potential. Moreover, contrary to the three members from Iran, India and Yugoslavia, they doubted the legitimacy of the Arab case rather than that of the Zionists. And it was with a sense of compromise that they suggested partition as the best viable solution.

Since the General Assembly had set up UNSCOP as an advisory commission to provide general remarks about the nature of the conflict and possible directions for solutions, the committee decided to present before the UN the opinions of all its members – that is of the majority, who recommended the division of Palestine into two states to be aligned in an economic union, and of the minority, the three members who favoured a federated Palestine composed of Jewish and Arab areas, autonomous but not independent. Both these views were discussed at length in the UN upon publication of the UNSCOP report.

The majority did not limit its recommendations to general principles. They clearly stipulated, in territorial and constitutional terms, what they meant by the principle of partition. The territorial framework was devised by the assistant to the chairman, Paul Mohn of Sweden. He based his plans on maps provided to the committee in Palestine by the British mandatory authorities. As these maps dated back to 1937, it is possible to argue that the UNSCOP partition plan was just another version of the Peel Report. It had been Professor Reginald Coupland of All Souls College, Oxford, who in 1937 had first suggested this solution.

Coupland, who had given his advice to the Jewish Agency in the 1940s, was in fact highly pleased with the partition plan of 1947. But it is important to note that these maps, so eagerly taken up by UNSCOP, were part of the colonial heritage left behind by the British and more appropriate to the mandatory period than the 1947 reality.[55] The two future states would be interwoven with one another, a situation that was feasible perhaps in a country such as Switzerland, where the last war to have been fought was only a dim memory, but not in Palestine, where such a geopolitical reality was a prescription for a continuation of the conflict.

There were two schools of thought within UNSCOP's majority group. The Uruguayan, Guatemalen, Canadian and Czech members wanted to grant the Jews most of western Palestine (with both the Negev and the Galilee). But the majority and, of course, the three members who favoured a binational state opted for a smaller Jewish entity. Notwithstanding intensive efforts, including the recruitment of Richard Crossman to appear before the committee, the Zionist movement failed in this respect.[56]

After a long debate, and at the last moment, the majority drew up a partition map, the essence of which was a division of Palestine into two independent states. The Jewish state was to include the Eastern Galilee, the coastal strip (excluding Jaffa, and due south as far as the Gaza Strip of today), and the Negev. The Arab state was to consist of the Upper and Western Galilee, the West Bank and the Gaza Strip. This partition line left more than 45 per cent of the Arab population in the designated Jewish state, but the committee believed this demographic reality to be temporary as they counted on an immigration of at least 150,000 Jews during the transition period – that is between the end of the mandate and the creation of the Jewish state – and thereafter open to all other Jews. The two states were required to conclude a ten-year treaty of economic union as a condition for their promised independence.[57]

The idea of an economic union was the brain-child of Rand, who supported the Zionist claim that a unitary economic system in Palestine could form the basis for co-existence. But what the Zionists wanted in 1947 was economic interdependence, and what Rand suggested was an economically dependent Jewish state.[58] The economic union meant, in practice, the use of a common currency and the adoption of a customs union and a joint pool of customs revenues. This joint revenue was meant to allow subsidy of the less productive Arab state by the more industrialized Jewish

one. After having adhered for years to the concept of a unitary
economy, the Zionists found it difficult to act against this part of
the report though it now threatened their economic and political
aspirations. As in the case of the borders, this chapter of the
discussions was also totally divorced from the economic and
political situation of the Palestine of 1947. Other stipulations were
the requirement to obey democratic precepts and constitutions and
the guarantee of a ceasefire until the end of a short transition
period between the end of the mandate and independence.

Strikingly absent from the majority report was the question of
implementation. Introducing a solution had been only part of the
assignment; the committee was also to suggest the mechanism for
its realization. Incidentally, the majority report did not of course
produce a new solution but only revived an old one. The question
thus remained one of implementation of old ideas and not the
introduction of new ones. A settlement could be achieved either by
obtaining an *a priori* consent of the parties to the solution or by
finding ways of forcing the ideas upon them. The majority report
counselled leaving these questions to the United Nations.

The minority report also took up an already existing idea – the
federated binational state – which had been suggested first by the
Morrison–Grady Committee, and thereafter by Ernest Bevin.
According to this solution the federated state was to be supervised
by an international commission consisting of nine people, three
from each of the warring parties and three from the UN, which was
to have sanctionary authority with regard to questions of
immigration and purchase of land. The country would be under a
federated legislature. The minority report argued that Palestine
was too small to contain two separate entities and that it was in
any case impossible to consider a solution which contradicted the
will of the majority of the population.[59] Thus, while it recognized
the need to consider the will of the majority, it ignored the
demands of the minority.

The principles of a federated binational state were particularly
popular among the senior officials of the State Department and
many of the British Foreign Office experts on the Middle East.
However, both the USA and Britain instructed their diplomats to
stay away from Geneva and allowed no public or private
intervention in the proceeding of the committee. The secretary of
state, George Marshall, despite his unqualified support for a
federated state had specifically directed his representative in the

UN to refrain from any action. Marshall would reintroduce the idea of a federated state in April 1948 when it seemed that partition had failed. He was then also acting upon pressure from the White House, where the Zionist and Jewish lobbies succeeded in convincing the American president of the preferability of the partition principle.[60]

Despite Bevin's support for provincial autonomy the British also remained aloof. UNSCOP was in fact extremely disappointed with Britain's lack of co-operation during the committee's discussions in Geneva.[61] While it is true that many members did not wish to contact Britain before formulating their own ideas about a desirable solution, one of the major components in the majority report was the call upon Britain to assist in the transformation of Palestine from a mandatory entity into two separate independent states. The total absence of prior consultations with Britain led to a chaotic transitional period preceding the civil war in Palestine in the first months of 1948. Incidentally, the British ambassador to the UN, Sir Alexander Cadogan, had suggested an *a priori* British consent to whatever UNSCOP would recommend, a suggestion which was ruled out by most Foreign Office officials.[62]

While the Jewish community in Palestine was overwhelmed with joy upon hearing the results of the UNSCOP proceedings, the leadership was more restrained; in particular because of those parts in the report which related to the economic union of the two states and the limited area granted to the Jews.[63] Nevertheless, the Jewish Agency decided to exert all its diplomatic energy to assure the acceptance of the majority report by the United Nations.

The Arabs never harboured any illusions about UNSCOP's intentions. The Palestinian leadership, however, had realized by now that a total ban on the UN process would be a mistake. Therefore on 3 September 1947 the Arab Higher Committee sent a Palestinian delegation to the UN, which by the end of September 1947 had led to a more active Palestinian involvement. But there was very little common ground between the Palestinian leadership and the UN. The Arab Higher Committee rejected both the minority and majority reports. In the words of its spokesman, 'the minority report was also a partition plan in disguise.'[64] This position left the battle for the Arab cause in the UN in the hands of representatives of the Arab states, who eventually came to see the minority report as a lesser evil and tried to convince the organization that partition was a disastrous solution which would lead to war. However, the leaders of the Arab world seemed already to have sensed that mere words and slogans were not sufficient to demonstrate their commitment to the cause of Palestine.

Both sides then had to prepare themselves for the second session of the General Assembly to which the UNSCOP recommendations were submitted. The Secretary-General of the UN decided to transfer the two reports to a special *ad hoc* committee. The natural choice might have been the Political Committee (the body which had conceived UNSCOP), but Trygve Lie at that stage wanted a committee composed of members with a more direct interest in Palestine. The new *ad hoc* committee chaired by Dr Herbert Evatt, the foreign minister of Australia, began on 25 September 1947. Until 25 October the committee reconsidered and reshaped the outlines of the report, but not its substance. A reappraisal of this kind was indeed called for as the questions of implementation and the hostile Palestinian reaction had now to be taken into account.[65]

The major problem facing the committee was that of implementation. The day after it commenced its deliberations, the British government made it perfectly clear that it would not accept responsibility for the implementation of the recommendations should they be accepted as a UN resolution. This British declaration raised the first reservations about the practicability of the plan. Loyal to Bevin's maxim that Britain would only support a solution which was acceptable to both sides, the attitude of the British cabinet forced the UN to add to the complex machinery it had already planned for Palestine the notion of an international force that would put it in motion.[66]

The British decision to shun any responsibility for the UN resolutions was first and foremost aimed at pacifying the Arab world. The total Arab rejection of both the majority and minority UNSCOP reports meant that Britain could not support the recommendations without alienating the Arab world, where Britain already had enough trouble. At the same time, Britain could not object to UNSCOP without endangering its relationship with the UN. The only alternative was a neutral position that did not satisfy anyone. Britain was particularly apprehensive about the reactions of Iraq and Egypt. In Iraq negotiatons had begun for the revision of the Anglo-Iraqi treaty of 1930 amidst allegations by nationalists of British exploitation of Iraqi soil and natural resources. In Egypt

Britain had found itself, from the end of the Second World War, in a continual crisis stemming from the Egyptian demands for a complete evacuation of the bases which Britain considered to be its main strategic asset in the area, and for the unification of the Nile Valley, i.e. Egypt and the Sudan, under Faruq's crown.

Many historians stress the role played by Attlee in this policy, asserting that what mainly worried the prime minister was the Indian precedent which had taught the British that staying on in an adverse situation was bound to result in more havoc for the nation in question and loss of prestige for Britain itself.[67] In any case, the British cabinet endorsed Ernest Bevin's view expressed in the Cabinet meeting of 20 September 1947 that the British must not allow themselves 'to be saddled with the responsibility for enforcing a plan which no minister was prepared to defend as either equitable or workable and which was certain to be rejected by the Arabs'.[68]

An interesting question emerges. As the British protestations had been made before the UN resolution, why did they have such a marginal affect on the final decision? The answer seems to be that no one took the British position very seriously. Although the Americans 'viewed with dismay the prospect of utter chaos in Palestine,' they felt unable to assist or guide the British in their predicament.[69] Most State Department officials found it difficult to believe Britain would stick to its word. The same was true of the Zionist leadership in Palestine. The Jewish Agency's delegates in London reported that although the British found the UNSCOP report problematic they would nevertheless co-operate with the United Nations.[70] Judging from Arab behaviour during the months which followed, it seems that they too based their strategy on the assumption that Britain would go along with the UN plan. The British, however, proved genuine in their decision not to intervene and persisted in their impartial position throughout the crisis, a position that secured their infamy in both Israeli and Arab historiography of the war.

It has also been suggested that the UNSCOP report helped Britain to finally make up its mind to evacuate after two years of frustration, as shown by Hugh Dalton's remark upon hearing about the report: 'This, if we stick to it, is a historic decision.'[71] The decision was historic in Dalton's view since he believed that it brought an end to British rule in Palestine. Since 1945 Britain had been on the horns of an intricate dilemma: because its diminished strategic importance no longer justified a continued British presence there, Palestine had become a liability, and yet it was impossible to leave the area without a proper solution in place.[72] While the UNSCOP report did not provide that solution, it did enable Britain to leave Palestine.

On the American side, the report heightened existing tensions between the pro-Zionist White House and the pro-Arab State Department. Caught in the middle, secretary of state George Marshall, who was totally unbiased and loyal only to American interests, found it most difficult to formulate the American policy: 'Had it not been for Truman's firm instruction to support the majority report of UNSCOP, it is probable that he [Marshall] would have pursued a course towards a binational solution in line with the arguments so vigorously presented by Loy Henderson.'[73] Henderson was the Director of the Office of Near Eastern and African affairs in the State Department with immediate responsibility for the Palestine question. He was also Marshall's oracle on the Arab–Jewish conflict. Truman saw himself as the commander in chief of American foreign policy, and as such tightened the chain of command over the Palestine policy.[74] Truman's commitment to Zionism was reflected in the composition of the American delegation to the UN which had very few State Department officials but a considerable number of the president's nominees. The Jewish Agency could not ask for more and indeed found it quite easy to co-ordinate its policy closely with the Americans.[75] The result was a less ambivalent American attitude and a greater involvement in the work of the *ad hoc* committee.

Nevertheless, throughout the discussions in this committee, the Americans often spoke with more than one voice. The head of the UN delegation was Warren Austin who, like most of the State Department officials, preferred a binational state to partition. In April 1948, he took the initiative and declared this to be official American policy, thereby infuriating the president and endangering the aspiring new Jewish entity. However, the presence of the various American viewpoints in the delegation ultimately made for a less biased American policy.[76]

Another important point about the American position during the month of the committee's discussions was that they were actually left with very limited choices because of the Russian support for the majority report, and a consistent pro-Zionist Soviet policy since May 1947. Had the Russians led the majority camp in the UN, the

United States would have lost the paramount position it had enjoyed in the organization since its establishment in 1945.

As it was, soon after the *ad hoc* committee began its work the positions of the superpowers, the Arab countries, and the Jewish community in Palestine all became known. The adamant Arab opposition to both reports and the British declaration of neutrality rendered the committee an impracticable body. There was very little hope therefore of devising the necessary machinery and setting a timetable for the implementation of the UNSCOP report. The solution offered by the chairman was a simple one dividing the committee into two main subcommittees – one to prepare a draft resolution according to the UNSCOP minority report and Arab points of view, the other according to the majority report. A third subcommittee was then established to seek a compromise between the two drafts.[77]

The first two subcommittees were primarily concerned with the question of implementation. The 'minority subcommittee' doubted whether the UK was vested with the authority to impose a settlement and suggested consulting the International Court in The Hague for advice. This was a substantial point and many members of the General Assembly who voted eventually for partition, nevertheless approved this precondition. On 25 November 1947, the General Assembly rejected the minority report but the motion to appeal to The Hague divided the voters into two numerically equal camps, and parity in the UN is considered as a rejection. Moshe Sharett, at the time Head of the Political Department in the Jewish Agency, commented as follows on this proposal: 'The acceptance of this suggestion would have opened up the possibility of forming a larger majority for a resolution that would have undermined the edifice built in anticipation of the decision of the General Assembly.'[78] In his elaborate way Sharett was saying that had an international court ruled that the UN lacked the authority to implement such a plan it would have been very difficult to find anyone to support partition. But the General Assembly deferred consideration of this issue, until the Americans brought it up in April 1948. At that moment it all depended on the subcommittee which had prepared the partition resolution.[79]

In the minority subcommittee there was very little discussion about the report itself. Most of its members came from the Arab world and used the committee to prepare a draft resolution representing the general Arab point of view and not the minority

recommendations. Thus, it called upon the General Assembly to
resettle the displaced persons in their original homelands and to
create an independent Arab state in Palestine in which the Jews
would be recognized as 'a legal minority'. Though granting the
Jews civil rights was a shift in the Arab position, it failed to win the
sympathy of most of the Assembly's members.[80]

The work of the subcommittee considering the majority report
was affected by three factors. First, it became the most important
of the three subcommittees, for the minority subcommittee was
marginal and the subcommittee seeking a compromise insignificant. A good indication of this is the fact that the British took
hardly any interest in the minority subcommittee, but participated
intensively in the majority one.[81] The second factor determining
the work of this subcommittee was the Arab indifference towards
its proceedings. While both Arabs and Jews were asked to appear
and present their case, the Jewish diplomats were in daily contact
with the subcommittee members but there was hardly any
interaction with the Arab side. Finally, it was affected by the active
part taken by the two superpowers. Under their guidance the
UNSCOP report turned into a draft resolution. An international
atmosphere that allowed co-operation and joint support for
partition by the superpowers was the most important Zionist
achievement at that stage of the diplomatic war.

But this consensus was not enough to overcome the technical
problems of implementation. The majority subcommittee was less
concerned with the legality of the UN intervention than by the
potential complexities arising from the British disinclination to co-
operate. Acting upon a recommendation from the State Department, the pro-partition subcommittee hoped to circumvent this
entanglement by shortening the period of transition from mandate
to independence from two years to two months. It was hoped that
such a tight schedule would induce the British to co-operate.[82]

To that end, the Americans persuaded the Russians to retract
from a demand for immediate British withdrawal. Jointly, the two
superpowers agreed that the mandate would end on 15 May 1948,
but that the British, for logistic reasons, would not be able to
complete the evacuation before 1 August 1948. The Americans
hoped that at least during the early stages of withdrawal Britain
would still be in Palestine to assist in the implementation of
partition. The Russians, for their part, backed this timetable since
they saw no harm in allowing the British to be dragged down in

the Palestine quagmire for a little while longer (or so it appears from the British documents).[83]

This countermeasure, however, failed to change London's views. In the cabinet a plan for withdrawal was being contemplated which had one, and only one, objective: to ensure the safe evacuation of British personnel and equipment. This left the problem of implementation to be resolved. Neither superpower wanted the other to be responsible for an operation that would inevitably involve the dispatch of troops into a vacuum created by Britain's withdrawal. A joint operation with the Soviets was ruled out by the Americans since Palestine, after all, was within the Western sphere of influence. In the event, such deliberations were somewhat premature. It was to take another few months and a considerable amount of violence in Palestine before the Americans realized that reconsideration of the partition plan was due.

Over a period of nine months no less than six committees had been created in the search for peace in Palestine. What then could be the harm of yet another one? This was the United Nations Palestine Committee (UNPC) which was saddled with responsibility for the orderly transition of Palestine from mandatory status into two independent states. This new committee, which started its work in January 1948 will be discussed in Chapter 2.

The other hurdle still to be tackled was the question of borders which was posed in arithmetical terms. In the view of the State Department officials there were two problems to be solved. The first was that the majority report allocated to the Arabs – who made up 63 per cent of the population – only 38 per cent of mandatory Palestine. The only way to alter this imbalance was by extricating parts of the Negev, which in the UNSCOP report had been promisd to the Jews, and reallocating them to the Arab state. Most of the subcommittee members supported this approach, since they realized that a Jewish Negev would drive a wedge between Egypt and the rest of the Arab world. Britain in particular was anxious that such a geopolitical reality should not materialize as it would jeopardize its own strategic set-up in the Middle East. When the State Department proposed that the area from Beer Sheba to the international border should be annexed to Arab Palestine, the pro-Jewish lobby in the USA succeeded in obtaining President Truman's intervention and foiled the plan. The successful prevention of such a serious shift in American policy has been claimed by Chaim Weizmann.[84] Although this is quite plausible, one should also take into account Truman's pro-Zionist approach which dated back to 1946. However, when the Americans regressed from their pro-partition policy in April 1948 Weizmann was again recruited. At the end of the day, the Jewish state was alloted 55 per cent of mandatory Palestine with most of the Negev, together with two-thirds of the coastal strip and the Eastern Galilee.[85]

The second problem with regard to the borders was the demographic balance: 498,000 Jews and 407,000 Arabs were to live in the Jewish state.[86] The subcommittee accepted UNSCOP's contention that this demographic imbalance would be settled once the displaced persons had settled in Israel. The superpowers' consensus even allowed the Jews one free port for immigration purposes during the transition period. This concession proved perhaps more beneficial to the Jews than was initially intended. For together with additional manpower, the port allowed easy transportation of arms and ammunition in the preparations for a military confrontation. The immigration settlement did not allay the Jewish Agency's fears *vis-à-vis* a binational state. As will be seen later, this apprehension clearly directed Jewish policy during the war.

The members of the subcommittee did not ignore the implications of the map they had drawn, but were hopeful that the abnormal features would be reduced by the concept of an economic union. Although the Jewish Agency had earlier failed to convince UNSCOP of the deficiencies of this concept, it now succeeded in persuading the subcommittee to limit the duration of the proposed union to ten years and leave the supervision of the union to a Joint Monetary Board. None of the members explained how this board was to stand in relation to the treasuries and economies of the two states.[87] In the final analysis therefore the idea of the economic union, rather than clarifying the picture, obscured it.

On the question of Jerusalem the subcommittee left the UNSCOP report almost intact. The Jewish Agency decided not to adopt an aggressive strategy on this question, realizing that for the final vote the goodwill of Catholic states was a necessity.[88] Although the Holy See and most of the Catholic establishments in the world were opposed to partition, they limited their involvement in the UN process to the question of the holy places in Jerusalem. The Vatican feared that any other solution might allow the Russians to become deeply involved in Palestine. In fact, the Pope himself did not voice his opinion until October 1948, thus allowing the Jews and the Catholic world to reach a tacit understanding about the internationalization of the holy places without entering into an open confrontation on partition.[89]

THE PARTITION RESOLUTION OF 29 NOVEMBER 1947

On 24 November 1947 the chairman of the *ad hoc* committee announced that the efforts of the third subcommittee to seek a reconciliation of the two positions had completely failed. On the same day the committee rejected one by one the recommendations of the minority report subcommittee. The next five days were devoted to the final formulation of the recommendations of the subcommittee dealing with the UNSCOP majority report.[90] On 25 November the world became acquainted for the first time with the final draft of the partition resolution, Resolution 181. This document became one of the greatest bones of contention between Israel and its Palestinian neighbours and the immediate cause of the 1948 war.

According to the UN procedure, a two-third majority in the *ad hoc* committee was required for the adoption of the draft as an official resolution. Two votes were lacking in the discussion in the committee, and the draft proposal for the partitioning of Palestine was therefore tabled by the committee to the General Assembly, which was already in session at Flushing Meadow, New York.

In the next few days, the Zionists and the Arabs were engaged in a race against time, as the vote could be scheduled for the next day or the day after. For the Jewish Agency it was a nerve-racking exercise in international diplomacy; for the Arabs and the Palestinians another desperate attempt to turn the tide.

Had the Arab delegates been more aware of the political developments in the four days leading up to the vote they might have been able to reorientate the political process. However, as they had chosen not to participate in the subcommittee on the majority report, they failed to understand the delicate balance which emerged at the end of the discussions. And indeed on 25 November, Nahum Goldman and Moshe Sharett learned to their dismay that some of the delegates who had spoken in favour of the partition plan had since changed their minds. It is quite possible that State Department officials were behind this as the countries concerned were supposedly allies of the USA. It is also possible, as the British documents indicate, that at the very last moment some Arab pressure was exercised. The Jewish Agency did not suspect the Americans and like the British attributed the last minute change of heart to Arab lobbying.[91]

But all in all, under the guidance of the White House and the Secretary of State, and despite State Department hesitations, it was eventually the Americans who saved the Zionist movement from an unfavourable outcome. Some Latin American delegates assisted also by delivering lengthy speeches postponing the vote from 26 to 29 November – thus allowing the Jews ample time to recruit the necessary votes for a majority.[92]

While the tactics employed to obtain that majority have been discussed in many historical and popular works on the war of 1948, 'the exact mechanics of the various lobbying activities remain obscure'.[93] Nevertheless, British, American and Zionist documents allow us to produce the following summary. It seems, first of all, that much of the work was done by the Zionists themselves. Through friends and supporters around the world the Jewish Agency succeeded in changing the position of some countries. Such was the case, for example, with the old socialist leader in France, Leon Blum, who helped to change French policy from abstention into support for the partition resolution; similarly Harvey Firestone, the owner of the large tyre industry, elicited a favourable vote from Liberia through his economic involvement there.[94] Secondly, we can quite safely assume a direct involvement by President Truman and pro-Zionist congressmen and senators on behalf of the Jews in other countries. This was particularly true of Latin and Central America, where a favourable vote from twelve out of the twenty Latin American members was secured.[95]

Finally, the diplomatic incompetence and political indifference of the Arab delegates also played an important role in the Jewish success. At the very last moment it seemed that the Arab camp realized the importance of the occasion, when on 28 November, Fadil al-Jamali, the Iraqi representative, tabled a compromise resolution. Jamali claimed before the General Assembly that, since hitherto no serious effort had been made to bring the two sides closer, the UN should allow a reconsideration of the resolution by the *ad hoc* committee.[96] However, these transparent tactics only persuaded the chairman of the session, Alexander Parodi of France, to postpone the vote by forty-eight hours. By then, the Zionists knew they had succeeded in recruiting the necessary majority. What was now required on the Arab side was a more substantial effort and the submission of a genuine compromise. But to the astonishment of the session on the following day, both the representative of the Arab Higher Committee and the most able spokesman for the Palestinians, the respected Pakistani foreign minister, Zafarullah Khan, failed to show up. Moreover, a dispute broke out between the remaining Arab delegates about the designate speaker in this discussion. The Jewish Agency had learned about these internal disputes from an informer who participated in the co-ordinating meetings of the Arab delegations. The Jews used this information about Arab disunity to persuade the other delegates that there was no need for further delay in the discussions.[97]

On Saturday morning, 29 November 1947, the General Assembly in New York voted in favour of partition and accepted Resolution 181. A historical event for both the Jews and the Arabs, for the former it meant international sanction for their state and the beginning of a war of independence. But for the Palestinians, it spelled the end of their hopes for an Arab state in the whole of Palestine and the start of a traumatic and tragic period in their history.

The problems of implementation emerged with a vengeance after the vote in the UN. Not only was there no change in the British position, the mandatory authorities were instructed by London not to allow the entry into the country of the UNPC, the transition commission, until two weeks before the final evacuation of British forces.

With the Arab attitude even more hostile than before the vote, the Arab League declared its duty to wage war against the implementation of the resolution. The majority of the State Department officials now concluded that carrying out the plan would be almost impossible. It could have been done jointly with the Russians who would have been more than happy to participate in the enforcement of peace in Palestine, but the Cold War prevented such co-operation. The State Department began reviewing the situation with fresh eyes.

In November 1947, UNSCOP had manoeuvred the UN towards a pro-Zionist solution and provided the Jews with an important victory in the diplomatic war over Palestine. But this in itself did not solve the Palestine question nor ensure the fulfilment of the Zionist dreams. The matter was returned to the United Nations headquarters where other members played an important role and where the balance could have been tipped against the Zionists. This did not happen owing to the skilful tactics of the Jewish delegation. Since the American commitment to Zionism had never been accepted by the State Department, the Zionists continued to face shifts in US policy towards the principle of partition in the period between the formulation of UNSCOP's recommendations and the creation of the state of Israel on 15 May 1948. The head of the Political Department of the Jewish Agency, its 'foreign minister' so to speak, years later regarded the days between the vote in the UN and the end of the mandate as the most anxious time for the Jews. Sharett's main worry was the attitude of officials of the State Department, where most of the Middle East experts were having second thoughts about the desirability and practicability of the principle of partition.

Meanwhile with almost all the Jews in Palestine dancing in the streets full of joy and elation, the Jewish leadership, sober minded as usual and realizing the struggle was not over yet, prepared its community for the next stages of the war. On the Palestinian side, very little was done. The Arab League had paved the way for a more united and committed Arab front, but all in all, these efforts were incompatible with the zeal and conviction that characterized the Jewish actions.

The partition plan was brought up for another round of discussions and revaluation before committees in which permanent members of the Security Council were present. The trend in the new discussion was very much against the Jews and in favour of the Arabs. However, at that crucial stage, the Arab Higher Committee, the body representing the Palestinians, again refused to participate in the proceedings, thus extricating the Zionist movement from an awkward situation.[98] The Palestinian leadership still hoped that it could prevent the establishment of a Jewish entity in Palestine by force of arms.

The State Department was to try once more, in April 1948, to revise the partition plan by suggesting an international trusteeship over Palestine as an alternative scheme. However, the Defence Department and the Russians both objected for their own reasons and, most important of all, the new idea was totally rejected by President Truman who by then had become one of the Zionists' most ardent supporters on the international scene.[99] With the failure of the trusteeship plan, the crucial stage as far as the Jews were concerned was over. As we shall see, the UN reopened the question of a comprehensive solution for the Palestine problem in September 1948 in the wake of the Bernadotte initiative, but on this occasion the Americans were the ones to foil these overtures.

Against the official Israeli version of the incipient state's attitude towards the UN partition resolution which argues that its acceptance by the Jews was actually a compromise – a concession dictated by the wish to restore peace to the war-torn Holy Land – it has been claimed it was merely a tactical move intended to pave the way for further territorial expansion through war whenever possible.[100] This argument is hard to prove, although it does not sound implausible. However, whether Israel accepted the partition resolution merely as a means of gaining international legitimacy for the state, or also out of acquiescence with the principle of partition, or even for its own expansion, are questions which historians will never be able to answer for they belong to the realm of speculation. Intriguing as they may be, the questions carry very little historical relevance and I suggest that the diplomatic effort in the UN before May 1948 should be viewed from a different angle.

The interest of the historian of the war should not focus on speculative assumptions but rather on discerning what effects each phase of the fighting had on the course of the conflict. The question which then becomes the most relevant is not why Israel accepted the UN resolution but whether or not it faced the danger of annihilation at that period. By recognizing the acute fear of another Holocaust among the Jews of Palestine at the time, we may understand part of Israel's behaviour both in the war of 1948 and that of 1967, and perhaps later also. But, was the Jewish community indeed facing another Holocaust? Was Masada under siege, and instead of committing collective suicide did the new Jews take to arms and in a miraculous way save their state? By explaining the emergence of the state in the context of the unique international political constellation of 1947, the historian certainly arrives at a rejection of the myth of annihilation, i.e. that the Yishuv was facing a potential national disaster in 1948.[101] This historical assessment of the degree of danger facing the community in Palestine is necessary when discussing the war of 1948 – both the unofficial 'civil war' that developed between December 1947 and May 1948 and the actual war between Israel and the invading Arab armies. This confrontation depended not only on diplomacy or military skill but also on motivation, adequate economic and social structures as well as competent leaders. While the Jewish side possessed most of the necessary means for winning the war, the Palestinians did not. Here again the annihilation myth seems to be unfounded.

2

The Civil War in Palestine

THE EMBRYO STATE:
THE JEWISH AGENCY'S PREPARATIONS FOR WAR

As early as 1917, and some would argue even earlier, the Jewish leadership considered the establishment of a state as the ultimate goal of the Zionist project in Palestine. The dream had always existed, but the yearning for a state until then had been no more than an idealistic aspiration directing the thoughts and actions of the Jewish settlers in the country. By the middle of the 1930s, the leadership had formed and maintained a clear sense of direction and henceforth was engaged in intensified state-building policies and activities. The infrastructure for a state had been partially established in the previous decade. A strong trade union movement, independent health and education organizations and an embryo army were the first manifestations of the Zionist propensity for efficiency and vitality in their accelerated settlement of Palestine.[1] In the late 1930s an autonomous transport association, agricultural marketing and building society were added to this structure.

Throughout the mandatory period the Jewish leadership in Palestine on various occasions declared its goal of turning Palestine as a whole into a Jewish state. A very clear reference to such determination was made by the Jewish leadership in May 1942, in the Hotel Biltmore in New York, and this became known as the 'Biltmore Programme'. The Jewish Agency had as yet neither specified a timetable nor outlined the practical steps it intended to take, and was still involved in efforts to influence the last British attempts to solve the conflict. But the slow stream of diplomacy concealed a faster flowing undercurrent of relentless energy and creativity on the part of the Jewish community in Palestine. The community was directed into this new phase by David Ben Gurion. Already in 1937 the Jewish leader had declared: 'The creation of a Jewish state should be our main objective, our actions abroad and in the country should all be devoted for this goal', and in the years preceding the end of the mandate 'the dream became an operative objective'.[2]

The transition to a more efficient and determined phase in the state-building process did not depend solely on the political leadership, important as this may have been. Other factors contributed to the Jewish success, the most notable of which was demographic change in Palestine. The increase in the Jewish population, after some initial disappointment, was impressive. By 1939 there were 470,000 Jews in 218 settlements; the additional 100,000 refugees from Europe, authorized by the Anglo-American Committee, and natural growth would bring the number to 660,000 by 1947. In that year, between 1.2 and 1.3 million Arabs were living in Palestine, in about 850 villages.[3] The Jews owned one and a half million dunams of land in the country, more than enough to sustain their agricultural needs.

Ownership of land, the size of the population and a determined leadership were the most important assets of the Jewish community in the struggle against the Arabs in Palestine. A closer look at the way in which this community was organized reveals another important asset – the existence of an efficient and strong political structure. The British mandatory authorities, although now less receptive and friendly than they had been in the early 1920s, continued to recognize the quasi-autonomous structure of the Jewish community. The community leadership and political practice were guided by democratic principle; the élite was incorporated into a national assembly, which acted as a kind of parliament and had a more limited executive body as its government.

The increased efficiency of the policy-making structure was arrived at by shifting the centre of Zionist power and leadership from Europe to Palestine, a process which had begun with the creation of the Jewish Agency in 1929 and the subsequent decline in the World Zionist Federation's authority throughout the late 1930s and 1940s. The World Zionist Federation was the organization which represented, epitomized, and led the Zionist movement from its inception until the end of the first decade of the British mandate. The Jewish Agency was created in 1929 and was originally intended to represent the World Zionist Federation's interests in Palestine; however, gradually, and particularly after the Second World War, the Jewish Agency succeeded in winning the recognition of the British authorities as the leadership of the Zionist movement both within and outside Palestine. The Agency was already established as a kind of government with an elaborate structure consisting of various departments acting as ministries of health, education, defence, employment, and so on. The World Zionist Federation was still in charge of the movement's 'foreign policy', but after the Second World War even that responsibility was taken over by the leaders in Palestine. Prominent members of the Federation who did not emigrate to Palestine, for example those who headed the Zionist Federations in the USA and Britain, would try to influence the Zionist 'foreign policy' – usually towards a more moderate path – but mostly with little success. Elections and selections to both organizations were held via political parties, so that the various Zionist parties of which there were about half a dozen – liberals, socialists, communists and extreme nationalists – were represented simultaneously in both organizations.[4]

Thus the Jewish Agency was the main political body leading and representing the Jewish community in Palestine. It was run by an elected committee – a kind of cabinet within the wider government – which was called the National Executive Committee and whose members came mostly from the main Zionist party, the Labour Party (Mapai). Mapai members had also dominated the Hagana. Most of the leaders held simultaneous positions or membership in all three of these important centres of power. The Agency's trade union organization, the Histadrut, was also an important scene for domestic politics. David Ben Gurion, for instance, reached his position as the community's leader via the Histadrut and then became the head of the Jewish Agency and the chairman of the National Executive Committee. In the 1940s he also headed the Defence Department. The ostensible diffusion of power vested in the different branches is therefore rather misleading as decisions were always taken by a small group of leaders. This group had to win the support of the Labour Party and to some extent, that of the more socialist parties such as Hashomer Haza'ir and Ahdut Ha'avoda, while the Revisionist Movement and the Communist Party were excluded by mainstream Zionism from the realm of policy-making.

During the Second World War the political structure described above was underpinned by a strong military foundation. The experience of some 27,000 Jewish veterans who had served with the British army and the establishment of commando units (Palmach) in 1941, enabled the political leadership to proceed with its plans in defiance of British and Arab opposition. Incidentally, it should be noted that of the Arab Palestinians only 12,000 had served in the British army during the war.[5]

The war also generated an open confrontation between the Jewish leaders and the British authorities, in which the main arena was that of illegal immigration. Holocaust survivors began to make their way into Palestine in the early 1940s and British attempts to stop the flow of these refugees led to the first serious clashes between British soldiers and the Hagana. The open conflict with the British strengthened the more extreme elements within the Jewish élite who had demanded the declaration of an independent state in Palestine irrespective of international or British consent for this action.

Yet the leadership remained pragmetic both during and after the Second World War. The relationship with the British was never too strained, at least not to the extent of preventing the continued, and necessary co-operation with the mandatory government. Likewise, the community diplomats were given a free hand in presenting outside Palestine the most moderate Jewish position possible. Such a policy, it should be stressed, was attained at the risk of dividing the Jewish community and alienating its more extreme parties from the mainstream. David Ben Gurion, who emerged as the main spokesman and leader of the pragmatic trend, often had to resort to intricate manipulations in his ultimately successful attempt to impose the 'realistic' point of view on his opponents from right and left. His main party often split over these issues and the other underground movements, LEHI and IZL were constantly threatening to take up arms against his authority in the country.

But internal feuding between the various underground organizations was set aside in October 1945, when Ben Gurion and his colleagues in the National Executive Committee decided to declare open war on the British in Palestine. The success of this step depended upon the unification of the military effort. The IZL and LEHI submitted to Ben Gurion's authority but retained the right to continue their independent purchase of arms (a compromise which was to bring the Jewish community to the verge of civil war when IZL tried to bring in arms on the ship *Altalena* in June 1948). Ben Gurion's instructions to confiscate this cargo led to an exchange of fire between the Hagana and IZL, endangering the stability of the new state. LEHI remained relatively autonomous and carried out its own attacks on Arabs often without either informing the newly-formed united military command or seeking its sanction.[6]

Yet, the overall picture was one of ability to mobilize the Jewish community in a joint military action against the Arab side. David Ben Gurion, who already held the most important political positions in the community, added to these the Defence portfolio of the Executive Committee, an appointment which was declared in December 1946, during the convention of the 22nd World Zionist Congress. As the principal decision-maker in the Jewish community, Ben Gurion now wielded more influence than any of his colleagues at the top, and almost single-handedly would orchestrate the Jewish preparations for the war of 1948.

Ben Gurion's two major contributions consisted in turning the Hagana into a proper army and in mobilizing Jews inside and outside Palestine, urging them to do their utmost, personally and financially, for the forthcoming struggle over the country. In November 1947, the united military command declared its intention to form a national army. The prevailing militia-like structure was replaced by an army based on regular conscription and professional training. Despite the Hagana's initial opposition, a new General Staff, *Hamifkada Haarzit* (the National Headquarters), was established, subordinated to what may be called an emergency war cabinet and headed by Ben Gurion. In the same month, a similar structural change was effected in the political sphere. The previous democratic edifice was now brought under the authority of a small committee, which took over the power of the National Executive Committee. Needless to say, Ben Gurion headed this body as well. Thus, the number of decision-makers in both the military and political spheres was considerably reduced in the course of 1947. These structural changes were deemed essential in order to co-ordinate the diplomatic and military activity of the community and proved their efficacy during the months of the civil war in the first half of 1948. The two new supplementary decision-making bodies overshadowed the older parts of the political infrastructure, which had until then governed the community along democratic and socialist lines. Concentrating the policy-making in two committees, one military and one political, the leadership in effect suspended both the external trappings and the practice of democracy for a more dictatorial way of life in the face of the crisis.

On 19 November 1947, the 'centre for the people's recruitment' was established. The office discovered, in February 1948, that a significant number of Jews had evaded conscription and evolved a more effective operation of mobilization. By 15 April 1948, about 82,500 men had passed through this centre but since those who lived in remote and isolated settlements were regarded as soldiers *ipso facto* the number of recruits was larger (it also did not include the commando units of the Palmach). The problem then arose how to arm this fighting force. Indeed, at the beginning of the war, the shortage of arms meant that only 30,000 of the total number of conscripts actually participated in the fighting.[7] It was only during the first truce, in June 1948, that arms were provided in sufficient quantities. When the fighting began in December 1947, about 20,000 young men from Jewish communities throughout the world joined the fighting force in Palestine. They were enlisted after a short training course. Some were ex-soldiers, mechanics or even pilots. These proved especially indispensable to the newly-established army and constituted the foundations of the Israeli air force, communication network and military medical service.[8]

The growth of the Jewish military potential is reflected in the increase in the number of infantry divisions. By the end of 1947, the Hagana had only one division under its command. By 15 May 1948 there were ten divisions, reinforced by newly-formed artillery units, armoured vehicles and an embryo navy and air force.[9]

Apart from unifying the military effort, the Jewish leadership also prepared the ground by expanding the settlement infrastructure. In the period between the Morrison–Grady report and the UNSCOP report the Zionist leadership tried to turn the Negev into a Jewish area. The Morrison–Grady committee had excluded the Jews from this part of Palestine. In order to face the UN with a *fait accompli*, eleven new settlements were established in the Negev by the end of 1946. Altogether, thirty new settlements were established during 1947 and were soon inhabited by fresh waves of immigrants.

With a new settlement infrastructure, a unified military force, and a clearer sense of political orientation, the Jewish leadership felt confident enough to tell UNSCOP that they were able to face the Arabs in Palestine, even if the latter were assisted by external Arab forces.[10]

The clearer sense of direction is also manifested in a detailed and determined Jewish master plan conceived at this junction for the takeover of the institutions and administration of mandatory Palestine. Consequently, in May 1946, the military command of the Jewish Agency declared itself the sole authority for the maintenance of law and order in the Jewish community. It assumed responsibility for the defence of factories and vital installations such as power stations, as well as the lives of all Jewish settlers.[11] The plan of May 1946 was based upon the assumption that the British would step aside the moment the fighting erupted. This assumption was vindicated in due course and the plan allowed the Jewish forces to take the necessary steps to fill the vacuum left by the British troops.

These preparations for a Jewish state were aided considerably by developments in the UN. In November 1947, the UN not only legitimized the Jewish state, it also offered to assist actively in its formation. UNSCOP's report and the subsequent UN partition resolution authorized the United Nations Palestine Committee to prepare the ground for the formation of an Arab and a Jewish provisional government. The committee was granted four months in which to accomplish this task, i.e., until 1 April 1948. Two weeks before this term expired the committee declared its failure and, like the British, left the warring parties to determine the shape and future of Palestine by force.

The failure of the Palestine Committee in no way hindered Jewish preparations for a takeover. Long before the transitional period was even conceived, Ben Gurion had already set the Jewish community on the path of state building. Upon hearing the British decision not to assist in the implementation of the partition resolution, Ben Gurion told the Jewish national assembly: 'We have to inform the world and the UN that we shall be the implementers. We ourselves, are able, capable and willing to function as a transitionary government from this very moment, from the beginning of the transitional period, instead of the withdrawing British government.'[12]

And indeed they were. Some minor problems had nevertheless to be solved before tackling the main stage in this project – the takeover of the mandatory system. One was the question of authority. The Jewish community in Palestine hoped to establish a democracy there. The legitimacy of authority depended therefore upon the community itself, although the community did not represent all the Jewish people and the state was not an established fact. It was therefore decided to form a transitional leadership upon whose authority all the political parties in Palestine and world Jewry concurred, instead of opting for the more complicated process of elections.[13]

In April 1948, the Jewish community complied with the UN partition plan by forming a 'transitional government' and a 'parliament'. The National Executive and Assembly were abolished, the Jewish Agency was transferred to London, and Jewish society in Palestine, to all intents and purposes, was transformed from an autonomous existence under a mandatory regime into the reality of statehood. The 'transitional parliament', the People's Council, comprised thirty-seven members who represented the political powers both in Palestine and in the World Zionist Congress. The 'provisional government' did not include the right-wing Revisionists or the Communists among its thirteen members. In Hebrew it was called the 'People's Directorship', but the UN accepted it as the provisional government aimed at in its 29 November partition resolution. As neither the 'emergency war committee' nor the 'political committee' were ever actually abolished, the structure in some respects remained heavily overburdened and indeed up to the last day of the mandate the question of authority was not resolved. But, as the vital and immediate issues of security and defence were handled by a small number of people, the system was efficient enough to conduct a war. Moreover, it was considered representative enough in the eyes of the local population, world Jewry and the international community. Hence we may say, that by April 1948 the Jews had virtually formed a representative government willing and able to take over mandatory Palestine.[14]

The takeover itself was carefully thought out and was part and parcel of an overall plan prepared by the Hagana on 10 March, 1948, Plan Dalet or Plan D. We shall have cause to return to Plan D in discussing the making of the refugee problem because of its bearing upon the exodus of the Palestinians. At this stage we need only view the plan as a component in the Jewish preparations for statehood.

Plan D was founded upon the assumption that Palestine was shortly to be freed of the firm control of the mandatory authorities, following which it would become – after a fashion – a no man's land. It correctly analysed the Arab camp as consisting of both irregular and regular forces and proposed to retaliate against any assault on Jewish settlements by attacking Arab villages and routes and occupying 'forward military bases in enemy's territory'. These 'bases' as named in Plan D were Arab villages lying within the area allotted in the UN to the Arabs. The plan also outlined the proposed capture of all the mixed towns in Palestine: Tiberias, Safad, Jaffa, Haifa and Jerusalem.[15]

An important part of Plan D, overlooked by most of those who have discussed it, is the reference it contains to a takeover of government institutions as well as the safeguarding of a continued normal functioning of services vital for the community. It was in fact meant to complete the process, begun in 1937, of creating an embryo state in Palestine. That is, it was not merely 'geared to achieve military ends', but rather intended as the final stage in the trasition between the Jewish community under the mandate and the Jewish state as it was to emerge on 15 May 1948.[16]

Parts of the plan had already been implemented even before March 1948. Once the British evacuation had started, Jewish forces took over any government services, offices and installations they could lay their hands on. Ben Gurion wrote in his diary on 21 March 1948: 'A Jewish government should be established; we should organize the necessary services: post, judiciary system, income tax, and a propaganda machinery.'[17] Even seemingly trivial aspects, such as the meteorological service, were included in the takeover plan; nothing in fact was overlooked in the Jewish effort to establish a state.[18]

In March–April the takeover was completed. This time not only deserted buildings, but also services which hitherto had been staffed mainly by Arabs were seized – for example the postal units, the revenue offices and the telecommunication centre.[19]

Not relying on direct taxation alone as a source of revenue, the leadership imposed a series of indirect levies and duties.[20] Even so, the main source of income which helped the community to establish its policy on a sound financial basis was the result of an appeal by the Jews in Palestine to Jewish communities all over the world, and in particular in the United States. Golda Meyrson, later Meir, was assigned to return to the States where she had spent her early years, and raise the necessary funds. For her success in this mission she would be warmly praised by Ben Gurion. Taxation, not yet a sufficient instrument to ensure a flow of funds, was, however, another expression of the new state's authority and therein lay its significance for the time being.

Apart from the structural takeover, the Jewish leadership in the last months of the mandate also concerned itself deeply with the morale and motivation of the community. This was a highly politicized and energetic community, but political disagreements abounded and, coupled with the common frailty of human nature, did not allow the leadership to remain complacent about the people's readiness to endure indefinitely a state of war and strenuous military service. The leadership therefore took steps to ensure that the mood of the community would not obstruct the conduct of the war: Ben Gurion set up a censorship authority, a kind of internal espionage agency, which kept a close surveillance on the direction of the people's feelings and the general mood in the country.[21]

When the hour struck on 15 May 1948, the Jewish community was ready. These were not easy days for the Jews in Palestine – the men and women in the street did not share the knowledge or the confidence of the leadership, while within the élite itself not everyone was equally sanguine about the outcome of the struggle. However, the leadership had prepared its community well for the challenge and, more importantly, it benefited from the absence of similar preparations on the Palestinian and the Arab side.

AN ÉLITE IN CONFUSION:
THE PALESTINIAN PREPARATION FOR WAR

It has already been pointed out, in our discussion of the diplomatic battle in the UN, that the Palestinian leadership failed in the guidance of its community at the most crucial time in its history. This failure becomes even more striking if one juxtaposes the two political élites in Palestine. In comparison with the commitment and effective performance of the Jewish élite in the last two years of the mandate, we find on the Arab Palestinian side a leadership crippled by internal strife and external pressures which prevented it from recruiting the necessary resources to confront the challenge ahead.

We shall offer two political explanations for the Palestinian leadership's failure. First, we shall endeavour to sketch the fragmented political organization of the Palestinian community which failed to withstand the crisis of 1948. This state of affairs led – and this is our second explanation dealt with in the next section – to the interference in local politics of Arab politicians from neighbouring states. In other words, the Palestinian leadership voluntarily surrendered its cause, and the community's fate, into the hands of the Arab League's mandarins. Thus, it lost the initiative and the ability to direct the political and military process in Palestine. At this point it might be useful first to consider the conduct and performance of the Palestinian leadership from a sociological vantage point.

From a comparison between the two rival élites there emerges a clear difference in their performance as political and social leaders of their communities. The Zionist and the Palestinian political élites had two basic functions or assignments, in view of the ongoing conflict in Palestine: they had to represent the political case of their societies in the international arena and at the same time manage the economic, military and political welfare of their communities. The Jewish élite fulfilled both these functions admirably, although with the necessary force of sanctions and at the expense of democracy. The Palestinian élite attempted to fulfil the first role, but lacked the requisite authority to maintain the second.

This failure cannot be explained without taking into account the nature of traditional Palestinian society. Analysing that society and its impact on the course of the conflict would lead us to the social history of the conflict – a fascinating subject but still virgin ground in many ways. However, recently a number of competent research studies have appeared with the help of which we can try and sketch a profile of traditional Palestinian society and particularly of its élite.[22]

Until the beginning of the nineteenth century a dominant component of the social élite of Palestine was the rural élite centred in the mountainous areas. In many sources a large section of this élite is described as feudal – a tricky term because of its European connotations. Hence, we should characterize its application in the Palestinian context, which is not totally different from that of the rest of the Ottoman Empire. As this system was still valid in many parts of Palestine until 1948, it is worth describing it in detail.[23]

The countryside feudalism of Palestine was based on three essential factors. It had an economic basis whereby the lords of the rural areas lived at the expense of the peasants' agricultural production. The agricultural means of production were in the hands of self-reliant peasants who, according to law and custom in the empire, had to transfer their surplus to their lords, although in Palestine it was not a strict or formalized system.[24]

The second basis for authority was a legal-administrative one. The Ottoman Empire, until the nineteenth century, was ruled on the basis of the 'parcellization of sovereignty'. The rule was secured via 'a network of loyalties culminating in loyalty towards the head of the Empire'.[25] This principle turned the local lords into representatives of the empire and together with their economic control it legitimized them as absolute leaders in their estates. More specifically, they were the local tax collectors and enjoyed a jurisdictional authority, not just as enforcers of the laws, but rather as interpreters, administrators and preservers of existing traditional customary laws.

However, for long periods in its history this system of parcellization of authority and total sovereignty was not in tact in the Palestine countryside. Rural landlords owed their rule not so much to the absolute power delegated to them by the Sultan but rather controlled their areas on the basis of tribal authority.[26]

The third factor, therefore, was the hereditary nature of the countryside élite. Their position was passed on within the clan or the family. Alexander Schölch, on whose analysis we rely here, speaks about 'clan or tribal solidarity' (*asabiyya qabiliyya*) as characterizing the relationship within the clan, and of 'feudal protection and allegiance' as characterizing the relationship between the peasantry and the lords.[27] This solidarity only rarely had a wider sectarian or religious framework, and hardly ever did it transcend the local region or district.

These family-based clans, with their dominant legal, economic, social and political position, continued to affect Palestinian society throughout the mandatory period, if only for the simple fact that society then was still predominantly rural. As an élite, the clans' position began to be challenged by the urban notables in the nineteenth century and even more so during the mandatory period. None the less it remained largely in place, although its function and behaviour were neither appropriate nor sufficient for the needs of the Palestinian community in time of crisis.

The second source of élite power was the urban centre. The élite there was composed of old families who had comparative wealth

and local influence because of their possession of religious offices
and *waqfs*.[28] Until the nineteenth century they did not wield much
political power in Palestine. Thereafter, two factors contributed to
the rising power of this élite, which endangered the status of the
rural lords: European economic penetration and the centralization
policy of the Ottoman Empire. European penetration led to the
integration of Palestine into the international market in the wake of
which a new and influential commercial bourgeoisie emerged in the
urban centres. Ottoman centralization policies generated a decline
in the power of those who had benefited from the 'parcellized'
system and was compounded by a change in the structure of land
ownership – the new orientation was towards private ownership –
thus creating in Palestine large areas of landed property. This
property was shared by the new commercial class and the old
landlords.[29] In both groups, the old and the new, family solidarity
was the paramount factor dictating the élite's policy.

Towards the end of the Ottoman rule, the Turks began to
intervene more actively in the Palestinian élite's affairs and
composition. They raised certain traditional noble families to
counterbalance others; this was the case of the Tuqan family in
Nablus and the Husayni family in Jerusalem.[30] These noble
families together with the newly-established bourgeoisie formed the
basis for the leadership of the Palestinian national movement in the
mandatory period. However, even in this new stratum, family and
clan loyalties were stronger than the novel national interest. In the
urban centres, Jerusalem, Nablus, and Jaffa emerged as national
headquarters for the movement with some success; however, in the
countryside the legacy of the long period of feudalization hindered
the efforts of the national leaders to induce the rural notables to
transgress beyond local patriotism.

The British conquest of Palestine did not alter the basic
characteristics of the élite and the society. It demanded of the élite
a more official political formation, but in essence not much
changed. The national leadership succeeded only once, during the
Arab Revolt in 1936–9, to wield political authority over large areas
of Palestine. It was a social protest no less than a political one –
that is, the Palestinians rebelled not only against the pro-Zionist
policy of the mandate but also against the socio-economic reality in
Palestine, one in which they lagged far behind the modernized and
thriving Jewish community. Only rarely did national or class
affinities supersede factional, communal, clan, patronage and

regional alignments; for most of the time the divisions of family more than anything else determined Palestinian politics during the mandatory period.[31] The traditional basis of the élite, it appears, was insufficient for the challenges of the modern era – it neither had the authority nor the legitimacy needed to fulfil the important tasks ahead.

The main success of the Jewish élite, as suggested above, was the creation of a state in anticipation of the termination of the mandate. There is no evidence to show that the Palestinian leadership was, at the same time, engaged in anything resembling the process of state-building or in mobilizing the community for the imminent confrontation. There was a total dependence on the mandatory government as the authority and the provider of services in the country. Thus, whereas the Jews had already established independent education and health systems, the Palestinians continued to depend on the government's respective departments. These departments were staffed by colonial officials whose career in the past had taken them to India, Egypt and Africa, and who treated the 'native population' with typical British paternalism. The policy of the Education Department is particularly illuminating as it shows a clear British intent not to go beyond providing an elementary school system in Palestine.[32] Only at the last moment, as we shall see, were some efforts made to create an infrastructure for a state but it was too little and too late to constitute a significant response to the Jewish challenge.

This overall failure had far-reaching political implications – it led to the appropriation of the Palestinian cause by the Arab states. The inability to form a leadership that could overcome family allegiances caused disarray and divisions within the Palestinian community and allowed external powers to take the lead. Hence, the fate of the local community and its national ambitions depended on the commitment and ability of Egyptian, Syrian, Lebanese or Iraqi politicians. This state of affairs was apparently the Palestinian leaders' own doing. Almost voluntarily they invited the Arab politicians to interfere and partake in local politics. Since many of the neighbouring states had strategic and political ambitions concerning Palestine, it is no wonder that any call for outside involvement in the politics of the country met with an immediate welcome in the capitals of the Arab world.

The appeal for interference in Palestinian politics dates back to the Arab Revolt. It is possible to discern a growing involvement of

Arab statesmen in Palestine's affairs from 1936. The monarchs of Egypt, Saudi Arabia and Transjordan regarded Palestine as a convenient venue for recruiting supporters and stirring up arguments in order to consolidate their respective claims for leadership in the Arab world. Their republican colleagues from Syria, almost unanimously, regarded Palestine as part of Greater Syria and could not therefore relinquish the scene to other Arab politicians. On the other hand the degree of involvement should not be exaggerated – it was impeded by the fact that all countries concerned were still engaged in a struggle for liberation from European colonialism. Thus, until the Second World War, Palestinian politics were relatively free from interference.

But even in those days of relative freedom the local political leadership failed in its main tasks. After its heyday during the Arab Revolt, the Palestinian leadership was severely affected by the harsh measures taken by the British to quell the local uprising; many leaders had been arrested, others expelled. The internal strife during the revolt had also claimed its toll: important leaders had been assassinated during the 1930s, others found it difficult to co-operate with their traditional foes and political rivals. The local leadership did not easily recover from the blow inflicted upon it. The entire Palestinian population went through difficult times during the Second World War. Unemployment coupled with the deceleration of economic growth created problems which strengthened parochial and local loyalties rather than national identification. The degree of political activity on the national level was again very low.[33] Local leaders took the initiative in some places but failed to have an influence on the general situation. National Palestinian activity in no way corresponded to the intensity and vitality shown by the Jewish politicians, who, unlike the Palestinians, assumed an active part in political developments both inside and outside the country.

For a brief moment, in 1943, it seemed that many Palestinians had suddenly become aware of the general and, for them, ominous course events were taking. The year 1943 was in more than one sense a watershed in the history of Palestine: it was the year following Rommel's defeat in al-Alamain, which was to reaffirm British paramountcy in the Middle East. It was also the year in which the Jewish leadership resolved to confront the British authorities, even at the risk of open conflict on the question of Jewish immigration. Both developments activated the Palestinian political scene for a short while. Local politicians were also aroused to some extent by the emergence of a new Pan-Arab movement, which eventually led to the foundation of the Arab League in 1945.[34]

These three factors, namely a renewed British interest in Palestine's future, the revival of Pan-Arabism and Jewish activism, together produced an independent Palestinian activity – independent that is of Arab interference – in the conflict. The main feature of this activity was an effort to institutionalize and unify the haphazard and split leadership. The first task was to seek a way of bridging the personal and ideological rifts that had paralysed the community in the aftermath of the Arab Revolt. In political terms this meant re-establishing a national consensus which could embrace all the political forces in the country. There were six parties in Arab Palestine. The leading force was the Husaynis' Arab Party, which was traditionally challenged by the Nashashibis' al-Difa'a (Defence) Party, but usually supported by Husayn al-Khalidi's Reform Party. A Pan-Arab party also functioned in Palestine, al-Istiqlal, led by Awni Ab'l-Hadi. The two remaining parties were the National Block, led by Abd al-Latif Salah, and the Youth Party of Ya'aqub al-Ghusain. There was a seventh party, the Communist Party, which had been dominated by Jews, although in the 1940s more and more Palestinians joined it.[35] The Communist Party did not join the Palestine camp as it adhered to an ideology that rejected nationalist identification on either side. Later on, its close association with Moscow led it to strongly support the principle of partition; a concept totally rejected by the other Palestinian parties.

All six parties professed their willingness to turn over a new leaf in their relatioship and remove past rivalries and enmities. Yet, when the moment came to choose a new Arab Higher Committee, a necessary step if the Jews were to be successfully challenged, ghosts from the past totally frustrated the attempt and sectarian and clan interests again took precedence over national and communal causes. The main contention was between the Husaynis, whose prominent leader Hajj Amin was in exile, and their rivals, centred around the Nashashibi clan. The latter sought to exploit the absence of the two exiled Husayni leaders to settle old accounts and to usurp their position of leadership in the community.[36]

Not only as a result of external Arab pressure but also in the face of intensive international diplomatic efforts to solve the question of

Palestine, the rival factions grudgingly agreed to co-operate under the auspices of one body – a newly-formed Arab Higher Committee. The establishment of such a committee had been the intention of all parties in Palestine, but they had aspired to select its members by consensus, even by democratic elections. In the event, the committee that was formed was imposed on the Palestinians by the Arab League. This came about when the Palestinian leaders approached the Arab League and appealed for its intervention when their own efforts were unsuccessful, thereby allowing the League for the first time to take an active part in local politics.

The Palestinian politicians sought this intervention when they realized that without it the community would have stood leaderless in the face of the growing international interest in a solution for the Palestine problem. In more concrete terms, we may conclude that it was the arrival of the Anglo-American Committee in Palestine which necessitated such a move since this important body would otherwise have communicated only with the Jewish leadership. The League was the only possible substitute for local leadership and, being a new phenomenon in Arab politics, many hopes were aroused by its creation. Its general secretary impressed the Palestinian public when he succeeded in persuading the British government to release Jamal al-Husayni from his forced residence in Rhodesia. This success at least led the Husaynis to withdraw their previous objection to co-operating with the Nashashibis and to assist in the League's efforts to form a new Higher Committee.

In June 1946, the League summoned the former members of the Arab Higher Committee in an attempt to establish a new representative body for the Arabs in Palestine. The League's secretariat acted on the principle of parity, inviting an equal number from the Husayni faction and from the coalition of those opposing the rule of the family. The Husaynis gave up their previous demand for a majority rule and were left with only five out of the twelve members who were to form the committee. Their compromise was not reciprocated by their rivals. Instead of participating together with the Husaynis in a new body, in June 1946 the competing families and ideological adversaries formed their own organization which they called the Supreme Arab Front.[37] The Front's challenge eroded somewhat the Husaynis' authority in Palestine but did not undermine the family's predominance. Yet, it transpired that the Arab Higher Committee

at the beginning of 1947 represented only part of the political
forces. This state of affairs was to have far-reaching implications
for the ability of the Palestinian community to cope with the crisis
of 1948.

The Palestinian predicament can be demonstrated by pointing to
the leadership's inability to recruit and utilize the community's
economic and military potential: it was this deficiency that led to
the final and decisive call for outside Arab intervention. Before the
crisis there were two competing 'national treasuries' in Arab
Palestine. One was owned by the Husaynis – this was *Beit al-Mal
al-Arabi* (the Arab Treasury). The other one was *Sunduq al-Umma*
(the Nation's Treasury) run by the Pan-Arab Istiqlal party. This
competition in the financial field had a crucial effect on the
Palestinians' ability to mobilize their resources in preparation for
the coming conflict. The failure to concentrate the financial and
economic assets in the hands of one single authority led to further
dependence on Arab aid, which proved sparse and insignificant.

In 1947 yet another 'national treasury' emerged, this was *al-
Mashru al-Inshai* (the Constructive Project), run by Musa Alami
and supported by the Iraqi government. Musa Alami was a
prominent Palestinian activist who had been chosen, because of his
excellent connections with both the British and the Arab leaders,
as the representative of the Palestinian Arabs at the conference in
Alexandria (1944) and Cairo (1945) at which the Arab League was
founded. The *Mashru* represented faithfully Alami's interest in
enlarging the area of cultivated Palestinian land. The *Mashru*
specifically provided funds for buying and developing lands.[38]
Alami would continue to believe in the value of land development
as a means of strengthening Palestinian nationalism long after 1948
and well into the 1970s – and would train Palestinian youth for
modern agriculture on his West Bank farm.

Under pressure from the League the unification of all three
financial bodies took place, but this did not provide the mechanism
required to unite the community and prepare it for the struggle
against the Jews.[39]

Not only was the financial infrastructure inadequate, but also
the military force. Private arms were abundant in the villages of
Palestine and some villagers had gained military experience during
the revolt of 1936, but neither of these was sufficient to organize a
serious fighting force. The difficulty in recruiting and mobilizing
the population lay in the fact that both the arms and the people

were divided between local forces. The Jewish underground, too, was beset by ideological disputes, but succeeded in uniting into one mighty force at the right moment. On the Palestinian side, paramilitary groups refused to co-ordinate their activities with the local leadership and in some cases even deserted the battlefield at the crucial moment.[40]

Yet, the Palestinians met with some success in 1947 when the Jihad al-Muqaddas (the Holy War Army) commanded by Abd al-Qader al-Husayni, was established. However, this was basically Husayni's own private army and the number of recruits testifies to the lack of voluntary zeal among the Palestinians. Muhammad Nimr al-Hawari estimated the number of conscripts at not more than a few hundred, a figure which tallies with the estimate of other sources.[41]

The failure to recruit an adequate military force has been ascribed by some to a general Palestinian aversion to participate in actual fighting, a tendency which was particularly evident during May 1948, after the state of Israel had been declared. At the time, most Palestinians preferred non-aggression pacts with their Jewish neighbours – so runs the argument – agreements which usually were violated by the Jews.[42] Evidence of this interesting and sympathetic view of the Palestinian community is scarce, but it is true to say that the number of Palestinians who ultimately participated in the war strengthens the suggestion that to serve in a Palestinian army did not rank high in the population's ambitions. By May 1948, the Palestinian fighting force consisted of four thousand soldiers. These were joined during the first months of 1948 by eight thousand volunteers, mostly irregular Arab soldiers. The Mufti later recalled that only a quarter of them were from Palestine. Another source, the Iraqi General Isma'il Safwat, estimated that the Palestinians made up even less than one-tenth of the overall number of volunteers.[43] In either case, this indicates that the Palestinian political leadership in fact governed no military power of its own and that without outside Arab assistance in the form of regular armies the Arabs of Palestine had absolutely no hope of achieving any significant military gain against the Jews. Even with the volunteers, the Palestinian fighting force numbered only 12,000, facing a Jewish force of 22,425 active military personnel. Numerically, therefore, the Palestinians themselves were a negligible force and even the overall Arab forces in Palestine towards the end of the mandate were no match for the Jewish military strength.[44]

Under pressure from the League, most of the military organizations expressed submission to the authority of the new Arab Higher Committee, but in practice very few organizations obeyed its instructions and orders.

The fragmentary political structure of the Palestinian community escaped the notice of UNSCOP's members when they visited the country in June 1947. UNSCOP perceived the Arab community as well organized and represented by one body – the Arab Higher Committee. This committee was able, as we have seen, to organize a general strike in the Arab community and lead an effective boycott of the UN investigation body. But the undercurrents of opposition and conflicting loyalties were to persist and determine the performance and conduct of the leadership in the days ahead. No sooner had UNSCOP left the country, than almost all members of the 'government of the Palestinians' – out of fear of the coming confrontation or to seek advice in Arab capitals – forsook their homeland and deserted their community. With the outbreak of actual fighting in Palestine later, they found refuge in the neighbouring Arab states and were never to return to Palestine to the end of their days. By July 1947, only three out of the twelve members of the Arab Higher Committee remained in Palestine. The others were in Damascus, while the leader of the movement, Hajj Amin al-Husayni, was in Cairo. The Mufti was prohibited from entering Palestine by the British; this prohibition was limited later to the area of Jerusalem but Hajj Amin never set foot in any of the towns or villages within mandatory Palestine. In August that year, Jamal al-Husayni, one of the three remaining members and the official head of the Arab Higher Committee, left for New York to plead the Palestinian cause in the UN sessions. Likewise, he never returned to his homeland but spent the rest of his time living in the various Arab capitals. As the Egyptian historian Khaled Ali rightly remarks, 'It was left to the two remaining members of the Committee, Dr Husayn Fakhri al-Khalidi and Ahmad Hilmi Pasha to carry the heavy burden of running the affairs of the Palestinians.'[45]

Al-Khalidi was the secretary of the Arab Higher Committee and in that capacity was now expected to substitute as chairman of the committee and co-ordinate the local forces in Palestine. He soon discovered that he did not wield the same authority as Jamal al-Husayni, and failed to smooth out the differences of opinion and constant frictions between the various political factions represented in each locality.[46] The absence of a guiding hand on the Palestinian side adversely compared with the unity of purpose that characterized the Jewish leadership – which both in organizing Jewish settlement in Palestine and in conducting the diplomatic campaign in the UN was performing well.

An élite is tested in times of crisis: the Palestinian élite had abandoned responsibility when it was most needed. This situation was sorely evident in Haifa, in April 1948, when the British tried to mediate between the two parties and found no one on the Palestinian side who would assume the responsibility of answering these overtures; eleven of the fifteen members of the local national committee, the governing body of the Arab community, had by then left the city. The only representative of the Arab Higher Committee, Chief Magistrate Ahmad Bey Khalil, had fled earlier during the fighting.[47]

The organizational structure of the Arab Higher Committee in 1947 illustrates the difference in the level of preparations between the two communities. The Jewish structure facilitated a relatively smooth transition from autonomy to statehood whereas the Arab structure was hardly sufficient to provide the needs of an autonomous community, let alone an independent state. The Arab Higher Committee delegated its power only to four departments: the department of land, of national economy, of general affairs which dealt with foreign policy, and of local affairs, which co-ordinated domestic policy. Education, health, police and many other aspects of public life were in the hands of the mandatory government and this ceased to exist in February 1947. On the Jewish side, we find not only an embryo government, with a differential division of authority and expertise, but also the departments necessary for running a state, such as a customs agency and elaborate education and medical systems.

The headquarters of the Jewish Agency were in Tel Aviv and Jerusalem; the main political office of the Arab Higher Committee was in Cairo, with branches in Jerusalem, Baghdad, Beirut and Damascus.[48] Arif al-Arif, the important Palestinian historian and an eyewitness, tells us that in December 1947 only one member of the Arab Higher Committee was in the country; that is, a few days after the UN General Assembly had announced its verdict only one Palestinian leader was actually present in Palestine. Of the Jewish leaders, on the other hand, most were present and took immediate action to recruit the community's resources for the coming conflict.

On a more local level the Palestinians were better organized. From November 1947, the Arab Higher Committee began forming local national committees. These, *al-Lijan al-qawmiya*, bore the same name as the committees which had instigated the revolt of 1936. Whereas in 1936 the members of these committees had been appointed by the Arab Higher Committee, this time they were directly elected by the local communities.[49] They formed an interesting phenomenon in the political life of the Palestinian community at the time and still await thorough scholarly attention; we do know that through this network the Arab Higher Committee distributed arms to the population and tried to supervise and co-ordinate the defence of the Arab villages and districts.

Co-ordination was, however, virtually impossible. We have already mentioned that Hajj Amin al-Husayni was in Cairo heading the political wing of the Arab Higher Committee. Abd al-Qader al-Husayni, carrying the title of Supreme Military Commander of the forces in Palestine, was in Jerusalem but it seems that there were other contenders for this title, such as Hasan Salameh from Jaffa. Leaders of the local national committees received orders both from Jerusalem and through wireless communication – intercepted regularly by the Jews – from Cairo. Not only did these instructions not always match, they often contradicted each other.[50] Khalil Sakakini recounts in his memoirs that the people of Qatamon, the neighbourhood of Jerusalem where he lived, were ordered to care for their own defence because of lack of co-ordination and guidance from above.[51] With a few exceptions, this seems to have been the rule for most of the Arab villages and neighbourhoods.

A very disparaging and critical view of the conduct of these national committees can be found in the memoirs of Muhammad Nimr al-Hawari. Hawari accused the committees' members of preferring their personal interest above the national one. He alleges that many members utilized community funds for their own ends and overtaxed the population in order to augment their personal income. The money was then smuggled out of the country and deposited in foreign bank accounts. Hawari's list of culprits is long and detailed and is therefore an important document, but one should bear in mind his own disloyalty when he defected to the Jewish side. Attaching a general stigma of dishonesty and corruption may have been intended to justify his own action. Nevertheless, he might be right and more research is undoubtedly warranted.[52] Hawari's memoirs reveal, among other things, the tangled relationship which existed between local magnates, like himself, and the elected heads of the national committees who were usually pro-Husaynis. The rift caused by clan loyalties and different ideological affiliations crippled the general Palestinian effort. King Abdullah was fully aware of this socio-political reality and used the knowledge to win over to his side some prominent members of the national committees in the West Bank. These members, like Muhammad al-Ja'abri in Hebron and the Tuqan family in Nablus, were to form the nucleus for the cadre of collaborators who assisted Abdullah in imposing Hashemite rule over the West Bank.

It is quite clear that the Arab Higher Committee's success in the period 1936–9 in organizing the community and preparing it for a common struggle, overcoming sectarian, clan and religious antagonisms, was not repeated in the years 1946–8. When the civil war broke out, the chairmen of several national committees expressed their frustration with and dismay at the lack of enthusiasm and steadfastness – especially when compared with the community's will and commitment in the days of the Arab Revolt.[53]

Palestinian historians have been engaged in a historiographical debate over the extent of Hajj Amin al-Husayni's responsibility for this failure. Samih Shabib is particularly derogatory about the former Mufti's role. Husni Jarar, on the other hand, accepts that al-Husayni made some critical mistakes but points out that he was overwhelmed by strong foes and that, all things considered, al-Husayni epitomizes both the achievements and the failures of the Palestinian people.[54] He was certainly responsible for allowing the gradual usurpation by the Arab states of the political initiative in Palestine and the 'expropriation' of the Palestinian cause – a process that prevented the establishment of independent Palestinian leadership and institutions.

THE AMBIGUOUS TAKEOVER: THE ARAB LEAGUE
AND THE QUESTION OF PALESTINE 1946–8

The critical situation in Palestine engaged the Arab League's attention from the very moment of its inception in December 1944.

During its first months the organization had many other issues on its agenda, such as the fate of Libya, Egypt and the Sudan, but no issue could hope to secure the united Arab sympathy as the case of Palestine. One of the first actions of the organization therefore was to voice general Arab support for the Palestinian cause. The crux of the matter, however, was that each Arab leader had his own notion of how that cause could best be served. And usually the cause of the leaders themselves, or at best that of their countries was incidentally to be served too. Very rarely did this diversity of ideas help the plight of the Palestinians.

Yet, the beginning was most promising for them. In the preliminary meeting in Alexandria, in October 1944, the League's commitment to an independent Palestinian state was firmly included among the basic principles for a Pan-Arab existence. Consequently, a representative of the Arab Palestinians was invited to join the inaugural session of the League and its subsequent meetings.[55] The League's covenant includes to this very day a special annex in which the Arab states one by one acknowledge their responsibility for Palestine's fate until independence is attained.[56]

The first significant discussion about Palestine's future took place in May 1946, at Inshas in Egypt. There and in another meeting shortly after in Bludan, Syria, the Arab leaders considered the implications of the Anglo-American Committee's report. The participants in both meetings were most vociferous in their support for the Palestinians' demands for full independence. The Arab states committed themselves to an unconditional financial, military and political contribution in aid of the Palestinian people. A special committee, the Palestine Committee, was formed to supervise the general Arab effort for Palestine. In a secret appendix to the Bludan resolutions, the members of the Arab League went even further and decided to impose economic sanctions on foreign countries that supported Zionism. This impressive clause was never put into effect as some of the Arab countries could simply not afford to sever their economic ties with either Europe or the United States. Transjordan, Iraq and Saudi Arabia in particular were vulnerable in that sense and their signature on the secret appendix was merely an exercise in Pan-Arab diplomacy.[57]

Notwithstanding their vehement rhetoric, the League's officials and the Arab leaders proved much more pragmatic than the Palestinians themselves in their attitude towards the international diplomatic effort. They were willing to allow some Jewish immigration into Palestine, whereas the Arab Higher Committee guaranteed the right of settlement only to Jews who had arrived in Palestine before 1919. After the UN partition resolution, however, the Arab Palestinians left the representation of their case entirely in the hands of the Arab diplomats and there is little point therefore in lingering over the niceties of the divergent opinions. The general Arab point of view and the Palestinian position therefore converged and became one, to all intents and purposes. It was not that the Arab diplomats failed in presenting the Palestinians' cause, but there was little they could do to save them from the impending tragedy which the complacency of the politicians and the incompetence of the generals was precipitating.

From December 1947 onwards, the Arab League began to play first fiddle in the Palestinian camp. It orchestrated the Arab reaction to UNSCOP's report, leaving only a minor role for the leaders of the Palestinians. What began as a Palestinian appeal for general Arab recruitment ended in the expropriation of the affairs of Palestine from the hands of its indigenous people. This situation was to further deteriorate and, as one historian has put it: 'During 1948, and in particular the second half of that year, the Palestinians would struggle for their independence not so much against the Jews as against the neighbouring Arab states.'[58] This description may be an exaggeration as the Palestinians were of course facing a Jewish threat, but it is correct in so far as it depicts the war of 1948 as a non-Palestinian war, fought between Israel and the Arab states. The Palestinians played at best a marginal role in the campaign over their country's future.

Hajj Amin al-Husayni had in fact sensed the new development quite early on, but his hands were tied and to his great dismay he became *persona non grata* in the successive Arab summit meetings intended to prepare the struggle against the partition plan. His attempts to convince the Arab leaders to include him in their preparations failed totally. Al-Husayni's troubles began in September 1947 when the League's Political Committee met in Soafar, Lebanon and decided to assist the Palestinian struggle by forming an Arab Liberation Army. They chose Fawzi al-Qawqji as its head. Al-Qawqji was a Lebanese who had served in the Ottoman army and won his fame during the Syrian revolt against the French in 1925. After being sentenced to death by the French he succeeded in escaping from Syria and joined the Iraqi army. In 1936, he arrived in Palestine heading a group of volunteers and established an alliance with the Nashashibi family, the Husaynis' main rivals. His service in the Iraqi army made him a favourite candidate in Baghdad. The government in Iraq did not forget for one moment al-Husayni's involvement in Rashid Ali al-Qa'yani's attempt in 1941 to overthrow the Hashemite regime. Abdullah had his own alliance with the Nashashibis and in any case regarded the Mufti as his arch-enemy in Palestine. No wonder therefore that al-Qawqji's candidacy was promoted by the two Hashemite kingdoms.[59]

The Mufti was strongly opposed to the nomination of Fawzi al-Qawqji but there was very little he could do. He tried to circumvent the appointment by declaring the establishment of a Supreme Command for Palestine. Since, as we shall see, the Arab League would form its own chain of command, the forces in Palestine thus came under the rule of two different authorities. There were in fact two separate Arab armies in Palestine up to May 1948: a local army subordinated to the Arab Higher Committee and the volunteer Arab Liberation Army, subjected to the League's authority. More often than not, these two forces were at loggerheads with each other and their clashes came to a head in March 1948 just when Palestinian unity was needed more than ever. The League's attempts to mediate between the two forces never had any success.[60]

The Mufti's endeavour to impose his own military authority irritated to no small extent the Arab generals who accused him of obstructing preparations for the war in Palestine.[61] He was subsequently urged by the Secretary-General of the League to cease any such activity and confine his role to the area of Jerusalem. Al-Husayni, nevertheless, did succeed in affirming the right of the two local Palestinian commanders, Abd al-Qader al-Husayni and Hasan Salameh to have the final word on military affairs within Palestine. However, al-Qawqji never felt subordinated to these local commanders, and was quite independent in deciding about offensives against – and alliances with – the Jews. In order to forestall the potential danger of internal strife the League confined al-Qawqji's mission to the north of Palestine. This division of authority was even more disastrous since it enabled al-Qawqji to pursue his own kind of war and furthermore served to ease the pressure on the large Jewish concentration in the centre of Palestine.[62]

In the months to come, the rift between al-Qawqji's forces and the local Palestinians became ever more marked. Like the politicians in the Arab capitals, al-Qawqji regarded the local population more or less as an obstacle to a successful military operation and generally seemed to have little respect for the peasants. His stay in Palestine between January and July 1948 had very little impact on the course of the war itself, but the somewhat brutal conduct and unscrupulous behaviour of his volunteer army, on the other hand, added to the misery of the local population in fighting the Jews. Due to the presence of foreign Arab troops in Palestine, and because he failed to fuse the local factions into a unified military force, the Mufti remained on the sideline. Thus, the local forces were entirely dependent on the Arab League in such matters as arms supply, where the Arab states proved more generous with Palestinian demands by both collecting and storing the required arsenal. Owing to the British embargo on arms transportation, which lasted until the end of the mandate, it was difficult to ship the arms into Palestine. In addition, Arab generosity had its limits, and the armament operation was to a large extent financed by Palestinian funds.[63]

The consequences of the military predicament were already evident during the civil war – the unofficial war so to speak in the first months of 1948. Then and later during the official war, the Palestinians were never the main fighting force on the Arab side and consequently had little say in political matters: 'The Palestinians were given no defined role in the Arab operations in Palestine, they were not assigned to any task, not even an auxiliary one, which is a proof for both their helplessness and the real nature of the general Arab position.'[64]

Being denied the leading military role in Palestine, the Mufti had now to struggle to maintain his political position. For this purpose he tried to engage the League in a discussion on Palestine's political constitution in the event of an Arab success in the war against the Jews. As a first stage he suggested the establishment of a 'government in exile' headed by himself. With this new message he began appearing, unasked, in the League's meetings dealing with the Arab policy on Palestine. He first did so in October 1947 in Aleyh, Lebanon, and obstinately persisted in this tactic almost until the end of the mandate. In Aleyh, where the Arab League was debating its reaction to UNSCOP's report, the Mufti suddenly walked into the meeting and presented what he considered the only possible answer to the UN decision: the public commitment of the League to establish on 15 May an independent administration in all Palestine. The Hashemite sister states rejected this suggestion out of hand and convinced the other League members to ignore the Mufti's proposals.[65]

Undeterred, al-Husayni tried his luck once more and made another uninvited appearance at the League's next session on Palestine, held in Cairo in December 1947. Here he was more successful since he persuaded the Egyptian prime minister, Mahmud Nuqrashi, to support the establishment of an independent administration in Palestine immediately after the country's liberation by the Arab armies. The Mufti named himself as the natural candidate for Palestine's future leadership, and even this suggestion was accepted by Nuqrashi. Nuqrashi had never previously expressed any great admiration for the Mufti and his personal attitude did not seem to have changed much. He was, however, aware of the fact that the alternative to a 'Mufti Palestine' was a 'Hashemite Palestine' or a 'Syrian Palestine', and he may have been moved either by a genuine belief in the Palestinians' right to rule the country themselves or by the hope that an independent Palestine would be less hostile to Egyptian interests than a Syrian one and certainly less than a Hashemite one.[66]

Similar considerations guided the Saudis and the Syrians. That is, either because of mutual suspicion or genuine support for the Palestinians' right of self-determination, Ibn Saud and the Syrian government were willing to join the Egyptians in helping the Mufti regain some of his political power. Thus, in December 1947 during the League's Council meeting in Cairo, the three delegations tabled a motion calling for the formation, upon independence, of a local administration (*idara mahaliyya*) in Palestine under the leadership of Hajj Amin. The Hashemites, however, again cast their veto and won the day, as no one wanted to be accused of sowing discord amidst the Arab ranks at such a crucial moment. Moreover, to forestall any future discussion on the matter, the Transjordanians and the Iraqis led the League to demote the Mufti to the position of supervising officer of the Jerusalem area alongside his relative Abd al-Qader al-Husayni.[67]

Yet, the idea of an independent representation was well received in Palestine itself. *Al-Difa'a*, like other Palestinian newspapers, called upon the Mufti to declare the establishment of a 'government in exile'.[68] The Arab Higher Committee tried to respond to domestic pressure by reaching some decisions regarding the political structure of the future independent Palestine. Thus was born, at least on paper, the 'new political framework' (*nizam siyasi*) for Arab Palestine. Six out of Palestine's seven political parties swore allegiance to the new body; the Communist Party, having accepted the partition resolution refused to participate. The preparatory committee to set up the 'new political framework' included besides the politicians two local non-partisan Christians and Ahmad Hilmi, the future head of the All-Palestine government of September 1948, who was appointed as the committee's treasurer.[69]

The 'political framework' was to include in its completed form the institutions of a modern state, such as a government, a national assembly, a judiciary system and a president as its executive head. In February 1948, a month after it was first proposed by the Arab Higher Committee, Hajj Amin asked the League to approve the new framework as a basis for an independent Palestinian state. The League's leaders met in Cairo that month and again it was the Hashemite members who refused to give their blessing to an independent move by the Palestinians. The Hashemite delegates instead presented a new draft resolution – which was accepted by the League's Council – suspending the decision on Palestine's future until after the liberation. The League, however, did promise that when the decision was made, it would be made by the Palestinian people themselves. Until such time, any part of Palestine falling into Arab hands would come under the temporary military regime of the occupying army.[70]

His setback in the League led the Mufti's own supporters in Palestine to doubt the wisdom of al-Husayni's political man-oeuvres. Some of the Palestinian leaders considered his efforts to be irrelevant in view of the harsh circumstances in which the Palestinian community found itself at the beginning of 1948.[71] The Mufti, however, did not relent and continued to ask for a firmer Arab commitment. The impending war had led to a more amicable rhetoric on the part of the Arab leaders. On 12 April 1948, for example, King Faruq addressed the Arab delegates to the League's assembly and promised that 'after the occupation Palestine's future would be determined by the Palestinians'.[72] But only three days before the end of the mandate, the Arab League succumbed to al-Husayni's pressure and promised to establish a civil administration in Palestine on 15 May, that is, immediately upon the mandate's termination.[73] However, as the war progressed and bigger areas of

Palestine fell into Jewish hands, other more urgent problems occupied the Mufti and the Arab League alike.

It has been argued above that the Jewish Agency was ready to take over as much as it could of the mandatory institutions and structure. It should be noted that not everyone on the Palestinian side was oblivious to the question of transfer of power; senior Arab officials serving within the British administration were prepared by the Arab Higher Committee for the eventuality of a take-over. The British authorities themselves were approached for this purpose but declined to co-operate.[74] Yet, even with British co-operation there would have been little hope for the establishment of the Arab 'new political framework'. Lacking the necessary military strength and the political support of the Arab League, it was a futile exercise in statehood. And the contribution of the League towards creating a state, always promised so vehemently by all the Arab leaders, failed to materialize. Rather the contrary happened: the policy of many of the Arab League members actually aimed to prevent the establishment of an independent and sovereign Palestinian administration – and they would attain their goal.[75] Without such a structure it was most difficult to win the 'civil war' in Palestine.

THE OUTBREAK OF VIOLENCE:
NOVEMBER 1947 TO MAY 1948

The morning after the UN General Assembly ratified the partition resolution, Palestine was swept by an outbreak of violence which signalled the beginning of a civil war that was to last until 15 May 1948. The first attacks were perpetrated by Palestinians against Jews. Two Jewish buses were attacked near Lydda airport and in Jerusalem Arab youths on 2 December ransacked the city's Jewish market and shopping centre. Beginning that same day the Arabs all over Palestine went on strike for three days. The first two weeks of December were marked by sporadic attacks on Jewish settlements in the north and along the coast of Palestine, and on the main routes connecting the cities. The Arab violence was soon met by that of the Irgun and the Stern Gang – three times between 23 December and 7 January the Jewish extremists threw bombs into the midst of Arab crowds near the Damascus and the Jaffa gates in the Old City of Jerusalem.[76]

Was this the beginnings of a 'Palestinian onslaught on the Jewish community' in Palestine? Sir Alan Cunningham – the last High Commissioner in Palestine – did not think so. He reported to London that the 'riots in Jerusalem were not the onset of an orchestrated offensive against the Jews, but rather spontaneous demonstrations against the partition resolution'.[77] Cunningham's analysis is shared by Palestinian historians who regard the violence as a natural consequence of the many demonstrations held in those days.[78] This was in contrast, however, to the view taken by the Jewish leaders, who declared to the world at large that a war of annihilation had begun.

The first day of clashes ended with the death of seven Jews and a few burnt down buildings and businesses in Jerusalem, and an equal number of Arabs killed in the wake of Jewish retaliation the morning after. As in the case of the civil war in Lebanon, limited events such as those occurring in Jerusalem can prove enough to ignite an entire country, especially when the will to put an immediate end to fighting is absent. The existence of this situation in Palestine is indicated in the following passage from Ben Gurion's diary in which he refers to the resumption of violence after a temporary lull in the fighting during 1947

Until five days ago [25 December 1947] Jerusalem was more or less quiet. There were isolated cases of attacks on Jewish visitors to the Old City and Damascus Gate. And then suddenly the Hagana Commander in Jerusalem decided that in Romema [a neighbourhood in the western outskirts of Jerusalem] lives an Arab, who owns a motorcycle and a petrol station and who is an informer [for the Arab side] about the movement of Jewish convoys to the city. The Jewish commander decides to kill him in his station in Romema and so he does. This Arab is from Kolonia (and not from Lifta, a village which was a source of trouble for the Jewish convoys to the city) so the people of his village retaliate by attacking a Jewish bus, seven people are injured. Then a vicious cycle evolves – a reprisal and a counter-reprisal.[79]

Ben Gurion's account is most important as it reveals that in some cases – and he cites quite a few – more restrained Jewish behaviour might have left the Arab population largely indifferent to the developing conflict. Ben Gurion gave as another example the village Silwan, in the Jerusalem area, which without provocation was attacked by the Hagana. Ben Gurion remarks cynically, 'Now of course Silwan is attacking the Jews.' In the same entry, Gad Machnes, Ben Gurion's adviser on Arab affairs, tells the Jewish leader that the riots in the Galilee were provoked and initiated by the Jewish side.[80]

The Arab attacks, which culminated in January 1948, were of such scope and force that they succeeded in shaking the confidence of the Jewish community, whose last experience of such a period of hostilities had been back in 1937. Israeli historians have called this period the 'nadir of the Yishuv' – summarizing the mood of the Jewish community in Palestine in those days.[81] The actions against the settlements and the major routes certainly caught the Zionist leadership off its guard, and it had already misjudged the intensity and severity of the Arab reaction.[82] The dismay and despair comes out very clearly from notes of the Mapai council meetings at the beginning of February 1948. Most members were particularly concerned about Jerusalem's fate and blamed Ben Gurion, who was present at those meetings, for inadequately preparing the community for the struggle.[83] The Arab siege of isolated Jewish settlements in the Negev was another sore point. Ben Gurion refused to describe the situation in dire terms and insisted – in this hindsight proved him right – that the local Arab effort in Palestine had failed.[84] He was ready to concede, however, that he had been surprised by the lack of steadfastness on behalf of the Jewish community in Jerusalem, and attributed the relative Arab success there to the pro-Arab position taken by the British forces and to the heterogeneous ethnic fabric of the city's population. The Jewish leader did not specify what he meant by this last remark – it could refer to the lack of commitment of the Sephardic Jews or, more likely to the local patriotism of the various sects.[85]

Within a few weeks bewilderment on the Jewish side was replaced by despair among the Arabs. The Arab Higher Committee's secretary, Husayn al-Khalidi, was in Jerusalem at the time and reported to the Mufti that lack of ammunition, absence of medical supplies and the British policy of disarming anyone they encountered, Jew or Arab, left the Palestinians defenceless in the face of a determined Jewish attempt to take over the city. He also complained that none of the Palestinian leaders stood beside him in that crucial hour.[86]

The war in Jerusalem spread in March 1948 into the

neighbouring Arab villages. Abd al-Qader al-Husayni, the Arab commander of the Jerusalem area, whose troops were based in the villages, tried to obstruct the daily communication between Jerusalem and the coast. The Jewish struggle to keep the road to Jerusalem open, and the retaliation operations carried out against the Arab villages in its neighbourhood, became an important chapter in subsequent Israeli war epics. Historically speaking, this campaign enabled the Jews to extend the area under their control in Jerusalem and the surrounding settlements.

The persistent Arab attacks on the Jerusalem road from the very beginning of the war generated a sense of siege among the Jewish population in the city and the leadership feared that its demoralized community would not be able to withstand this feeling for long. In reality, however, although the Arabs succeeded in capturing the main water supplies and their frequent attacks on the routes to the city created a shortage of food in the Jewish neighbourhoods, the city was never completely encircled by the Arab forces.

By February 1948 the local Jewish leadership had overcome most of the problems by ably organizing and distributing the city's resources and the days of hardship for the community were over. Two months later, at the beginning of April, the Jews defeated al-Husayni's forces, a success that placed them at a considerable advantage when the war in Jerusalem entered its second stage, the Legion–IDF battle of June to July 1948.

The two other major urban centres of Palestine, Jaffa-Tel Aviv and Haifa, were also highly affected by the ongoing war. The city of Jaffa-Tel Aviv was sharply divided between the two communities with the exception of the Arab villages of Sheikh Munis, Semeil and Jamusin, which were situated within the boundaries of the predominantly Jewish Tel Aviv area. The Jews had the upper hand from the onset of the fighting and at an early stage of the war the inhabitants of Sumeil and Jamusin were chased out and the villages destroyed. Moreover, whereas in Jerusalem the routes leading to the city were controlled by Arab villages, Jaffa was at the mercy of Jewish settlements commanding the main entrances to the city.

Very shortly after the first exchange of fire in Jaffa, the local leadership consisting of Mayor Yusuf Haykal and Nimr Hawari, head of the Najjada paramilitary movement, were willing to enter negotiations with the Jews. On 9 December 1947 a cease-fire agreement was concluded between the mayors of Tel Aviv and Jaffa. The agreement was supported by the rich Arab merchants of Jaffa as the cease-fire enabled the resumption of normal economic activities and their livelihood depended upon the citrus trade. This unique situation was shortlived, however, as other elements from both sides did not respect the cease-fire agreement. On the Jewish side the Irgun and LEHI (Stern Gang) refused to put down their arms and on the Arab side the Arab Liberation Army continued fighting. Neither did the military commander of Lydda and Ramleh, appointed by the Arab Higher Committee, abide by the agreement.

The local Arab leaders in Jaffa at that stage beseeched the military committee of the League to send ammunition and reinforcements, but in vain. The Jewish forces encircled Jaffa in accordance with Plan D but went no further than besieging it as the British officers in charge prevented an overall attack on the city. The siege, however, sufficed as there was no one who could come to the rescue of its inhabitants, and on 11 May 1948 Jaffa capitulated.[87]

The Arab quarters of Haifa were also safe until the last days of the mandate owing to the British presence. As in Jaffa, local exchanges of fire, sniper shots and explosives planted by Jews in Arab territory and vice versa led to more extensive fighting. The location of the Jewish neighbourhoods on the Carmel mountain gave them an important strategic advantage, fully utilized by the Jewish forces. Moreover, the Jews outnumbered the Arabs in Haifa, were better equipped, and well organized under the command of efficient officers such as Moshe Carmel.[88] Carmel did not wait for his superiors' instructions before retaliating against the Arab attacks. This resulted in a wave of refugees from the poorer neighbourhoods of the city, following their more affluent fellow countrymen many of whom had already fled in December 1947. One of the first objects of the Jewish offensive was the harbour. Built in 1925 by the British, it was practically the only reasonable port in Palestine and thus coveted by both sides. The Jewish operation aimed at the expulsion of the Arab dockers and their replacement by Jewish workers.[89] In February 1948 a Jewish director was appointed to the port and all Arab workers were expelled from the docks.

Worse was the fate of two villages on the north-eastern outskirts of Haifa (Balad al-Sheikh and Hawassa), following clashes between

Jewish and Arab workers in the refinery complex nearby which had resulted in the death of forty Jews. The operation against these two villages, which ended in their total destruction, had wider objectives however: 'The Hagana's command decided to execute a large scale operation to deter the Arabs and boost morale, and the objectives were the villages Balad al-Sheikh and Hawassa.'[90] Carmel suggested, and the General Command approved the massacre that took place in the two villages. The order was to kill as many men as possible but 'to avoid the killing of women and children as far as possible'.[91] All the men of the two villages were dead by the end of the operation as were a number of children and women. On the ruins of these villages the Jewish neighbourhoods of Ben-Dor and Tel-Hanan were later erected. A discussion followed among the politicians of the Jewish community about the desirability of actions of this kind, but no operative conclusions were drawn.

If an Arab convoy sent from Beirut with men and ammunition had arrived, it might have altered the situation in March 1948. But it was ambushed by the Hagana units and the Arabs of Haifa were left to fend entirely for themselves. The Jewish forces in the city waited with their takeover operation until 12 April 1948, when General Stockwell, the British military commander of Haifa, announced that his forces were relieved of any responsibility for the city. Immediately the Jewish forces began their offensive and in three days occupied the Arab districts. The last service rendered by the local British commanders was the mediation between the defeated Palestinians and the Jews which resulted in a relatively large number of Arabs being allowed to remain in Haifa. The general atmosphere soon improved, which may explain the relatively good relationship existing there between the two communities today.[92]

Winning the battle in the urban centres was the most decisive Jewish achievement in the course of the early phases of the war. This success was due to two main causes: first, in Plan D, capturing the mixed towns was singled out as one of the major objectives of the war. On the Arab side, whether in the perpetration of acts of violence in some cases, or when responding to Jewish attacks in others, there was an absence of that clear sense of direction and objectives which Plan D provided for the Jews.

Also important in deciding the outcome of the fighting within the cities was the difference in the quality of the intelligence units on both sides. It would seem that the Palestinian headquarters was totally ignorant of the size and strength of the forces facing them. The Jewish intelligence service, on the other hand, assessed correctly the disarray, weakness and confusion existing on the Palestinian side and had a fair estimate regarding the malfunctioning of the various national Arab committees. Most of the telephone conversations between the local leaders and the Arab Higher Committee were intercepted by the Jews and the internal feuding between the various factions was thus known to them. The Jewish intelligence was also acting as an *agent provocateur* trying, successfully in a number of cases, to augment already existing tensions and to strengthen anti-Husayni elements. The Jews were particuarly interested in promoting Suliman Tuqan, the mayor of Nablus, a known anti-Husayni politician. Tuqan, however, had already pledged his allegiance to the Hashemites.[93]

Compared to their failure in the cities, the Arabs were quite effective when it came to controlling the main routes of the country, i.e., the road between Tel Aviv and Jerusalem, the road from Tel Aviv to the Negev, the coastal way leading to Ras al-Naqura in the north and its parallel in the eastern part of Palestine leading from Tiberias to the Jewish settlement of Metula. The Jews tried to circumvent the problem by using secondary routes and by escorting civilian transportation with armed vehicles. But they put most store by retaliation, attacking Arab villages along the roads. Local Hagana commanders were authorized to use any means deemed fit for retaliation. Moshe Carmel in the north was particularly 'active', as already illustrated by the massacres of Balad al-Sheikh and Hawassa, in retaliating immediately after an incident, and many of his operations resulted in massive casualties in Arab villages in the north of Palestine.

The desirability of such a policy had already been discussed by some of Ben Gurion's advisers on Arab affairs in January 1948. Among them, Ezra Danin was a stout supporter of the retaliation policy, and favoured utilizing it as widely as possible. Danin told Ben Gurion that 'our friends among the Arabs inform us that a severe blow, with a high rate of casualties to the Arabs would increase Arab fear and would render external Arab intervention ineffective'.[94] His words were echoed by Gad Machnes, who told Ben Gurion that 'we need a cruel and brutal retaliating policy, we have to be accurate in time, place and number of dead. If we know that a family is guilty, we should be merciless, and kill the women and the children as well, otherwise the reaction is useless. While the forces are in action, there is no room for checking who is guilty and who is not'.[95] While these last two faithfully represented the mood of virtually all those around Ben Gurion, the exception was Eliahu Sasson who suggested limiting the military activity to those areas from which the Arab attacks emanated. Showing a comprehensive grasp of the situation, Sasson thought that since the Arab Liberation Army had performed so poorly against the Jews it would be expedient to limit Jewish actions so as to furnish no inducement to the League to send reinforcements into Palestine – a unique strategic thinking that was not approved by Ben Gurion, who was in agreement with his other advisers on Arab affairs. Danin and Machnes won the day and the Jewish community decided upon an overall offensive as the best protection of the embryo state.[96]

But a policy of retaliation did not redress the difficulties of transportation, aggravated further by the Jewish determination to hold on to every settlement, even the more isolated ones. The Jewish concept was that each settlement signified a hold over the area around it. The Arab Liberation Army took the major part in the campaign against these isolated settlements. Only after al-Qawqji's total defeat did they again become relatively accessible and the routes open.

The first attack on an isolated Jewish settlement occurred on 9 January 1948. A Jewish kibbutz in the north, Kefar Szold, was attacked by a unit of the Arab Liberation Army coming from Syria. This was followed by two successful operations by al-Qawqji's troops against two Jewish convoys, one in the north and one near Jerusalem in January and February. These, however, were the first and last victories; attacks on kibbutz Yehi'am and kibbutz Tirat Zvi were successfully rebuffed. By March and April, the Arab Liberation Army was already becoming less effective in determining the course of the civil war. Its final significant contribution to the campaign was an attack on kibbutz Mishmar Ha-emek on 4 April 1948. Although al-Qawqji threw into the battle almost all his forces, and outnumbered the Jewish defenders, he failed to overpower them.[97]

Al-Qawqji's failure can be attributed to the fact that no reinforcements or ammunition were available to him. His troubles began when the Jews blew up many of the bridges on the main routes leading from Transjordan across the river to Palestine, thus

cutting him off from his logistic hinterland. But his main problem
was Abdullah's decision to disallow all transport and movement of
volunteers through his territory. The Hashemite ruler, who in
former days had been al-Qawqji's ardent supporter, was persuaded
in January 1948 by Sir Alec Kirkbride to stop the transfer of troops
through his domain. Kirkbride was convinced that these forces
would eventually be directed against the Hashemites and used in a
coup in Transjordan.[98] Abdullah himself was more concerned with
a possible threat in the south – where the Saudis suggested sending
their volunteers via Transjordan into Palestine – and went to the
length of sending his army to block the way of these volunteers.[99]

It should be noted that there is no evidence to support
Kirkbride's suspicions. Al-Qawqji owed his allegiance and appointment to the Iraqis and to a certain extent to the Transjordanians. He harboured no ambitions for the overthrow of
Abdullah, nor, it would seem, was he the proxy of the Syrians or
anyone else for such a mission. Later, in his diaries he would
glorify his role in the war, but Jewish sources reveal him to have
been seeking a *modus vivendi* with almost anyone, including the
Jews, in order to establish his rule in the north of Palestine.[100]

Egypt, on the other hand, did allow its own brand of volunteers
to enter Palestine. These were mainly members of the Muslim
Brotherhood who participated in attacks on isolated Jewish
settlements in the Negev. Their operations were quite successful,
and consequently many on the Jewish side felt that some of these
settlements should be evacuated. Already in December 1947 one of
Ben Gurion's advisers had strongly advocated the evacuation of the
more isolated settlements.[101] However, Ben Gurion recognized the
importance of a Jewish presence in an area designated by the UN
as part of the Jewish state and adamantly refused to heed such
advice. In January 1948 he declared:

> In the Negev the problem is not defending the settlements.
> There are hardly any settlements. The problem of the Negev is
> defending the whole area as part of the future Jewish state. I will
> say it more bluntly: the occupation of the Negev. We should
> regard every settlement in the Negev as a military garrison, see
> in each Jew a soldier and we need a force that would assure total
> control of the Negev.[102]

Ben Gurion's strategy was ultimately vindicated. In the final analysis the Muslim Brotherhood were no true match for the Jewish forces, and the Jewish commander of the Negev could report on 15 May 1948: 'The whole of the Negev is under Jewish rule. The fighting had ceased, there are no more ambushes on convoys, and the water pipes are safe from sabotage. The local population, the Bedouin, have accepted our authority.'[103]

To conclude, then, the only Arab success was in obstructing Jewish transportation, laying siege to Jerusalem and in a few isolated attacks against settlements in the south of Palestine. The more extreme Arab factions for a while terrorized daily life in Jerusalem, Haifa and Tel Aviv (the notable cases being the blowing up of the Palestine Post and the Jewish Agency buildings, in Jerusalem in February–March 1948). However, only very small units were counter-attacking the Jewish posts and most of the time the Palestinians were engaged in defence.[104]

The Jews moved from defence to an offensive, once Plan D was adopted. The plan, *inter alia*, aimed at extending Jewish rule in Palestine. It was decided to move to more aggressive operations owing to the temporary American revocation of its unconditional support for the partition plan and the failure to regain mastery of the main routes in the country. Thus, from 1 April 1948 to the end of the war, Jewish operations were guided by the desire to occupy the greatest possible portion of Palestine. *Ipso facto* this policy ensured safe transportation and communication with isolated settlements. The first Jewish thrust was concentrated in the narrow strip connecting Tel Aviv and Jerusalem. It was there during the battle over the road to Jerusalem that Abd al'Qader al-Husayni was killed. A day later Deir Yassin was occupied and its population massacred. The massacre was carried out by a group of soldiers belonging to the Irgun, who killed about 200 villagers. The Irgun later claimed that its operation had been authorized by the Hagana and was part of a larger Jewish operation in Jerusalem. Deir Yassin was located on a strategic hilltop overlooking one of the routes leading to Jerusalem.[105] It is therefore possible to assume that its destruction was indeed approved by the Hagana, and that the massacre was the Irgun's 'interpretation' of the military comand's orders.

Elsewhere, in the rural areas, Plan D was fully implemented. The plan specified thirteen operations towards the occupation of Palestine of which only one failed totally – the occupation of the Jewish quarter in Jerusalem. By April, the Jews had completed the occupation of the mixed towns, had almost secured Jerusalem, and inflicted a blow to al-Qawqji's Arab Liberation Army from which it never recovered. Ben Gurion's diary reflects the relief felt by the Jewish leaders before the second phase of the war – the invasion by the Arab armies. Between 4 and 12 April, Ben Gurion was preoccupied primarily with relatively mundane questions, such as the nature of the relationship between the Jewish Agency and the provisional government of the state after victory.[106]

On the Palestinian side, there was neither leisure or place for any mundane matters. A tragedy was in the making as hundreds of thousands of Palestinians, some fleeing, most of them expelled, left their homeland to become the refugees who haunt the Middle East to this very day.

3

The Making of the Refugee Problem

Any war fought in an inhabited area is bound to create a refugee problem. In some cases the civilians who flee or leave their homes return once the fighting is over; in others, they become refugees, uprooted from their country and waiting to be either repatriated or resettled elsewhere. In this sense the making of the refugee problem in the war of 1948 is no different from its historical precedents. Yet, there are two aspects which distinguish it from all other cases. The first is that embodied in the allegation made by historians both Arab and Western, that the exodus of the Palestinians was the result of a deliberate action on the part of the Zionist leadership in Palestine. The second is the fact that almost all the Palestinians (90 per cent to be exact) were uprooted from their original homes in the area occupied by Jewish forces during the war. The two aspects are interrelated of course. For some historians, it was exclusively Israeli or Jewish policy which turned so many Palestinians into refugees.

Until recently, the historiographical debate on this question was characterized by political convictions rather than academic criteria. Israeli historians have claimed that it was the Arab leaders who had ordered the flight of most of the Palestinians, and Arab historians have accused Israel of a deliberate policy of expulsion. The debate, thus, centres around the question of responsibility.

Let us first set out what has been accepted and agreed upon by historians of both sides. It seems that no one questions the fact that the flight of the Arab leadership from the country as early as September–October 1947 seriously undermined the steadfastness of the population, and that it was followed by the departure of about

70,000 Palestinians by the end of January 1948. There is no argument between historians that this group left voluntarily. Moreover, it is accepted that the Jewish Agency, at the time, did not have coherent or specific plans for eviction and expulsion. As one historian put it: 'Official Jewish decision-making bodies – the provisional government, the National Council and the Jewish Agency Executive – neither discussed nor approved a design for expulsion, and any proposal of the sort would have been opposed and probably rejected.'[1] It would seem that the first group of Arabs to leave Palestine was composed of members of the upper classes of Palestinian society, who did so as soon as they sensed the approaching winds of war. They fled without their possessions, nor did they sell their property – clearly they left in the hope of returning once the storm subsided and a solution was found one way or another. Yet, some of them had been forced to leave following Jewish reprisals – in the wake of Arab hostilities – which included attacks and the destruction of villages located on the main routes of Palestine.[2]

But all in all, the movement out of the country of so many Palestinians took the Jewish leadership by surprise, and a pleasant one at that. Without any transfer of population the Jewish state envisaged by the UN would have been a binational state – a concept accepted as viable only by a marginal group of a-Zionist Jews. However, a large number of Palestinians were still left within the designated Jewish state. Most of them lived in the rural areas and were villagers strongly attached to their lands and homes and not easily intimidated by acts of war.

It is on the exodus of the Palestinians from March 1948 onwards that the historical debate evolves. The question it poses is: how can the phenomenon of the departure of a whole nation be explained? Israeli historians talk about the 'domino effect', arguing that the élite set the example and with the continued Jewish successes on the battleground the population chose not to stay.[3] This official Israeli explanation is best described by Ben Gurion himself in a speech he gave to the Knesset on 11 October 1961:

The Arabs' exit from Palestine . . . began immediately after the UN resolution, from the areas earmarked for the Jewish state. And we have explicit documents testifying that they left Palestine following instructions by the Arab leaders, with the Mufti at their head, under the assumption that the invasion of

the Arab armies at the expiration of the Mandate will destroy
the Jewish state and push all the Jews into the sea, dead or
alive.[4]

Arab historians, on the other hand, even those who accept that the
first wave left by its own will, argue that the remainder, that is the
majority – conservative accounts talk of 750,000 refugees – were
expelled by force. They point to Plan D, as proof of the existence of
Jewish plans to drive the Arabs out of Palestine.[5]

The publication of *The Birth of the Palestinian Refugee Problem*, by
Benny Morris has shifted the direction of this debate. His was the
first book to be written on the subject after the declassification of
the Israeli documents relating to the 1948 war; hence its
importance. The book rejects most of the explanations given till
then by Israeli historians, but also argues with some of the
allegations made by Palestinian and Arab historians.

Like the Irish journalist Erskine Childers before him, Morris
found no evidence of instructions or directions by the Arab Higher
Committee, or any Arab government for that matter, to the local
population of Palestine to leave the country.[6] All he could trace
were instructions by the Arab Higher Committee to local
commanders to secure the evacuation of women, children and old
men from areas of danger. Furthermore, based upon documents
from the Israeli military archives, Morris discovered that in many
incidents and during many campaigns the Arab population in
certain villages or city quarters was evicted by force of arms and
expelled. But, he stresses, there was no Israeli master plan to expel
the Arabs; quite the contrary. The actions of eviction, expulsion
and massacres were, according to Morris, a by-product of the war
and a consequence of a certain mood prevalent among Israeli
soldiers – in other words they were local initiatives and not guided
from above. Most of these actions, apart from rare incidents, won
retrospective affirmation and understanding from the superiors
concerned.[7]

This explanation is deemed unsatisfactory by the leading
Palestinian historian of the war, Walid Khalidi. Khalidi, even after
Morris's research, still recognizes Plan D as the master plan for the
expulsion of the Palestinians. Khalidi and Morris disagree in their
interpretation of the plan, each stressing a different aspect. Plan D
is now accessible both in Hebrew and in English. Anyone
examining this text will agree that the document is quite

straightforward yet, it has generated a great amount of historiographical debate.

Morris views it more as a military programme:

> not a political blueprint for the expulsion of Palestine's Arabs: it was governed by military considerations and was geared to achieving military ends. But given the nature of the war and admixture of the two populations, securing the interior of the Jewish state for the impending battle along its borders in practice meant the depopulation and destruction of villages that hosted hostile local militia and irregular forces.

He further maintains that Plan D was,

> a blueprint for securing the emergent Jewish state and the clusters of Jewish settlements outside the state's territory against the expected Arab invasion on or after 15 May. The plan was born out of a feeling of losing the diplomatic battle due to the shift in America's policy and the initial success of the Arab irregulars.[8]

Morris's main argument for the marginal importance he attributes to Plan D rests on the way the war developed: 'However, during April–June relatively few Hagana commanders faced the dilemma of whether or not to carry out the expulsion clauses of Plan D. The Arab townspeople and villagers usually fled from their homes before or during the battle: the Hagana commanders had rarely to decide about, or issue, expulsion orders.' And he summarizes the question: 'Plan D aside, there is no trace of any decision-making by the Yishuv's or Hagana's supreme bodies in March or earlier April in favour of a blanket, national policy of driving out the Arabs.'[9]

Walid Khalidi, on the other hand, regards the plan as the last of many plans to destroy the Palestinian community:

> Plan Dalet, or 'Plan D', was the name given by the Zionist High Command to the general plan for military operations within the framework of which the Zionists launched successive offensives in April and early May 1948 in various parts of Palestine. These offensives, which entailed the destruction of the bulk of the Palestine Arabs, were calculated to achieve the military *fait accompli* upon which the state of Israel was to be based.[10]

It is true that the plan reflected a specific Jewish predicament. In March 1948 when the Jews faced initial Arab successes in the civil war and an unsympathetic American State Department, the Jewish command decided to react by a *fait accompli* policy. Thus, Jewish forces were instructed to occupy not only the area allocated to the Jews, but also the mixed towns of Palestine and many areas outside the designated Jewish state. The clear purpose was to win firm control over most of western Palestine and by that to precipitate the Arab invasion, thereby putting an end to the fluctuations of the American policy-makers. The Jewish élite, by way of moral justification, based the new policy on the repudiation by the Arab side of the UN partition plan. That being the case, went the argument, the Jewish side was no longer obliged to respect the UN resolution regarding the allocation of territory to the Arabs. But it did signify more than Morris would have us believe and some of the points made by Khalidi deserve our attention. It would be wrong to focus on the plan as if it epitomized the conflict, as Khalidi does. Its significance lies in the means by which the Jews hoped to solve the predicament of March 1948, as detailed in the plan itself. They include, as Khalidi notes, the uprooting, expulsion and pauperization of the Palestinian community; all signifying an escalation in Jewish actions against the Palestinian community. Until then the efforts were towards establishing a state, building an infrastruture, contemplating a takeover of the mandatory system – but Plan D spoke of the destruction of the other party to the conflict. The strategy was the same – establishing a Jewish state, with or without Arab consent. However, the Arab rejection of the partition resolution had altered the Jewish tactics and in that respect, Walid Khalidi justly attaches more importance to the plan than Morris does.[11]

Moreover, it does seem that Plan D was an important factor accounting for the exodus of so great a number of Palestinians. A thorough analysis of the plan as a military stratagem reveals its importance. The principal aim of the plan was to offer a strategy *vis-à-vis* the results of the civil war at that point, and to prepare for the impending invasion by the regular Arab armies. According to the plan, the best military strategy was to establish:

A fixed defensive system to preserve our settlements, vital economic projects, and property, which will enable us to provide government services within the borders of the state (based on defending the regions of the state on the one hand, and on blocking the main access routes from enemy territory to the territory of the state, on the other).

The 'defensive system' was a euphemism for what in fact was the establishment of a security zone to be controlled entirely by Jewish forces. This zone covered all the regions surrounding Jewish settlements and quarters as well as the areas along important strategic routes. Plan D went on to outline a plan of action. This referred to 'enemy bases' and dealt with the need to attack them as a preventive measure. The term 'enemy bases' refers to Arab villages or quarters from which hostile actions had been launched against Jewish settlements and convoys. They were not proper military bases yet, they were civil locations accomodating army personnel and ammunition. Hence when Plan D called for their destruction, it was calling for the destruction of certain Arab population centres. The 'enemy bases' designated for attack as military objectives fell within three distinct categories: those located in the security zone defined above (i.e., the surroundings of Jewish settlements and all strategic routes); on the borders of the territory designated by the UN to become Arab Palestine; and those within the Jewish state as defined in the UN resolution.[12]

The subsequent fate of these 'enemy bases' is also discussed in the plan. The Jewish forces were ordered to mount:

> operations against enemy population centres located inside or near our defensive system in order to prevent them from being used as bases by an active armed force. These operations can be carried out in the following manner: either by destroying villages (by setting fire to them, by blowing them up, and by planting mines in their debris), and especially of those population centres which are difficult to control continuously; or by mounting combing and control operations according to the following guidelines: encirclement of the village, conducting a search inside it. In case of resistance, the armed force must be wiped out and the population expelled outside the borders of the state.[13]

If we consider the geographical scope of the three categories mentioned we find that only some of the Arab villages existing in Palestine at the time were regarded as such by the composers of

Plan D – the rest, more than half of the villages, were simply regarded as military targets. Accordingly, in areas defined by the Jews as theirs, only those villages which would surrender unconditionally would stand a chance of not being submitted to the harsh treatment mentioned above. In fact, application of this treatment had in some cases preceded the formulation of the plan, so that even if no master plan existed, one finds that there was a certain preconception shared by many in the Jewish armed forces of how to deal with 'enemy bases.' Plan D did not, therefore, only provide guidelines for the future, it also reflected an existing notion prevalent among the policy-makers of the Jewish community – the notion that a Jewish success in the struggle over Palestine might involve the destruction of the Palestinian community. The concept of a zero-sum game was not adopted by the Jews alone; the other side accepted the role thrust upon it much as if the ongoing conflict was a Greek tragedy of sorts.

The Jewish and Arab perceptions were both nourished by emotions of hatred and the desire for revenge. One should not underestimate these psychological factors on both sides when discussing particular atrocities. Both parties had ample reasons for implementing the biblical imperative of 'an eye for an eye'. In some cases emotions of this kind led soldiers to ignore standing orders or general instructions. Nevertheless, along such lines an explanation may account for sporadic incidents but cannot explain the phenomenon which occurred in Palestine – the exodus of most of its Arab population. This is the real significance of Plan D, although it is true that it was not the only factor causing the flight, and one cannot explain what happened by concentrating on Jewish policy alone. The absence of Arab leadership and the traditional structure which we described above, certainly played a role. Yet, we are left with the impression that of all these factors, the Jewish policy as exemplified by Plan D is the principal explanation for the departure of most of the Arabs of Palestine. This was not an expulsion plan, it was a plan demanding the surrender of the population – had most of the villagers and townsfolk waved the white flag, refused to allow the entrance of armed men into their midst, their fate would have probably been different. The Israelis did not expel out of the blue, there had to have been a 'provocation'.

On this score one should point out that Plan D in some places in Palestine was not implemented at all. Local commanders in the towns of Haifa and Tiberias tried to persuade the Arab population to stay. But in the wake of the massacre of Deir Yassin the inhabitants of these towns had little trust in the Jewish side.

One last point to consider is the fact that in many cases the population had already fled before the completion of the occupation process. According to the plan, the final stage in all cases where the occupation was met by local resistance consisted of the expulsion of that population from the area controlled by the Jews, thus in those cases actual expulsion did not take place. But this state of affairs does not underrate the significance of Plan D as a blueprint for the expulsion of villagers and townsfolk refusing to surrender. In the final analysis, if I plan to throw someone out of his flat, the fact that he had left before I had a chance to expel him, in no way alters the fact of my intention. So Plan D was, in many ways, just what Khalidi claims it was – a master plan for the expulsion of as many Palestinians as possible. Moreover, the plan legitimized, *a priori*, some of the more horrendous atrocities committed by Jewish soldiers. In some cases, particularly in the north, in the area under the command of Moshe Carmel, the order 'to destroy', meant also to kill off the local population. Hence, those responsible for the Deir Yassin massacre could have legitimized their action by referring to Plan D, as almost every village in the vicinity of Jerusalem was considered an enemy base.[14]

Thus, if we continue to survey the fate of the Palestinian population from March 1948 on we can see that those villagers and townspeople living within the designated Jewish state, or within the areas indicated by Plan D as essential for the state's survival, stood very little chance of being left in peace. In many of these villages units of the Arab Liberation Army had established their bases and were thus transforming the villages into 'military objectives'; others were attacked just for their location in areas considered by the Jews as strategically vital. Only exceptional cases, such as Abu Ghosh, near Jerusalem, withstood the tumults of war. To that end they had to actively assist the Jewish war effort or at least adopt a neutral policy benevolent to the Jewish side. Very few of the villages in fact followed such a policy and by August 1948, 286 Arab villages had been destroyed as a direct result of the war, many others were considerably damaged and later abandoned.[15]

The differentiation between friendly and hostile villages was committed to paper but seems to have been totally ignored by the energetic officials working in the Jewish Agency's Land Department. It was in particular the head of the department, Yosef Weitz, who tried to evict as many Arabs as possible regardless of their 'friendliness' or 'hostility'. Weitz was very active in searching for fertile land, in encouraging local commanders to evacuate Arabs and generally in exploiting the state of anarchy for the acquisition of more and more land. The Jewish policy of reprisals provided the best opportunity for such activity. Thus, in places where the reprisals had already resulted in a large number of ruined and empty villages, as in Yadjur and Balad al-Sheikh near Haifa, all that remained to do was to take over the land of the village. It seems that if Weitz had had his way, even more evictions would have taken place, but as there was no general plan or coherent policy, his more 'ambitious' plans were left unaccomplished.[16]

Weitz's plans met with greater success during the first days of May 1948 once a more coherent policy had been formulated. He was appointed to head the 'transfer committees'. The headings of some of the internal memoranda left by these committees are rather telling, such as 'Retrospective Transfer', 'A Scheme for the Solution of the Arab Question in the State of Israel' and similar references to acts of expulsion. Weitz was very close to Ben Gurion, and very much in his trust, but there is no evidence that the provisional Israeli government ever supported or executed all the plans of the transfer committees.[17] The Jews did not retaliate by standard military steps alone but resorted to some biblical warfare procedures as well. These methods included the setting on fire of Arab fields and stealing their crops. Burning the field of the enemy was first exercised in modern Palestine by the Arabs, in the revolt of 1936, and has again been used by the Palestinians in the Intifada. We may say therefore that the struggle in Palestine was not only over the land but also over its yield. The 'war over the crops' was waged from March 1948 onwards.[18]

Here, too, we can see once more the significance of Plan D, since before it came into being the Palestinian harvest had not been considered a strategic objective. In the plan the Jewish Supreme Military Command was ordered to ensure the state not only by military means but also by the 'application of economic pressure on the enemy'. In the cities this meant cutting water and food supplies; in the villages it meant preventing the farmers from cultivating their fields. In May 1948 the Jewish Agency decided that the harvest of all the abandoned villages was to be confiscated by the newly-born state.[19]

The 'agricultural' retaliation was widely implemented during the war itself, in the summer of 1948. Local commanders were encouraged to harass Palestinian farmers and set fire to their fields. It was particularly common in the Negev where a close link seems to have existed between agricultural considerations and military operations. There seems to be ample evidence to indicate that the 'harvest war' was initiated from above and was thus a 'national policy'.[20]

If the upper classes left voluntarily, it does seem that the lower strata of the Palestinian society were driven out through the implementation of Plan D and because of the developing civil war which reached a climax in April 1948 with the Jewish takeover of the mixed towns of Haifa, Jaffa and Tiberias. The massacre in Deir Yassin played an important role in driving these groups out of Palestine in April and May 1948: it is the contention of many historians that the Deir Yassin massacre had a psychological effect on the Arab community and acted as a catalyst to the exodus.[21]

By 15 May 1948, about 380,000 Palestinians had become refugees.[22] By the end of the war the number was doubled and the UN report spoke of 750,000 refugees.[23] Some Israeli historians claim that this was the result of the civil war sparked off by the Arab League and by the Arab Higher Committee's rejection of the partition plan. This argument may be valid when one is concerned with alternative history. That is, it is possible to assume that had the Arab side accepted the UN partition resolution, bloodshed as well as expulsion might have been prevented. However, this ignores Ben Gurion's determination to enlarge the Jewish state at any cost and for that purpose to carry the war forth into the areas designated by the UN as the Arab state. Nor does it take into account the non-involvement of most of those expelled. These were not active soldiers and very few of them had ever engaged in hostilities against the Jews.

Moreover, this argumentation fails to account for Plan D with its specific orders of destruction and eviction. Between the beginning of the official war and the conclusion of the second truce in July 1948 an additional 100,000 Palestinians left their homes. The most notable case, about which more will be said when we present the course of the official war, was the exodus of the people of Lydda and Ramleh.[24] Yitzhak Rabin (later one of Israel's prime ministers), took part in the military operation to extend Jewish control in the Jerusalem area. From his account and Morris's description it emerges that the population was marched out of the towns by the Israelis, as part of an explicit policy to leave as few Arabs as possible in the Jewish state.[25]

The last waves of refugees – about 150,000 – left Palestine in October and November 1948, but Arabs from various parts of Palestine occupied by the Jews continued to be transferred outside Israel until the middle of 1949. In October and November the Israeli forces swept through both the north and south of Palestine. It was then that the bulk of the Gaza refugee population left in the wake of the Egyptians' defeat in the south.[26] Both in the Galilee and in the southern coastal areas large numbers of Palestinians left their homes even before the Israelis reached them. The Christian Arabs tended to stay behind, whereas the Muslims fled. A considerable number of cases of expulsion occurred, on two accounts: populations of villages that did not immediately surrender were expelled as well as refugees from the previous waves who had found asylum in other villages.[27]

Some of the worst atrocities against local Palestinians occurred during that phase, among them the massacres in Ilabun, Sa'as'a. Dawaymiya, Safsaf and elsewhere in the Galilee and Hebron areas.[28] Still, one can argue, as Morris does throughout his book that *À la guerre comme à la guerre*: atrocities are inevitable in war. Morris mainly challenges the pretension of some Israeli historians that the Israeli army in the 1948 war was particularly moral and exceptionally humane. This myth, of the 'purity of arms' of the Israeli army, was conceived during this war – an oxymoron if ever there was one.

From October 1948 on the Israelis did their utmost to create a *fait accompli* that would render repatriation impossible. The prime objective was to demolish what was left of the abandoned Palestinian villages, almost 350 in all, so that the term itself would become meaningless. Moreover, Israel's policy-makers required the land and the property for the absorption of the waves of new Jewish immigrants, not only from Europe but also from the Arab countries. Thus, in a sense, the Israelis could view the Palestinian exodus as part of a possible exchange of populations.

Be that as it may, it would seem that even before the war 'it was clear to many of the Jewish leaders that the Arabs who left would not be allowed to return'.[29] In June 1948, Yosef Weitz wrote in a

memorandum that there was a consensus among those responsible
for the 'Arab problem' that the best way to deal with abandoned
Arab villages was by 'destruction, renovation and settlement by
Jews'. In August 1948 the Israeli government decided to
implement Weitz's ideas to the letter.[31] As we shall see, once the
war was over neither world public opinion nor the UN and the
Americans would envisage a solution that did not include
repatriation. Aware of this tendency in the international arena, the
Israelis acted on two levels. Officially, it was decided to deposit the
abandoned urban property in the hands of a custodian, and to
declare a willingness to include the refugee problem as part of a
comprehensive peace agreement. However, in practice, Ben Gurion
continued the *fait accompli* policy. He, and most Israelis, regarded
would-be repatriated refugees as a potential fifth column and an
additional economic burden which would impede Israel's ability to
integrate Jewish refugees. Every possible measure was therefore
taken to prevent mass repatriation. One method was rumour-
mongering, activated by Moshe Dayan, with the aim of deterring
the refugees from even contemplating a safe return. More
important were the steps taken by the Jewish National Fund.
Aided by the government, they turned the empty Arab villages
either into agricultural plots or into a no-man's land in order to
prevent repatriation.[32] This policy and the initiatives of some local
military officers to settle Jewish immigrants in the Arab neighbourhoods of the mixed towns, despite the law of absentees (which
charged the government with responsibility and ownership of the
property and land left by the refugees) were irreversible steps
perpetuating the conflict between Jews and Palestinians.

In summing up the making of the refugee problem we would like
to raise again the question of responsibility. We have noted that, in
our opinion, Plan D can be regarded in many respects as a master
plan for expulsion. The plan was not conceived out of the blue –
expulsion was considered as one of many means for retaliation
against Arab attacks on Jewish convoys and settlements; nevertheless, it was also regarded as one of the best means of ensuring
domination of the Jews in the areas captured by the Israeli army.
The plan reflected the mood of the Jewish soldiers before and after
the war, a mood which is echoed very concisely in Ezra Danin's
words to Ben Gurion: 'The Arabs of the Land of Israel, they have
but one task left – to run away.'[33]

Moreover, one is tempted to point to the possibility of a certain

link between the Jewish expulsion activities against the Palestinians, and the demographic situation in the Jewish state as
delineated by UNSCOP. The UN suggested a binational state of
1.1 million citizens of whom 45 per cent would be Arabs: only the
a-Zionist Jews in Palestine were reconciled to binationalism, all
other political groups regarded such a state as the shattering of
the Zionist dream. However, the evidence that the demographic
situation engendered the decision to expel the Arabs of Palestine is
merely circumstantial.

The Palestinian leadership, as we have shown in a different
context, played an important, albeit a negative role in the
dynamics of the exodus. Not only did the political élite forsake its
constituency in its most crucial hour; it also failed to give coherent
guidance from its exile to the besieged communities in Palestine.
The escape of those who were able to flee in relative security – the
professional and business class from the major cities – augmented
the terror and confusion.

However, it is not only the Jews and the Arab politicians who
share responsibility for the creation of the problem: the first refugee
wave took place when the British were still in charge of law and
order in Palestine. Therefore, they may be held partly responsible
for the making of the refugee problem as well as for the chaotic
situation in Palestine after their withdrawal.

THE BRITISH SHARE AND INVOLVEMENT IN THE CIVIL WAR

There were two main components to the British policy towards
Palestine between January and May 1948. The first related to
activities in Palestine itself and the second to ideas about the post-
mandatory era. The latter coincided entirely with Transjordan's
ambitions and aspirations and has therefore been addressed in the
chapter on the secret negotiations between the Jews and the
Hashemites. It is our intention to focus here on the actual British
behaviour in Palestine.

We have already noted that Britain was at variance with
UNSCOP's proposal for peace in Palestine. Consequently His
Majesty's Government refused to take part in the implementation
of UNSCOP's plan. This was a neutral position, as the British did
not wish to undermine the UN effort to establish peace in the Holy
Land. But as they were still the government in the land their

indifference and lack of co-operation hindered the UN attempts to assume control over Palestine and to introduce a period of transition between the mandatory era and independence.

In practice, the British confined their activity and concern in Palestine exclusively to those areas where Britons still lived or held property. The main priority of the High Commissioner was to ensure the well-being of British soldiers and the safety of British installations until the final date of withdrawal. According to Britain's understanding, and probably in accord with international norms of behaviour as well, Britain was responsible for law and order in Palestine util 15 May 1948. By limiting its responsibility to areas under Britain's immediate control, London clearly shirked its duty.

Two main problems troubled the last High Commissioner, Sir Alan Cunningham: he had to stop and prevent large-scale incursions of Arab irregulars into the areas under his control, since he feared an attempt by one Arab country or more to invade Palestine before the end of the mandate. He was also apprehensive lest the Jewish state be declared before that date, which would have precipitated a general Arab invasion. The cabinet in London, if somewhat late in the day, supported its representative in Palestine by deciding that it would oppose by force both a large-scale Arab intervention and a premature Jewish declaration of independence.[34]

Minor Arab incursions and Jewish preparations for statehood on the other hand were treated with growing indifference. There exist in the relevant literature both Jewish and Arab accusations of British partiality during the civil war, which should be treated with circumspection because Britain officially pursued a policy of non-interference in Palestine. Any actions in favour of one or the other of the warring parties – and there were many – should be attributed to the decision of local commanders and officials, each acting according to his inclinations and affiliations.[35] Some of the British officers in Palestine even took an active part in the fighting on both sides, others confined their solidarity to the passing of vital information about the course and timetable of the intended evacuation.[36]

None the less some of the criticism was warranted. One of the principal Jewish allegations concerned the British refusal to allow the UN to prepare the ground for Jewish independence. The British cabinet prohibited the entry of the United Nations'

Palestine Committee into Palestine during the civil war. The British foreign secretary, Ernest Bevin, tried to justify this policy by arguing that the arrival of the committee would affect the security situation to the extent of rendering impossible the task of maintaining law and order in the country.[37] The British also annoyed the Jews by blocking their passage from the country's economic hinterland to the sea port in Tel Aviv; a passage that the partition resolution promised to keep free in order to allow Jewish immigration.

Yet, most of the time the British let the local actors run the show. The Jewish Agency tried to persuade the UN at least to replace the British in those places from which they withdrew, and suggested that the UN employ an international force to supervise the areas abandoned by the British. The UN Palestine Committee considered this request favourably, but none of the Western powers was willing to risk involving Russian forces in such a sensitive part of the world. It is difficult to imagine the possible consequences of an alternative British policy: the Arab camp would probably have taken up arms against the UN forces with the inevitable result of further alienating world public opinion. To move from alternative history to firmer ground, let us conclude this assessment of the British role by commenting that the local British initiatives, all in all, had very little effort on the consequences of the civil war. In places like Jaffa and Haifa British involvement delayed the final outcome but could not prevent it. Elsewhere it was only the balance of power between the two sides that determined the course of the struggle and its issue.

4

The Arab World Goes to War, or Does It? The General Arab Preparation

In the period between the publication of the UNSCOP majority report (September 1947) and the end of the British mandate (15 May 1948) several Arab summit meetings took place, in which the leaders unanimously demanded the establishment of an Arab state in all of Palestine. In practice, those meetings reduced almost to nothing the authority of an independent Palestinian representation and drastically limited the freedom of action of the local Palestinian leadership. In this chapter we would like to determine whether this neutralization of the Palestinians was followed by any significant Arab interference on their behalf.

As mentioned earlier, the Arab League began its discussions on the fate of post-mandatory Palestine in Aleyh, Lebanon, in October 1947.[1] The one practical consequence of that meeting was the formation of the Arab Liberation Army and the establishment of training courses for the volunteers who signed up for it in Qatana near Damascus.[2] On a more theoretical level, the participants discussed the question of direct Arab military involvement, but no specific plans for operation were put forward and the meeting on the whole was characterized by mutual suspicion and zealous rhetoric about the need to liberate Palestine. The pattern set at Aleyh was repeated in the subsequent League meetings until the outbreak of, and even during the war.

In Aleyh the first doubts were raised about the ability of the Arab world to pursue a successful armed intervention in Palestine – though only behind closed doors. To the outside world the League's members appeared confident of their ability to decide the future of Palestine. The Lebanese were the only ones who continued publicly to advocate diplomacy and proposed to address a joint appeal to Britain to prolong its stay in the area. While individual Arab leaders in private conversations with British and American officials were later to express similar wishes, in Aleyh such advice was given in public for the last time. It was the Syrians who set the tone in that and subsequent meetings by demanding firm military action. Syria's president suggested instigating guerrilla warfare in Palestine, to be followed by direct military involvement. The Syrian army, in fact, was the first Arab army to deploy forces near the border, and it did so immediately after the Aleyh meeting. This Syrian enthusiasm raised the suspicions of the Iraqi government; the politicians in Baghdad told the resident British diplomats that Damascus was contemplating and actually pursuing a policy in Palestine which was aimed at furthering Syrian territorial ambitions in the area. Consequently, the Iraqis decided to counter the Syrian move by requesting the permission of Abdullah to transfer an Iraqi unit through Transjordan to the Palestine border. The Egyptians meanwhile appeared quite indifferent at this stage to the inter-Arab squabble. In reality, this brandishing of swords and patriotic ramblings did not amount to much: only a few small Iraqi units eventually crossed Transjordan, and the Syrian units deployed on the border were not strong or active enough to influence the course of the civil war in Palestine.[3]

Before rounding up their discussion in Aleyh the Arab delegates decided to leave the co-ordination of the overall Arab aid to the Palestinians in the heads of a technical-military committee that was to operate on a permanent basis from Cairo and was headed by the deputy Iraqi chief of staff, General Isma'il Safwat, who was joined by high-ranking officers from Syria and Lebanon and representatives of the Arab Higher Committee. Although the Transjordanians selected their delegate for the military committee he never participated in its meetings.[4]

In his first report to the League Safwat presented a very realistic evaluation of the balance of power in Palestine. The Jews were better organized, had a numerical advantage and more abundant financial resources. Only an immediate deployment of the Arab armies on Palestine's borders and shipments of armaments and ammunition would help to tip the balance in favour of the Arab states. He suggested a contribution of £1 million to the Palestinians.[5] The League's Council rejected most of Safwat's recommendations, accepting only the need for financial assistance. Yet, the League had no sanctional authority and none of the Arab governments actually followed up the organization's request to finance the campaign in Palestine.[6] Moreover, the Council had to obtain the Political Committee's approval for any decision it made; the latter was composed of the heads of all the Arab states. Any decision that failed to win the blessing of the Political Committee was meaningless. As we shall see, till the end of the mandate, apart from the appropriate rhetoric, the leaders of the Arab world were very careful not to commit themselves to the Palestinian cause.

After the adoption of the 29 November resolution by the General Assembly, military preparations on the Arab side were somewhat intensified, probably also because of massive demonstrations in the Arab capitals. The change of pace was manifested in the proceedings of the Political Committee's meeting in Cairo in December 1947. The Arab leaders decided to reciprocate Arab public demand for firmer action by forming a general military command comprising all the Arab chiefs of staff, with Safwat, head of the military committee, appointed chairman. Immediately he reiterated his plea for more active Arab involvement in Palestine, only to discover again that the Arab politicians preferred to postpone any decision until the end of the mandate.[7]

The League's Council met in Cairo again in February 1948 to discuss its military preparations. It repeated the call for financial and military aid to the Palestinians, as most of the Arab states did not seem to be doing much to comply with the League's earlier appeals.[8]

The Arab governments hoped that military actions by the Arab Palestinians aided by volunteers from Arab neighbouring countries would succeed in persuading the world community to desist from implementing the partition resolution. All hopes for local successes were shattered, however, during the month of April. The loss of Haifa, Jaffa, Tiberias and Safad, and the Deir Yassin massacre caused a great deal of despair and apprehension in the Arab capitals. Perhaps this was the moment of truth – in which Arab leaders were called to match patriotic rhetoric with visible actions. But the confusion and indecision within the Arab ranks in those crucial months of March and April were such that most of the leaders tried to postpone a decision on their course of action and if possible to avoid entering Palestine altogether. Their distress was accentuated by their own rhetoric and it soon became impossible to maintain the improbable imbalance between the vociferous commitment – heard first in October 1947 in Aleyh and repeatedly thereafter – to fight the UN partition resolution and the unimpressive and inadequate military preparations for the anticipated war in Palestine.

Arab public opinion certainly demanded a more drastic approach. The pressure from the crowds in the Arab capitals reached a crescendo in the wake of the Jewish successes in Palestine in April – precluding any public declaration of withdrawal from the battlefield. A glimpse at the Arab newspapers of the period reveals the enormous pressure brought to bear by the populace on their leaders in the quest for action in Palestine. Daily demonstrations, petitions and violent strikes gave vent to a growing 'pro-Palestinian' public stance. Most of the Arab regimes at the time were quasi-democracies, where press reports and parliamentary speeches played an important role in shaping the attitudes of the people in the street. Unlike the press, the Arab governments had urgent concerns other than Palestine. We do not possess protocols of government meetings in the Arab world at the time, but we do have daily reports on these meetings sent by foreign diplomats, particularly British, to their own governments. It seems that virtually all the Arab countries who eventually became involved in the war of 1948 had a similar 'national agenda': the preservation of domestic stability in the face of internal and external pressures. Palestine was not, and could not be, their main concern. For Iraq and Egypt the major item on their national agenda was the termination of British domination and this overshadowed the economic and social problems, which in themselves were abundant in the post-war era. An accelerated process of modernization had impoverished the rural areas and created new classes of unemployed and underemployed masses in the cities. The unemployed in particular were easily incited by political parties to mob behaviour. Only success within their own countries against British colonialism could assure popularity for Egyptian or Iraqi politicians.

Egyptian historians claim that many segments of Egypt's society were much more committed than the rest of the Arab world to the Palestinian cause. It seems, however, that such a commitment was confined to the activities of both the political left and the right wing who, unlike the main-stream politicians, saw a clear link between the struggle against British colonialism and the war against Zionism.[9] Only one group in Egypt was indeed totally committed to the Palestinian cause and this was the Muslim Brotherhood; its members were not content with words alone and many of them volunteered to fight alongside the Palestinians in the war against the Jews.[10]

In Syria after it was liberated from French colonialism, the causes of political instability were somewhat different. The leading political force in the country was the National Bloc, headed by Shuqri al-Quwatli and Jamil Mardam, which in the years immediately after the liberation was struggling to maintain its dominant role in a country torn by rivalries between parties and politicians. Syria's leaers were trying to sustain a parliamentary system and frequently were forced to defend their policies in national elections. The opposition would thus blame the government for its passivity in the face of Palestine's plight and urge it to play a more decisive role in the war against Zionism. This may explain why Syria was the most active member of the Arab League in promoting the general preparations for the war. And yet, even the Syrians in the final analysis did not send a significant contingent into the battlefield in Palestine. One Syrian writer retrospectively justified this by pointing to the danger of leaving Syria undefended and a prey to Hashemite ambitions.[11] Indeed, it seems that the limited involvement on the part of Syria was involuntary. The historical data reveal a genuine Syrian will to send a larger force and a desire to extend their sphere of operations as far as possible. Nor did the Syrians object to submitting their force to a foreign supreme commander, be it an Iraqi general or even Glubb Pasha of the Arab Legion. The truth is that they were simply not asked by the military committee of the Arab League to contribute more troops than they sent in the end.[12] Syrian commitment to the Palestinian cause did not save its leadership from the downfall brought upon it largely by the Arab defeat in Palestine. Al-Quwatli found some consolation in a letter which Abd al-Rahman Azzam, Secretary-General of the Arab League sent him and which stated: 'You have done more than was expected of you.'[13]

The Iraqis for their part had a taste of the Palestine 'syndrome' – the effect the affairs in Palestine had on the domestic scene – in January 1948 when the government tried to negotiate a revised defence treaty with Britain. Baghdad's streets were seething with demonstrators who, among other things, accused the government of conspiring with Britain at the expense of the Palestinian cause. The Iraqi government could ill afford to let such accusations go unanswered since its main objective was to present to public opinion both at home and abroad an Iraq which was completely independent of foreign domination. But allegations by the demonstrators and the opposition forces continued and eventually forced the Iraqi parliament to revoke the new treaty. The treaty of Portsmouth, as it came to be known, did not include any deal with Britain about Palestine, but it did leave Iraq as a quasi-independent state. Britain asked for its two air bases in Habaniyya and Sh'iba to be maintained and to retain its mandatory strategic privileges. The British government wished to commit the Iraqis to British defence interests throughout the world, to such an extent that should a war in the Falklands break out, for example, the Iraqi army would be required, according to the treaty, to stand by and be ready to participate if necessary. The political leadership of the country and the Hashemite dynasty, represented by the Regent Abd al-Ilah, did not find these British requests in the least exaggerated – they shared London's apprehensions regarding the threat of Communism and radicalism in the Middle East which could only be challenged, so they believed, by aligning Iraq to the West. However, this point of view was not shared by other segments of the political élite: the professional middle class, students, army officers and the underemployed stratum of society were showing growing resentment towards Baghdad's concessions to Britain.

The nationalistic sections of Iraqi society posed only one of the problems facing the Sunni government of Baghdad. Shi'i tribes in the south and, more important, secessionist Kurdish groups in the north threatened the regime's stability and its ability to rule. Palestine could not therefore be an issue of high priority. Yet, because geographically Iraq was more remote from the Palestine scene than the other Arab countries Iraqi politicians were encouraged to sound more extreme than their colleagues during meetings of the League, and to adopt an uncompromising position before, during and even after the war – when the other Arab participants in the fighting on the contrary were willing to negotiate a peace agreement with Israel. As we shall see, Iraq in the end did not sign an armistice with Israel and did not participate in the Lausanne Conference. Actually, the Iraqis were double-crossing everyone: while ostensibly leading the Arab world into firm action in Palestine, they simultaneously assured King Abdullah that they sympathized with his territorial ambitions there.[14] Everyone in the Arab world was thus led to believe that they had the Iraqis on their side.

It was for these reasons that the Arab politicians were less than anxious to be dragged into a military adventure over Palestine's destiny. As a further main reason for their disinclination one may add their perception of the balance of power in Palestine. When the heads of the Arab states met in Cairo on 12 April 1948 to discuss the implications of the Palestinian defeat in the civil war, they were duly presented with assessments of the state of the Arab armies compared to the Jewish forces. The next moves in the Arab world were based on these assessments. Before continuing therefore with our analysis of the Arab preparations in the four weeks remaining till the outbreak of the war on 15 May 1948, it is only right that we first try to arrive at an evaluation of the balance of power in Palestine.

THE BALANCE OF POWER

One of the most reliable sources of information about the strength and potential ability of the Arab armies involved in this war is the assessments written by the British chiefs of staff and presented to the British government. These generals estimated that most of the Arab armies had no previous combat experience and were generally used as a domestic police force. British intelligence asserted that the Iraqi army could, logistically, only maintain one battalion under battle conditions, and even then only if Syria or Transjordan agreed to assist. The Syrian army was less dependent in its logistics on other Arab states owing to its proximity to the Palestine border; its shortcomings were lack of ammunition and poor maintenance and the British felt certain that as a result its endurance in the battlefield would be limited.[15]

The Saudis had no regular army – and their irregular troops had no ammunition to speak of so they ended up as an auxiliary force to the Egyptian troops. The British had very little faith in the ability of the Egyptian army. It was undoubtedly the largest of the Arab armies, but only a small number of its units were sufficiently well trained to be sent to the front. From the end of the nineteenth century the Egyptian army had been left out of all significant battles and, as Nasser's memoirs indicate, its soldiers were poorly motivated and demoralized during the Palestine campaign. Egyptian ammunition reserves were also limited. The military adviser in the British embassy in Cairo summed up the situation as follows: 'The Egyptian army hardly warrants consideration as a serious invading force.'[16] The Egyptian War Ministry affirms this gloomy assessment in its report of March 1948: apart from the newly-established navy, the report estimated that as far as ammunition, equipment and maintenance were concerned the army was not ready for battle.[17]

Of all the Arab armies the Arab Legion in Transjordan was the only one to which the British attributed any standing power should it be sent into the battlefield against the Jews. The 7,400 strong Legion possessed genuine war experience and was relatively modernized. Its capability, however, depended entirely on British supply of arms and ammunition. With sufficient supplies the British believed it could withstand eight months of fighting.[18]

The military committee of the League estimated that it needed an army comprised of at least five divisions and six air wings for the battle in Palestine. Acceptance of this estimate would have meant deploying the bulk of the Arab armies. Jewish intelligence estimated the overall strength of the Arab armies in 1947 to be 165,000 soldiers with a military budget of almost £28 million. Had this massive force indeed been pitched into the battle, notwithstanding the pessimism showed by the British about its potential performance, the war could have developed less favourably for the Jewish state than it eventually did.[19]

But it seems that already in Aleyh and again later in the Political Committee's meeting on 12 April 1948 the heads of the Arab states – who were at the same time the titular heads of their armies – ruled out the possibility of sending such military strength into Palestine. The chiefs of staff of the Egyptian army explained to their war ministry that they could only dispense with one infantry brigade with auxiliary forces as 'the rest of the forces are required for internal security operations, safeguarding the army bases in the country and guarding the communication lines'.[20] The report estimated that similar considerations would force the other Arab states to limit their involvement in Palestine. Indeed, the utilization of their armies as a political tool prevented the Arab governments from sending more than a small part of them, which in addition suffered shortages of ammunition and lacked any significant military experience.[21] Their situation was further aggravated because the small units which were designated to Palestine did not even have adequate time to prepare themselves for the eventuality of war. The only exception, as noted before, were the Syrians who by 11 October 1947 had already concentrated some units near the Hula lake. The British authorities, however, had reacted immediately and firmly by dispatching some of their army units and forcing the Syrians to withdraw.[22] The Syrians tested British readiness to intervene on behalf of Jewish settlements once more at the beginning of January 1948. When the British again proved that they would not tolerate large-scale Arab incursions, the Syrians gave up these attempts.[23] The Syrians delayed their mobilization to 30 April 1948, that is until after the League's meeting in Cairo. At that time, the Lebanese and Iraqi armies joined Damascus in preparing for battle but by then they were left with precisely two weeks in which to complete the process.

As for the training of the Egyptians for battle conditions we again refer to the war ministry report: 'It is known that the situation of the field exercises is unsatisfactory as the Egyptian forces had never exercised battle manoeuvring above the level of infantry brigade.' An infantry brigade, accompanied by armoured troop-carrier units, was all the Egyptian government was willing to send into the battlefield. Although a combined action by such a brigade with auxiliary units needed further training, the army commanders informed the government in March 1948 that there was not enough time to carry out such manoeuvres. Moreover, they reported that it would be very difficult to find suitable troop-carrier units as the war ministry estimated that '60 per cent of the overall carriers were not ready for operations'.[24] Of the 38,000 combat troops of the Egyptian army, which was the largest army in the Arab world, only about 10,000 troops in the end participated in the battlefield. These 10,000 Egyptians were joined by 3,000 Syrians, 1,000 Lebanese, 3,000 Iraqis and 2,000 Arab volunteers. The Arab Legion deployed almost 60 per cent of its forces, 4,500 out of 7,400; it was the only Arab army to devote such a large proportion of its troops to the campaign of Palestine. It was also the only force in the Middle East enjoying a regular training programme as well as an adequate maintenance level. Thus, it was intended to be the natural backbone of the Arab forces sent to Palestine, which explains Abd al-Rahman Azzam's eagerness to integrate the Legion in the all-Arab army.

Therefore when one of the official Israeli histories of the war states that, 'on 15 May 1948, a day after Israel's establishment, the armies of five Arab countries: Egypt, Transjordan, Iraq, Syria and Lebanon, invaded the newly born state', we may safely say that this gives a somewhat misleading portrayal of the actual situation.[25] The overall force prepared by the Arab League for the May 1948 confrontation amounted to no more 23,500 men. It was to be added to the Palestinian forces already engaged in war in Palestine itself – estimated at about 12,000 irregulars including the volunteers who had already entered the country. We may also consider the unidentified number of *ad hoc* armed villagers as part of the Arab fighting force. Small units of artillery, a few dozen tanks and three air-squadrons completed the military lay-out on the Arab side.[26]

The 35,500 regular and irregular Arab troops were facing a similar number of Jews. On 1 May 1948 Ben Gurion was told by the head of the personnel department in the army that there was a fighting force of 22,425 ready for action. On 4 June 1948 the number had risen to 35,368. The Arab numerical and aerial advantage in the first two weeks of the war will become evident when we describe the major developments on the battleground in the next chapter. But by 4 June this advantage had been mollified and thereafter the Jews enjoyed parity with the Arab armies facing them. Both camps had succeeded in recruiting altogether 100,000 soldiers when hostilities ceased in January 1949.[27]

The actual Jewish preparations for the war began on 7 November 1947 with the formation of four new brigades. A fifth brigade was added in February 1948.[28] These forces were trained and equipped in underground conditions aided by purchasing operations abroad and an embryo military industry at home. Until the first truce (9 June 1948) the Arab armies had an advantage over the Jewish forces in that they were better equipped, but the balance tipped in Israel's favour during that truce when armament factories in the Eastern bloc began sending equipment and ammunition to the Jewish state; simultaneously three of the major Arab armies – the Egyptian, the Iraqi and the Legion – due to a UN embargo not respected by the Eastern bloc, were cut off from their main supplier, Britain.

The Jews also enjoyed a financial advantage. The funds promised by the Arab League to the Palestinians failed to reach Palestine. In the final analysis only £143,000 (Palestinian pounds) were received, most of it provided by Syria.[29] But even if the budget for the Arab military effort had reached the sum promised by the Arab League, it could still not have compared with the Jewish Agency's military budget, which in December 1947 allocated $28 million for defence purposes.[30]

This then was the balance of power between the Arabs and the Jews on the eve of the war over Palestine. The strength of the Jewish forces was quite accurately assessed by the Egyptian intelligence before the war, so we may assume that the rest of the Arab generals shared the same information.[31] It led Nahum Goldman, a member of the Jewish Agency's directorship, to tell British and American officials that he was very confident about the Jewish military prospects.[32] It led Azzam Pasha, on the other hand, to approach the British government and ask it to prolong its stay in Palestine for at least another year. Similar appeals were made by the Saudi king and Lebanese statesmen. The balance of power was then perfectly known to the Arab side; the Arab leaders had hardly entertained any illusions about the outcome of the war. In fact, local politicians, in Cairo, Jedda and Beirut, were quite terrified at the prospect of the possible repercussions to their own life and career.[33] In Baghdad and Damascus there was a display of more self-confidence, but here too, one wonders what the actual feelings were.

The balance of power as presented to Azzam Pasha and the heads of the Arab states in April 1948 had taken for granted the Egyptian and Transjordanian contributions to the war effort. However, both these governments, the first with the largest and the second the most efficient Arab army were by then still reluctant to approve their participation. It follows that when in April 1948 the Arab leaders declared their intention of preparing the Arab armies for direct military intervention in Palestine, they actually struck a rather presumptuous note since neither Abdullah nor the Egyptians had as yet given their consent to join in such an operation. If any success was to be achieved against the Jews, the participation of these two armies had to be secured. Therefore, immediately after the April meeting in Cairo, a delegation composed of the Iraqi regent, Abd al-Ilah, the Lebanese Prime Minister, Riyad al-Sulh, and General Isma'il Safwat, was urgently sent to Amman with the task of persuading Abdullah to join forces. In Amman, the three men found a king who had already developed his own ideas of how to save Palestine, and at the same time fulfil old territorial and dynastic ambitions. Abdullah's vision of post-mandatory Palestine owed much to a series of negotiations he had held with members of the Jewish Agency. The understanding reached in the negotiations led the king to assign only limited objectives to his army in the war against the Jews, thus further weakening the Arab side.

DIVIDING THE SPOILS: THE JEWISH–HASHEMITE UNDERSTANDING OVER PALESTINE

The UN debate and its final outcome could not prevent the war from breaking out in Palestine after the British withdrawal. The UN stumbled over the same predicament as had the British in their efforts to reach a settlement during the mandatory period – the inability of an outside mediator to secure *a priori* consent for what could only be an arbitrary solution. However, the UN initiative was not the only attempt made at the time to solve the question of Palestine, nor would it prove the most successful. Long before the UN began its deliberations in New York, the Jews had found one Arab country willing to reach a compromise with them over Palestine – the Hashemite kingdom (emirate) of Transjordan under Abdullah.

The beginnings of this unique relationship can be traced as far back as January 1919 when Sharif Husayn's son, Amir Faysal, had come to an understanding of sorts with Chaim Weizmann about the validity of the Balfour Declaration.[34] Faysal was not particularly keen on the Jewish presence in Palestine, and the agreement with Weizmann had simply been a tactical move: Faysal wanted British support against the French in Syria and was willing to please the British by signing a piece of paper with Weizmann. This may also explain why three months later Faysal denied that the event had ever taken place. Other members of the family, however, notably Abdullah, took up and continued this positive attitude towards the growing Jewish community in Palestine. Abdullah's first encounter with a Zionist leader came in 1922 when he met Chaim Weizmann in London.[35] By that time only the head of the family, Husayn, King of the Hejaz, still echoed the Palestinians' opposition to the Jewish settlement in Palestine.[36]

Once Faysal was transferred from Damascus to Baghdad, his interest in the Zionist movement declined and from then on until his death in 1931 his main concern was to be the future of the Fertile Crescent in general and his own role as its ruler in particular. Abdullah, however, could not afford to lose interest in Palestine or in Zionism. After being stranded, of his own choice, in historical Palestine, his fate was ineluctably intertwined with that of the Holy Land.

While this explains why Abdullah took such a keen interest in the affairs of Palestine, it does not answer the question why he chose to back the Zionist horse, so to speak, rather than align himself, much more naturally, with his Palestinian brethren.[37] Behind Abdullah's unique approach to the Zionist movement lay two principal motives. One was sheer *realpolitik* in the face of Zionist strength and lack of Arab unity to match it. The second was 'an expectation of gains – gains which, at least in part, could be realized at the expense of the Palestinian Arabs'. These gains included Jewish financial support in return for pro-Zionist political stands, and territorial concessions on the part of the Jews which would enable the king to extend his desert kingdom. Such territorial expansion in turn meant partial realization of Abdullah's ambition to rule Bilad al-Sham, ancient Greater Syria (including contemporary Syria, Lebanon, Israel and Jordan). Abdullah sought this kingdom not out of megalomaniac ambitions but because of his growing apprehension that without such territory the legitimacy of his presence in Transjordan would be forever questioned by his Arab peers.[38]

Another plausible explanation of the unique stance adopted by the Hashemite ruler is his lack of anti-semitism – unlike some of his contemporaries – and a common interest with the Zionists in confronting the aspirations of the Palestinian national movement.[39] Needless to say, not everyone on the Zionist side was happy with the budding alliance. The Revisionists opposed it even when in the last years of the mandate it became obvious that Abdullah's approach was unique in the Arab camp. It was the pragmatic mainstream of Socialist Zionism that at first grudgingly and later enthusiastically accepted the appearance of a third actor in the arena of conflict. Abdullah thus became the ideal interlocutor for the Zionist leadership, someone who 'would appreciate the blessing and progress which the Zionist movement would bring' in its wake to Palestine.[40] To the hard core of Marxists in the Labour movement, he probably represented no more than a decadent and reactionary despot, but Marxist-Zionism, like Social-Zionism, became gradually more pragmatic in the face of political and economic realities and put national interests over and above its universalistic ideologies and values.

Signs of Abdullah's exceptional attitude first appeared in 1933 when he negotiated with the Jewish Agency over the possibility of settling Jews in Transjordan. Although these contacts bore no tangible results, they paved the way for more significant meetings in the future and acquainted the king with some of the principal policy-makers in the Jewish Agency.[41]

Further proof of Abdullah's unique position towards Palestine was presented to the Jews during the Arab revolt in the years 1936 to 1939. It was then that for the first time, both the British and the king suggested solving the question of Palestine by annexing densely Arab populated areas to Transjordan. This new notion was officially introduced in 1937 by the Peel Commission which advocated the partitioning of Palestine between the Jews and the Hashemites. The idea became the cornerstone for the policy of both Abdullah and of the Jewish Agency in the last two years of the mandate. In the final analysis, it determined the outcome of the war of 1948 and was advocated by the Israeli Labour party well into the 1980s. The British, with whom the formula originated, were to consider many other solutions before reintroducing it again shortly before the outbreak of the 1948 war.[42]

Until August 1945, Hashemite–Jewish discussions about the desirability of partitioning Palestine between them remained largely academic. Towards the end of the Second World War, however, they gave way to serious bilateral diplomatic negotiations about the future of post-mandatory Palestine, and two significant meetings took place in Abdullah's winter palace during August 1945. While the palace was to become the venue for even more important landmarks in the history of the negotiations, at that time the meetings 'were useful in identifying at least some common ground between Abdullah and the Zionists and in providing a basis for future co-operation between them'.[43]

The direct contact between King Abdullah and the Jewish Agency with regard to the future of post-mandatory Palestine was resumed in the summer of 1946. The talks then held coincided with the last British and American efforts to solve the conflict by introducing the cantonization of the country. The simultaneous

Hashemite–Jewish accord in effect indicates both the mistrust that the two sides felt towards outside mediation and, some would argue, their political foresight. By developing their own independent solution, Abdullah and the Jewish leaders completely disregarded not only the general Arab point of view, but also that of the Americans, the British and the Palestinians. Not only was Attlee's cabinet strongly committed in those days to the principle of cantonization, it was the first time that Britain's loyal ally in Amman had directly challenged London's policy in the Middle East. The American State Department supported the British plans at that stage, while President Truman was still studying the question. The Arab League and the Palestinians strove to create an Arab Palestine and opposed both cantonization and partition.

By challenging Britain, Abdullah won the sympathy and allegiance of many of the Jewish leaders. The Jewish Agency was apprehensive of cantonization, fearing that it would lead to the creation of a unitary Arab state in Palestine. The only way of frustrating such plans was by strengthing the alliance with Amman. Hence, on 12 August 1946, Eliahu Sasson, head of the Arab section of the Jewish Agency's Political Department, contacted King Abdullah with the aim of furthering the understanding over Palestine's future.[44]

Sasson could not have chosen a more propitious moment. He arrived in Amman at a time when Abdullah sought ways of improving his image and that of his kingdom in the eyes of the Arab world. From the beginning of his rule in Transjordan in 1921, the king had been regarded by the other Arab states as a British puppet. His dependence on the British indeed had forced him, at intervals, to prove his usefulness and importance to Britain, which he did, for example, first by participating in the Allies' Second World War efforts in the Middle East and later by putting himself forward as the protector of British interests in Palestine.

This tension between Abdullah's desire to appear as an independent ruler on the one hand, and his complete dependence on and obligation to Britain on the other, explains many of the fluctuations in the king's foreign policy after the Second World War. The British did very little to accommodate Abdullah on this point. They either stood in the way or remained aloof when the king sought possible ways of extricating himself from his predicament. One of the most notable attempts in this direction was Abdullah's Greater Syria plan. It should be remembered that the Hashemites had interpreted the Husayn-MacMahon accord as a British commitment to establish a Hashemite kingdom in Greater Syria. In the early 1940s Abdullah seriously advanced the notion that in order to attain Pan-Arab sanction for the fact that he was ruling at all, he must be the ruler of a clearly defined new kingdom comprising Syria, Palestine, Lebanon and Transjordan. This ambitious plan found most of the British policy makers bemused, a few apprehensive, but none willing to lend a hand. Needless to say, the people in the countries mentioned did not exactly queue up to be ruled by the Hashemites. In fact, it seems that no one in the Middle East took Abdullah's Greater Syria plan seriously. Instead, it was the plans of Nuri al-Said, the Iraqi statesman, for the unity of the Fertile Crescent which contributed to the creation of the Arab League. Nevertheless, Abdullah persisted in his attempts to fulfil the scheme until as late as July 1947. In that month, shortly before the Syrian national elections, Abdullah contemplated the annexation of Jabal al-Druze through the help of the leading Druze family in Syria, the al-Atrash family. The scheme failed owing to the opposition of the British chief of staff of the Arab Legion, Sir John Glubb.[45] Abdullah then realized that only in Palestine did his ambitions and British interests coincide.

Only towards the end of 1946 was London prepared to assist Abdullah in his efforts to refute allegations of British dominance in Transjordan, that is when they terminated their mandate there and concluded a defence treaty with the king, who thereby had officially become an independent ruler. But Abdullah remained a British protégé in the eyes of his neighbours and needed more substantial prompting of his self-image as an important figure in the Arab world. In these circumstances Sasson's overtures could not have come at a better time.

The message carried by Sasson to Abdullah was that the Jewish Agency sought an agreement about partitioning post-mandatory Palestine between Transjordan and the future Jewish state. Sasson hoped to induce the two countries to join a front against the Morrison–Grady plan. Abdullah, however, was not the only Arab leader approached by Sasson in 1946. The Jewish emissary also travelled quite often to Egypt where he inquired about Cairo's position towards the future of Palestine. He soon found out that a deep chasm separated Cairo and Amman. Abdullah talked of annexation of vast parts of Palestine to his kingdom, whereas the Egyptians envisaged the creation of an independent state in the

Arab parts of Palestine. Nevertheless Sasson was gratified when he heard not only from Abdullah, but also from the Egyptian prime minister, Isma'il Sidqi, that neither of them would object to the creation of a Jewish state in Palestine.[46]

Sasson's mission to Egypt failed in the end when the Egyptian government succumbed to domestic pressures and adopted a more pro-Palestinian policy. To his great dismay, Sasson learned that it was the Egyptian delegates in the League who persuaded the organization to declare its unconditional support for the creation of a unitary Arab state over all of Palestine. One of the Israeli historians of the period argues that British diplomats in Cairo and elsewhere in the Middle East shared in the responsibility for preventing a possible Jewish–Egyptian reapprochement, fearing the formation of a strong anti-British alliance in the Middle East.[47]

This situation left the Jews as the only possible ally for Abdullah in a tactical agreement over Palestine. Negotiatons between the two sides continued until the crystallization of a Hashemite–Jewish understanding over the future of post-mandatory Palestine. This accord is commonly desribed as the 'divide and annex' solution of the Palestine question: dividing Palestine and annexing the Arab parts to Transjordan. The common ground for the agreement was a mutual objection to the creation of a Palestinian state. Both sides were convinced that such a state would be ruled by Hajj Amin al-Husayni, the Mufti of Jerusalem. They believed that a 'Mufti State' would prevent both of them from realizing their national and territorial ambitions. The Jewish Agency in particular abhorred such a possibility, asserting that the creation of a Palestinian state would perpetuate the ideological conflict in Palestine. Unlike the Revisionists who coveted Transjordan as well, the main Zionist stream was in favour of partition, as it implied recognition of the Jewish state. This is why they gave wholehearted support to UNSCOP's report, although they preferred the Hashemites to the Palestinians as partners in the division of Palestine.

This meant, of course, that the Palestinians were entirely left out of any solution, an implication which they had already realized in 1936, when Abdullah attempted to end the Palestinian strike by suggesting the annexation of Palestine to his emirate. In many ways, the Peel Commission adopted Abdullah's solution. The paper *Filastin* termed it then 'The Greater Transjordan' solution, an expression later adopted by the British Foreign Office to describe its own chosen solution to the Palestine problem.[48]

The British decision to withdraw from Palestine forced the Jewish Agency and King Abdullah to consider more seriously the significance of their thus far precarious connection. After the UN resolution, the territorial and political framework of the solution they had arrived at became even clearer. At the beginning of 1947, the gist of their scheme was the annexation of the populated Arab areas of Palestine to the king's territory in return for his tacit recognition of the Jewish state; the UN resolution from November 1947 forced the two partners to define more specifically the territories allotted to Abdullah.

For that purpose in November 1947 a meeting took place between Golda Meyrson (Meir), the acting head of the Political Department of the Jewish Agency, and King Abdullah. At this meeting Abdullah presented a new vision of Palestine in which a Jewish republic would be integrated into a newly-formed Hashemite kingdom – consisting of Transjordan and Palestine. When, not surprisingly, this was rejected out of hand by the other side, Abdullah asked for Jewish consent to the annexation to Transjordan of the UN-defined Arab state. To this the Jewish Agency's representative did give her assent, in return for the king's promise not to attack the Jewish state in the event of a war breaking out.[49] A month later these mutual promises were reiterated in a meeting between Eliahu Sasson and the king's personal physician, Dr Shawkat al-Sati.[50]

The Jews never promised Abdullah the whole area allocated to the Arab state by the UN, but asked him to decide first, as indeed he did, which parts were vital to him. His natural choice was the regions of Samaria and Judea for the dual reason that these were both fertile and closest to his current borders. Once he had designated that area, he obtained an unwritten Jewish consent not to fight him over these territories. Abdullah may have contemplated at that stage (November 1947), the annexation of more Arab territory, for example in the Galilee or Gaza, but as the war progressed he made no apparent effort to reach those areas, let alone fight over them.[51]

At the beginning of 1948, Abdullah sought British approval for his plan. Since it was impossible for him to visit Britain personally to discuss the future of post-mandatory Palestine, as this would have aroused suspicions in the Arab world, the king looked for a pretext which would make it possible to conduct secret negotiations with the British. This was found in a Transjordanian request for a revision of the 1946 Anglo-Transjordanian treaty. The Hashemites claimed that such a revision was necessary in order to further strengthen Transjordan's image as an independent state. Thus, in February 1948, a delegation headed by the prime minister, Tawfiq Abu'l-Huda, went to Britain to discuss the future of Palestine as well as the revision of the treaty. In the course of those talks, the Transjordanians revealed to their British interlocutors the scope and content of their negotiations with the Jews and it was then that the king obtained Britain's blessing for the tacit understanding he had reached with the Jewish Agency about the partitioning of post-mandatory Palestine.[52]

The British, in fact, went further than just supporting the tacit understanding – they turned it into the cornerstone of their own policy towards the question of Palestine. The 'Greater Transjordan' idea suited Britain eminently since it allowed London to remain loyal to its only staunch ally in that part of the world, and at the same time to maintain a certain amount of involvement in Palestine in spite of the decision to withdraw. The British position was due also to the pragmatic attitude of the foreign secretary, Ernest Bevin, under whose guidance the Foreign Office pursued an *ad hoc* policy in the Middle East. Together with the backing of 'the tacit understanding' between Abdullah and the Jews, a major outcome of his policy was also Britain's recognition of the state of Israel.[53]

Once he had secured London's approval Abdullah advanced and intensified the negotiations with the Jews. In talks held in January and February 1948, the king demanded an outlet to the Mediterranean as a condition for his recognition of the Jewish state. The Jewish refusal to grant Transjordan this corridor was one of a number of loose ends left unresolved at the outbreak of the war.[54] On the whole, as we shall see, the king vacillated up until May between strong commitment to the agreement and hostility towards the Jewish community in Palestine. Abdullah's doubts evaporated after the impressive Jewish successes in the battles over the mixed towns in Palestine.

The Jewish achievements in April indicated how dangerous was the path Abdullah had chosen to follow in his relationship with the Arab world. He wished to retain his place there, perhaps even to attain a leading role, while at the same time adhering to his secret agreement with the Jews. In the eyes of some of his ministers this was an impossible and perilous position. The British representative in Amman, Sir Alec Kirkbride, also regarded Abdullah's policy as hazardous. Kirkbride gradually, though never wholeheartedly, reconciled himself to the secret accord, but Abdullah's ministers never came to terms with it. Notwithstanding his absolute rule in the kingdom, Abdullah could not ignore his ministers' position. Unwilling to reveal the full extent of his ties with the Jews, he would, therefore, at times burst into a barrage of anti-Zionist rhetoric. While this was meant to satisfy his opponents at home and abroad, it also undermined Jewish confidence in him, especially toward the end of the mandate, since naturally Abdullah echoed the League's resolve to oppose by force the UN partition resolution and to send the Arab armies to occupy Palestine. In public the king continued to adhere to that policy while privately conveying to the Jews a different message. Despite its obvious benefits – the extension of Transjordan's territory and enhancement of Abdullah's position in the Arab world – it remained a risky option to take. But he persisted in his belief that only through this double game could he achieve these objectives. Hence his refusal to accept Jewish demands that he should declare in public what he had promised them behind closed doors. His double game caused the Jews to question the sincerity of his promises, but in order to soothe Arab doubts as to his loyalty to their cause he was willing to take that risk.

Thus, when Azzam, Abd al-Ilah and Riyad al-Sulh arrived in Amman in April 1948, they did not, and could not, find any tangible evidence of contacts Abdullah might have had with the Jews. Whatever rumours had accompanied Abdullah's talks in London or however longstanding the knowledge of the king's ambitions for a Greater Transjordan, the Arab world had difficulties in discovering Abdullah's real intentions. None of the scholars dealing with this episode have been able to establish how much in fact the Arab leaders knew. In his memoirs the Iraqi general and adviser to the Arab League's committee on Palestine, Taha al-Hashimi, states that the king was suspected all through the Arab world of having cut a deal with the Zionists.[55] Two contemporaries of his, who were both also eyewitnesses, Sir Alec Kirkbride and Glubb Pasha, believed that at least the secretary-general of the Arab League, Azzam Pasha, knew of the king's policies.[56] If so, he did not stand up and accost the king directly – rather he urged him to join the League's efforts and send his army into Palestine.

LAST MINUTE PREPARATIONS, APRIL–MAY 1948

Whatever the Arab leaders may have suspected Abdullah of, in April 1948 he was indispensable to them. Transjordan's Arab Legion was the only able and experienced Arab army – without it there was very little scope for Arab ambitions in Palestine. Faced with this reality the League had to do its utmost to persuade the king to join in.

The delegation from the League was surprised to find Abdullah reluctant to oblige his visitors by immediately consenting to send his army to Palestine. He demanded first a firmer commitment from the other Arab states, particularly Egypt. In reality, however, Abdullah had long been waiting for this moment. He was more than willing to co-operate and in fact coveted the leading role in the operation, since without it he felt he would be unable to realize his territorial ambitions. His close relationship with the British made him one of the best informed actors on the Palestine stage; thus he must have been well aware of how slim the chances were for success in the war against the Jews. Yet, he did everything possible to become the head of the military intervention in Palestine, even though he may have realized it would turn into a fiasco; for how else could he hope to navigate the dangerous straits between secret agreements with the Jews and ostensible commitment to the Palestine cause? The path certainly was a slippery one, and at times it seemed Abdullah might lose his balance; but in the final analysis he succeeded both in commanding the Arab Palestine campaign and keeping his understanding with the Jews.

On purely military grounds, Abdullah, of course, was the best candidate to lead the Arab armies into battle – he was the only ruler who could offer to send most of his troops, and the best, for internally his country was the only tranquil one in the stormy Arab world: 'while Egypt, Iraq and Syria were preoccupied at this time with internal upset and could ill afford to send their best, or any troops at all, to Palestine, Transjordan was firmly controlled allowing the bulk of the Legion to be stationed in Palestine without fear of internal problems at home'.[57]

Abdullah's political manoeuvring began by depicting Egypt as the last stumbling block on the road to a successful war in Palestine; he therefore suggested to his guests that together with his friend, Riyad al-Sulh, the Lebanese prime minister, he would go to

Egypt and try to convince the reluctant Egyptian politicians to join the offensive. The two flew to Cairo towards the end of April.[58]

As no one in the Middle East at the time seemed able to understand or predict the Egyptian position, their task was not simple. British intelligence, usually successful in deciphering the intentions of the Arab armies, found it impossible to ascertain whether or not the Egyptian army would participate in the overall military operations.[59] Egyptian politicians themselves were unable to make up their minds until the very last moment. Muhammad Hassanein Heikal, then a young journalist working for the daily *Akhbar al-Yawm*, has recently recalled the days of Egypt's indecision. At the time he wrote a series of articles on Palestine for which he interviewed the Egyptian leadership in March and April 1948. In March 1948 all the Egyptian senior politicians he met were convinced Egypt would not venture beyond sending volunteers to fight in Palestine. In April, in Heikal's words: 'The Prime Minister ultimately changed his mind and it was decided to send the Egyptian army into the battle, because there were strong indications that war would break out with the creation of a Jewish state on 15 May.' Heikal rightly attributes this change of plans to the pressure of King Faruq who had set his mind on playing a leading role in the Arab world.[60] Faruq, it seems, was not motivated in this by patriotic urges but was seeking rather an outlet from his domestic unpopularity and may also have been bent upon securing for himself a place in posterity.[61] Muhammad Hassanein Heikal, on the other hand, sympathized to a certain extent with Egypt's prime minister, Mahmud Nuqrashi, who was disinclined to divert forces from Egypt at the time of its struggle against the British.[62] Another Egyptian historian has claimed that since Egypt was under foreign domination it could do very little for Palestine.[63] This apology was reiterated in 1988 by the commander of the Egyptian forces that entered Palestine in 1948, General al-Mawawi, in an interview he gave to an Egyptian newspaper.[64]

The Egyptian government was in the midst of delicate negotiations with Britain over the future of the Suez Canal zone and the Sudan. It won the sympathy of most of the UN members and the Arab world in its demand for complete independence. However, legally speaking, the Anglo-Egyptian treaty of 1936 (which had allowed both for a British military presence in Egypt and for the co-rulership over the Sudan), was valid for another eight years. Both the left and the right in Egyptian politics attacked

Mahmud Nuqrashi's liberal government for its incompetence in the domestic and the foreign arenas. The leaders of the Egyptian national movement were as anxious as King Faruq to play a decisive role in Arab affairs; however, in 1948 they gave precedence to local national interests over Pan-Arabism. The struggle for the liberation of Egypt was in fact just entering its final and crucial stage, and there could be no room for the concerns of others, not even Palestine.

Abdullah wanted Egyptian participation for two reasons. He needed Egyptian military pressure on southern Palestine in order to facilitate his own takeover of the central areas. The Jews, so it seemed to him, would be more agreeable to concessions if Egyptian troops entered the Negev – an area he had promised the Zionists and the British he would not encroach on as it was part of the UN Jewish state. Secondly, we may assume that the thought of subordinating the Egyptian army under his command brought Abdullah considerable pleasure – for he had been mocked for years of Egyptian politicians as a British puppet.

Arriving in Egypt, Transjordan's ruler in fact found a receptive Egyptian government, willing to participate after a long period of hesitation. It is somewhat ironical that the Egyptians assumed that by their participation they could prevent Abdullah from fulfilling his ambitions in Palestine, whereas Abdullah believed that their enrollment would only serve his plans. His intended involvement in the war and the actual move of some of his units into Arab Palestine, just a few days before he went to Egypt, called for an Egyptian reaction in order to avert any possible Transjordanian expansion into the south of Palestine near the Egyptian border. If Palestine were to be divided, even if only into spheres of influence, the south naturally was Egyptian territory. It seems that it was above all Abdullah's determination to enter Palestine with or without general Arab blessing which put an end to Egypt's hesitations. It suddenly became feasible that if no other Arab country entered the war with him, Abdullah might keep his side of the long suspected agreements with the Jews. Such prospects were particularly offensive to King Faruq:

An invasion by Abdullah and the partition of Palestine between him and the emergent Jewish state, regardless of whether accomplished peacefully or as a result of an armed conflict, would have dealt a death blow to the vision of Arab unity, to

Egypt's hegemonial aspirations, and to Egypt's prestige in the Islamic world.[65]

Immediately after Abdullah and Riyad al-Sulh left Egypt, King Faruq did his utmost to coerce the Egyptian government into a clear commitment to participate fully in the war effort. To this end he recruited the religious establishment of al-Azhar who contributed to the already tense atmosphere in Cairo by declaring the war in Palestine as a *jihad* against Zionism.[66] The frequent meetings of the League in the Egyptian capital also added to the frenzy in Cairo's streets and on 12 May 1948 the Egyptian Upper House, the Senate, approved the intervention of the Egyptian army in the offensive. The army demanded parliamentary approval so as not to become the scapegoat in case of a defeat.[67] The government soon realized the immediate advantage of a war situation; a day after the Senate's decision to enter Palestine, an *état de siège* was declared and the prime minister became the military governor-general of the country. The military regime was ostensibly to facilitate a safe transfer of troops to the border, but it also served as a means of restoring law and order.[68]

The timing of these last inter-Arab manoeuvres is very important, for it proves that a fortnight before the war the leaders of the Arab world were unable to guarantee Transjordanian and Egyptian participation in the war. In the two weeks left till 15 May they did succeed in enlisting Amman and Cairo, but one wonders to what extent the Arab armies could prepare themselves for an offensive in such a short time.

Nevertheless, by the end of April it was possible for the Arabs to draw up a plan for the Palestine war. Prepared by the military committee of the Arab League, the plan stipulated that the tiny Lebanese army would move along the coast as far as Nahariya on the way to Haifa and Acre; the Syrians would use the Lebanese town of Bint Jbeil as a launching pad on the way to the Galilee where they were to occupy Safad, Afula and Nazareth; the Iraqis were to cross the river Jordan at Naharaim and meet the Syrians in Afula; the Legion would meet with the other forces in Afula after it had occupied Samaria and Jerusalem; the Egyptian army would complete the operation by entering Palestine in a pincer movement, meeting the Jordanians in Jerusalem and the Syrians somewhere between Afula and Tel Aviv.[69]

This plan troubled Abdullah on two scores. He was displeased with the limited role designated to his army and he objected to the appointment of the Iraqi general chief of staff, General Nur al-Din Mahmud, as the supreme commander of the invasion force. To be able to determine the assignments of the invading force in such a way as to fulfil his own ambitions in Palestine, Abdullah naturally desired the post of supreme commander for himself. In the event, there was no need for drastic action on the part of the Hashemite ruler to bring this about. On 13 May 1948, two days before the outbreak of war, Azzam Pasha, in a move which surprised the king offered the post of commander in chief of all the Arab armies in Palestine to Glubb Pasha, and the honour of becoming the titular commander of the Arab forces to Abdullah himself; whereas the king after prolonged hesitation accepted this position, Glubb declined his. The British general and Sir Alec Kirkbride believed that Azzam was actually looking for a scapegoat once it had dawned upon the secretary-general that the chances for success in Palestine were slim. Glubb surmised as much when Azzam presented the League's invasion plan to him; upon hearing the number of soldiers intended for the campaign, he remarked bitterly to Azzam that the entire Arab attitude was naïve and impractical.[70]

Azzam's move was indeed quite surprising in the light of the fact that all other Arab states rather mistrusted Abdullah: it was one thing to draw the Legion into the battle but quite another to ask Abdullah to lead the campaign. It becomes less puzzling if we accept Kirkbride's and Glubb's explanation, which after all was quite plausible, that Azzam was searching for a future scapegoat. But even this is inadequate to explain the comparative ease with which Palestine's future was left in the hands of the most unlikely candidate. We should stress again that at that point very few of the Arab leaders were sanguine about the chances of winning the military confrontation; it was impossible for them to avoid participating so late in the day, but they did everything possible to limit the disastrous repercussions which they expected in the wake of a defeat in Palestine. Abdullah's appointment, therefore, should be seen more as a matter of lack of choice, or rather of candidates.

Thus, quite reluctantly, the member states of the League convened in Cairo immediately upon Azzam's arrival from Amman to approve the appointment. The following summary of that meeting was given by Azzam's head of office, Wahid al-Daly, and shows the League's fundamental discomfiture:

The League's council decided to appoint King Abdullah as the supreme commander. Some of the Arab states had at first been strongly opposed to the appointment, but were convinced eventually to accept it. There was no other choice. The position, *vis à vis* Palestine, of the Transjordanian army was better than that of the other armies, since several units of this army had already been in Palestine at the time as part of the Mandatory Police Force. Therefore, the Arab states had to accept Abdullah's appointment as the supreme commander. General Nur al-Din Mahmud was duly appointed as his deputy.[71]

In other words, without the efficient Legion any hopes for even partial success would be vain. Consequently, even if Abdullah's own ambitions had been known, he was indispensable for the general Arab effort.

With the League's approval and Glubb's refusal to accept the post, approximately seventy-two hours before the war was to break out Abdullah became the supreme commander of the all-Arab force sent into Palestine.[72] From his new vantage-point, Abdullah immediately set about revising the League's invasion scheme to suit his own ambitions and plans. In the new plan, which he drew up the night before the war, Abdullah cancelled the intended Syrian entrance into Palestine from the north and instead diverted Damascus's forces to the areas allocated by the UN to the Jews, near the southern tip of Lake Tiberias. In the original plan he had been assigned to those areas himself but by sending the Syrians there he could now ensure that his own forces would not transgress the borders of the Jewish state, thereby keeping to his agreement with the Jewish Agency.

In addition, Abdullah himself took over almost all assignments originally given to the Iraqis, confining the Baghdad contingent to Samaria (the northern part of the West Bank of today) where he had already established a *de facto* rule in April 1948, and where the Iraqis were now to be a police force. Abdullah needed the Iraqis all the more for this purpose as it became increasingly clear that he would not be able to reach an agreement with the Jews over Jerusalem and thus would require all his fighting men for the campaign over that city. At the same time the king was aware of his unpopularity in many towns and villages in Arab Palestine and deemed it expedient to keep a watchful eye on the Arab

Palestinians.[73] The Iraqi presence in Samaria had in addition one other objective – to disperse any allegation of Transjordanian monopoly in this area. Leaving the Egyptians to tackle the Jews alone in the Negev, an area designated by the UN to the Jewish state, Abdullah was prepared to interfere in the Galilee, an area that fell within the Arab state. There he contemplated sharing the burden of the fighting with the Syrians, the insignificant Lebanese army, and the Arab Liberation Army. The latter force had already been expelled by Abdullah from the towns of Hebron and Bethlehem after it had allegedly looted the local population (there is no evidence to substantiate this allegation).

Why did the Arab armies end up by accepting Abdullah's obviously underhand plan? It seems that the Arab world had little choice for Abdullah presented them with a *fait accompli*. His forces had already entered Arab Palestine and could not be halted. Moreover, some of the Eyptian troops had by that time moved into Palestine proper and their retreat was unthinkable given the already tense atmosphere in Cairo's streets. Neither the Egyptians nor the other Arab armies could hope to achieve anything without the Legion, and this made it possible for Abdullah to dictate a new plan at zero hour. By forcing the Syrians to change tactics, giving an impossible task to the Lebanese soldiers and turning the Iraqis into his proxies in the area, Abdullah saw his chance to annex the West Bank to Transjordan.

However, his success on the general Arab front had led him into serious troubles with the Jewish Agency. The Hashemite palace's patriotic, warlike declaration which accompanied the king's manoeuvres in the Arab world caused Abdullah's Jewish friends in Tel Aviv to doubt his commitment to their joint understanding. A parliamentary decree to commence full mobilization of the Transjordanian army only made things worse. As a consequence, Abdullah's relationship with the Jewish Agency deteriorated sharply in the weeks of April and May 1948.

Abdullah became more careful and for a while he tried both publicly and privately to present a coherent position and suggested autonomy to the Jews in a Hashemite Palestine. In private correspondence with his Jewish friends he even declared that he would desist from further negotiations with the Jews 'until both sides were in a more reasonable mood'.[74] By 'a reasonable mood' he evidently meant one in which his autonomy proposal would be accepted. The king's new rigidity may be best understood by the fact that in April Amman became the hub of the inter-Arab preparations for war. Abdullah was clearly playing the role of Palestine's liberator.

This shift in policy was naturally not well received on the Jewish side. In March some of the principal protagonists of Jewish–Hashemite understanding had already shown signs of impatience and dissatisfaction with the king's hesitations and his overt support for the general Arab line. As they equated Jewish victory with a successful implementation of the agreement with Abdullah, they even went as far as suggesting to Ben Gurion that he ask the British to prolong the mandate for a year, and in the meantime he should seek a new agreement.[75]

Ben Gurion, however, had become less interested in the political implications of the understanding with the Hashemites and more and more aware of the fact that even partial neutralization of the Arab Legion would facilitate the establishment of the Jewish state. Partial neutralization meant that the Legion would have only limited military objectives in Palestine and would undertake not to enter the ares allocated to the Jews in the UN partition resolution. Already in May 1947 Ben Gurion had striven to attain this goal. At that time, he received the following report from the heads of the Hagana: 'The Arab Legion is so far the most serious military force. It has at its disposal approximately 25,000 men [the British estimate as we have seen was 7,400]. It is well-equipped, and commanded by the British. Its main problem is the absence of an air force.' The report was wrong in its numerical estimation, but not in its overall prediction. It stressed the indispensibility of the Legion for an Arab military success in Palestine. The report's conclusion influenced the war plans of the Jewish side later on. The knowledge of the Legion's importance was one of the principal reasons that convinced the Zionist leadership to seek diplomatic ways of neutralizing the Legion, even at the cost of political concessions.[76]

In April 1948, despite the pessimism among his advisers on Arab affairs, Ben Gurion continued to assert that as a result of the previous negotiations with Abdullah the danger of the Legion was considerably reduced. He expected the Legion to participate in the battlefield, but to pursue only limited objectives.[77] In this vein, in April 1948 Ben Gurion informed the leaders of the Jewish Agency that the newly-formed Jewish state would have immense difficulties in occupying the areas allocated to it if the Legion were to go beyond the Arab areas, thereby hinting that everything possible should be done to prevent it from taking part in the fighting. Many members of the Jewish Agency shared Ben Gurion's assessment and regarded the *modus vivendi* with Transjordan as an important asset that would contribute to the successful establishment of a Jewish state. Indeed, Ben Gurion made every possible effort to ensure that Abdullah would adhere to his original scheme. In this context, it is understandable why Ben Gurion decided to send a letter to Abdullah denying the Jewish Agency's part in the Deir Yassin massacre.[78]

Had Ben Gurion been able to read the reports sent from Amman to London he would have found them echoing his own evaluation of the situation. The British officers in the Legion reported that Abdullah's public declarations about his intention 'to go to war against the Zionists' were made only in order to cater to Arab public opinion.[79] The British representative in Amman reported to the foreign secretary that, Abdullah's new military title not-withstanding, what was important for Transjordan was its agreement with the Jewish Agency. This view was accepted by Bevin and the Foreign Office and influenced British policy towards the conflict in the years ahead.[80]

By May Abdullah's friends in the Jewish Agency could again view things in a more relaxed way. The consolidation of his leading role in the Arab war effort, with no visible opposition, allowed the king once more to pledge allegiance to the Jews. At the beginning of that month, the two sides for the first time attended to the specific understanding and military arrangements between them, and senior Hagana officers and two senior British officers of the Legion (Colonel Goldie and Major Crocker) met to discuss these issues. Sir Alec Kirkbride reported that the purpose of these 'top secret' meetings was 'to define the area of Palestine to be occupied by the two forces'.[81] All the participants expressed their desire to prevent a war between the Jews and the Hashemites, and the Hagana's impression at the end of the meeting was that although it would participate in the general Arab effort, the Legion had no intention of occupying other than the Arab areas.[82]

The meeting took place after the Legion had already clashed several times with the Jewish forces. However, the British officers indicated in their reports to London that these incidents were the result of misunderstandings and not a shift in the king's policy.[83]

With the tactical arrangements completed between them it was time to try once more to attain a firmer strategic understanding. The last political meeting between the Jewish Agency and the king took place on 11 May 1948. The Jewish emissaries tried to elicit a clear commitment from the king to the military arrangement and Abdullah tried to clarify his ultimate intentions to them. Golda Meir, who again on this occasion met the king, was deeply disappointed when he announced that only a Jewish consent to defer the proclamation of their state could avert a war. He also demanded the cessation of Jewish imigration. The king hinted that his inflexible position stemmed from the fact that he was not alone in the game but rather 'one out of five' Arab armies entering Palestine – but he promised to allow Jewish representation to his parliament should he be successful in occupying all of Palestine.[84] This gamble failed, perhaps because Abdullah underestimated the Jewish strength and self-confidence. As she had done in November 1947, Meir rejected all the king's proposals and urged Abdullah to stand by the original promise he had made to her not to invade Jewish territory. According to some reports the king replied that indeed he would never go back on a pledge he had made to a woman.[85]

Apparently, neither party ever intended to depart from the original understanding. The first president of Israel, Chaim Weizmann, was later to recall that both sides left the last meeting with the impression that, divergences of opinion notwithstanding, they had succeeded in preventing a major clash between the two armies. The Israelis who participated in the meeting reported that they felt Abdullah might want to improve his position by extending his territory slightly beyond that outlined in the 29 November UN resolution but would not attempt to occupy part of the Jewish state. American intelligence at the time reached similar conclusions.[86]

Nevertheless, Abdullah's reluctance to sign a written agreement must have left the Jews in the dark as to whether or not he would stick to his promises. The progress of the war from 15 May 1948 onwards indicates that most of the Legion's operations did not in fact constitute a breach of the promise first given to Meir in November 1947 and again in May 1948. The lack of a written agreement means of course that we shall never know whether this was intentional or the result of circumstance. The Legion's attacks on the Jewish potash plant in the Dead Sea and the electricity plant in the north, as well as the Jewish attempt to occupy Jenin, and above all the bloody battle over Jerusalem, underline the vagueness of the terms of this understanding.

It still seems remarkable today that two partners who had settled an arrangement for all of Palestine, could not concur over the fate of one city. Indeed, this question was raised by the British Legion officers in the meeting they had with their Hagana counterparts at the beginning of May 1948. The Jewish officers promised the Legioners that 'Jerusalem is a Hebrew town, but if the road to the city and its vicinity is free, there is no need for a military confrontation'. As the routes to Jerusalem were under constant attack from Arab irregulars and because the Muslims regarded the city as a holy place, this remark was tantamount to stating that the fate of the city would be determineed on the battlefield.[87]

The absence of any understanding on Jerusalem was as important for the effect this would have on the course of the war as was the existence of the agreement itself. It seems that neither side felt it could give up its ambition to hold all of Jerusalem *a priori*. Abdullah was moved by Pan-Arab, family and religious considerations; as Kirkbride put it in a letter to Bevin: 'How could the King reach the frontiers of the Jewish state and remain passive, he had to fight at least over Jerusalem, the third holiest place for Islam.'[88] As we shall see, Abdullah later justified his early withdrawal from the battlefield by the need to protect Jerusalem. By occupying the city he could assume the ancient role of the Hashemite family as protectors of the places holy to Islam. He probably also hoped to appear to the world as the guardian of all major religious sites. Moreover, he counted on gaining Arab recognition for his annexation of the Arab areas of Palestine due to the very fact that he had gone to battle over Jerusalem.[89] Finally, we may add that his father, Husayn, was buried in the city, a fact which may have played an emotional part in the king's decisions.

As for the Jews, it is not difficult to appreciate the strength of their position on Jerusalem (owing to their large numbers there) and the depth of their feelings for Zion. After all, could the Zionist movement have fought a war for independence without obtaining Zion? Ben Gurion, in particular, regarded the security of Jerusalem as of top priority to the Jewish war effort. He would have refused any agreement which did not make provisions for Jewish control over at least the Jewish quarters of the city.[90]

Tragically, and despite all the efforts to prevent this very outcome, the battle over the city continued intermittently until September 1948 and ended in the *de facto* division of Jerusalem. Most of the Legion's casualties were sustained in that battle; while the toll of Jewish lives was heavy too.

Except in the Jerusalem area, the Legion did not engage in any significant manner in the war against the Jews. Hence, the limited objectives tilted the balance of power, which at the onset was basically equilateral, in Israel's favour. The indispensibility of the Legion to a successful Arab war effort was known to the Jewish side; so were Abdullah's objectives. Even without a clear sense about the Legion's plan for the war itself, the newly-born Jewish state thus knew it would not be facing a formidable force. Considering the general quality of the other Arab armies, their size and the minimal amount of time they had to prepare themselves for war, as well as Abdullah's meandering politics, it is no wonder that Goliath was so definitively defeated by David.

The balance of power between Jews and Arabs in May 1948 of course looks different if one juxtaposes the numbers of the entire populations involved in the 1948 war. This is a comparison which corresponds more to the prevailing Israeli myth and the rather general recollection that few were pitted against many. On the battlefield, however, the situation was near parity. This does not mean that sorely imbalanced battles did not take place. Many Israeli historians in the past have dwelt upon some of the bloody and severe confrontations between Arabs and Jews before and during the war. Some of these determined various developments in the course of the war and the military history of the 1948 war would be incomplete without them. We, however, wish to maintain that these incidents belong rather to the microhistory of the war.

The numbers of soldiers employed, the level of preparation and the performance on the battlefield all clearly point to the ambivalent attitude of the Arab states towards the problem of Palestine. It seems that only in the case of Faruq, but not his government, can we assume a genuine wish to join in the battle for Palestine. The other Arab leaders were primarily engaged in jingoistic rhetoric, against their better judgment, hoping the mandate would not really come to an end and that international public opinion would repudiate the UN partition resolution. That the rhetoric did not match the reality can be inferred from the postponement, to April 1948, of their actual decision to enter Palestine. In the case of Egypt it was delayed even further – until

12 May 1948, that is until three days before the end of the mandate.

An evaluation of the nature and development of the Arab commitment to the Palestinian cause is beyond the scope of this book. Suffice it to comment that although the Arab leaders were motivated by individual interests in their involvement in Palestine, they were, and still are, under pressure from within to salvage Palestine. These leaders tried first to confine their commitment to words, then to a limited military effort – their failure in the moment of truth was their undoing.

5

Seeking a Comprehensive Peace – Count Bernadotte's Mission and the Development of the Military Campaigns

THE FIRST STAGE OF THE WAR (15 MAY – 11 JUNE, 1948) AND THE FIRST TRUCE

Of the events that followed upon the outbreak of the war on 15 May perhaps the most remarkable were the immediate efforts made by the outside world to end the fighting. Not only did the Great Powers and the UN Security Council early on in the campaign attempt to bring about a cease-fire; even more surprising was their simultaneous endeavour to introduce a new and different peace plan, as though the first signs of hostilities were sufficient to convince the members of the UN and the officials of the American and British administrations of the inadequacy of the barely six-month old partition plan. The question of Palestine was at no time put aside or even ignored, but remained throughout on the agenda of the UN sessions. And yet, these relentless efforts came to nothing. The fighting was to end only after the Israelis had decided that they had accomplished their goal of occupying as much as possible of western Palestine without jeopardizing their understanding with King Abdullah. In the final analysis, the only achievement to come out of the peace proposals was that once the parties agreed to a cease-fire the subsequent mutual military arrangements between Israel and the Arab governments were set up through UN services.

Who carried the blame for the failure of the endeavours for peace? Was it the United Nations officials, to whom the mission was entrusted; or the respective governments, who in their action and decisions showed themselves to be stubborn and narrow minded and thereby condemned their societies to a continuing cycle of violence and bloodshed? Was only one side culpable – and if so, which? Such questions can best be approached by a careful examination of the UN mediation and conciliation efforts and by an analysis of the Israeli and Arab responses to them. No definite, unequivocal answers are of course possible. We shall try and provide only the facts. At the same time, however, we would also point to the alternative courses of action which were open to all involved but which were not followed. One thing we do know for certain – the course chosen brought in its wake more violence, close to a million Palestinian refugees and no peace for either side.

The quest for a settlement to end the fighting was entrusted by the United Nations to Count Folke Bernadotte. An extraordinary man, Bernadotte was the first of a long line of Swedish mediators in regional conflicts around the world. Like the Swiss, the Swedes had succeeded in pursuing a neutral policy towards international as well as regional conflicts. Their persistence in this course throughout the grim Second World War era had annoyed many people and governments in the anti-Nazi alliance. And yet, this neutral position made them eminently suitable to act as mediators in places where others would not have been welcome.

Bernadotte was in many ways best qualified for the task: during the Second World War he had headed the Swedish Red Cross and had won international acclaim for securing the release of about 20,000 Jews from German concentration camps. He had also taken part in the negotiations ending the Second World War in April 1945, and so had gained some experience in armistice negotiations. But Bernodotte knew very little about the Middle East and probably even less about Palestine. Such lack of familiarity need not be a drawback, but if one accepts that the failure of UNSCOP was partly due to the inexperience of its members in Middle Eastern affairs, then it seems that in this particular instance the United Nations failed to draw a lesson. As we shall see, Bernadotte first relied on common sense in outlining a peace plan. When this plan was rejected he relied on British expertise in Middle Eastern affairs and introduced a second plan. This was turned down as well by all the parties, which means that actually Bernadotte fared neither better nor worse than mediators before or after him.

Bernadotte was appointed mediator by the Security Council on 20 May 1948. The General Assembly authorized him to seek an immediate solution to the conflict, and to work towards a cease-fire.[1] To judge by the evidence of the Israeli foreign minister at the time, Moshe Sharett, the beginning of Bernadotte's mission was promising: it became instantly the focus of Middle Eastern political life, and a glimpse at the Arab and Israeli newspapers of the day seems to confirm this. However, since it was the military operations and not the diplomatic moves of this or that mediator which dominated daily life this interest was not sustained for long.[2] Bernadotte's first task was to try to impose a truce on the warring parties.

In the week following the end of the mandate the Arab armies entered Palestine and attacked Jewish settlements in the north and south. At the same time an Egyptian contingent began a long journey along the coast and into the Negev capturing areas which in the partition resolution had been designated to the Jewish state. Another Egyptian contingent was stationed in the Bethlehem area and captured Kibbutz Ramat Rahel. Tel Aviv was bombarded from the air by Egyptian aircraft and Jerusalem remained cut off from the coast by Palestinian and Legion forces. The Syrians meanwhile succeeded in establishing a bridgehead in the Jordan Valley, whereas the Iraqis, who had failed to do so, entered Samaria thereby facilitating the annexation of that area to Transjordan. Only Abdullah frustrated the general Arab war plan by concentrating most of his troops in the vicinity of Jerusalem, rather than having them join forces with the Arab armies in the north.

In the face of the Arab offensive, the Jewish state did not merely retaliate but implemented Plan D which called for the military takeover not only of the areas designated to the Jewish state in the partition resolution but also those within the designated Arab state where Jews were living. It seems that only the president of the newly-born state was unaware of his country's strategy. Shortly after meeting Truman, Weizmann told a press conference in the United States that Israel would of course evacuate Jaffa and Acre, which formed part of the designated Arab state and had been captured by the Jews in April and May 1948.[3] Sharett by way of correction, immediately cabled the Jewish Agency's representative in the United States: 'This is unwarranted. We cannot foresee all eventualities arising as a result of the present war and must avoid commitments.'[4] Couched in diplomatic language, this of course meant that Weizmann was deviating from Plan D, for which he was reprimanded.

Israel's adherence to the plan was particularly evident in the case of Jerusalem. On 14 May, the British left the city. The Jews, following arrangements made privately with British officers prior to Britain's withdrawal, immediately took over 'Bevingrad', the former quarter of the mandatory government offices. An Arab attempt by local Palestinian paramilitary groups to prevent the operation was repelled. The Jewish leadership had decided already in March 1948, when Plan D was first devised, that on the last day of the mandate the Jewish forces in Jerusalem would take over all Arab neighbourhoods adjacent to Jewish ones.[5] These included Sheikh Jarah, Baqa'a, Abu Tour and the Arab residential areas to the north of the Old City wall. Plan D also stipulated the capturing of the Armenian quarter in the Old City. In the words of the head of the Hagana intelligence in the city:

> In the final analysis, Plan Dalet, in the case of Jerusalem, ignored the political limitations and called for the occupation of most of Jerusalem, apart from the Christian and Muslim quarters of the Old City. The assumption was that the isolation of the Old City would anyhow cause the exodus of the Arabs from Jerusalem and engender the city's unconditional surrender.[6]

The Israelis began the war over Jerusalem immediately, engaging Abdullah in it. The Arab Legion foiled most of the Jewish plans, and even succeeded in capturing the Jewish quarter in the Old City on 18 May.[7] While the Israelis conquered the neighbourhoods of Baqa'a, Talbia and Qatamon, they failed to fully carry out the instructions of Plan D, partly due to the resistance put up by the Legion, but mainly because Ben Gurion decided not to transfer troops from isolated settlements around Jerusalem to the city itself.[8]

The United Nations had tried to stop the fighting even before Bernadotte's arrival. Already on 23 April 1948, the Security Council had appointed a special truce committee for Jerusalem. As both were assigned to the same mission this committee initially acted at cross purposes with Count Bernadotte. However, since the committee was seated in Jerusalem, it was cut off from the rest of the country when the war started, after which it merely supervised the Jerusalem area, on Bernadotte's behalf. Its members were the consul-generals of Belgium, France and the United States. And as the Arab forces in the city – the Legion and the Palestinian groups – refused to co-operate with it, the committee gradually lost its significance. However, the committee acted as if the Holy City formed a Corpus Separatum; it appointed a UN official (Pablo de Azcarate) as the municipal commissioner for Jerusalem – a position soon to become as meaningless as the committee itself.[9]

This then was the atmosphere in which Bernadotte was to operate and given the circumstances he fared relatively well. As mediator, he was facing two stubborn parties, each of which refused to enter into negotiations either because it was just then enjoying the upper hand in the fighting or because it had not yet quite secured a military success. To this day, some forty years after the war, certain Israeli historians view the attempt made by the Security Council to impose a truce after only one week of fighting as an anti-Israeli act.[10] Actually, the Israelis eagerly accepted the first time the Security Council proposed a truce, on 22 May 1948.[11] The Israelis at that point feared a deeper Arab invasion, aiming at the heart of the Jewish settlement. For this very reason the Arab delegates in the United Nations withheld their assent, in which they were strongly supported by the British delegate who used procedural arguments to demand a postponement of a cease-fire for thirty-six hours – hoping that by then Abdullah would have completed the occupation of Arab Palestine, that is today's West Bank.[12] Since the Americans had initiated the call for a cease-fire, Britain's position put some strain on the Anglo-American relationship, though not for long: on 25 May, when it became clear that the Hashemite king had fulfilled his territorial ambitions in Palestine, the British removed their objection. Abdullah had by then annexed Arab Palestine to his kingdom, without actually firing a single shot.[13]

It took a few more days before Abdullah, then still the supreme commander of the Arab forces in Palestine, succeeded in persuading the rest of the Arab armies to accept the truce offered by the UN.[14] As is evident from the telegrams they sent to their headquarters, the Egyptian officers on the front, who had captured a few Jewish settlements and controlled a good deal of the UN Jewish state, were desperately asking for two things: ammunition and a clear definition of the political and military objectives of the campaign in which they were engaged – in other words 'What next?' These demands from the front encouraged the Egyptian prime minister, Mahmud Nuqrashi, who had opposed the campaign from the outset, to follow Abdullah's suit and accept the truce.[15]

Bernadotte also played an important part in bringing the Arab states to the conclusion that a truce was inevitable. He had arrived in Palestine on 31 May 1948, after having spent time in Cairo awaiting the Security Council decision on a cease-fire. Meanwhile, he founded the UN truce supervision and observation units, a force which the UN still employs today.[16] By the time Bernadotte entered Palestine, the Arab armies were no longer as successful as they had been and, on 8 June 1948, they agreed to accept a truce. Now, however, it was the Jewish side which was unwilling to go along, for they wished to conquer as much as possible before the diplomatic effort froze the geopolitical map of Palestine.

At the beginning of June, the Israelis could view their achievements in the war with satisfaction. In spite of the initial shock and anxiety during the first week of fighting, by June they were in control of the mixed Arab–Jewish towns in Palestine that they had captured in April; they had driven back the invading Arab armies from the north of Palestine, and also caused an Egyptian débâcle in the south. One of the primary reasons for this outcome was the Legion's deviation from the original plan of the military committee of the Arab League and the fact that the Iraqi contingent in Samaria had collaborated with King Abdullah in his side-plan and had confined its actions to a single attack on the Jewish settlement Gesher, otherwise engaging only in the maintenance of law and order in the Palestinian areas under its control.

The Jewish state at this stage of the war had two main strategic problems: the predicament of settlements isolated from the populated coastal area, and the still precarious connection between the coast and the besieged city of Jerusalem. While the Israelis managed to recapture some of the settlements and ease the blockade around others, they were to find their match in the Arab Legion. In the first weeks of the war, the experience and competence of the Legion had become apparent, particularly in the fighting over Latrun, a valley on the road between the coast and Jerusalem. The Israelis tried to capture the police station which overlooked the valley but failed time and again. This post gave the Transjordanians an important stronghold on the way to the city, and formed a valuable bargaining card once the Israeli–Transjordanian negotiation began at the end of 1948. Yet, the Transjordanians did not transgress into the areas of the Jewish state – in other words, Abdullah kept his part of the tacit understanding and excluded the best equipped and trained Arab army from participating on any other front in the course of the first Arab–Israeli war.

All in all, the Israelis had little difficulty in confronting the rest of the Arab units. Many lives were forfeited and the Jewish quarter in the Old City was lost, but the Israelis seemed to be on the path to victory when the truce went into effect. This was clearly reflected in the euphoric mood of Ben Gurion who seems to have felt that the skies were his – the Israeli successes led him to write in his diary at the time:

> We should establish a Christian state [that is, a Lebanon controlled by the Maronites] whose southern border would be the Litani [river]. We shall conclude an alliance with it. When we have broken the force of the Arab Legion we shall annihilate Transjordan, and then Syria would fall. And if the Egyptians dare continue fighting, we shall bombard Port Said, Alexandria and Cairo.[17]

Ben Gurion's mood even led him to risk the understanding with the Hashemites. Animosity between the two sides was augmented by the continued fighting over Jerusalem where, despite its numerical advantage over the Legion, the Israeli army was unable to capture the Jewish parts of the city.[18] The Israelis then deviated from the understanding by attacking Jenin in Samaria, an abortive attempt that was not to be repeated in the course of the war.[19]

Ben Gurion postponed his consent to a truce since he hoped to be able to lift the Transjordanian siege of Jerusalem. After failing in the attempt to capture Latrun, the Israelis found a solution on 1 June. Resorting to British war-time tactics they bypassed the Latrun area forcing a new and quickly paved road through the mountains leading to Jerusalem, which they called the 'Burma Road'. Ben Gurion, who seemed to be obsessed with taking the Latrun stronghold, continued to send reinforcements (including immigrants who had just arrived in Palestine and had no military experience) into the battle there. When the third Jewish attack on Latrun, on the last day before the truce, also failed, all obstacles on the road to a general cease-fire were removed.[20]

After twenty-seven days of fighting a truce was declared between the warring parties in Palestine on 11 June 1948. While it had taken Bernadotte twenty days to persuade them to agree to a cease-fire, the first part of his mission was successfully accomplished.

Indeed, the most effective aspect of international intervention in the Arab–Israeli conflict (be it by the UN or the two superpowers), has always been their ability to separate the sides in times of war and end the fighting; while in subsequent peace negotiations they meet with little success in bringing the conflict closer to a solution.

The Israelis emerged triumphant in more than just military respects. The circle of states granting Israel recognition, which had begun with the two superpowers, expanded and very soon others followed their example. On 14 May, the United States and the Soviet Union granted the Jewish state *de facto* recognition. And had it not been for the State Department officials, particularly the assistant secretary of state, Robert Lovett, Truman would already have granted *de jure* recognition.[21]

On the domestic front, meanwhile, the Israeli army became institutionalized: all three underground movements were merged into one force, and while it still took a few months and the threat of a civil war before all factions were subordinated to a central authority, the state was firmly on its way. Other, more mundane issues were also tackled in that period: a central censorship was established and an efficient information service for foreign news correspondence was formed.[22] On the Palestinian side, as suggested in the previous chapter, it was too late to engage in the act of state building.

The Arab disadvantage was felt also in the shift in the strategic balance which occurred during the first truce. Towards the end of the first three weeks of fighting the predicament of both sides was lack of ammunition and equipment. By the end of the first truce the Israelis had solved the problem, whereas the Arabs found it increasingly difficult to strengthen their frontline units. The truce was accompanied by an arms embargo imposed on both sides, initiated jointly by the Americans and the British. It was an act of reconciliation between the two powers after the American recognition of Israel had caused some disturbance in their relationship – joint policy on embargo mended the fences to a certain extent.[23] The new policy mainly affected Transjordan, Iraq and Egypt, which all depended on British arms supplies and found it almost impossible to replenish their armies when these were stopped. Where the Israeli arsenal was concerned, the decision had very little impact as the Jews purchased their weapons and ammunition in the Eastern bloc. On the other hand, the Israeli army was affected by another clause in the truce resolution – the

prohibition on the entrance into Palestine of 'fighting personnel
and men of military age'. The resolution left it to the mediator's
discretion to determine who of the Jewish immigrants and
detainees in Cyprus fitted this description.[24] But all in all, and
notwithstanding the limitation it imposed, the military balance
tipped in favour of the Jews during the truce, a situation which, as
will be elaborated below, stiffened the Israeli attitude *vis-à-vis* the
United Nations.

THE FIRST BERNADOTTE PLAN (JUNE 1948)

Bernadotte's main mission was to form and introduce a viable
peace plan for Palestine, and he utilized the lull in the fighting to
carry out negotiations with the Arabs and the Jews. He set up his
headquarters on the Island of Rhodes, perhaps hoping that the
tranquil atmosphere would induce the parties to respond favourably to his suggestions. The main discussions, however, took place
in the respective Arab capitals and in Tel Aviv. Thus, Rhodes
became the venue for military discussions and the Middle East
itself for political negotiatons.

The count's energetic efforts to negotiate with the parties before
proposing a solution indicate that he was determined to obtain the
prior consent of the two sides to his plan, thereby hoping to
circumvent the pitfalls which had led to the failure of the UN
partition resolution. However, he soon discovered that neither side
was in a mood for compromise, that after all he would have to
formulate a settlement irrespective of their consent. He found
himself back at square one, in a repeat of precisely the same tactics
that had been pursued by UNSCOP, and in this case with less
success. The partition plan was at least accepted by one party;
Bernadotte's first proposals were rejected by both.

Even before he presented his solution, Bernadotte must have
realized that neither the Arabs nor the Jews were likely to accept
any settlement that did not fully correspond to their pre-war
positions: a demand for a state on the Jewish side and a rejection of
the partition plan on the Arab side. The Israelis gathered from
their meeting with the count that he wished to reopen the question
of Israel's legitimacy: an intolerable thought to most Israelis,
especially after the *de facto* recognition granted to Israel by many

states including the two superpowers. But the mediator ignored this sensitivity and in his recommendations referred to Israel's right to exist only implicitly.[25]

The Arab governments co-operated with Bernadotte in the hope that he would revoke the partition resolution, though they doubted the UN would accept such a proposal even if the mediator chose to introduce it. The Political Committee of the Arab League set the tone in its meeting on 3 June 1948 when the Syrian, Saudi and Lebanese delegates proposed to expel from the League any Arab state that would recognize Israel and to condemn such a state as a traitor to the cause. The Transjordanian representative suspected that this threat was particularly directed at his king who was already engaged in negotiations with the Jews, negotiations which naturally implied recognition. He suggested to his colleagues that they should not discuss the matter at all, and when his proposal was rejected he angrily left the meeting. No resolution was reached, which therefore left room for a more moderate Arab point of view at a later stage. For the time being, the Arab states refused to discuss recognition of Israel.[26]

Bernadotte must have found some comfort in strong British and American support. The British and the Americans gave the count not only logistic assistance but also a good deal of advice and information about their vision of a solution. They differed mainly on the question of recognizing Israel: the Americans regarded it as a *sine qua non* for a settlement; the British, although acknowledging the existence of the Jewish state, supported the mediator by adopting a more evasive position on its *de facto* recognition.[27] It was this backing that made the mediator decide, in spite of the obvious opposition of both sides to the conflict, to present a peace plan of his own in June 1948.

Bernadotte's plan proposed that Palestine as defined in the original mandate entrusted to Great Britain in 1922 (i.e., with the inclusion of Transjordan) would form a union consisting of two member states: one Arab, one Jewish. The Arab state was to include the Arab parts of mandatory Palestine as well as Transjordan. At this stage the count's proposal did not define the national identity of the Arab state, but in Transjordan it was taken as a recommendation to annex Arab Palestine to the kingdom. This interpretation, incidentally, was shared by Ben Gurion at the time.[28] The US State Department was also in favour of an extension of Abdullah's rule over a new Arab entity in Palestine.

The State Department officials in charge of the area concluded at the end of June 1948 that only Abdullah had a substantial 'material bargaining point' whereas the Arab Higher Committee and the Mufti had ceased to count.[29] This was an accurate assessment of al-Husayni's situation in June 1948. The way in which Abdullah had abolished all Palestinian authority in the West Bank, including that of al-Husayni, has been described above. The Mufti was in Cairo at the time, trying desperately to co-ordinate the Palestinian policy but with very little success, though he was to regain some political importance once the fighting subsided.[30]

In fact, there was a certain resemblance between the solution envisaged by the State Department and Bernadotte's recommendations – with one important difference.[31] The mediator did not dwell on the question of who would rule the new Arab Palestine, but was more interested in impressing upon the parties the need for a federation. Instead of the two nation-states as proposed by the UN in its partition resolution, Bernadotte suggested that the two member states would rule jointly through the economic, military and political institutions of the union, which he hoped would form a solution to the conflict.[32]

Although Bernadotte left the final demarcation of the frontiers to future negotiations, he did provide a territorial framework. In this he was inspired by ideas developed by the State Department in early June. Loy Henderson, head of the Near Eastern office, and Philip Jessup, a member of the American delegation to the UN, suggested that given the position of the armies at the end of the first truce common sense dictated that the Negev should be given to the Arabs and the Galilee to the Jews.[33] Needless to say, Britain was delighted with the new map, since it promised a territorial continuity between its strategic bases in the Middle East. This suggested exchange of territories and reversal of the UN partition plan was adopted by Bernadotte and included in his peace plan (it was later referred to as 'the Jessup principle').

For some reason, the internationalization of Jerusalem was regarded by the mediator as an unworkable solution. He preferred an Arab Jerusalem with administrative autonomy for the Jews. However, he did apply the principle of internationalization to the ports of Jaffa and Haifa and the airport of Lydda.[34] On this question the mediator produced his own solution. He could not have derived his ideas from either the Americans or the British, since the former believed, at the time, in incorporation of the

Jewish quarters of Jerusalem into Israel and internationalization of
the rest of the city. The British supported partition for Jerusalem
as well, provided Abdullah was to rule the eastern parts of the city.
It is possible that Harold Beeley, a senior Foreign Office official
dealing with Palestine's affairs and one of the few objecting to the
British support of the Transjordanian–Jewish accord, suggested to
the count that without an Arab Jerusalem there was very little
hope for a solution – although Beeley himself doubted whether the
Israelis would accept such an idea.[35]

On the question of Jewish immigration, Bernadotte had nothing
new to offer, and was guided by the British mandatory proposals
which had always ruled that Jewish immigration depended on
Arab consent. A novel feature of his plan, however, was the
suggestion that 'after two years, either member would be entitled
to request the Social and Economic Council of the UN to review
the policy of the union (on this issue)'.[36]

Finally, he recommended extending the truce to allow time for
both sides to consider and to implement the proposals should they
be accepted. Bernadotte presented his recommendations to the
rival parties in Palestine on 3 July 1948.

Before we continue with the sequence of the historical events, let
us stop to ponder for a moment the historical significance of
Bernadotte's plan. We would like to suggest that Bernadotte was
the first peacemaker to propose a comprehensive solution to the
Arab–Israeli conflict. For it to be successful, a comprehensive
settlement had to cover as many aspects as possible of the conflict
and, more importantly, had to satisfy the demands of the Israelis,
the Palestinians and the various Arab states involved, or at the
very least those of Transjordan. It had to deal with three major
areas of dispute: sovereignty, the Palestinian refugees, and the
future of Jerusalem.

As an extrernal observer, free of all prejudice and with no
particular axe to grind, Bernadotte aimed from the outset for a
comprehensive solution to the conflict. First he combined the Arab
demand for a unitary state with the Jewish ambition for a separate
national entity by suggesting a binational union. This was by no
means a new solution: such a union had been suggested previously
by the Jewish Brit Shalom movement and by the British.
Bernadotte came to the Middle Eastern bazaar to buy first and
only then to sell. Amidst the many draft proposals introduced by
the British during their long stay in Palestine he found and selected

both the idea of partition and the proposal of a unitary state. To this recipe he added the concept of Greater Transjordan, first suggested by a British Royal Commission in 1937, which envisaged the annexation of Arab Palestine to the emirate of Transjordan. Understandably, this solution became very popular with the Hashemite court in Amman. It was also the solution favoured by most of the Israeli leaders.

It is quite obvious that after only a short stay in the area Bernadotte was convinced that only Transjordan among the Arab states was interested in annexing parts of Palestine. The Egyptian disinclination to absorb the Gaza Strip underlines the plausibility of this assertion. Indeed, ever since Bernadotte entered the scene, most of the peace plans for Arab Palestine had taken Transjordan's status with regard to the proposed solution into consideration. The most difficult task of all future mediators would be to satisfy the demands of all sides of this Israeli–Transjordanian–Palestinian triangle. Bernadotte suggested weakening the independent identity of each of the three parties by basing the solution on an economic and political federation and joint sovereignty. The problem with this approach was that it assumed complete mutual confidence between the parties and their commitment to peace. The conditions necessary for such confidence might perhaps be expected to develop towards the end of the process but were certainly unfulfilled at that early stage. In his second efforts, Bernadotte abandoned the idea and accepted the British point of view that it would be better to satisfy two members of the triangle, Transjordan and Israel, rather than trying to satisfy all three. The UN, on the other hand, would try to find an answer to the wishes of Israel and the Palestinians as the best solution to the conflict. We shall try to argue that in view of the development of the conflict the latter approach was closer to a comprehensive settlement than the Israeli-Transjordanian accord.

By adopting the concept of a federation between two member states and reversing the territorial framework of the UN partition plan, Bernadotte treated only some of the aspects involved in the confict, while at the same time he had to address himself to new problems which arose from the war itself and had not existed during the mandatory period. Most important of these was the problem of the Palestinian refugees. Bernadotte recommended repatriation of all the refugees who wished to return and compensation for those who preferred to stay where they were.

This proposed solution to the refugee question was to be adopted later by the United Nations and became a UN General Assembly resolution. The Palestine Liberation Organization today still adheres to the solution as first suggested by the count only a month after the outbreak of war.

As to the future of Jerusalem, the last ingredient in a comprehensive settlement, Bernadotte's solution differed from that of all former and subsequent would-be peacemakers. His suggestion to include Jerusalem in the Arab state was surprising since everyone else advocated turning the Holy City into a Corpus Separatum. Moreover, the Jews were the largest religious group in the city, numbering more than 100,000. Bernadotte's position astonished even those American and British officials who had wholeheartedly supported his mission.[37] Robert McClintock, President Truman's adviser, wrote in response: 'Jerusalem is as much a Jewish City as it is an Arab Metropolis and it contains sacred shrines to three of the principal world religions. To permit it to be made the capital of King Abdullah would rouse Jewish passion and irredentism.'[38] Bernadotte may not necessarily have meant to make Jerusalem Abdullah's capital but rather the capital of the Arab state as envisaged in his plan. Beside the Jewish attachment to it, Jerusalem was a focal point for the Christian world as well. In his final proposals Bernadotte revised his suggestion once more and advocated internationalization – as did the UN after him, and still does.

The Arab governments authorized the secretary-general of the Arab League, Azzam Pasha, to reject the plan on their behalf. Azzam told the mediator that he had been led to believe that the count would revoke the partition resolution, instead of which all he had done was to present a revised version of it. Moreover, he claimed that the territorial framework of the whole scheme was based on the false assumption that there existed a historical connection between Transjordan and Palestine. It should be noted that, at a meeting with them in Cairo, Bernadotte had in fact been warned by the Arab leaders that any mention of the UN partition resolution in his recommendation would result in a categorical rejection of his plan.[39]

The Transjordanian delegate in the Arab League joined the secretary-general in questioning the assumption of an historical link between his country and Palestine. This is somewhat surprising in view of the fact that the court historians of the Hashemite kingdom went to great length to prove the unity of Palestine and Transjordan.[40] Perhaps the Transjordanian rejection stemmed not just from considerations of the territorial issue but rather from the ambiguous stand taken by Bernadotte on the question of sovereignty. Bernadotte's first proposals left open the possibility of Palestinian sovereignty over the Arab state: theoretically, a Greater Palestine rather than a Greater Transjordan may have been intended.

In Bernadotte's vision there was no room for an independent Israel, only a tortuous recognition of its existence. This part of the proposal irritated the Israelis more than any other, while at the same time the very minor reference to Israel's right to exist was pointed out by the Arabs as one of their main reasons for objecting to the plan. The count later tried to assuage the Israeli annoyance by pointing out that the union *ipso facto* meant the creation of a Jewish state and that he had used the term 'member-states' in order to placate Arab sensibilities.[41]

It seems, however, that Bernadotte intentionally obscured the Jewish political entity in his plan. This becomes especially striking when compared with the trouble he took in specifying the legal machinery for the proposed union and its political structure. In any event, the mediator amended this in his second proposal with an explicit recognition of the right of Israel to exist.

One of the rewarding features of writing history is the occasional chance to trace patterns of continuity in the behaviour of individuals or nations. As an historian one can also try to pinpoint precise historical moments in which certain personal or collective modes of conduct changed and new patterns of behaviour emerged. These tasks come to mind when one reviews the Israeli reaction to Bernadotte's proposal. Up to that point, ever since the beginning of the Zionist settlement in Palestine, it was the Jewish side to the conflict which invariably responded favourably, or at least tactfully, to international peace proposals, such as the UNSCOP plan. Its reaction to Bernadotte's proposals, on the other hand, was an out-of-hand rejection just like that of the Arabs. According to Roger Louis there was good reason for this: 'Bernadotte's impartiality . . . was tempered by a sense of justice more sympathetic to the Arabs than to the Jews.'[42] Previous mediators, who were mostly British, could not all be considered pro-Zionist, but then the Jewish Agency had always been willing to negotiate new proposals or at least to listen. It would appear that it was the success in establishing a *fait accompli* in Palestine in the face of Arab and Palestinian hostility that caused this transformation in the Jewish attitude. From that point onwards impartial mediation was no longer possible and was invariably treated as antagonistic by the Jews as well as by the Arabs. Only in Lausanne, as we shall see, did the Arab states, but not Israel, deviate from this course, and become willing at least to consider proposals for a solution from an external source. On the Israeli side a complete mistrust of outside mediation was to develop, in particular of UN attempts, which has continued to affect Israeli policy to this very day.

One of the Israeli leaders of the time who expressed his concern at this change in the Zionist policy was Moshe Sharett, Israel's foreign minister. Since he will be an important actor in our story, it may be appropriate to state clearly at this stage that Sharett was a loyal civil servant who pursued a foreign policy formulated by an Israeli government entirely dominated by David Ben Gurion as its prime minister. Moreover, whereas he seems to have possessed a unique outlook on the course and future of the conflict, he very rarely dared to stand up to the majority in the government, let alone to confront Ben Gurion. Consequently, his original thoughts regarding Israel's policy and the future of Palestine were rarely expressed anywhere other than in internal memoranda or his personal diary. Ultimately, like many Israelis of his political hue – a group one might call 'the pragmatic doves' – Sharett was ambiguous in his attitude towards the Arabs, and alongside remarks about the need to compromise with the Arabs and the Palestinians there are derogatory anti-Arab expressions and wishful thoughts about transfer and expulsion. None the less, and this for us is the relevant point, in his list of priorities peace with the Arabs in general and the Palestinians in particular was the primary goal that the state of Israel should pursue after the 1948 war. Within the Israeli political élite his was a voice in the wilderness and in stark contrast to Ben Gurion.

Throughout this period Moshe Sharett featured as a politician who was willing to consider favourably the concept of a comprehensive solution for the Palestine problem and who did not reject out of hand the possibility of multilateral discussions, for example the international conference which would be proposed in the summer of 1949. Sharett had already shown this inclination when the Morrison–Grady plan for the cantonization of Palestine was introduced by the Americans and the British in the summer of 1946, which Sharett had been willing to consider while everyone else in the Zionist camp was opposed to it. His attitude stemmed from a desire to leave all options open before making a final decision on Palestine's future.[43]

Sharett's views, however, had very little effect on the development of the Arab–Israeli conflict. He was defeated by Ben Gurion who between 1948 and 1954 became the almost uncontested chief Israeli policy maker. By the time Sharett could exercise more authority as Israel's prime minister, the relatively propitious post-1948 climate for negotiations was gone.

Sharett, however, did express his unique stand during the discussions within the Israeli government about the attitude to be adopted towards Bernadotte's proposals. He cautioned the Israeli provisional government against an out-of-hand rejection of the Bernadotte plan, and even demanded that a government press release should emphasize the positive aspects Israel had noted in the count's proposals. Sharett called on the government to publicly welcome the UN peace initiative since this action on the part of the UN amounted to a recognition of the state of Israel. He did not accept the plan *in toto* but only as a basis for negotiations, and was opposed to many items in the plan – such as the territorial arrangements, especially the inclusion of Jerusalem in the Arab state, and the demand for the repatriation of the Palestinian refugees. He also wanted a more explicit recognition of Israel.[44] His main suggestion to the Israeli government was to adhere to the 1947 partition plan as the most likely basis for negotiations. The American administration, for one, would have understood such an Israeli policy. The opening Israeli position in future negotiations should be, Sharett believed, a claim for Israel's right to hold on to all the territories it had occupied up to the first truce. In such negotiations he would be willing to seriously consider ceding the southern Negev to the Arabs in return for the western Galilee.[45]

Sharett made another significant contribution to the academic debate over a possible solution. He felt that Bernadotte had failed to deal thoroughly with the question of sovereignty. To him it was apparent that it was in Israel's interest to see the Arab Palestinians govern the Arab parts of the country. At least, as he put it, it would constitute a feasible solution to the Arab–Jewish conflict in Palestine. He left this question to the Arabs themselves to decide.[46]

Sharett belonged to a Zionist school of thought headed by Weizmann which attached considerable importance to diplomacy. While he did not underestimate the activism to which the Zionist leadership attached such importance – i.e., first creating *faits accomplis* in Palestine and only then seeking international blessing for these, if at all – he preferred to base Israel's policy upon the sanction of the United Nations.[47]

By adopting such an attitude Sharett found himself at loggerheads with Prime Minister Ben Gurion. The leader of the Jewish state, in contrast to Sharett, cared very little about the UN's response to Israel's policies, and asserted that it was *faits accomplis* in Palestine which would determine the policy underlying external intervention (such as that of the UN or the superpowers) and not *vice versa*. As soon as he learned about the Arab refusal to accept the partition resolution and realized that a separate agreement on the division of post-mandatory Palestine could be reached with Transjordan, Ben Gurion regarded the partition resolution as a dead letter. In his view, frontiers were to be decided only on the basis of the position of the respective armies at the end of each round of fighting. This meant that Israel should gain control over the largest possible areas in Palestine before a permanent cease-fire was achieved. The Israeli government paid no heed to Sharett's warnings and followed the prime minister's lead, as it had done often before and would do frequently again.[48]

In later years Sharett and Ben Gurion would set out their respective arguments about the validity of the partition resolution. Sharett claimed that Israel owed its existence to that resolution while Ben Gurion attached little value to its role in the creation of the state.[49]

Ben Gurion was annoyed, in particular, by Sharett's willingness to give up part of the Negev (the southern part) in return for the western Galilee. He was afraid that this idea might win American support. Undoubtedly it would have done, since it corresponded to the 'Jessup Principle' which reversed the partition map and advocated exchange of territories. Sharett's readiness to give up part of the Negev also perfectly suited the British desire to see that part of Palestine annexed to Transjordan.[50] Sharett might have won the sympathy of the Russians, too, had Israel stressed its commitment to the partition resolution. By supporting the resolution he was also accepting an international Jerusalem, which Ben Gurion, and with him most of the other members of the Israeli government, absolutely rejected. Only some of the members of the Israeli delegation in the UN dealing with Israel's admittance to the organization supported Sharett's policy because they saw it as a necessary condition for Israel's acceptance to the UN.[51] Another supporter who shared most of Sharett's views at the time was the Israeli minister for the 'affairs of the minorities', Bechor Shitrit.[52] But Ben Gurion won the day, and it was he and not Sharett who shaped Israel's policy.

The British and the Americans were not surprised by the total rejection of Bernadotte's plan by both sides. Philip Jessup had commented that the prospects it contained were vague and stood little chance of being accepted without international pressure.[53] Both Washington and London recognized that in order for mediation to become an effective tool for peace, more vigorous support from their side was required. However, at that point the British and Americans were more concerned with an extension of the truce and less by the rejection of Bernadotte's peace plan.[54]

THE TEN-DAY WAR (9–18 JULY 1948) AND THE SECOND TRUCE

Whereas the Israelis were prepared to extend the truce, the Arab League decided it could not admit defeat and resumed the fighting on 8 July 1948.[55] Ten days elapsed before the Security Council managed to impose a second truce. In those ten days, the Israelis gained more territory in the south and in the north, fresh streams of refugees left the country and the Arab governments found themselves in an even more precarious position.

Very few were surprised by the results of the second stage of the fighting. According to a CIA report, dated 27 July 1948, the Arab forces in Palestine were estimated at 46,800 and the Israeli army had expanded by then to total 97,800 troops.[56] While the CIA numbers included 50,000 of the Israeli militia whose members were not placed in the front line, nevertheless numerical parity was not the only determining factor and it should be viewed together with the Israeli superiority in ammunition and above all, the continued disunity within the Arab ranks which spread even further in those ten days.

Hence, while Bernadotte was considering the possible alternative solutions, the fighting in Palestine continued. Hardly had the first truce ended when the Egyptian forces in the Negev tried to improve their positions and strengthen the link between their two main contingents, the one in the southern suburbs of New Jerusalem and the second in the northern and western parts of the Negev.[57] The Egyptian troops were reinforced by fresh units of volunteers from the Sudan and Saudi Arabia and even by soldiers from the Yemen and Libya, who jointly in the initial stages of this campaign succeeded in extending the area under their control.

While the Egyptians succeeded in maintaining some momentum in the Negev, the Legion was confronting a strong Jewish offensive on Jerusalem and its outskirts. The Legion had entered the Arab parts of the city on 15 May and had been engaged in fierce fighting with Jewish forces ever since. Abdullah realized that he needed all his forces to defend the part of Jerusalem he had occupied, even if this meant the risk of leaving other fronts vulnerable. He was particularly exposed in the area of the two Arab towns of Lydda and Ramleh. The Israeli attack on the two towns was part of an operation codenamed 'Dani' intended to open the way from Jerusalem to Tel Aviv and enlarge the territory of the Jewish state. Abdullah nevertheless ordered the commander of the Legion, General Glubb Pasha, to withdraw the forces which had been defending these two towns to the Jerusalem area.[58] The official Jordanian history of the war accuses Glubb of having foresaken Lydda and Ramleh, claiming that he acted on his own initiative. The Arab leaders, meeting in Amman a day after the end of the campaign over the two towns, on 12 July 1948, held Glubb responsible for the defeat. In his memoirs, however, Glubb justified the action and contended that he had acted upon explicit orders from the king.[59]

While for the Arab states the surrender of the two towns meant some loss of prestige, for the Palestinians it spelt tragedy. Almost the entire population from both towns was expelled by the Israeli forces. Those who tried to stay on left after Israeli soldiers massacred about 250 people.[60] Lydda and Ramleh constituted the first serious Israeli attempt to occupy areas allotted to the Arab state by evicting the resident Palestinian population.

The Lydda and Ramleh exodus turned the refugee problem into a central aspect of any proposed solution. Bernadotte was to focus his attention on their plight in his final recommendations, and the Palestine Conciliation Commission, his successor in the mediation efforts, was to regard it as the centre of the conflict.[61]

Could the other Arab armies have helped turn the tide? The

Egyptians provided air cover for the retreating Legion, and did try to send a few units to Lydda and Ramleh, as indicated by the telegrams of the commander in chief of the Egyptian forces in the Negev. These, however, were intercepted by the Israelis.[62] Abdullah told the Arab leaders who gathered in Amman immediately after the fall of the two towns that Lydda and Ramleh had been lost due to Egyptian indifference and disinclination to assist the Legion.[63] For a reconstruction of Abdullah's words we only have Egyptian sources, that is, interviews given long after the events, and may never know whether this was what Abdullah in fact said.[64] What we do know for certain is that when in the winter of 1948 the Egyptian forces in the Negev desperately called for help, Abdullah justified his inaction by referring to the Egyptian conduct in the Lydda and Ramleh affair. However, as we shall see Abdullah had other reasons for adopting this position, which facilitated the Israeli takeover of the Negev and the expulsion of the Egyptian forces from Palestine. In addition to the populace of Lydda and Ramleh, most of the Muslim population of southern Galilee, which had been captured by the Israelis in the ten-day war, fled either to Lebanon or Syria. The units of Syrian and Iraqi volunteers under the command of Fawzi al-Qawqji were totally defeated by the Israeli forces and were in fact expelled from Palestine.

At that stage, 12 July 1948, Bernadotte counselled the Arab League to accept another cease-fire. Abdullah agreed immediately; happy to be able to extricate his Legion from the battlefield. The Egyptians and the Syrians, on the other hand, rejected the suggestion and jointly pressured the Transjordanian king to resume the fighting. The Egyptians still felt that some political gain could be had by continuing the war. The other League members, lacking a clear sense of what they wished to achieve in Palestine, simply followed the Egyptian leadership and authorized the secretary of the organization to make anachronistic stipulations for ending the fighting, such as stopping Jewish immigration and banning the supply of arms to Israel.[65] Not that the Egyptians had at that stage any clear notion of their political aims. It is possible that they still hoped to merge with the Legion and jointly occupy the Negev. As the Negev had been designated for the Jewish state in the UN partition resolution, such a conquest would have granted them a valuable bargaining position should Bernadotte reopen the discussion on Palestine's future.

As for the Israelis, although for the time being they were unable to defeat the Egyptian forces in the south, it seems that their main concern was to occupy as much of northern and central Palestine as possible before a new truce was concluded. Ben Gurion's diary from that period reveals his constant apprehension of a premature truce.[66] But apart from the southern front, the Israeli military success on the other two fronts was impressive, and curiously Palestine was now divided in the manner advocated by Bernadotte and the American State Department and in complete reversal of the UN partition plan: the south was Arab and the north was Jewish.

Since both sides were reluctant to stop fighting, the fact that on 19 July 1948 a second truce was finally declared should be attributed to the success of the Security Council in imposing its will, by threatening the parties with sanctions according to Article 39 of the UN charter, if it failed to obtain affirmative responses to its demands. On the Arab side, the Transjordanians, guided by the British Foreign Office, were most active in persuading the rest of the Arab leaders to agree to a second truce.[67] In fact, by then it had become clear to all involved that the Transjordanians were on their way out where the fighting was concerned. Without the assistance of the most efficient Arab army and with the Syrian and Iraqi contingents defeated, little hope remained for the Egyptians once the Israeli offensive in the south began.

The Israeli foreign minister, Moshe Sharett, termed the period of the second truce a war of attrition.[68] Indeed, there never was a lull in the actual fighting for though the intensity and persistence of the military action diminished, each side continued to try to improve its positions. This was particularly true in the south where the Israelis tried time and again to open the way to their besieged settlements in the Negev. In the centre it was the Transjordanians who attempted to tighten the encirclement of Jerusalem but with less success than in the earlier stages of the war.

Notwithstanding the sporadic outbursts of fire, the truce gave each side respite to reconsider its tactics and politics. Some of the most crucial Israeli decisions were taken at that time – decisions that were to have far-reaching repercussions on the possibilities for a solution. The official Israeli committee dealing with the refugee problem decided to erase from the face of the earth some 400 Arab villages which had been declared hostile (i.e., active in the fighting) and were by then deserted. Most of these were turned into agricultural land, and on the rest new Jewish settlements were built.[69] From an Israeli point of view repatriation thereafer became an impossibility. The Israeli foreign office, in fact, informed the State Department on two occasions, once on 27 June and again a month later, that Arab refugees would not be allowed to return.[70] Even James McDonald, an ardent pro-Zionist, and the first American ambassador to Israel, resented this stand. He wrote to George Marshall that the Israeli position would cause future bitterness amongst the refugees.[71] In practice, it has done more than that: the refugee problem has become the principal bone of contention between Palestinians and Israelis.

All in all the positions of the armies *vis-à-vis* each other did not change much during the second truce and the diplomatic process was held in check for a while. Towards the end of August 1948, after weighing the objections of both sides to his earlier proposals and considering the new military reality, Bernadotte decided to leave the area for a few weeks and return to Sweden, where, in the relatively cool Swedish summer, he tried to formulate an alternative peace plan. When in mid-September of that year he returned to his headquarters on the island of Rhodes still lost for new ideas, he appealed to the British and the Americans to take a more active part in the peace process.

BERNADOTTE'S FINAL REPORT

Bernadotte's first attempt to find a solution to the conflict had met even greater resentment than the November 1947 UN resolution. However, he did not despair and thereafter treated his first proposals as mere feelers sent out to discover what were the main bones of contention between the two sides. To his British interlocutors, who had learned of his failure, he explained that his proposals had been no more than tentative ideas that were 'put with no intention of finality'.[72]

It had been the total rejection of his proposals by both sides which forced the mediator to seek and formulate another plan. This time he decided to work closely with the British and was greatly influenced by their concepts and policies.[73] Bernadotte's final report could be described as a virtual attempt to impose a Pax Britannica in the area, though he was by no means 'a British agent' as Ben Gurion suggested. Bernadotte never saw himself as a vehicle either for British or for American ambitions and was genuinely interested in establishing peace. After his own ideas had failed, he was, naturally, more susceptible to external influence, but still only because he felt that the British ideas together with the American power of persuasion could pave the way to his own objective.

Bernadotte's close association with the British was also due to the British logistic and communication networks which he needed in his mediation and supervision efforts. The principal liaison between London and Bernadotte was the British Middle East Office (an organization that assumed the function both of the war-time Middle East Supply Centre and the resident-minister in the area). The office was mainly responsible for assisting the Arab countries in development projects but was handicapped by the fact that in the Arab world, in the post-1945 era, Britain was regarded more as a political rival than a philanthropic benefactor. The head of the office, Sir John Troutbeck, was mostly engaged in nurturing the precarious relations between the Arab League and the Foreign Office. The British ambassador to Cairo, Sir Ronald Campbell, also assisted in the liaison work with Bernadotte. But in actual fact the two were mainly messengers, transmitting to the mediator the ideas and schemes formulated by the Foreign Office Middle East experts.[74]

It is therefore essential for us first to try to fathom the basic guidelines of British policy towards the conflict. London's main concern seems to have been to protect the interests of its only loyal ally in the Arab Middle East – the kingdom of Transjordan. The Foreign Office advised its government to back Abdullah's ambitions in Palestine. The Transjordanian ruler in a desire to create a Greater Transjordan sought the expansion of his kingdom at the expense of Arab Palestine; a scheme which had tacitly been approved by the Jewish Agency before the war. In order to legitimize this plan internationally, the British Foreign Office convinced Bernadotte to base his final report on the Greater Transjordan concept. While a comparison between the two Bernadotte plans immediately reveals that they both fused Transjordan and the Arab Palestine into one political entity, in his first proposals the mediator had left the question of sovereignty open and suggested a federation with the Jewish state. Accepting the Greater Transjordan concept meant an explicit proposal for the creation of two new political entities in the Middle East: a Jewish state and an extended Transjordanian state which would include Arab Palestine. At the time Bernadotte's first proposals were made there was no longer a clear notion regarding the borders of Arab Palestine, in the main because the war was still raging on and the final borders depended, to a large extent, on the ultimate position of the armies. Moreover, there was a difference between Arab Palestine as envisaged by the UN in its partition resolution of November 1947 and the one portrayed by the count in his first proposals: Bernadotte had reversed the territorial framework of the plan and allocated the Negev and central Palestine to the Arabs and the Galilee to the Jews.

For such a solution to be viable it was necessary to recruit the Americans. And indeed Bernadotte himself wished to secure *a priori* American agreement to the plan.[75] During August and September 1948, many State Department officials began to withdraw their early support for the partition plan and came closer to the British point of view. The Israeli success, the lack of unity and purpose on the Arab side and the deadlock in the UN mediation efforts increasingly persuaded the Americans that the Greater Transjordan concept was the least of all evils.[76] The Americans, in fact, worked very closely with the British on this occasion. Senior diplomats from both countries devised a timetable for the execution of their ideas on the desired solution (the Greater Transjordan concept). The schedule included a week for persuading the count to accept the British Foreign Office's ideas and, in fact, that was all it took to convince him. Another ten days were estimated to be needed to convince the Israelis and the Arabs, and another twenty days for lobbying in the Security Council and eliciting the approval of the other three global powers.[77]

Only the first stage was successfully carried out. A senior American official, Robert McClintock, was sent to Rhodes especially to convince the count that the Greater Transjordan idea was the best solution for the conflict. Sir John Troutbeck joined his American colleague a few days later for a concerted effort. The American envoy reported in the middle of September 1948: 'Two days devoted to discussions of substance of what may eventually be called "the Bernadotte Plan".'[78] The *New York Times* suspected as much and reported from Rhodes that the Americans and the British had jointly drafted the Bernadotte report in the mediator's headquarters on the island.[79]

It is just as likely, however, that the mediator was affected not only by the envoy's pressure but also by the changing cir-cumstances in Palestine. A longer stay in the area may well have convinced him to reconsider his earlier conviction concerning the desirability of a federated Palestine. With less confidence in human nature and a more cynical approach, Bernadotte might even have discerned the unity of purpose and interest – at least for the near and foreseeable future – between the Hasemites and the Jews.[80]

The following points were included in Bernadotte's final report: an explicit recognition of the right of Israel to exist; Jerusalem was declared once again a Corpus Separatum; the Negev was defined as Arab territory, as it had been in the first plan, while Ramleh and Lydda, the two towns already occupied by the Israelis in July, were added to Arab Palestine; the Galilee was defined as a Jewish area. Basically, the map had not changed much but the mediator added a clause on the refugees – they should be given the right to return to their homes or receive compensation should they choose not to exercise their right. He also recommended that his mediation efforts be replaced by a conciliation commission that would continue the quest for peace.

As for the question of sovereignty of the Arab areas, the count was most careful in his choice of words. On the one hand he presented two possible options for the disposal of the Arab areas: they could become an independent state or be divided between either Transjordan and/or Egypt. He added his own recommenda-tion that the areas be annexed to Transjordan: 'In view of the historical connection and common interests of Transjordan and Palestine, there would be compelling reasons for the merging of the Arab territory of Palestine with the territory of Transjordan.'[81]

The British foreign secretary was convinced that the other stages in the planned timetable would be just as successful. Bevin explained to the cabinet that he considered the first Bernadotte proposals unacceptable since they would have forced Britain to compromise Abdullah's position. Moreover, they could only have been enforced by the Security Council, which would have led to the same problem faced by the implementers of the partition resolution.[82] Though Bevin seemed to have overcome the first difficulty by altering the original proposals, he was nevertheless left with the second dilemma. Nothing in the new proposals could help implement them without the force of the United Nations, which became glaringly obvious when the two sides voiced their reaction

– both parties once again categorically rejected and condemned the final recommendations of the UN mediator.

It should be pointed out here that Bernadotte was still hoping to attain a comprehensive peace, which as mentioned above meant solving three major problems: the question of sovereignty, the problem of the refugees and the future of Jerusalem. The issue of sovereignty he addressed by adopting the Greater Transjordan concept. The most obvious attraction of this approach was that it advocated the partitioning of Palestine between the Hashemites and the Jews. However, it meant the transformation of the ideological struggle waged between two antagonistic national movements into a territorial dispute between two neighbours in Palestine, and thus totally ignored not only the ambitions but even the very existence of the Palestinian side of the Palestine triangle.

On the two other aspects upon which a comprehensive settlement depended, Bernadotte was much more attentive to the interests and the positions of the parties involved in the conflict. On the question of Jerusalem he now took a less partial position and advocated the internationalization of the city, although according to American documents Bernadotte still felt even during the negotiations on the final report in September 1948 that in the case of Jerusalem justice lay with the Arab side.[83] In any event, during these negotiatons he came to accept a statement made by the head of the Eastern Department in the British Foreign Office: 'The internationalization of Jerusalem in some form is one of the few things on which there is almost a universal agreement between the Powers.'[84] The British faced difficult times convincing their Transjordanian allies that this was indeed the best solution. After all, an Arab Jerusalem was the most significant trophy for King Abdullah to present both to the rest of the Arab world and to the Palestinians. Fortunately for the king, the Israelis harboured even stronger objections to the idea and reacted in such a way as to render any action by Abdullah redundant. Working under American and British guidance what Bernadotte proposed was in the final analysis the demilitarization of the city and the creation of a Corpus Separatum in it.

As to the refugees, their numbers increased enormously during the ten-day war and the period of the truce that followed. No one was certain about the actual numbers but by September 1948 Palestinian refugees must have amounted to about 450,000. The Israeli objections to and measures against their repatriation were not taken into account and Bernadotte (and later the Americans who took over the mediating efforts), advocated repatriation as well as compensation to those who did not wish to return, as the sole basis for any future solution.

An attempt to overcome two other salient and recurring obstacles to peace between Israel and the Arab world is also incorporated in Bernadotte's final report. The first obstacle was the Arab refusal to grant explicit recognition to the State of Israel. The problem in 1948 was not just to find a territorial framework for the Jewish state acceptable to the Arabs but to gain Arab acceptance at all of Jewish statehood in the Middle East. In this respect the surprising development of the following year was that through the armistice agreements and the Lausanne conference, the UN succeeded in inducing the Arab governments to grant Israel at least implicit recognition.[85] The second stumbling block was Israel's refusal to withdraw from any of the territories it had occupied during the fighting. The Israelis asserted that the cease-fire situation at the end of each stage of the fighting should determine the final demarcation of the borders.[86] It was this conviction of course which led Israel both to occupy as much territory as possible and to adopt an intransigent attitude in the peace process.

THE ASSASSINATION OF BERNADOTTE

Bernadotte decided that his second attempt would not be subjected to the scrutiny of the parties alone, but would also be tabled as a draft resolution at the third session of the General Assembly, scheduled for 21 September 1948. He sincerely believed his report contained the new peace plan that was to replace the unworkable partition scheme. Sadly, however, Count Folke Bernadotte did not live to see that day. On 17 September 1948, on one of his many visits to Jerusalem, three members of LEHI (the Stern Gang) assassinated him.

His last days had been spent in shuttling back and forth between the various Arab capitals and Jerusalem, in an attempt to assess the reactions to his ideas, although his fateful trip to Jerusalem was concerned more with the problems of the UN observation force. From May 1948 UN observers had been posted on the front lines to report on breaches in the cease-fire. Jerusalem was one of the most dangerous places to be in as the crossfire there never really ceased. It had been Bernadotte's intention to encourage his personnel by paying them a visit. He also believed that the supervision would be more efficient if his own headquarters were moved from the Isle of Rhodes to the former Government House on the southern outskirts of the Old City of Jerusalem, which was a demilitarized zone supervised by the Red Cross. Although he had been warned by Dov Yosef, the Israeli governor of Jerusalem, that the Israelis did not regard the area as neutral and that should war start they would try and capture the place, Bernadotte decided he wanted to take a closer look at the house. He was warned by the Israeli governor too, that the area was notorious for the activities of the Jewish terrorist organizations. In addition, in Government House he would have been completely at the mercy of the irregular bands all around him.[87] Nevertheless, in the morning of 17 September, accompanied by members of his staff, Bernadotte drove out to the house – and on his way back, in the afternoon, his car was attacked by Jewish terrorists and he was murdered.[88]

The Stern Gang suspected that joint Anglo-American support for Berndaotte would lead to the implementation of his report by an international force. The group had already sent a manifesto on 25 June to the American Consulate in Jerusalem declaring that the UN observers were not neutral but serving the British government. Some members of the group decided to vent their discontent in the most violent way. The assassins were never brought to trial.[89]

The UN was convinced the Israeli government knew who the perpetrators were and accused it of taking a lenient attitude. The government indeed did very little in that respect – no genuine effort was made to find the culprits – a policy which indicates the unpopularity in Israel of mediation and in particular Bernadotte's.[90] It reflected Israeli determination not to allow outside peace negotiations to undermine Israel's achievements on the battlefield. The Israeli government went on to challenge Bernadotte's report by creating more *faits accomplis* before the actual negotiatons began. The Arab states, apart from Transjordan, waited patiently for the UN session on Palestine, realizing that after the assassination at least a more favourable atmosphere and understanding of the Palestinian cause would be found. The Israelis became progressively less successful in the diplomatic sphere, but maintained their lead on the battlefield, which seemed to matter most as far as they were concerned.

6

The Complete Takeover and the Israeli Struggle Against Bernadotte's Legacy

The Arab world, with the exception of Amman, rejected Bernadotte's report. The Syrian government completely disapproved of the initiative, with the Lebanese government obediently echoing the Syrian opinion – which was its usual policy when dealing with Pan–Arab matters. The Saudis were showing very little interest in the whole affair and in the end joined the nays with the Syrians and the Lebanese in the Arab League. The Iraqi court and government privately conveyed to Abdullah their support for the idea of a Greater Transjordan but offered no public backing and preferred to toe the general Arab line.[1]

The only support for the final report, as might have been expected, came from Amman. Moreover, the Transjordanian prime minister was confident that he could remove Egyptian and Syrian opposition by offering those countries parts of Arab Palestine.[2] There was very little basis for this supposition. According to the American ambassador in Cairo, the Egyptian government saw Bernadotte's final report as a British plot to secure a Transjordanian takeover of Arab Palestine and the Negev.

Indeed, Britain believed at the time that together with Transjordan it could win the day. The two governments concurred upon the necessary tactics to ensure a favourable reaction in the Arab world. The Hashemites were neither to declare nor advocate publicly their support for the Greater Transjordan concept. Both London and Amman hoped this would help allay Arab fears that an 'imperialist' deal had been struck behind their backs and mitigate the existing tensions between Transjordan and the other Arab states. Sir Alec Kirkbride, the British representative in Amman, commented that this was the best policy to pursue since time was working in Transjordan's favour.[3]

The success of Bernadotte's final report, on the other hand, depended on the ability of the UN to enforce its implementation rather than upon time. And this, in turn, required a strong American commitment. After the mediator's assassination it seemed for a short while that both Washington and London were willing to apply pressure to the stubborn parties in Palestine and thus implement what soon came to be regarded as Bernadotte's legacy. It was not clear, however, to what extent the Americans were interested in pressuring the Israelis and whether Britain was still capable of exerting an influence on the Arab side. With the wisdom of hindsight we know the answers to these questions, but at the time it seemed that Bernadotte's report was virtually his last will and testament and that the Great Powers ought to play the part of executors. Thus, contrary to the ambitions of those who had murdered him, the international community became more stead-fast in its support of Bernadotte than it had ever been when he was alive. Before the report was made public on 21 September 1948, no one had viewed Bernadotte's proposals as a final plan. Both the Americans and the British regarded it merely as a measure to stabilize the political situation in the Middle East. Bernadotte himself had emphasized throughout that he saw his role merely as 'offering suggestions as the basis on which further discussions might take place'. These suggestions were submitted, he said 'with no indication of preciseness or finality', while there would be 'no question of their imposition'.[4]

The Americans had actually argued against enforcing the plan in June 1948. The idea of an imposed solution, however, took ever stronger hold among British policy makers and from the moment of his death the British energetically tried to persuade everyone – and in particular the Americans – that Bernadotte's report should be treated as a 'sacred' testament.[5] As Bevin told the House of Commons: 'The best way for us to commemorate his death is to complete his work on the basis of the proposals he put forward just before his death.'[6] He added: 'We do not expect that either side will welcome these proposals in total, but the world cannot wait forever for the parties to agree.'[7]

For some time, at least until it became evident how strong the Israeli opposition to the plan was, this point of view was also popular in Washington. As was usually the case with the American Palestine policy, the State Department fully accepted the British contention whereas the White House had to consider its domestic implications. Clark Clifford, the president's special counsellor on Palestine, tried to persuade Robert Lovett, the under-secretary of state, that accepting Bernadotte's report in its entirety would considerably damage the president's relationship with the Jewish community at home. The president was facing general elections in December that year, and was therefore more susceptible to Jewish lobbying. As Clifford told Lovett: 'The pressure from Jewish groups is mounting, the time is as bad as during the trusteeship period.'[8] Clifford and Lovett had to compromise and carefully phrase Truman's speech for the coming Jewish New Year's eve. The result of the compromise between the unqualified support demanded by Lovett and the vague commitment suggested by Clifford was the following: 'It seems to me that the Bernadotte plan offers a basis for continuing the efforts to secure a just settlement.'[9] One could hardly have expected firm action on the Palestine question on the basis of such a statement.

The Israelis agreed with the mediator on the principle of partitioning Palestine between them and the Hashemites, but objected to the final demarcation of the proposed frontiers. Most of Palestine west of the river Jordan had already fallen into their hands, and they were unwilling to retreat as dictated by the map drawn up by Bernadotte. In view of their understanding with Abdullah, they believed that he should be content with what later became known as the West Bank – and it is doubtful whether Ben Gurion was even willing for all of the West Bank to come under Hasemite rule, given his suggestion to occupy part of it in retaliation for the Transjordanian siege on Jerusalem. Most of Israel's politicians, and certainly most of its military officers, agreed with what the prime minister told the American representative, James McDonald on 7 September 1948. In his diary, Ben Gurion recalls his words as follows: 'According to my conviction we are entitled to all of Western Palestine [i.e., the whole of mandatory Palestine], since a Jewish state there hardly encroaches upon the vast Arab areas in the Middle East.' Nevertheless, Ben Gurion indicated that for the sake of a peace agreement he would be prepared to settle for a 'smaller' Israel, but, as he told the State Council in July 1948 not at the expense of territories already occupied by the Jews.[10]

There was, however, a second and different Israeli opinion concerning Bernadotte's final report. Like Ben Gurion, Sharett rejected the plan but, unlike the prime minister, he did not object to mediation. Sharett's reasons were both ideological and tactical. If Israel did not come up with an alternative solution, it would for ever be up against the mediator's legacy, and the international support it had gained after the count's assassination: 'Bernadotte in his death can be more influential a factor than during his life. There exists a moral obligation to persons who died as martyrs at the hands of political assassins.'[11] The alternative, as envisaged by Sharett, was to adhere to the partition plan of November 1947 as a basis for negotiations, as he told the Israeli State Council: 'My mission in the General Assembly would be to prevent the acceptance of the Bernadotte proposals by a majority of two thirds and to duly retain the 29 November resolution as the legitimate international basis for the settlement of the Palestine conflict.' Moreover, in anticipation of his debate with Ben Gurion over the validity of the partition resolution, he declared: 'There is no contradiction between the Zionist demand for the whole of Western Palestine and the [Jewish] consent to establish a state only in part of Western Palestine. The first demand was a just one, and the subsequent compromise was also just. We demanded what had been our right but settled for what we could obtain.'[12]

Sharett did not wish to see the partition plan implemented in its original version. As mentioned before, he demanded the inclusion of the Galilee and most of the Negev in the Jewish state. Nevertheless, he continued to believe in the principle of partition between a Jewish and an Arab-Palestinian state. After Bernadotte's death Sharett was even more convinced that an independent Arab Palestine was to be preferred to the concept of Greater Transjordan. While he had never opposed the Greater Transjordan idea, he did not see it as an exclusive path for future peace negotiations. An independent or autonomous Arab Palestine on the West Bank seemed to Sharett as viable a solution as the annexation of that area to Transjordan.[13] He also accepted the principle of the internationalization of Jerusalem which was a keystone in the partition plan.

Since Sharett's views were the exception, his line of thinking was never adopted by the Israeli government. As on virtually all other occasions the government followed Ben Gurion's lead also on this matter. The prime minister reiterated his declaration that the UN partition plan was to be regarded as null and void because of the sweeping changes that had taken place in the battlefield. Ben Gurion laid little store by Sharett's chances of opposing Bernadotte's legacy in the UN. He told the Israeli State Council that

the only way to effectively counteract Bernadotte's report was by
military force, asserting that, eventually, the UN would have to
accept the final positions of the armies as the only criterion for
determining the demarcation of Israel's borders. Ben Gurion
wasted no time and indicated there and then that he intended to
launch an attack on the Egyptian forces in the Negev and on the
other Arab forces in the north in order to complete the annexation
of the Galilee and the Negev.[14]

In the final analysis, Sharett did convince the UN to re-adopt
the partition resolution. The Palestine Conciliation Commission,
which replaced Bernadotte as the mediator in the peace process,
guided the UN back to a pro-partition line. The Arab and Israeli
delegations to the Lausanne conference followed suit for a short
while and committed themselves to Resolution 181 (the partition
resolution) as a basis for future negotiations.

The debate between Ben Gurion and Sharett, of which only the
gist is reported here, took place on 27 September 1948, one week
after the publication of Bernadotte's report. On 6 October Ben
Gurion presented the Israeli government with his plan for the
occupation of the Negev.[15] Since the second truce was still in force,
it was not easy to put this decision into effect. The Israelis,
however, found a pretext for violating the cease-fire in the situation
of the twenty-one Jewish settlements in the Negev, which had been
cut off from the rest of Israel by the Egyptian forces. Some of them
had been under siege for a considerable time already and probably
would have been starved into surrendering but for the Israeli
operation. Their predicament was real but the timing of the Israeli
offensive was not in the first place determined by their plight but
by the political developments – that is, the UN intention to
implement the Bernadotte report.[16]

Ben Gurion was particularly worried about London's position.
The British delegation in the UN unreservedly supported the
proposals as the final peace plan and as the substitute for the
partition scheme of November 1947. As noted above, the British
and the Transjordanians were satisfied with Bernadotte's final
report and did not wish the UN partition plan of 1947 to re-
emerge. The Americans, however, described the report as a
possible basis for peace negotiations which left it to the warring
parties to determine their future frontiers and relationship.[17]

The British wanted no negotiations at all but rather for the two
sides to accept Bernadotte's report as a final verdict. Ernest Bevin,

in particular, was distressed by the American position feeling that they ought to have been as firmly committed to Bernadotte's legacy as was Britain.[18] Apparently, not only had the White House relinquished its formal support for the plan by October, but even the State Department veered towards a negotiated rather than an imposed solution – though it remained committed to the principle of territorial exchange, namely an Israeli quid pro quo for every Arab concession.[19] Not so the president, who by then seemed to have abandoned altogether the 'Jessup Principle', and it was in the White House that Ben Gurion's fait-accompli policy first bore fruit. After Israel had successfully captured the northern parts of the Negev, the White House accepted the inclusion of both the Galilee and the northern Negev in the Jewish state. In view of their special strategic interests in the area, nothing could have been more alarming to the British, but there was very little they could do to stem the tide.[20] As the days went by and the American election campaign entered a crucial stage, the president became even more reluctant to antagonize Israel. The State Department still accepted the principal guidelines of Bernadotte's report but gave in to pressure from the White House.[21] Truman, in fact, could do little else. The Republican presidential candidate, Senator Thomas Dewey, had alleged very early in the campaign that by supporting the Bernadotte plan Truman was betraying the commitment, embodied in the Democratic platform, to the security of the state of Israel.[22] None the less, it should be noted that Truman stood by his new position after the elections as well. He wrote then to President Chaim Weizmann: 'I agree fully with your estimate of the importance of that area [the Negev] to Israel, and I do deplore any attempt to take it away from Israel.'[23]

While American support for Bernadotte's legacy was dwindling, the British watched the lightning Israeli offensive in helpless dismay. The Foreign Office feared that the Israeli forces would presently cross the international borders into Egypt and Transjordan, which would have immediately invoked the defence treaties Britain maintained with these two countries. A year after their historic decision to leave Palestine, the last thing the British government needed was a direct involvement in the fighting there.[24]

The British had ample reason therefore to assume the active role they took upon themselves in the United Nations' discussion in the winter of 1948 over the war in the Negev. They were driven not only by concern for Egypt and Transjordan, but also by their own concepts regarding the geopolitical importance of the area. Britain still hoped at that time to see the Negev in Arab – preferably Hashemite – hands. This wish was in accordance with all the territorial solutions offered by Britain during the mandate: from the Peel Report (in 1937) to the Morrison–Grady plan (in 1947), the Negev was always included in the Arab area. The UNSCOP report of November 1947, which awarded the area to the Jews was the first deviation from this principle. When Bernadotte and the US State Department thereafter changed international public opinion once more, the Negev was again considered an Arab area. This view in turn, was strongly questioned yet again by October 1948.

What most annoyed the British government was that it had assumed a swift and harmonious Anglo-American action would secure an overwhelming UN majority in favour of Bernadotte's report. Indeed, it is hard to imagine who, apart from Israel and the Arab states, would have opposed it. However, in practice the American delegation to the UN had been instructed by Truman, in October 1948, to postpone the debate until after the presidential elections, and it was this circumstance which allowed the Israelis to operate in the Negev where, though violating various Security Council decisions, they were not breaching any General Assembly resolution as none had as yet been reached.

Truman was wholeheartedly supported by the secretary of state, George Marshall, on this point. Marshall reasoned that discussions in the General Assembly would have compelled the president to commit himself one way or another regarding the Bernadotte report, which, in the one case would have antagonized the Jewish voters and in the other complicated America's relations with the Arabs. He expressed his apprehension that, 'if matters arise, a bitter debate will be provoked during which, if we are entirely silent, slurs and insinuations will be heaped upon us to the serious injury to our prestige and our influence in this session of the Assembly'.[25]

The secretary of state, therefore, suggested diverting the UN to another issue. His choice was Greece, and while it was not difficult to persuade the UN of the urgency of the Greek situation – in October 1948 it seemed as though the northern Greek districts were falling to the Communist rebels – it proved more difficult to convince anyone that these were sufficient grounds for postponing the debate on Palestine where the situation was just as critical.[26] Marshall was persuaded to seek a different pretext or other tactics after reading his assistant's remarks on his plans: Robert Lovett cautioned the secretary that his ideas were no more than a transparent cover-plan.[27]

Ultimately these overtures ended with an American refusal to back the British initiative to present the Bernadotte report to the General Assembly. The American delegation to the UN explained to its British counterpart that this plan could never win the necessary two-thirds majority. They proposed therefore to postpone the debate in the General Assembly and instead devote their energy to utilizing the Security Council to conclude a permanent truce in Palestine.[28]

This was a serious blow to the British policy-makers. In one final attempt they argued that a new inquiry commission be established, similar to UNSCOP, and assigned to submit a new peace plan to the General Assembly. When the Americans rejected this procedure, the issue was referred to the already overworked UN Political Committee.[29]

All the British Foreign Office could do at that juncture was to concentrate its efforts in the Security Council to bring the Israeli offensive to an end. This could perhaps have been obtained by threatening Israel with sanctions unless it withdrew northwards, to its truce-time positions. The Americans were all in favour of another truce but a negotiated and not an imposed one. Thus, to British dismay, the Americans refused to join them in presenting such a proposal and even voted against it when, together with the Chinese, the British submitted it.[30] But according to the memoirs of the Israeli foreign minister, it was due to the Russians even more than the Americans that this decision did not turn into a serious condemnation of the Israeli acts. Sharett later wrote that the Russians acted as if they were 'our envoys in the UN'.[31]

It seems that Washington was now more interested in the short-term objectives of the mediation effort (namely, the conclusion of a prolonged truce in Palestine) than in the imposition of a final settlement. An extended truce meant then, as it probably still does today, an armistice agreement. This hybrid between a situation of peace and a truce suited the American Palestine policy. The Israelis could not, of course, ask for more than firm American support for armistice negotiations.

From the very outset they had wished to impress upon the world that the final position of the armies should constitute the ultimate demarcation of the state of Israel. Sharett should be credited with having been the first to suggest an armistice if it is true that, as he claims in his memoirs, this was originally his idea. The Israeli Foreign Office, according to Sharett's memoirs, assisted the Canadian delegation in the UN to prepare a draft resolution calling for the initiation of armistice negotiations. Sharett wrote that this was introduced mainly as a countermeasure to the UN attempt to implement the Bernadotte report. Israel itself could not have submitted such a proposal since in November 1948 it had not yet been admitted to the UN. This draft resolution won the support of the French, the Belgians and the Americans and was passed by the Security Council. It is difficult to ascertain whether the armistice idea was Sharett's initiative – indeed most scholars have credited it to the acting mediator, Ralph Bunche.[32] At the end of September 1948, Bunche had already expressed opinions which resembled the Israeli point of view. He told Michael Comay, a member of the Israeli delegation to the UN, that:

> the Security Council could not order the various armies to go home or to demobilize themselves, and the United Nations could not, therefore, effectively dismantle the present state of war. What could be done was to finalize political frontiers, guarantee them, and compel armed forces to adjust themselves to these frontiers, even if it meant withdrawals from certain areas.

In Bunche's view the boundaries 'should be based, as far as possible, on the *de facto* position, as officially crystallized in the present [the second] truce fronts'.[33] In any case, the Americans were the principal propounders of this concept. The armistice negotiations were a necessary step on the way to the multilateral discussions in Lausanne and for the bilateral contacts between Israel and the Arab states.

While these discussions went on in the UN, the Israelis continued to accumulate military victories. Fearing a premature truce, the Israelis diverted many of their units from Jerusalem to the southern front. As shown above they also resumed negotiations with Transjordan while the Legion, at that point, was in fact out of the cycle of fighting. In September 1948, there was still talk in the Israeli government of the need to react to the Transjordanian siege on Jerusalem. Ben Gurion suggested that the Israeli army should occupy part of the West Bank, but failed to win a majority in the government. When this proposition fell it marked the end of the military campaigns between the two sides.[34]

In October Ben Gurion and the other Israeli leaders were no longer engaged on the eastern front but concentrated all their efforts in the Negev. After some initial failures, Operation Yoav, the campaign for the occupation of the Negev, met with success. This was on the night between 19 and 20 October 1948, when the Israeli forces succeeded in driving a wedge in the Egyptian lines, isolating two main groups within garrison posts. By the end of October those two forces were besieged. During the first week of November the Egyptians began to withdraw, leaving the besieged garrisons to their fate.[35] In the course of that attack, the Israelis captured the town of Beer Sheba. General Shakib, the Egyptian military historian, sees the fall of Beer Sheba as a turning point in the Israeli–Egyptian confrontation: 'It became apparent that after Beer Sheba's fall the Egyptians lost their control over all of the Negev and our forces were divided into three besieged factions.'[36] Basing himself on Egyptian government documents from the period, Shakib presents the desperate but unavailing Egyptian appeals for Iraqi and Transjordanian assistance. The courageous behaviour of one of the besieged Egyptian units became something of a legend in Egyptian military ethos, probably also because Gamal Abd al-Naser was an officer of that unit.[37] On the Israeli side, David Ben Gurion wrote in his diary: 'The occupation of Beer Sheba is most valuable for us – [since] it is internationally known because of the bible. And a cease-fire (if accepted by the Egyptians) guarantees the [validity] of the occupation. Whatever the fate of this town, the debate in the UN would be different altogether after our occupation.'[38]

The Egyptians' troubles were not limited to Beer Sheba. At the beginning of the war, in accordance with the military plan of the Arab League, the Egyptians had dispatched contingents to south Jerusalem. These units controlled Hebron and Bethlehem and succeeded in occupying the Jewish settlement Ramat Rahel. They were curbed by both the Arab Legion and the Israeli army. First, the Israelis cut this force off from the rest of the Egyptian army in the Negev. Then Abdullah, who wanted to establish complete control over the West Bank, refused to assist the Egyptian soldiers besieged in that area.[39]

A temporary lull in the fighting was achieved at the end of

October 1948 when the Security Council adopted a resolution calling upon the sides to cease fire and start negotiations for an armistice. Having failed to secure military assistance from either the Arab states or Britain, the Egyptians began to consider the possibility of an armistice with Israel.

On the last day of October 1948 the entire Galilee fell into Israeli hands. Moreover, in the course of the operation – Hiram – the Israelis captured 14 villages inside southern Lebanon. Carried away once more, Ben Gurion contemplated again violating the tacit understanding with the Hashemites and occupying some of the areas controlled by King Abdullah.[40] However, his colleagues again prevailed upon him to stand by the understanding.

In November the Egyptians offered Israel a permanent aristice in return for Israeli withdrawal from the Arab parts of Palestine and consent to the annexation of the southern Negev to Egypt. The private papers of Egyptian General Sa'ad al-Din Sabur reveal that the army officers put forward this suggestion because of the considerable Israeli advantage in manpower and ammunition at that stage, and the lack of co-operation from Iraq and Transjordan.[41]

Israel rejected the proposal and fighting broke out again in December. This time the Israelis penetrated into Egypt proper and almost came into open confrontation on the ground with the British forces there. A clash with the British did eventually occur in the air at the beginning of January 1949, when the Israelis shot down five RAF planes. These had been on reconnaissance flights and not on offensive missions and, furthermore, were shot down above the Sinai.[42] Consequently, the British forces were put on alert and only at the last minute was open warfare between Israel and Britain averted. The incident reinforced the pro-Israeli lobby both within and without the British government and led to the British *de facto* recognition of Israel: the incident occurred on 6 January 1949, recognition was accorded on 30 January 1949.

As for the Egyptians, their reluctance to enter armistice negotiations without prior Israeli concessions only benefited Israel. The longer the Egyptians delayed the more territory they lost to Israel. The war between Egypt and Israel ended on 7 January 1949 and the two sides sent delegations to the acting mediator's headquarters in Rhodes to commence armistice negotiations.

From that point on, we have to distinguish between two major courses of action pursued by the UN in its attempt to solve the

Arab–Israeli conflict. The first consisted of efforts to end the hostilities by persuading the sides to conclude a long-term armistice; the second, to resume the mediation efforts in order to find a political solution to the conflict. UN determination in pursuing these two courses was based on the agreement the Arabs had revealed in their discussions with Bernadotte to accepting the partition plan of November 1947 (Resolution 181). Most of the Arab states now seemed willing to seriously consider the advantages of the plan. This trend culminated in the Arab consent at Lausanne in the summer of 1949 to recognition of the partition plan as a basis for peace negotiations with Israel. Very much like the efforts of Bernadotte himself, the UN was successful in the first task and failed utterly in the second. The two efforts were launched simultaneously and they were conducted by two different UN agencies. The task of bringing about a permanent cease-fire in the area was entrusted to the acting mediator, Dr Ralph Bunche. The mediation operations, on the other hand, were consigned, as Bernadotte had recommended, to a commission to be known as the Palestine Conciliation Commission.

Following the chronological order of events we shall first summarize the armistice discussion which lasted until June 1949 and then survey the conciliation efforts which in a way continued until 1955.

7

The Armistice Agreements

The task of mediation was passed to the person who had been Bernadotte's deputy, Dr Ralph Bunche. Bunche had served earlier as head of the Trusteeship Department in the UN General Secretariat, and was selected by the secretary-general as his special envoy to the mediator's team. For his conduct and achievements as acting mediator and as the principal armistice negotiator he was awarded the Nobel Peace Prize in 1950.

Bunche had an impressive record with African affairs as his speciality. He had toured Africa in the 1930s and 1940s as part of his research on colonialism, in which his focus had been racism in European colonial policy. After his return to the United States he took an active part in the civil rights movement. In Palestine, where he dealt mainly with the nitty-gritty of military arrangements – the task of finding solutions to the delicate and susbtantial questions of sovereignty, refugees or the future of Jerusalem were assigned to others – his political knowledge was hardly put to use.

With Bunche's guidance, between January and June 1949 armistice agreements were signed between Israel and, in chronological order, Egypt, Transjordan, Lebanon and Syria.

THE ARMISTICE WITH EGYPT

The first round of negotiations was held with the Egyptians at the beginning of January 1949. By the end of January the governments of Syria, Jordan (as Transjordan was renamed that year) and Lebanon announced their willingness to join the armistice negotiations at Rhodes. Initially, Bunche wanted to widen the range of the Rhodes talks, but the Israelis (who feared that this would stiffen the Egyptian position), insisted on conducting separate armistice negotiations and their position was eventually accepted by the acting mediator.[1]

The Israelis hoped that the encounter in Rhodes would result in UN recognition of the armistice lines as the definitive borders of Israel and it was this which prompted their desire to turn the armistice negotiations into political discussions. To that end, Israel sent not one but two teams to Rhodes, one political and one military. The political delegation was headed by the director-general of the Israeli Foreign Office and consisted of the office's most senior experts on Arab affairs. The military team included high-ranking officers of the Israeli Defence Force. Between the two delegations tension reigned more often than harmony, with the diplomats asserting that the government should adopt a more moderate approach towards the Arab demands and the military delegates pressuring their government to stiffen its position even more.[2]

The political team was strongly supported by the Israeli representative in Washington, Eliahu Elath, who advised his government to compromise as much as it could in Rhodes lest the political issues be diverted to the Palestine Conciliation Commission (PCC) composed of 'unfriendly Turkey, unreliable France and vacillating US [sic]'. Elath favoured a direct and partial agreement with the Arab world which he believed would suffice to secure Israel's image in the eyes of the world.[3]

This attitude annoyed some of the Arab delegates at Rhodes. In an interview with Sam Souky, the United Press representative there, an Egyptian delegate complained that Israel was trying to use the armistice negotiations to obtain more territory than it had already acquired.[4] The crux of the matter was not the presence of expansionist tendencies on the Israeli side, but rather Israel's determination to refuse any peace offer based on territorial compromise – everything was negotiable except the state's borders.

There is ample evidence that the acting mediator at first shared the Israeli viewpoint and hoped to steer the armistice negotiations towards political issues. Already at the start of the Israeli–Egyptian armistice negotiations, he expressed his wish to introduce some political issues. However, realizing the rigidity on both sides, he soon abandoned this attempt and thereafter concentrated on military affairs. Some informal political discussions between the Israeli and the Egyptian delegates none the less took place.[5]

In any case, Bunche's assignment was very clear, and as manifest in his opening remarks to the Israelis and Egyptians gathered at Rhodes in January 1949 it did not include conducting a peace conference: 'We are not holding a peace conference here; we are not expecting to settle the complicated political issues which bedevil this problem and to which the Conciliation Commission will soon direct its attention.'[6] According to the senior Israeli representative in Rhodes, Bunche set little store by the chances of the PCC and acted upon the conviction that a series of armistice agreements was all the UN could hope to contribute towards pacifying the area.[7] If that was indeed the terms according to which the acting mediator operated, they would prove tragically prophetic.

On 24 February 1949 the first armistice was signed between Egypt and Israel. The main issues agreed upon were Egyptian military rule in the Gaza Strip and the withdrawal of the Egyptian units besieged in the Negev. The occupation of the Gaza Strip by Egypt left about 300,000 Palestinians under Egyptian rule. However, unlike Transjordan, Egypt did not officially annex the area and it remained under military rule. The Egyptians, therefore, favoured repatriation as the best solution for the refugee problem, which would leave them with the territory, but with only half its population. The alternative solution was resettlement of the refugees in more affluent Arab countries such as Syria and Iraq. At one point, as we shall see, the Egyptian government was willing to consider annexation of the Gaza Strip to Israel, but King Faruq objected and nothing came of it.[8] In putting their signature to the second issue the Egyptians as good as recognized Israeli control over the Neveg. Later, in March 1949, the Israelis exploited the armistice with the Egyptians to advance their troops via the southern parts of the Negev to the Gulf of Aqaba, without fear of Egyptian reaction.

The armistice with Egypt, more than anything else signified a shift in Egypt's attitude towards the Palestinian cause. This shift can be traced back to October 1948.[9] A month earlier, when they established the All-Palestine government, the Egyptians were still officially committed to Palestinian nationalism. They were prepared then to negotiate a compromise with Israel over the Negev, but not to give it up.[10] In Rhodes they were willing to go even further.

The political advisers of the Egyptian delegation (whose

appointment may suggest that the Egyptians regarded the talks as more than just military discussions) were the most forthcoming in this respect. In an unofficial conversation with Eliahu Sasson of the Israeli political team, Abd al-Muni'm Mustafa and Omar Lutfi emphasized the Egyptian preference for a separate peace with Israel. According to Sasson's testimony, the Egyptians refused to be linked in the peace negotiations either to Iraq or to Jordan – though the Iraqi statesman, Nuri al-Said, suggested at the time that the three countries form a united front in the negotiations.[11] Al-Said proposed that the Arabs stipulate three conditions for their consent to meet the PCC: repatriation of all the refugees, inclusion of Jerusalem in the Arab state and for the PCC to negotiate first with the Jews. Taha al-Hashimi, the Iraqi general and a reliable historian tells us that al-Said's proposal was part of a scheme devised in order to induce the rest of the Arab world to resume the fighting in Palestine. That is, al-Said was confident his conditions would be rejected, thus enabling the Arab League to justify a renewal of hostilities in which they hoped that this time the British would take their side.[12] Regardless of the intrigue (if such there was), the two Egyptian diplomats conveyed their government's determination to continue peace negotiations with Israel on the question of Arab Palestine, which they wished to turn into an independent state rather than see it annexed to Transjordan. We have, however, only Eliahu Sasson's word for this surprising Egyptian position and it should be regarded with circumspection.[13] Still, even later, in Lausanne, Egyptian diplomats continued to express these sentiments and conveyed the impression that Egypt, the most reluctant Arab country to enter the war, would be the most enthusiastic to end it.

Why the Egyptians took this position is readily explained. Since 1945, Egypt's Pan-Arab and Palestinian concerns had given way to the crucial problems in its relation with Britain. Securing a complete British withdrawal and the unity of the Nile Valley were the two main objectives of the Egyptian liberal-led government, and its negligible breakthrough on these fronts activated vehement and sometimes violent opposition. Mahmud Nuqrashi, Egypt's prime minister during the 1948 war, forfeited his life for lack of progress in the struggle against Britain and Zionism. He was assassinated in December 1948 by the Muslim Brothers who paved the way for another yet more potent opposition group, that of the free officers. Nuqrashi's successors concentrated all their efforts in struggling against both domestic opposition and British imperialism.

The Israelis were satisfied with the results of the first armistice agreement. The bilateral procedure seemed to serve Israel's interests very well. Would Egypt have been as accommodating in a multilateral forum? Probably not. The Egyptians, in fact, attempted to convince Bunche and the Israelis to postpone the final ratification of the agreement so that the UN could review it. Both the Israelis and Bunche rejected the suggestion and the agreement of January 1949 was accepted and approved by the Egyptian and Israeli governments.[14]

The armistice with Egypt paved the way for Abdullah to complete his armistice negotiations with Israel.

THE ISRAELI–TRANSJORDANIAN ARMISTICE AGREEMENT

From the end of the 1948 war until the assassination of King Abdullah in July 1951, Jordan and Israel made a genuine effort to conclude a peace treaty. Indeed, in that respect those years were unique in the history of the Arab–Israeli conflict. During this period Israeli officials were frequent visitors in Amman and helped to lay the foundation for a long-term understanding between the two countries which, in a way, still holds today.

The first phase of this mutual understanding was completed in April 1949 when the two countries signed an armistice agreement. The armistice had been Abdullah's aim since the end of the war, in order to elicit an Israeli acceptance of his ambitions in the West Bank. For the sake of clarity, we shall begin this section with a brief survey of the contacts between the two countries from May 1948 and until the conclusion of the agreement.

Abdullah had already achieved most of his goals in Palestine by the end of the first week of the fighting. Hence, one may argue that it was general Arab pressure and the Israeli offensive in Jerusalem which kept the Legion in the battlefield, rather than Abdullah's own military plans. No wonder, therefore, that at a very early stage in the fighting the king sought ways of conveying to the Israelis his desire to renew the pre-war understanding despite the continuation of the war.[15]

The Israeli position at the time was a mixture of a genuine wish to end the hostilities and a strong conviction that each day on the battlefield could gain additional territory for the Jewish state. Thus, a division of labour occurred whereby the diplomats engaged in peace efforts while the military and political leadership contemplated the next stages in the conquest of Palestine.

Already in May 1948 the Israeli Foreign Office had asked the US State Department to inquire through its diplomatic network whether any of the Arab states was willing to negotiate a peace settlement with Israel. The only serious response came from Amman. The first contacts between the two parties took place in the American consulate in Jerusalem in June 1948, which convinced American officials that a sincere desire for peace existed on both sides. In these talks, Abdullah delivered a promise not to allow large-scale operations against the Israelis.[16]

It took some time and considerable effort on Abdullah's part to persuade the influential British representative in Amman, Sir Alec Kirkbride, to fall in with his new policy. Kirkbride and his government agreed that in order to safeguard Arab Palestine some sort of agreement with Israel would be required. However, the British and the Transjordanian governments from the very outset of the negotiations were doubtful about the king's determination to conclude a formal peace with Israel. They asserted that to consolidate the understanding between the two countries a *de facto* agreement was sufficient. These were the first signs of a serious rift between the king and his ministers. Abdullah wanted a formal and proper peace treaty with the Jewish state probably because he believed it would be more binding than an armistice. It would commit the Israelis to desist from any attempts to change the political status of the West Bank. Moreover, the king had by then lost interest in securing a leading position in the Arab League, a body which he considered to be totally hostile towards the Hashemites. Abdullah valued his relationship with the West more, for he assumed that such an alliance with a European power would ensure the survival of his kingdom. One way of being helpful to the West was by settling the Arab–Israeli conflict, for this would pacify the increasingly vital and strategically important Middle East. This line of thought corresponded with the main themes developed by the principal policy-makers in the West who assumed that instability in the region would facilitate the infiltration of communism. Thus, Abdullah aspired to become the stabilizing agent in the Middle East.

The basis for the king's enthusiasm (and not just mere readiness) to reach an understanding with the Jews however, was, we believe, his apprehension of secessionist Palestinian ambitions. His worst enemy, the former Mufti, Hajj Amin al-Husayni, was still enjoying the active support of Egypt and Syria and popularity in the West Bank. Abdullah needed an assurance that the Israelis would not join these Arab countries in an attempt to expel the Hashemites from that part of mandatory Palestine which he had been able to annex to Transjordan.

The king's eagerness to achieve peace with Israel may be attributed to yet another reason. One may plausibly assume that he realized the advantages to be reaped from co-operation with the Jewish state. The traditional forefathers of Zionism had certainly always hoped to persuade at least some Arab leaders of the potential benefits of a modern Westernized Jewish state in their midst. That no one else in the Arab world was thinking along these lines is beyond doubt. Abdullah's ministers most certainly did not – although they were, in many ways, more Westernized than the king, they did not regard a link with Israel as part of a pro–Western attitude. In a sense they were Pan-Arabists, that is, they sought to strengthen Transjordan's precarious standing by toeing the general Arab line. The British Foreign Office also resented the idea of a formal peace treaty which would have incurred the animosity of the rest of the Arab world.[17] In a letter to Abdullah, Bevin suggested that all political matters be left in the hands of the UN for further discussions. Both the Transjordanian prime minister and Sir Alec Kirkbride predicted that the Arab world albeit reluctantly would eventually come to terms with Hashemite rule over Arab Palestine (the West Bank) but would not tolerate a separate peace treaty between Jordan and Israel.[18]

Be that as it may, after several preliminary meetings between the two sides in Jerusalem negotiations continued in Paris, where representatives from both countries attended the Security Council session. In the French capital, the Israelis sought a united front with the Transjordanians in order to block the acceptance of the final Bernadotte report. However, as mentioned earlier, Abdullah had very little cause to object to the report. Therefore, so long as it seemed that the Bernadotte plan would be adopted as a United Nations resolution, the Jordanians were disinclined to join such a front.[19] When it became apparent in November 1948 that the

British attempt to turn the Bernadotte scheme into a binding UN resolution had failed, the talks in Paris became more substantial. The king sent his personal secretary, Abd al-Ghani Karami, to join the negotiations in Paris, but it seems the two sides were at that stage merely going through the moves, that is only exploring the possibilities of serious negotiations. This was mainly because Ben Gurion felt he had little to discuss with the king before completing the occupation of the Negev, and was content simply to attempt to keep the process going.[20] Nevertheless, one of the direct results of the Paris talks was that the king refrained from assisting the Egyptians who were then being attacked and besieged by the Israelis in the Negev. Arab writers have claimed that there was an official Israeli–Transjordanian agreement to that effect, but it seems that Abdullah pursued this policy for no other reason than lack of interest in the fate of the Negev. This area was of more concern to Britain than to Jordan and the king did not deem it necessary to intervene to assist the Egyptians.[21]

In December 1948 the negotiations were again resumed in Jerusalem. In the second round the Transjordanians secured Israel's blessing to the Jericho congress's resolution. The congress was convened as part of the struggle between Egypt and Jordan over who had the right to represent the Palestinians. As mentioned the Egyptians established the All-Palestine government, most of whose members were former members of the Arab Higher Committee. Abdullah reacted by first convening a meeting of refugees in Amman in October 1948 and then the Jericho conference attended by local residents of the West Bank. Both meetings acknowledged, of course, Abdullah's right to represent the Palestinians. The Israeli assurance was a welcome gesture in the face of fierce opposition in the Arab world.

The two sides agreed on the imposition of a permanent cease-fire and the *de facto* partition of Jerusalem, which meant that the city could be divided according to the respective positions of the two armies.[22]

In the course of the Jerusalem meetings it became apparent that the presence of Iraqi troops in Samaria (the northern part of the West Bank) was a major stumbling block to an Israeli–Transjordanian armistice. The Iraqis had declined the UN invitation to participate in the armistice negotiations in Rhodes since, as Baghdad claimed, they shared no border with Israel and in any case regarded the armistice accord as an unwarranted recognition of the Jewish state. Indeed, the Iraqis could only take such a position precisely because they had no border with Israel. From December 1948 onwards the Israelis exerted pressure on Abdullah to repatriate the Iraqi contingent stationed in Samaria, and even concentrated troops and initiated military manoeuvres near the cease-fire line in order to underline the seriousness of their demand.[23]

Abdullah had consented to the Iraqi presence in the West Bank in April 1948 for two main reasons. He needed them, as we have already seen, to maintain law and order in Arab Palestine while his forces were engaged in the battle over Jerusalem. Secondly, he perceived the Iraqi presence as a means of allaying Arab suspicions concerning his true intentions in Palestine. However, by December 1948 the Hashemite ruler had good reasons to wish the Iraqi forces gone. Although the politicians in Baghdad were sympathetic towards his ambitions to enlarge Transjordan, the Iraqi rank and file in Palestine was supporting the cause of the local Palestinian inhabitants and inciting the population in the rural areas against the Hashemite rule. This behaviour questioned the wisdom of keeping the Iraqi contingent in Samaria. Furthermore, the Israelis made it quite clear that they would not tolerate the Iraqi presence there for long and threatened Abdullah that unless he evicted the Iraqis Israel might attack the area. These ultimatums were accompanied by intensive military activity on the border between Samaria and Israel.

And yet, despite the unrest caused by the Iraqi soldiers in Samaria and the Israeli threats, Abdullah did nothing about withdrawing the Iraqi contingent. In fact, he even persuaded the Iraqi government to further delay repatriation of the forces when Baghdad was about to withdraw of its own accord since it needed them to quell the Kurdish insurrection in the north of Iraq.[24] The best explanation for this seemingly unreasonable policy is that Abdullah surmised, quite rightly, that the Israeli threats had very little to do with the Iraqi presence and were in fact part of Israel's attempt to compromise the king's position before the final stages of the armistice negotiations. Indeed, until the conclusion of the agreement at the beginning of April 1949, whenever the negotiations reached a dead end the Israeli negotiators threatened the king with the use of military force unless he conceded to their demands.

Moreover, the tough Israeli stance was born out of second thoughts in Tel Aviv about the desirability of maintaining the tacit understanding with Transjordan. The balance of power in early 1949 was such that the Arab Legion was no match for the strong Israeli army which numbered about 120,000 soldiers at the time. With or without the Iraqi forces in Samaria, there were several army commanders who thought that at least part of the area annexed by Transjordan should be occupied by Israel, whether for strategic reasons or national sentiments. In fact, three times in the period under review the Israeli government, responding to pressure from the army, considered the possibility of launching an attack on the West Bank.[25] So long as the Israeli threat was looming on the horizon the king could not give up the Iraqi help. Moreover, inspite of Kirkbride's persistent efforts, the British government refused to promise immediate military intervention in the event of an Israeli attack on the West Bank. The Foreign Office maintained that the alliance treaty between Transjordan and Britain only applied in the event of an Israeli offensive against Transjordan proper. This fact, incidentally, was unknown to Ben Gurion; indeed his fear of open confrontation with the British was quite probably one of the reasons for his hesitation in approving an Israeli operation in the West Bank.[26]

It is probable that the Iraqi presence did strengthen the king's position and allowed him to make some demands of his own, instead of merely responding to those presented to him by the Israelis. Thus, the king demanded the annexation of Ramleh and Lydda to Transjordan. Throughout the Arab world Abdullah was held responsible for the fall of these two towns and although he had tried to cast the blame on Glubb, he probably still felt that in order to redeem his reputation he had to regain them. When Israel dismissed his demand out of hand, it seemed that the only practical outcome of the December talks in Jerusalem was the consolidation of the *de facto* partition of that city by introducing mutually agreed military arrangements.

The American and the British representatives in Amman both felt that the king had been pushed into an inferior bargaining position. They feared the Israelis could compromise his position even further and urged their respective governments to exert pressure on Israel to moderate its demands. But both London and Washington were more interested in the UN efforts to find a replacement for Bernadotte and did not intervene in the development of the bilateral accord.[27]

The UN attempt in December 1948, to establish a body that

would assume the mediating role that had been Bernadotte's indeed complicated the Israeli–Transjordanian negotiations. Abdullah, however, saw no reason to stop the direct contact with the Israelis and for once the British foreign secretary supported him.[28] Bevin was doubtful about the precise role the UN could play in the peace process. The Americans, who would later strongly support a UN involvement and object to any parallel negotiations, were at that time still undecided whether or not the direct approach hindered the efforts of the UN.[29]

Hence, the armistice negotiations duly continued without outside interference in Jerusalem. The Israeli side was represented by Reuven Shiloah of the Foreign Office, who was also a close aide of Ben Gurion, and Moshe Dayan. Their counterparts were Abdullah al-Tal, the commander of the Jerusalem area, and Abdullah's physician and adviser, Shawkat al-Sati. On both sides the seniority of the negotiators was marked not by their official position but rather by their intimacy with the leaderships.[30] The atmosphere at those talks may not have been as charged and ominous as Wells Stabler, the American representative in Amman, and Alec Kirkbride described in their reports to Washington and London. It should be noted that neither of them was an eyewitness to the negotiations and both relied on the king's evidence. And Abdullah deliberately created the impression that the Israelis would not do with less than a formal peace treaty. The king wanted to persuade the two diplomats that if they withheld their full support, particularly as he did not have the solid backing of his own government, they would be responsible for the resumption of hostilities.[31] Tawfiq Abu al-Huda, the Transjordanian prime minister for one did not believe the king. He knew that Abdullah's rhetoric about an imminent resumption of the fighting was an attempt to elicit his support and forestalled the king by tendering his resignation. Kirkbride persuaded Bevin to send a special message to Abu al-Huda urging him to reconsider and remain in office, which he did until April 1950.[32]

Thus, despite Kirkbride's apprehensions, the negotiations continued. The December 1948 round of talks ended with a decision to appoint official delegates on both sides to pursue the process. In January 1949 the contact was resumed both in Jerusalem and in Abdullah's winter palace at Shuneh. From these meetings emerged a mutual consent to accept the truce line as the border between the two states, which meant that the territorial changes proposed by

Bernadotte and implied by the American policy were disregarded.[33] But Israel still withheld its recognition of the annexation of the West Bank for the sake of which the king – believing that Israeli approval was a *sine qua non* for the successful implementation of his ambitions – had entered into negotiations in the first place.[34]

That Israel was still in a belligerent mood was evident from the vigour with which it pursued the last phases in the battle over the Negev. In January 1949 the Israelis were thrusting forward in two major directions. One, which did not concern the king, was the operation in the western Negev, on the border with the Sinai and the Gaza Strip. The other was an attempt to reach the Gulf of Aqaba in order to allow the new state an outlet to the Red Sea. The Israeli forces advanced towards the Gulf via Wadi Arava, almost within Transjordanian territory. This proximity alarmed both Amman and London. The British forces in Aqaba were put on the highest alert and Israel was warned that encroaching on Transjordan proper would lead to the invocation of the Anglo-Transjordanian treaty of alliance. Due to these warnings or out of sheer common sense, the Israelis felt no desire to risk opening another front in the south, and their march to the Red Sea, which ended two months later, did not cross the border nor did it lead to any significant fighting. By March 1949 the Arab fishing village of Um Rashrash, on the Red Sea shore had become Eilat.[35]

All in all, the Israeli operation, codenamed Uvda (Hebrew: 'fact', i.e., *fait accompli*), had only a marginal effect on the pace of the armistice negotiations. Other developments were more crucial, notably the opening of the armistice negotiations between Israel and Egypt in January 1949. These official discussions held under the auspices of Bunche alarmed the king even more than the Israeli advance in the south. Abdullah's main concern was that the Israelis would reach an agreement with Egypt at the expense of Transjordan, although, as it turned out, because the Egyptians preferred to leave the final decision for later discussions, the talks were purely military.[36]

On 15 January 1949 Moshe Dayan and Reuven Shiloah were invited to the king's winter palace at Shuneh. The Israelis expected the meeting to end with both delegations accepting Bunche's call to Rhodes to commence armistice negotiations. The king explained, however, that owing to considerable opposition from his ministers and from the British, he was unable to embark on proper armistice talks. The British reports and a few other sources indicate that, in fact, there was no governmental opposition to the Rhodes talks since they accorded with the general Arab line and that Kirkbride did not object to them. It seems that the king was reluctant to negotiate an armistice while other Arab delegates were still in Rhodes. He also preferred the talks to continue in Shuneh because there he could personally intervene whenever a deadlock seemed to be reached.[37]

The Transjordanian ministers and the British approved of the Israeli–Transjordanian negotiations – even if they took place in Shuneh – provided the secret discussions were within the framework of the armistice accord. Thus, in February 1949, the negotiations continued in Abdullah's winter palace. The king requested that Jordan should have an outlet to the Mediterranean in the form of a corridor through Israeli territory. The Israelis were willing to allow the Transjordanians such a passage pending the conclusion of an overall peace agreement.[38]

Because of pressure from his own government and the British, the king at this stage could no longer postpone the dispatch of an official delegation to Rhodes. In Shuneh the two sides agreed that they would participate in the Rhodes negotiations so as to please the British and the Americans, but that the actual negotiations would take place in Shuneh. The idea was that the two states would reach a prior agreement in Shuneh and then sign the Armistice agreement in Rhodes, a formula concocted by Abdullah and Moshe Dayan.[39]

Fortunately for both parties, the Arab League did not decide to negotiate en bloc in Rhodes and so the bilateral negotiations could be carried on even there. The Egyptians, moreover, had informed Bunche that until they had completed their negotiations no other Arab state should finalize terms with the Israelis. This position suited the Israelis well and led them to announce that they for their part would not negotiate with a joint Arab delegation.[40]

The Transjordanian delegation proceeded to Rhodes only at the end of February, instructed by its government not to discuss political matters. The king approved this guideline as he knew political negotiations could continue in Shuneh.[41] By the time the two delegations began discussions in Rhodes, the Israelis had completed their territorial expansion in the Negev. The king, with some justification as we shall see, still suspected Israeli intentions regarding his rule over the West Bank, and had not yet repatriated the Iraqi forces positioned in Samaria. But this issue did not prevent an agreement in Rhodes over the formalization of the partition line in Jerusalem.[42]

In March 1949 direct negotiations continued both in Jerusalem and in Shuneh. The Israelis then claimed that they would not be content merely with Iraqi withdrawal from Samaria but wanted to reconsider the future of that area. In other words, the Iraqi evacuation could reopen the discussion over Samaria's political status. Since the annexation of Samaria with its refugee and local Palestinian population could have served no specific Israeli interest, this may well have been a tactical move only to raise the price extracted from Abdullah for Israel's approval of its annexation by Transjordan.

The Israelis named an area, later known as the Little Triangle (to be distinguished from the Large Triangle, a term applied to Samaria at the time) which it wanted as compensation. It included Wadi Ar'ara (Ara nowadays), its immediate surroundings and the road which runs through it connecting the two Israeli towns of Afula in the valley and Hadera on the coast. Fifteen Arab villages dotted the valley with a total population of 12,000. The area also contained strategic high points overlooking the Wadi Ar'ara road.[43]

Abdullah agreed to the territorial concession and told the Israelis he did not envisage any particular difficulties with his government on this issue. The main reason for Abdullah's assent was the Iraqi decision at this point to recall its contingent from Palestine, which left the king facing the Israelis alone.[44]

Once again the British representative in Amman appealed to London and this time Kirkbride managed to alarm his superiors somewhat, not so much on account of the substance of the Israeli demand but because he insisted that Israel was preparing to attack the West Bank. This was a misunderstanding of the nature of the Israeli political system at the time. Some army officers were indeed still calling for a limited operation in the area, but the final decision was left to Ben Gurion who in October 1948 had already given up the idea. As a precaution the British conveyed yet another warning to Israel via the Americans, though Whitehall was reluctant to intervene in any political sense unless tangible evidence of Israeli preparation for an attack could be provided.[45]

Following the meeting in Jerusalem, the Transjordanian government assembled to discuss the Israeli demand, though without the

prime minister, Abu al-Huda, who was in Beirut with other Arab
leaders at a meeting with the UN officials. The king was correct in
assuming that his government would not raise objections but it did
demand that a ministerial delegation meet with the Israelis in
Jerusalem to finalize the agreement.[46]

This ministerial meeting took place on 23 March 1949. It was
decided that the ceremonial signing of the armistice would be held
on the following day in Abdullah's palace at Shuneh. Another week
elapsed, however, before the final ceremony materialized, for which
Sir Alec Kirkbride was solely responsible: he persuaded the
Transjordanian government to demand a postponement until Abu
al-Huda's return from Beirut. This was done purely in order to
gain time. Kirkbride hoped to achieve two things: first to convince
London of the gravity of the situation and secondly to make
Abdullah appeal personally to President Truman to pressurize
Israel to modify its position. In this last endeavour the British
representative enjoyed the full co-operation of his American
colleague in Amman, Wells Stabler.[47] The British and American
representatives were equally disappointed with their governments –
neither of which was prepared to do more than voice its protest to
the Israeli government.

Meanwhile, the Jordanian prime minister returned from Beirut
to participate in the last meeting of the Transjordanian cabinet
before the final ceremony. He suggested accepting the Israeli
demands and ratifying the agreement as finalized at the meeting in
Jerusalem. During that session Abu al-Huda accused Britain of
having manoeuvred Transjordan into a position that left it no
choice but to surrender to Israeli pressure.[48]

Thus, on 30 March 1949, in the presence of the Israeli and
Transjordanian delegations to Rhodes and the entire Transjordanian cabinet, but with no Israeli ministers present, the formal
armistice between Israel and Transjordan was signed. The
agreement was the first written, official Israeli consent to the
annexation of the West Bank to Transjordan, in return for which
Israel gained control over the Little Triangle. The other major
component of the agreement was the establishment of a special
committee to finalize the partition of Jerusalem. In the following
years this committee became the principal medium for Israeli–Jordanian negotiations.[49]

The Little Triangle passed to Israel on 1 June 1949. The Israelis
lost no time, and on the very same day began transferring some of

the indigenous villages to make room for new Jewish settlements.[50]
In the view of Palestinian nationalists Abdullah had committed yet
another act of treason. But at the time, the agreement, though
strongly criticized was nevertheless accepted by the Arab world, as
it constituted one of the armistice agreements approved by the
Arab League.

By 1 April 1949, Israel had settled its eastern and southern
borders and was left the task of reaching similar arrangements with
the Syrians and the Lebanese.

THE ARMISTICE WITH SYRIA AND LEBANON

The negotiations with Lebanon began on 1 March 1949. It was
believed in Israel that, if it had been less vulnerable to pressure
from other Arab countries, Lebanon would have been the second
Arab country to sign a peace treaty with Israel. But, in fact, the
Lebanese vulnerability was an integral part of its existence and
hence the government was less forthcoming than it seemed to the
Israelies. Given the present state of the Arab–Israeli conflict it
seems most unlikely that Lebanon could today adopt the policy of
rapprochement upon which it ventured during the armistice
negotiations of 1949.[51]

The final terms of the 1949 Israeli–Lebanese agreement were
signed through direct contact between military officials in Ras al-
Naqura. As in Rhodes, the Israelis attached diplomats to the
discussions in order to enhance the importance of these negotiations. Guided by Bunche's assistant, the Frenchman Henri Vigier,
the Lebanese demanded Israeli withdrawal from the parts of
southern Lebanon that Israel had occupied at the end of 1948.
While the Israeli diplomats, in the spirit which also characterized
their behaviour in Rhodes, were willing to accept an unconditional
Israeli retreat from the fourteen villages occupied during the war,
the military representatives were unwilling to compromise. No one
could envisage the Lebanon of the time as a threat to Israel, so
eventually Ben Gurion decided to accept his Foreign Office's
advice.[52] Lebanon could afford even less than Egypt to be involved
in the affairs of Palestine. The armistice negotiations coincided
with an especially tense situation in Lebanon caused by the return
of the leader of the Syrian nationalist party, Anton Sa'ada, from
Brazil in 1947 and who caused unrest until his execution in 1949.

Another destabilizing factor was the attempt by the Maronite President Bishara al-Khury to be re-elected in 1948. A majority of amenable members of parliament revised for his sake the main precepts of the delicately balanced Lebanese constitution.[53] Hence, the Lebanese were far too busy with internal affairs to consider a front with Israel.

The armistice negotiations with Syria lasted longer than with any other Arab country. Syria held out against Israeli military efforts to push its forces back into Syrian territory and it took four months, from March to July 1949, to conclude an armistice (mostly due to the rapidly changing political circumstances in Syria). In the summer of 1947 free elections in an independent Syria were held for the first time. A feeble parliament was formed with no one party strong enough to take the lead, though the National Bloc, which led the struggle for independence against the French after the Second World War, was still the predominant party. It was headed by Prime Minister Jamil Mardam and President Shuqri al-Quwatli. Their inability to control parliament exposed Syria to external, regional and international pressures and intervention. This government could not sustain the criticism cast upon it in the wake of the defeat in Palestine, and the continued uncertainty about its future led to a greater involvement of the military in the political scene. The inevitable coup occurred in March 1949. The head of the Syrian army, Colonel Husni Zaim, took over in a bloodless coup and created a new political system of which he was absolute ruler. As such he could indulge in some unconventional ideas about the Arab–Israeli conflict. Concerned mainly with building a strong army against foreign intervention and domestic insurgency, Zaim sought the financial assistance of the West and particularly American aid. This priority led him to make a generous offer for the resettlement of the Palestinian refugees, as we shall see when discussing the Lausanne conference.

Zaim's singularity was also revealed in his direct approach to the question of an armistice with Israel. In the summer of 1949 he proposed to meet Ben Gurion personally and discuss with him the terms not only of an armistice but even of a peace treaty.[54] By that time, Ben Gurion was content with the armistice with Jordan which, to his mind, had solved the problem of post-mandatory Palestine. Peace with other Arab countries did not feature high on his list of priorities, so he rejected the offer despite Sharett's advice to explore it and discover whether Zaim was a genuine peace seeker.[55] Though there is historical evidence to support the assumption that Zaim's intentions were earnest, we will never know how far he might have been prepared to pursue this priority; after only several months in power Zaim was overthrown and his successor reverted to the traditional Syrian anti-Zionist policy. It is true that the quest for peace often has an irreversible dynamic, and Zaim might have opened a new chapter in the Israeli–Syrian relationship. What we may learn from this episode is that contrary to opinions held by many Israeli historians and the Israeli myth concerning the 1948 war, there were indeed Arab leaders who sought peace with the new Jewish state in their midst, and that some of them were rebuffed by Israel.[56]

Nevertheless, before an armistice was concluded between the two countries there was a preliminary Israeli–Syrian meeting which discussed peace. This took place between the Israeli acting chief-of-staff, General Yadin, and Zaim's representatives in Rosh Pina, but not much came of that meeting.[57] The armistice agreement was signed after the Syrian forces withdrew and a demilitarized zone was created around the river Jordan – one of the main sources of water in a region suffering from scarcity of it. This buffer zone became an endless source of friction between the two countries over the years and contributed to the heightening of tension which precipitated the June 1967 war.[58]

In the final analysis, as Bunche had observed, while the armistice agreements were an important stage towards ending the war on a military level, they did not suffice to end the ideological and political struggle over post-mandatory Palestine.[59] The most important political facet at this stage was probably the implicit recognition granted to the state of Israel by all the Arab co-signatories to the armistice agreements. This view was voiced at the time by Walter Eytan, the director-general of the Israeli Foreign Ofifice, and is accepted by many Egyptian historians.[60]

No matter what views one holds of the result of his Middle East mission, Bunche was a very able negotiator – one of only a few in the chronicles of the conflict. A recent assessment shared also by Bunche's contemporaries states that he stands out among the intermediaries as 'highly successful and abundantly praised', which it attributes to the 'the fortuitous coincidence of circumstances, his own astute political judgement and flexibility, and bargaining power'.[61] It should also be borne in mind that Bunche had never succeeded in achieving more than territorial arrangements between the warring parties, even if he aspired to more. Those, however, contributed little to the political solution of the Arab–Israeli conflict. Moreover, it should be stressed that Bunche was never perceived as such an able negotiator on the Arab side, where he was and still is regarded as someone who assisted the Israelis in completing the occupation of Palestine by diplomatic means.[62]

Readers familiar with European history will recall that both the First and Second World Wars ended in two stages: an armistice agreement which brought a cease-fire, and a subsequent peace conference which officially terminated the state of war. Unfortunately for all concerned, in the Palestine conflict this pattern, though adopted, was never completed.

8

From Mediation to Conciliation: The Establishment of the Palestine Conciliation Commission

By September 1948 it had transpired that the General Assembly would not adopt the Bernadotte report as the basis for a peace plan. The Assembly regarded the report as a dead letter after both sides in the conflict had refused to comply with it, and also because of American reservations. Instead, the UN embarked upon a new initiative and replaced the mediator by a mediating body.[1] The basis for the new effort was a UN General Assembly resolution, Resolution 194(III), which was adopted on 11 December 1948.

The new resolution was drafted by the UN Political Committee, which acted as yet another inquiry commission on Palestine. Like Bernadotte before, the committee's first task was to try and stop the fighting in Palestine. Thus, on 15 November 1948, the Canadian delegation submitted a draft resolution calling upon all the countries involved in the conflict to enter armistice negotiations. The Security Council adopted this call on 16 November.

The next stage was to prepare a draft resolution for the General Assembly about the future of post-mandatory Palestine. The committee had two choices – either to adopt the Bernadotte report as a basis for the new resolution or to revert to the partition resolution. It seems that a small majority was leading the members to hold a renewed vote of confidence on the viability and desirability of the partition principle.

The members of the committee were equally divided between support and rejection of the Bernadotte report. As expected, the British led the ayes; less expected was the Russian leadership of the opposition. A sensible way out of the deadlock was found in early December 1948: a synthesis between Bernadotte's report and the general outlines of the partition resolution.[2] The new resolution did not relate to territorial arrangements, which were the backbone of the Bernadotte report. In other words, the UN rejected, or at least did not actively uphold the concept of Greater Transjordan, as it had been devised with the blessing of the British and the backing of the mediator, by the Israelis and the Jordanians.

This, therefore, was an important juncture in the history of the peace negotiations since it meant that the bilateral Israeli–Jordanian accord, which moreover had been conducted with disregard for regional sanction did not attain international recognition. And yet, as we shall see, the two architects of the concept, Ben Gurion and Abdullah, would try to turn this accord into the main peace process in the area.

The late mediator's ideas on the refugees and on Jerusalem, on the other hand, were included in the resolution and were introduced with even greater conviction and clarity. The same is true of the mechanism suggested by Bernadotte: the task of mediation was entrusted to a committee entitled the Palestine Conciliation Commission (PCC).

On 11 December 1948 the third UN General Assembly adopted the draft resolution calling the creation of the PCC. Comparing this resolution to a memorandum prepared already in October 1948 by the American secretary of state, George Marshall, reveals a striking verbatim resemblance between the two documents.[3] This is, in fact, less surprising than it may seem. Since April 1948, and in spite of all the unexpected developments that occurred, the American State Department had become a strong advocate of the partition principle. The 'Jessup Principle' meant that the State Department tried to adapt the UN resolution to the new reality in Palestine. The Americans felt that an exchange of territory between the Jews and the Arabs within Palestine would turn partition into a workable solution. They deviated from this line of reasoning under British influence, during Bernadotte's deliberations over his final report, but reverted back to partition after the mediator's tragic death.[4] Thus, although the Americans gave only silent support to the draft resolution in the committee, in the hall of the Assembly it was John Foster Dulles, the American delegate, who vigorously and persuasively led the Assembly to accept the new resolution.

Dulles's speech also marked the beginning of an intensive American involvement in the peace process. It would not be an exaggeration to say that this was a historical turning point, at which the Americans replaced the British as the peace brokers. The resolution, therefore, ended a period of more than thirty years of British mediation in the conflict and marked the beginning of a new era characterized by American diplomacy which lasts to this very day.

The resolution called upon the parties to enter peace negotaitions either directly or under the auspices of a new mediating body, that is the PCC. The goal of these negotiations would be 'the final settlement of all questions outstanding between them'.[5]

Count Bernadotte had been the first to suggest the creation of a conciliation commission. The State Department officials, however, were now the first to take his proposals seriously. In October 1948 the State Department declared that the commission should consist of three delegates from among UN member-states. The naming of these delegates was left to a committee composed of representatives from the five permanent members of the Security Council. All these proposals were duly followed by the UN after the resolution was adopted.[6]

Another American proposal was also implemented. This was the recommendation by the assistant secretary of state, Robert Lovett, to appoint a technical boundaries commission to assist in delineating the frontiers in Palestine. The commission was to be subordinated to the PCC.[7] Thus, the UN General Assembly in its resolution empowered the PCC to demarcate the frontiers of Palestine on the basis of Bernadotte's recommendations. However, as will be pointed out later, the commission, in consultation with the parties concerned, decided to base the negotiations upon Resolution 181 and not upon Bernadotte's report.

The PCC resolution also set guidelines for future negotiations on Jerusalem and the refugees; without such guidelines no solution could be considered complete. The General Assembly resolved that the holy places in Palestine, namely Jerusalem, Bethlehem and Nazareth, should be accessible to worshippers of all religions. It had also instructed the PCC to present 'detailed proposals for a permanent international regime for the territory of Jerusalem'. That decision in fact reiterated Resolution 181 on the future of Jerusalem. In 1947, a Truce Commission had been entrusted with finding means of implementing the UN decision. This was a body composed of the American, Belgian and French consuls in the city. In December 1948, the same mission was assigned to the PCC.

The General Assembly's views on Jerusalem disregarded the *de facto* partition of the city between Transjordan and Israel as concluded in the agreement signed by the two respective military governors of the city, Abdullah al-Tal and Moshe Dayan. Moreover, the resolution robbed both Israel and Transjordan of a city which the Israelis had intended for their capital and the Transjordanians regarded as a holy one; hence the adamant refusal of both states to comply with that part of the resolution.

In any event, the UN was determined, as reflected in Article 8 of the resolution, to be the sole arbitrator on this question:

> The General Assembly resolves that, in view of its association with three world religions, the Jerusalem area, including the present municipality of Jerusalem plus the surrounding villages and towns . . . should be accorded a special and separate treatment from the rest of Palestine and should be placed under effective UN control.

However, the Jews and many Muslim religious leaders (unlike the heads of Arab states) expressed no wish to see Jerusalem as a Corpus Separatum and only the Christian powers (in Europe and in Latin America) had lobbied in the UN for internationalization. Be that as it may, the General Assembly decided to leave the fate of the holy city to the discretion of the international community.

The resolution's most famous article, which was endorsed by all the parties concerned except Israel, was Article 11, which stated:

> The General Assembly resolves that the refugees wishing to return to their homes and live at peace with their neighbours should be permitted to do so at the earliest practical date, and that compensation should be paid for the property of those choosing not to return and for loss or damage to property which, under the principles of international law or in equity, should be made good by the governments or authorities responsible.

As we shall see, for the Israelis the 'earliest practical date' was only *after* peace was concluded with the Arab world; for the Arabs the 'earliest date' was *before* any agreement with Israel was signed. As for compensation, only the Israeli foreign minister was prepared to consider the demand.

To sum up, one may say that the General Assembly aptly defined the three topics which were to be on the PCC's agenda – the frontiers of the Arab and Jewish states in Palestine, the refugee problem and the question of Jerusalem. Once more, the UN had covered what it clearly considered to be the three prerequisites for a comprehensive settlement.

The General Assembly appointed three members to serve on the PCC: an American, as the first chairman, a Frenchman and a Turk. The American was Mark Ethridge, the publisher of an American newspaper and with very little experience in Middle Eastern affairs who won the appointment because of the services he had rendered President Truman during the presidential elections of 1948.[8] The French delegate was Claude de Boisanger, a Foreign Office official, and the Turkish delegate Husayn Jahed Yalcin, an elderly journalist who was probably chosen for the fierce anti-communist articles he wrote in his paper.[9] One Arab scholar claims that Arab officials in the UN distrusted Yalcin since he was Jewish by birth and a convert to Islam (he was in fact a member of a crypto-Jewish community).[10] As he was equally distrusted by the Israelis, who suspected his principal assistant of being an anti-semite, he seemed fully qualified for the job of mediator.[11] The Turks were eager to participate in the commission as part of their efforts to parade as regional peacemakers, particularly before the American administration. Asserting that a solution to the Palestine conflict was high on the American list of priorities, the Turkish government hoped to become Washington's principal ally in the Middle East. Moreover, since the end of the Second World War Ankara had sought the establishment of a regional defence pact, which it hoped would protect Turkey from Soviet threats. Therefore, it is possible that the Turkish government perceived an Arab–Israeli peace as a prerequisite for the formation of a regional alliance with the West.

Each of the three members had a team of assistants, deputies and advisers. The commission's secretary was a Spaniard, Pablo de Azcarate, whose appointment was a controversial issue in Israel. During the Israeli–Egyptian armistice negotiations he had managed to antagonize the Israeli officials who felt he was prejudiced in favour of the Egyptian side. This allegation, though denied by de Azcarate, was echoed loudly by the Israeli press at the time. On the other hand, the head of the Israeli Foreign Office held de Azcarate in high esteem for his integrity and objectivity and reined in the attacks against him in the press.[12] James McDonald, who was the first American ambassador to Israel and was never suspected of hostility to the Zionist cause, singled de Azcarate out as most impartial and professional among the PCC's staff.[13]

De Azcarate's staff, that is, the secretariat of the commission, was seated in New York and was thus rather cut off from the rest of the PCC members who spent most of their time between Switzerland and the Middle East. In his memoirs de Azcarate claimed that there was an unspoken rivalry between the secretariat and the PCC, which could not have enhanced the commission's effectiveness.[14]

The PCC began its work in January 1949, and after a preliminary meeting in Geneva was due to set itself up in Jerusalem. The initial effort was to be confined to bringing the parties into direct negotiations.

In March 1949 the PCC published its first progress report, in which it also declared its intention to establish its headquarters in the Government House (the former residence of the British high commissioner in Palestine) in Jerusalem.[15] This move indicated that the commission intended to tackle the future of the city first. In any event, it could hardly deal with any other issue as long as the armistice negotiations had not been brought to an end. Possibly the decision to move to Government House was a tribute to Bernadotte who, as mediator had been murdered while exploring the possibility of making it his headquarters. In any case, the commission, like Bernadotte, encountered Israeli opposition to its attempt to settle in Jerusalem, and it took some time before the Israeli governor of the city enabled the PCC to install its headquarters there.[16] During its stay in the Middle East the commission's principal achievement was to induce the Israelis and the Arabs to participate in a joint peace conference in Europe.[17]

The Arab world as a whole welcomed the idea of the PCC. Taha al-Hashimi who as mentioned is considered one of the most reliable sources for the history of the conflict, sheds light on the deliberations in the Arab capitals which preceded the Beirut conference.[18] Apparently al-Hashimi and others asserted that there was no sense in refusing to meet the PCC. Al-Hashimi went even further, declaring in a conversation with Iraqi politicians that 'the Jewish state is a *fait accompli* and there is nothing the Arabs can do to change this fact'. The only thing they could hope for was a solution imposed by the powers that would be favourable to the Arabs.[19] The question of what policy to follow *vis-à-vis* the conciliation efforts was first discussed in a meeting of the Arab League in Cairo. There the Arab leaders decided to negotiate *en bloc* with both the PCC and the Israelis. This atypical decision stemmed from their desire to use the PCC primarily to solve the refugee problem: not one of the Arab countries wished to negotiate individually on a subject which concerned the Arab world as a whole. Indeed, the issue was discussed only in the multilateral meetings and never mentioned in the bilateral negoations.

There were additional reasons for the Arab decision to appear as a united front. It was the best way to resist Israeli pressure and to avoid the pitfalls of the Rhodes negotiations.[20]

The first meeting between the commission and the joint Arab delegation was convened in Beirut on 21 March 1949. The Israeli press and government, as well as James McDonald, the American ambassador, regarded the PCC's policy in this matter as a grave mistake. In the words of the official paper of Mapai, the leading political party in Israeli: 'Israel preferred separate negotiations with each Arab state. Any attempt to form a united front against Israel would aggravate the situation and diminish the chances of peace.'[21]

But the Americans, who had become the prime movers behind the peace process, were all in favour of such an approach and the meeting proceeded. The Beirut conference was attended by representatives from Lebanon, Iraq, Syria, Jordan, Saudi Arabia and Egypt.[22] Most of them were of the highest ministerial level, the prime minister of Jordan and the foreign minister of Egypt being the most prominent.[23] Apart from these representatives, the PCC invited various groups of refugees, such as members of the All-Palestine Government of Gaza, members of committees from Nazareth, Haifa and Jerusalem. However, it declined the former Mufti Hajj Amin al-Husayni's demand to participate in the meeting and was only prepared to correspond with him. Al-Husayni, feeling insulted, refused to co-operate, though later he sent his representatives to Lausanne.[24]

The Jordanian delegation had to carefully negotiate its way between the commitment to the intensive peace negotiations it had already begun with the Israelis and the wish to remain within the general Arab camp. This predicament had already troubled the Jordanians before the war of 1948 owing to the secret negotiations of King Abdullah with the Jewish Agency. It seems that the Jordanian prime minister, who was always more worried about this dichotomy than his king, was quite sincere about his government's ambivalence towards the PCC. Tawfiq Abu al-Huda warned the PCC members that Abdullah preferred separate negotiations with

202 The Making of the Arab–Israeli Conflict, 1947–51

the Israelis and aspired to a bilateral agreement with the Jewish state. The commission, however, ignored this vital piece of information that so clearly corroborated the existing tension between the bilateral and multilateral efforts. Looking back there is little doubt that this tension was one of the principal reasons for the PCC's failure.[25]

The conciliation team must nevertheless have felt extremely successful when it persuaded the Arab delegations to give up their demand that the refugee problem be solved as a precondition for peace negoations. All the Arab representatives, except the Iraqis, concurred on this concession. Furthermore the PCC managed to obtain Arab acceptance to negotiate with the Israelis in a neutral place with separate adjournments and indirect talks.[26]

In Jerusalem Israeli consent for a multilateral conference was secured and it was David Ben Gurion who suggested that the sides should meet at Lausanne in Switzerland. The sessions in Lausanne opened on 28 April 1949. The favourable reactions to the PCC overtures must have stimulated the members' expectations and created the right atmosphere for the forthcoming peace negotations.

9

The Lausanne Conference

FRAMEWORK, OBJECTIVES AND PROCEDURE

During the last days of April 1949 the delegations of Israel, Egypt, Jordan, Syria and Lebanon arrived in Lausanne for the international peace conference. Also present was a delegate of the Arab Higher Committee which represented the Arab Palestinians. The meeting was to be one of high-level delegates. The Lebanese and the Israelis sent the heads of their respective foreign offices. The Jordanian defence minister also attended the discussions, whereas the Egyptians sent the heads of the political and Palestinian departments within the Egyptian Foreign Ministry. The Syrians attached their ambassador in Paris to the conference and appointed Ahmad Shuqayri, a Palestinian who was to become the first chairman of the Palestine Liberation Organization (PLO), as their delegation's adviser.[1]

The opening ceremonies propitiously enough took place in an atmosphere of optimism, as reflected in the words of Walter Eytan, the director-general of the Israeli Foreign Office and the head of his country's delegation:

> We come to Lausanne determined to do everything possible towards the attainment of an honourable and lasting peace under the general auspices of the UN Conciliation Commission and through direct contact with the delegations of the Arab states which in recent months have signed armistice agreements with Israel.[2]

Though they also mentioned their peaceful aspirations the Arab delegates were more cautious. They were troubled from the very beginning by the implications of direct contact with the Israelis. For them, negotiating with Israel was tantamount to a tacit recognition of the Jewish state and in their mind recognition was a concession on their part that required an Israeli quid pro quo. The official position of the Arab states throughout the conference was that the negotiations were with the PCC and not with Israel.[3]

The question therefore arises, to what extent can Lausanne be considered an ordinary peace conference and, whether everyone concerned regarded the objective as 'the attainment of an honourable and lasting peace'? It seems that for the UN, the international community and the delegates themselves Lausanne was indeed a peace conference, a view shared by the Israeli press, which reported the opening ceremonies in an optimistic mood and widely quoted the following promise made by Mark Ethridge, the American member of the PCC, upon his arrival in Lausanne: 'The conference efforts to reach a final and comprehensive peace in Palestine will be successful.'[4] The Arab press, however, took a more sceptical approach and refused to describe Lausanne as a peace conference, a judgement shared by many Arab historians today. The Arab papers told their readers that the conference had only two objectives: 'The PCC will discuss only the questions of refugees and Jerusalem and if the Jews think otherwise they delude themselves.'[5] This was a warning directed towards the Arab governments as well – not to widen the scope of the discussions.

In those days, the Arab press reflected the mood in the street – and was believed to do so by the Arab leaders. Hence it is possible to say that by these articles the press imposed restrictions upon the Arab delegates in Lausanne – restrictions which forced the PCC to spend much valuable time on questions of semantics and procedure rather than substance. Readers acquainted with the course of diplomatic efforts in the Middle East since 1948 up to our own days will recall that problems of procedure can form dangerous pitfalls not always successfully bridged. The dilemma for Arab delegates in Lausanne, as it has been for the PLO since 1974, was that simply sitting next to an Israeli representative implied recognition. The Israelis, on the other hand, insisted again and again on direct and joint sessions precisely for that reason – that such sessions could be perceived as tacit Arab recognition. At Lausanne, the problem was solved by allowing the negotiations to operate on two levels: an indirect, official one and a direct, unofficial one. This was a particularly effective method of advancing the negotiations but not of leading them to a fruitful conclusion. There was no point in secret agreements as final guidelines to a peaceful settlement unless they could be made public. And therefore we shall find considerable discrepancies between the two levels at which the conference was conducted, both in terms of subjects discussed and degree of agreement reached.

The official discussions took place through the mediation of the Conciliation Commission, which also dictated the agenda of the talks. In these official meetings, the commission's members (primarily due to their own personal ambitions), did not simply limit themselves to passing the demands of one party to the other, but also tabled their own proposals. It was in a way a departure from the mandate entrusted to the PCC's members. The General Assembly had authorized the PCC only to facilitate negotiations between the parties; that is the PCC should convey the positions of one side to the other. However, it seems that the commission members soon abandoned this form of mediation and took upon themselves the role of arbitrary conciliators presenting the sides with solutions of their own. It is quite apparent that all three aspired to be remembered as the peacemakers of the conflict and that none was content with a position of go-between.

The PCC services were not required for the unofficial bilateral talks. These contacts were initiated by the Israelis who were great believers in the usefulness of this channel. Though most of the Arab delegates were quite willing and even eager to participate in these clandestine meetings, they had to consider the Arab League's strict directive not to conduct official i.e. open bilateral contact with the Israelis. The League insisted that the Arab delegations would only negotiate *en bloc* with Israel. Yet this meant that only problems which concerned the Arab world as a whole could be brought to the negotiating table. For example the refugee question, the fate of Jerusalem, and the sovereignty of Arab Palestine. Egypt, for one, had no wish to bring these three problems into discussion with Israel but was more interested in a territorial arrangement in the Negev. Thus the direct Israeli–Egyptian negotiations in Lausanne did not come in the way of the official discussions there. Syria, Lebanon and Jordan also had separate particular issues to discuss with Israel and could therefore make a similar distinction between their contribution to the general Arab effort and their own interests *vis-à-vis* Israel. It is important to stress again and again that we are talking about an Arab readiness to enter discussions on several issues, not in the first place to reach official agreements. It is very likely that each of the Arab delegates knew about the others' bilateral talks with the Israelis. The main obstacle was not arriving at a separate agreement, but reaching and finalizing an understanding shared by all sides and making that public.

The Israelis, for their part, were only too happy to avoid the Palestinian refugee problem in their bilateral discussions; moreover, it soon transpired that owing to the geographical distribution of the refugees any bilateral agreement could only partially solve the problem. They took a similar stand on the question of Jerusalem and Arab Palestine – two issues they were not interested in discussing at all as they were satisfied with the status quo. Not surprisingly Israel persisted in its efforts to convince the Arab delegates of the advantage of bilateral contact. The energetic acting head of the Israeli delegation, Eliahu Sasson, soon discovered that the lack of unity in the Arab world, particularly where Palestine was concerned, enabled him to conduct unofficial discussions about bilateral subjects with most of the Arab delegates. Sasson also knew many of the delegates personally from his previous travels and missions in the Arab world and cleverly used this intimacy to Israel's advantage.

The bilateral talks were held in the corridors of the Hôtel Trois Couronnes in Vevey where the delegations were staying, and in several little towns near Lausanne, where the two sides engaged in secrete dialogues characterized by great flexibility on the part of all concerned. The main problem that arose, however, was that usually the respective governments, including the Israeli one, did not back up the positions taken by the negotiators on the spot and were not prepared to be as forthcoming in their public declarations as they were in their confidential discussions.

THE MAY PROTOCOL – A FIRST SIGN OF HOPE

The conference officially opened on 27 April 1949. On 12 May the PCC reaped its only success when it induced the parties to sign a joint protocol on the framework for a comprehensive peace.

Like its predecessors, Bernadotte and the UN Political Committee, the PCC set out to reach a comprehensive settlement that would solve the three outstanding problems of post-mandatory Palestine: territories, refugees and Jerusalem. The problem was the directly opposing Israeli and Arab attitudes on prioritizing the issues. The Arab delegates refused to discuss a general settlement before Israel declared that it accepted the repatriation of the refugees. The Israelis refused to consider solutions for the refugee problems before a general Arab consent to a peace settlement was granted. The Israelis were in particular interested in an Arab recognition of the territorial status quo which emerged after the war, namely in the state of Israel. It did not take long before the energetic members of the commission recognized that in its two respective resolutions of November 1947 and December 1948 the UN Assembly had been responsive to exactly these two contradicting stands: the partition resolution included both recognition of the Jewish State and a state for the Palestinians, thus providing a basis for a territorial agreement while the 11 December resolution called for the repatriation of the refugees, mutual recognition between the Arabs and Israel and the internationalization of Jerusalem. If the two sides could be induced to accept these two resolutions as a basis for a settlement, both the question of territorial arrangements and refugees could be simultaneously discussed.[6]

A reasonable assumption, no doubt. But what would bring the Arab states to accept a partition resolution against which they had gone to war in the first place? And what could induce the Israelis to retreat from a position of power from which they reasoned that they were entitled not only to the territories allocated to them in the partition resolution, but also to those they had occupied during the war?

One assumes that it took a considerable measure of courage and hopeful expectations on the part of the PCC members to envisage such dramatic shifts in the two parties' positions. It was the French delegate, Claude de Boisanger, who decided to chance this bold opening gambit. Being the chairman of the commission at the time (the three members alternated in this job) he approached the delegates on 9 May 1949 proposing a concise synthesis of the two UN resolutions in the form of a joint protocol as a *base de travail*. De Boisanger promised Walter Eytan that the proposed protocol would be 'a knock in the eye for the British', assuming probably that the Israelis, given their struggle against Albion during the mandatory period, would gladly join any anti-British overture.[7]

Despite this attractive wrapping, the pill itself was still a bitter

one for the Israelis to swallow – accepting the partition resolution
was against everything Ben Gurion believed in at that stage. And
yet, once Washington gave its blessing to the French initiative, the
Israelis had no choice but to accept de Boisanger's proposal. The
American administration had pinned its hopes on the PCC and
gave a clear indication to the Israeli government that it would not
tolerate any attempt to prevent a successful start to the Lausanne
conference.[8] An Israeli appeal to the UN to be accepted as a full
member was due to be voted upon only two days later, on 11 May,
and its acceptance by the UN depended to a large extent on the
American position. This would have been the worst time for Israel
to refuse an American demand. Though President Truman
informed the Israelis beforehand that the USA would support
Israeli's admission unconditionally, the State Department did not
hesitate to insinuate the possibility of a different course. With this
in mind, Eytan convinced his government to accept the protocol,
which it did on 12 May, the day when the Arab delegates also gave
their consent to the document.[9]

There were, in fact, two identical protocols and maps attached to
them (of the partition resolution) – one signed by the Israelis and
the other by the Arab states. In this way the Arabs could remain
loyal to their refusal not to negotiate directly with Israel. In the
protocol the two sides recognized both the UN resolution of
11 December 1948 and the map of the 1947 partition resolution as
a basis for negotiations.[10] The protocol resembled, one could even
say reiterated, Bernadotte's first proposals, which back in June
1948 everyone had ridiculed and rejected but which now seemed
more reasonable and acceptable than his final proposals.[11]

Before submitting their approval the Arab governments also
hesitated. They were asked to sign a document which in essence
implied recognition of the Jewish state. In the words of the
Egyptian historian Salah al-Aqad:

> In Lausanne a unique development occurred which would not
> recur in the Israeli–Arab relationship. This was an Arab
> acceptance to discuss with Israel political issues. During these
> discussions the Arabs accepted for the first time the principle of
> partition, which was a dangerous regression in their position
> caused by their earlier consent to sign the armistice agreements
> which allocated to Israel more territories than determined by
> the UN.[12]

These words, one should remember, were written before Sadat's visit to Jerusalem and reflect more or less the situation until 1973.

We do not have any of the memoranda of the inner-circle discussions of the Arab delegations, which could have helped us to undertand better the motives behind the Arab acceptance of the protocol. According to the published memoirs of the Syrian foreign minister, Adil Arslan, decisions at Lausanne were taken by the delegations themselves and only later approved by the Arab governments. Arslan wrote in his diary, a few months later, that the whole Arab attitude towards the partition resolution had changed: 'The Arab governments that had rejected partition, before and after the creation of the UN, now regard the UN resolution as a political Arab achievement.'[13] Indeed, it seems in retrospect that the main Arab objective in Lausanne was to revive the partition resolution and to force Israel to repatriate most of the refugees. It is unthinkable that anyone among the Arab delegates hoped or believed that an international conference, such as Lausanne, would end in, for example, a worldwide consensus on the abolition of the Jewish state. The admission of Israel to the UN a day before the Arab delegates were due to hand in their consent to the protocol must have persuaded those in the Arab camp who still needed persuasion that the Jewish state was a *fait accompli*. The best their governments could hope for was to try and turn the clock backwards somewhat by accepting the partition resolution. The Egyptians in particular attached considerable importance to Israel's admittance to the UN. The Egyptian government in May 1949 saw only one obstacle to peace, as can be inferred from the cable it sent to its delegation in Lausanne: 'Israel is now a member of the UN – if she accepts the principle of the right of the refugees to return, you are authorized to discuss territorial settlement.'[14] The Egyptians had already in October 1948 changed their attitude towards partition. Whereas in August of that year the prime minister, Mahmud Nuqrashi, repeatedly declared that the division of Palestine was unrealistic, in October he told the American ambassador to Cairo that the concept of partition was acceptable.[15] Elsewhere, the shift in the general Arab policy was thus made public, when the Arab press publicized the protocol.[16]

The protocol reflected therefore much more the Arab than the Israeli position. It expressed dissatisfaction with the status quo, a dissatisfaction which was shared by the Arab countries who wished to re-open the discussion over the future of Palestine – despite the fact that most of that country now was under Jewish control. The new Arab position consisted of support for the partition resolution or, alternatively, for a new territorial settlement that would force the Israelis to withdraw their forces from the areas granted to the Palestinians in the resolution.

The Israelis, at least until Lausanne, had had no wish whatsoever to alter the status quo. The end result of the armistice accord was a reflection of their desire to see the cease-fire lines as the definitive borders of the state of Israel, give or take a few minor border rectifications. The protocol questioned many of the Israeli military achievements in the 1948 war. Hence, it is not surprising that immediately after it had given its consent, the Israeli government developed second thoughts about the protocol. Whereas the Arab states' commitment to the protocol would increase and solidify as the months went by, the Israelis with every passing day regretted their consent more and more. It is surprising that the Israelis signed the protocol in the first place, and we have already attempted to explain their attitude at the time by stating that they did so as a mere exercise in public realtions aimed at strengthening Israel's international image. Had the proposal for the protocol not coincided with the vote in the UN on Israel's admittance, it is a matter of conjecture what the Israeli position actually would have been. This does not mean that the conference as a whole was treated as an exercise in public relations – for most of the Israeli diplomats Lausanne was a peace conference; for Eliahu Sasson, the acting head of the delegation, it was an opportunity to pursue bilateral talks; for others, such as the Israeli foreign minister himself, it was even an opportunity to discuss possible solutions for the refugees and the Jerusalem problem. But the protocol demanded of Israel a willingness to discuss withdrawal from land occupied in the war and it seems that no one in Israel or Lausanne was even thinking of conceding territory in return for peace. That signing the May protocol actually consisted of an Israeli agreement to that extent, even in principle, the Israelis only realized after the document had been signed. One might conclude that although the May protocol in practice did not indicate a change in Israeli policy, it could none the less have created a different momentum and orientation in the peace process. This, however, did not happen.

In fact, in later years, both the Arabs and the Jews would repudiate their actual commitment to the protocol. However, it is important to emphasize that eighteen months after the Arabs had rejected the partition resolution, they accepted it as a basis for negotiations when they signed the protocol. Similarly, it should be borne in mind that Israel for the first time accepted the principle of repatriation and the internationalization of Jerusalem.

The international community was impressed by the significance of the protocol. The Americans in particular were satisfied with the new course of development as it reflected their own way of thinking: a revival of the partition plan meant that Israel was entitled only to either the Negev or the Galilee, but not to both – as embodied in the 'Jessup Principle' which demanded territorial compensation from Israel for land occupied in addition to the UN Jewish state. The other principle incorporated in the protocol – the repatriation of the refugees – had always been acceptable to Washington.

Only in London were less enthusiastic voices heard. There the Greater Transjordan concept remained the favourite solution and full support was granted therefore to the Israeli–Jordanian negotiations. This was not by any means a dogmatic position. The Foreign Office was more than willing to join the Americans in preparing any peace plan that could be brought for a vote, if possible without a debate, in the UN General Assembly. Unlike the Americans, the British diplomats had very little confidence in the UN – they never regarded it as an independent body capable of contributing by itself to a solution. For Britain the partition resolution was a good example proving this point, and also explains why Britain refused to participate in the PCC when first asked to do so by the Americans.[17] In fact, the British government in those days was interested only in one objective – extracting an international and in particular an Israeli recognition for the annexation of Arab Palestine to Transjordan. Washington, how-ever, though not objecting in principle to Greater Transjordan, nevertheless argued that the disposing of Arab Palestine was a matter for consultation between the Arab states and the Arab Palestinians themselves.[18]

The Russian position was very close to the American one. In the UN they had been persistent in their support of the partition resolution from the very beginning. Moscow, quite rightly, regarded itself as one of the principal forces that helped to bring the resolution to the UN.[19]

Thus any Israeli change of mind concerning the protocol would have brought Israel into a direct confrontation with both the USA and the USSR, though not with Britain or Jordan. Lausanne, one could say, was on the whole an American show and Israel's main concern became how to appease the Americans in order to be able to undo the harm caused by the protocol.

Walter Eytan, the head of the Israeli delegation, soon found the tactics which emptied the protocol of its content. On 14 May the Israeli delegation stipulated a number of additional conditions which in fact formed a reversal of the Israeli position. Eytan wrote to Sharett, who was in New York at the time:

> At formal meeting with commission this morning we stiffened our necks began talking [*sic*]. Stressed 20 November gave Arab states no rights in Palestine, demanded withdrawal of all Arab forces, suggested plebiscite [in Palestine]. Explained difference our holding Galilee and Arab states holding parts of Palestine, stressing latter without shadow legal basis. *Commission startled, confused* [my italics], by all above propositions.[20]

The Israelis also refused to discuss the refugee problem as the first issue despite a surprising change in the Egyptian position, who 'softened their necks', so to speak: they now instructed their delegation to discuss with Israel the principle of repatriation and no longer, as in the past, held on to an unequivocal demand for the return of the refugees.[21]

In June 1949 Eytan defined Israel's main policy in the conference in these words:

> My main purpose was to begin to undermine the protocol of 12 May, which we had signed only under duress of our struggle for admission to the UN. Refusal to sign would, as Boisanger at the time openly threatened, have immediately been reported to the Secretary-General and the various governments . . . I felt the important thing was to begin to get the commission used to the idea that the protocol was not the main thing and that we should sooner or later base ourselves on the armistice arrangement.[22]

But the protocol was 'the main thing' in the eyes of the Americans.

Washington became annoyed with these tactics as time passed by and Israel was to carry the blame for causing a deadlock in Lausanne.

THE GAZA PROPOSAL OF MARK ETHRIDGE (MAY 1949)

Within only a few days of the protocol being signed, the Americans realized that Israel had to be pressured into co-operating with the PCC's agenda. Israel's main predicament stemmed from the fact that the Americans concurred with the Arab demands to first discuss the repatriation of the Palestinian refugees – once the armistice accord had been completed, the world's interest, at least for a while, focused on the humanitarian aspects of the conflict. The US State Department insisted that the problem of the refugees should be given precedence over the others. Thus the dilemma the Israelis faced at this point was either to address the question of repatriation which they were quite reluctant to do, or be subject to increasing American pressure.

The position of both Israel and the USA depended to a large extent upon their respective estimates of the numbers of refugees involved. When the conference opened, there were conflicting estimates: the International Refugee Organization talked of 910,000 refugees, the Israelis of 530,000 and the PCC, whose account seemed to be the most reliable one, reported about 750,000.[23] All accounts agree that most of the refugees (about 55 per cent), were living in Jordan (including the West Bank), which meant that if Israel refused to consider repatriation and the other Arab states declined to accept additional numbers of refugees, the entire burden of caring for them would fall on Jordan. Together with the permanent residents of the West Bank, the Palestinians constituted 75 per cent of the population of the Hashemite kingdom. This state of affairs did not satisfy anyone and the Americans led the way in focusing general attention on the need to find a solution that would combine repatriation with resettlement of the refugees in other Arab countries.

Officially, the Israelis declared that only explicit recognition of the Jewish state by the Arabs would open the way to serious negotiations about repatriation. In practice, however, they were doing everything to ensure that repatriation would soon be impossible. A decision followed in June 1949 to block the return of the refugees by taking irreversible measures with regard to their property and lands.

Already in July 1948 a senior official in the Israeli Foreign Office had written the following explanation to the State Department:

> The government of Israel must disclaim any responsibility for the creation of this problem. The charge that these Arabs were forcibly driven out by Israeli authorities is wholly false; on the contrary, everything possible was done to prevent the exodus. The question of return cannot be divorced from its military context. As long as the state of war continues, the refugees would be a disruptive element in the maintenance of internal law and order and a formidable fifth column for external enemies.[24]

The Israeli position on the refugee question can be condensed into two basic guidelines. The first stated that Israel had not been responsible for the creation of the problem, but that, nevertheless, it was willing to assist in solving the question on humanitarian grounds; the second was that never should any solution to the problem jeopardize Israel's security. Ben Gurion stressed the last point in the few meetings he had with the PCC's members in Palestine before the convention of the conference.[25] On this question the Israeli policy-makers were united. The Israeli foreign minister, Moshe Sharett, had declared that the Israeli refusal to discuss repatriation was irreversible.[26] However, as we shall see, during the Lausanne conference and later in the negotiations on the refugee question in 1950–51 Sharett would develop his own ideas about the need to compensate the refugees – regarding an Israeli gesture in this direction as a prerequisite for solving the conflict.

Israel's firm and rigid position on repatriation had practical as well as psychological reasons. In practical terms, the Israelis decided they needed the land and property abandoned by the Palestinian refugees for the resettlement of the waves of Jewish immigration from Europe and the Arab world. These immigrants had been put in transit camps in Israel, where thousands of them were living in rather dismal conditions, unemployed and frustrated. Any repatriation of the Palestinian refugees would have cast an additional economic burden on Israel and would have restricted its ability to absorb Jewish refugees.[27] An important influence was also the mood of the country and the anti-Arab feelings of a society which had just concluded a bloody war with the Palestinians and believed that repatriation of their former enemies could result in the continuation of the war from within the Jewish state.

For the first few days after the start of the conference, however, there were no signs of a breach in Israel's attitude. This led the American representative in the PCC, Mark Ethridge, to portray the Israeli position as obstructive. Like most officials in the State Department he was of the opinion that Israel ought to accept, publicly at least, the principle of repatriation. The State Department realized that the hope for a solution to the refugee problem had been the main, some argue the sole, reason for the Arab willingness to participate in the conference. Moreover, as the Israelis themselves stressed again and again, the territorial question had been solved, at least temporarily, through the armistice accord. The same was not true of the refugees whose situation in the relief camps around the Arab world since the end of the fighting in the winter of 1948–9 had only grown worse. Since their relief was mainly financed by American voluntary organizations, there were thus also practical grounds for American support for the Arab position.

In response to Ethridge's pressure, the Israeli delegates in Lausanne hinted at a possible change in Israel's position. However, these insinuations did not satisfy Ethridge who demanded a clear statement from Ben Gurion on the matter. To Washington Ethridge wrote that he very much doubted Ben Gurion's willingness to reach a compromise and expressed considerable pessimism about Israel's sincerity: he was now convinced that Ben Gurion had permitted the participation of the Israelis in the Lausanne conference solely in order to facilitate the admission of Israel to the UN.[28]

Ethridge succeeded in inducing his government to exert pressure on Israel in order to force it to modify its position on the refugee problem. Even before the protocol of May was presented to the sides, Ethridge had worked out a draft proposal which, he thought, would enable Israel to accept the principle of repatriation. He suggested that in return for the annexation of more Arab territory Israel would agree to the repatriation of at least some of the refugees: more specifically, he proposed the annexation to the state of Israel of the Gaza Strip with all its inhabitants, refugees and permanent residents.[29]

In the debates that the Israeli government held on this proposal at the beginning of May, Moshe Sharett began by suggesting that the offer be declined. He declared that despite the attraction of gaining more territory Israel could not afford to absorb such a large number of Arabs (300,000). Here, Sharett hinted for the first time that he might consider repatriation, provided it did not undermine Israel's economic capabilities or threaten its security. Ben Gurion, on the other hand, pulled the rest of the government behind him when he explained that the geopolitical advantages of this offer were enormous and that it held the promise of a relaxation in international pressure on Israel. The government decided therefore to accept Ethridge's offer.[30]

By supporting the Gaza proposal Ben Gurion admitted Israel's willingness to accept a large number of refugees on condition that it was allocated more territory. As we shall see, the Americans would later exploit this admission in order to try and persuade Israel to absorb a considerable number of refugees without annexing more territory.

The PCC transmitted the Gaza proposal in the middle of May to the Egyptian government. Cairo's initial reaction was favourable. However, after three days of discussions between King Faruq and his ministers, the offer was rejected. It seems that whereas some members of the Egyptian cabinet were willing to give up the Gaza Strip, it was Faruq who was opposed to cede the only Egyptian trophy in an unfortunate Palestine war. The Egyptian government realized the difficulties of both maintaining Gaza and controlling its population and therefore was more inclined to respond positively to the Israeli offer.[31] But it would be wrong to attribute the change in the Egyptian position only to Faruq's opinion on the matter. The proposal had put the government in an uneasy position: if it accepted, it would mean that all of Arab Palestine would have fallen under either Hashemite or Jewish rule. Since the Hashemites had decided to annex the West Bank, the Egyptians were the only Arab state possessing parts of Palestine whose sovereignty had not been determined.

This was a source of strength as well as a cause of concern to the Egyptian government. On the one hand, the Egyptians were sponsoring the last remnants of independent Palestinian representation – the Gaza government; on the other, they had never gone so far as to grant Gaza independent status but had left it under military rule.[32] Conceding Gaza to the Israelis would have been tantamount to Egypt's withdrawal from the Pan-Arab arena – where the Palestinian question formed the focal point – and at the same time granting implicit recognition both to the Jewish state and the enlarged kingdom of Jordan. Such a wholesale retraction of their ideals and declared objectives naturally would have been worth the Egyptians' while only if a very high price were extracted from the other side, that is Israel. The Gaza proposal did not contain any concessions to the Egyptians. In fact, Sasson had learned in his unofficial conversations with Abd al-Mun'im, the head of the Egyptian delegation to Lausanne, that in return Egypt demanded the southern Negev, an area which not only had great strategic importance for Egypt but also would have left it with part of Palestine. Sasson refused to consider this suggestion seriously and the Gaza proposal fell. Egyptian ambivalence toward the question of Palestine could be observed in the constant tension between a desire to invest energy only in purely Egyptian problems and a feeling of solidarity – kindled by ambitions for Pan-Arab leadrship and genuine identification – with the Palestinians. And these conflicting desires seem to continue until this very day.

The Egyptian delegation therefore continued to toe the general Arab line in Lausanne. After Ethridge had come up with the Gaza proposal, the Arab delegations submitted a number of memoranda to the PCC that stressed the need to tie the fate of the refugees to that of the land of Palestine, in other words the Arabs were not only looking for a humanitarian solution, nor were they satisfied with repatriation – above all they wanted parts of Palestine to remain under Palestinian sovereignty. Not that there was a consensus among the Arab governments with regard to the question of sovereignty; a clear rift existed between the Transjordanian decision to annex part of Arab Palestine, a decision that had been implicitly supported by Hashemite Iraq, and the other Arab states which called for the creation of an independent Arab Palestine.[33]

Incidentally, the French PCC member, de Boisanger, supported the Egyptian position. The Israeli delegation thought that this was due to traditional Anglo-French rivalry in the area – though this is quite possible, one can find other reasons for close Egyptian–French co-operation at a time when France was seeking a more amiable Egyptian attitude towards its ambitions in North

Africa. And one can of course also adopt a less cynical approach and accept that French support for the idea of Palestinian independence was genuine. In any case, after the Gaza proposal had fallen through France joined the other members of the PCC in their search for a different approach to the problem. Under American guidance the commission tried to induce Israel to offer another substantial gesture on the refugee problem.

THE AMERICAN PRESSURE ON ISRAEL–JUNE 1949

It would seem likely that the receptive response of the Israelis towards the Gaza proposal together with its rejection by the Egyptian side would have improved Israel's image in Ethridge's eyes. This, however, was not the case: somehow the Israeli conduct in this question failed to satisfy both Ethridge and the American administration as a whole. Eight days after Israel announced its willingness to annex the Gaza strip. President Truman sent a sharp note to the Israeli premier, Ben Gurion, in which he accused him of causing the stalemate in Lausanne. The American president threatened Israel with sanctions and political repercussions if it did not soon show a more flexible stand.[34] The protestations of the clearly pro-Israeli American ambassador at Tel Aviv, James McDonald, did not save Israel from Washington's wrath. Truman wrote:

> The government of the US is seriously disturbed by the attitude of Israel with respect to territorial settlement in Palestine and to the question of Palestine refugees ... The US government is deeply concerned to learn from Eytan's statements that the suggestion both on refugees and on territorial questions which had been made by it for the sole purpose of advancing prospects of peace have made so little impression upon the government of Israel.

Truman was annoyed by Israel's unwillingness to reiterate its support for the May protocol, and he went on to state that 'the US government is gravely concerned lest Israel now endanger the possibility of arriving at a solution of the Palestine problem in such a way as to contribute to the establishment of sound and friendly relations between Israel and its neighbours'. Truman's message ended in a direct warning that unless Israel changed its attitude 'the U.S. government will regretfully be forced to the conclusion that a revision of its attitude towards Israel has become unavoidable'.[35]

American impatience with Israel also stemmed from the fact that the conference was an American 'show'. Having been excluded voluntarily from the peace process during the British mandate period to its very last days, the Americans for the first time had taken the initiative. The American delegation to Lausanne very shortly after its arrival had come to the conclusion that the Israelis were there for all the wrong reasons. It accused Israel of doing all it could to bring the conference to a premature end. This was a harsh judgement since the Israeli Foreign Office and the foreign minister had come to Lausanne seeking a peace settlement. It was Ben Gurion who regarded Lausanne as a futile exercise, or rather as a trap set up by pro-Arab US State Department officials. In Ben Gurion's eyes peace was not the first priority of Israel in the spring of 1949. Securing the armistice agreements and concentrating on the integration into society of the wave of about one million Jewish immigrants were Israel's main concerns. Hence, a significant shift in Israeli policy depended on Ben Gurion. After a while, the Americans seemed to appreciate this reality and directed their criticism to Jerusalem rather than pressurizing the Israeli delegation in Lausanne.

The failure of the Gaza proposal thus led to more American pressure on Israel. To this end, the American delegation in Lausanne was reinforced by a number of senior officials from the State Department. The personal composition of the group of newcomers indicated also an American willingness to accept the Arab contention that priority should be given to the problem of the refugees, which clearly stood out in the personality of George McGhee. McGhee, who would reorient the direction of the diplomatic effort in Lausanne, was able to play such an influential role owing to his personal friendship with the American Secretary of State, Dean Acheson, and his association with the American oil industry. Roger Louis has described McGhee as one of the principal antagonists of British policy in the Middle East, and as such most receptive towards Arab national sentiments and ambitions.[36] In 1949, when he arrived in Lausanne, McGhee came as a newly-appointed co-ordinator for Palestine refugee affairs in the State Department.[37] He had already made his debut as a potential peacemaker by offering, in a public speech in April 1949, a scheme for economic development of the Middle East – a kind of Marshall Plan for the area. McGhee asserted that only vast development projects throughout the Middle East and particularly in Israel and its Arab neighbour states could induce the warring parties to settle ther refugee problem.

It was this 'Middle Eastern Marshall Plan' of McGhee that became the cornerstone of American policy towards the refugee problem in the years 1949 to 1955. McGhee's plan hoped to solve the refugee problem by inducing Israel to repatriate 200,000 refugees and persuading the Arab governments to resettle the remaining 550,000 in the various Arab states. It contained the necessary mechanism for fund-raising and had placed responsibility for its execution on the PCC.[38] Barely three months later, when the Americans had given up their attempts to pressure Israel into changing its attitude and the PCC had lost interest in changing the territorial status quo in Palestine, McGhee's plan became the major initiative in the peace process. In June 1949 McGhee's influence increased further when he was appointed senior assistant to the secretary of state for Near Eastern and African affairs.

Our discussion of the American attitude towards the conference in the first half of June 1949 would be incomplete without a reference to the American views on the Arab position and conduct in Lausanne until that time. To the Americans, the Arab delegation seemed more reasonable than the Israeli for two reasons. First was their adherence to the May protocol. Secondly, the Arabs had accepted the Jessup Principle and demanded an Israeli public recognition of it.[39] However, despite the similarity between the Arab positions and the State Department's principles of a settlement, it should be noted that American ideas of territorial compensation were always merely tentative and never really insisted upon.

McGhee's arrival brought the Arab and the American positions even closer. He accepted the Arab insistence that no territorial solution could be finalized before Israel made some gestures to ease the predicament of the refugees. The Arabs suggested in June 1949 that Israel might agree to the repatriation of the 'rich' landowners and religious dignitaries as a sign of goodwill and demanded that Israel stop putting impossible conditions in the way of repatriation.

As briefly mentioned above, in the summer of 1948 Israel had already decided that repatriation of Palestinian refugees was out of the question. Four hundred Arab villages subsequently were turned into cultivated land, Israelis were allowed to enter Arab neighbourhoods, and Arab property everywhere was expropriated by the state and taken over by Jewish occupants. Officially, the Israelis were committed to keep in custody Arab property and land, in practice only a very small portion would ever be saved under this commitment.[40]

Under McGhee's influence the American pressure, which had begun with Truman's message of 29 May 1949, culminated on 13 June in a decision of the American administration to condition a promised loan of $100 million to Israel by an American bank on Israel's attitudes towards the refugees.[41] As we shall see, this severe measure did eventually help to soften the Israeli position.

American irritation with Israel stemmed not only from Washington's identification with the Arab position. There were two other notable bones of contention: the Israeli policy towards Jerusalem and Eliahu Sasson's clandestine meetings and negotiations with individual Arab delegates in Lausanne.

The PCC had formed a sub-committee to discuss the future of Jerusalem. The head of the Israeli delegation told this committee at the end of May 1949 that 'the integration of the Jewish part of Jerusalem into the economic, political and administrative framework of the state of Israel has taken place as a natural process arising from the conditions of war, and has been paralleled by a similar process on the Arab [Jordanian] side'. In that respect Jordan and Israel differed from the other participants in Lausanne. The Arab countries supported internationalization since they feared that the alternative would be a Jewish Jerusalem, and several Arab leaders were not enthusiastic about the idea of a Hashemite Jerusalem.[42] The partition of Jerusalem had indeed been a natural outcome of the war; it was also a consequence of the pre-1948 tacit Israeli–Transjordanian agreement. The Jordanians, however, could hide under the Arab umbrella in Lausanne, thus appearing to support internationalization of the city. They succeeded in attracting little or no attention to this double-game since they took no spectacular measures in Jerusalem, as the Israelis did when they officially turned the city into their capital.

As to the second source of irritation, the Americans had come to Lausanne seeking a comprehensive agreement for problems that related to the Arab world as a whole, whereas the Israelis, i.e., Sasson, were pursuing the objective of partial agreements. This, in the American mind, would only have perpetuated the conflict. The State Department saw Sasson's overtures as a deliberate attempt to foil the conference.[43] They somewhat misjudged his intentions, for Sasson did not seek to obstruct the conference, but wanted to turn it into a forum of bilateral talks between Israel and the Arab countries and did not see it as a means of attaining a comprehensive settlement. For Sasson, the general Arab insistence on dealing first with the refugee problem was only a matter of tactics; he had very little belief in or respect for the Arab commitment to the Palestinians.[44] The Americans were particularly annoyed by the continued negotiations between Sasson and Fawzi al-Mulki, the Jordanian defence minister and the head of the Jordanian delegation in Lausanne. Mulki represented Abdullah's ambition to reach a separate peace with Israel. The bilateral negotiations with Jordan were conducted in Palestine itself, but the extension of the talks to Lausanne had succeeded in undermining the international effort to impose a comprehensive peace settlement.[45] The Americans had sent an endless series of notes to the Israeli Foreign Office expressing their utter dissatisfaction with Sasson's initiative.[46]

Did anything at all come out of these negotiations? Sasson, for one, was very enthusiastic in the reports he sent back to his government and boasted about the progress he was making in the out-of-court contacts. The Lebanese and Egyptian delegates, for instance, had told Sasson that their governments would accept Israel's borders provided it ceded territory in the north to Lebanon and in the south to Egypt. Incidentally, it was also in these meetings that the head of the Egyptian delegation gave Egypt's final negative answer on the Gaza proposal. But all in all, the information Sasson collected and conveyed, whether accurate or not, did not alter either the Israeli position or the official Egyptian or Lebanese attitudes.

Sasson also met several of the Palestinian dignitaries who attended Lausanne in either an official or unofficial capacity. His meetings with them form one of the most intriguing chapters in the history of the Arab–Israeli conflict, and the importance of this development deserves further elaboration. As it occurred during the first stage of the Lausanne conference, its analysis here fits into the chronological order of events.

ISRAELI–PALESTINIAN NEGOTIATIONS IN LAUSANNE

The Palestinians were only marginally involved in the negotiations over the fate of Palestine. The permanent residents of Arab Palestine, those who had succeeded in staying and now fell under Israeli, Jordanian or Egyptian rule, had no say whatsoever in the discussion in Lausanne. Several representatives and leaders of the refugee community, however, appeared in Lausanne – some of them former members of the Arab Higher Committee – and they were the ones Sasson met.[47]

The two groups of Palestinians, refugees and permanent residents alike, did still have a leader: the former Mufti of Jerusalem, Hajj Amin al-Husayni. It is difficult to assess al-Husayni's popularity at the time of Lausanne but judging from the amount of effort invested by the British and the Hashemites to curb what they called the 'pro-Mufti' elements one gets the impression that the former Mufti was still very popular. The Egyptians, as mentioned before, had allowed him to stay in Gaza and later in Egypt during the short-lived All-Palestine government. At the end of 1948 this government was dissolved and a department for Palestine affairs was established in the Arab League, headed by al-Husayni. In this capacity he would send two delegates to Lausanne towards the end of the conference. However, in the first stage of the discussions, in June 1949, the only representative of the refugees was Muhammad Nimr al-Hawari. Hawari was a lawyer from Jaffa who, during the mandate, had commanded the 'Najjada', a paramilitary scout movement. He had no connection with the al-Husayni family; on the contrary, he was one of their main rivals during the war and was accused by them of collaboration with the Jews. After the war Hawari, together with Aziz Shehadeh, a lawyer from Ramallah, opened an office for refugee affairs in the West Bank. The PCC, wishing to secure some independent Palestinian representation there, encouraged Hawari to come and appear before the commission in Lausanne. Hawari did not concern himself with the Gaza Strip and came only to discuss the future of the West Bank. He immediately contacted the Israelis and suggested to them that the best solution for the refugee problem would be either to annex the West Bank to Israel, or to turn it into an independent state closely linked to Israel, two suggestions which were particularly attractive in the eyes of Moshe Sharett.[48] Hawari proposed that the refugees would themselves negotiate with Israel about their problem with no external Arab interference. Sasson found this last proposal most appealing and cabled his enthusiasm to Sharett explaining that it would allow Israel to discuss only territorial problems in Lausanne; that is, if Hawari's position was acceptable to the other Arab delegates.[49]

These suggestions were made in May 1949. In June two Palestinian refugees from the Gaza Strip, Sa'id Baidas and Francis Jelad, appeared as well. They had better connections with the former Mufti, but seemed to co-ordinate their activity with Hawari. After consulting with them Hawari proposed to Sasson that a refugee committee should be allowed to tour Israel which, so went Hawari's argument, could possibly convince the refugees of the impracticability of repatriation. By then, he seemed to have abandoned the idea of annexing the West Bank to Israel and demanded the creation of a Palestinian state with the help of Israel and the USA. Sharett considered the idea favourably, so would Bechor Shitrit, the minister for minority affairs, but Ben Gurion and the rest of the Israeli government would not even discuss it.[50]

Yet, even though they agreed in their positive attitude towards Hawari's proposal, there was a substantial difference in the way Sharett and Sasson viewed the affair. Sasson tried to induce Hawari, Baidas and Jelad to propose to the PCC that the refugee problem would be exclusively dealt with between Israel and these Palestinians.[51] Ever pragmatic, Sasson saw this suggestion as being, in his words, another good 'trick' that could be used to embarrass the other side. Sharett quickly discerned Sasson's wish to use Hawari as a means of advancing Israel's position in Lausanne and warned him against 'dangerous profiteering' and 'resorting to temporary tactics'. Furthermore, Sharett believed that any objective observer would soon see that vast areas in Israel were still uninhabited, which might convince the refugees to demand repatriation even more rigorously.[52] Hence, he supported only that part in Hawari's programme which talked about the creation of an independent Palestinian state, under Israel's influence. But even this was not accepted by Israel, and this short episode of direct Israeli–Palestinian negotiatons, which would continue until 1956 in the form of correspondence between refugee leaders and the Israeli Foreign Office, left no mark on the development of the conflict.[53]

All in all, the unofficial negotiations did not bear much fruit. However, they do tell us something about the uniqueness of the period in question. A year after the first round of fighting between

Israel and its Arab neighbours, Lausanne opened the way to all kinds of possibilities for peace. That these possibilities were not properly explored, let alone tested, stemmed mainly from an Israeli preference for a peace with the Jordanians which completely excluded agreements with the Palestinians and left unresolved the problems of the refugees, Jerusalem and Israel's acceptance in the Arab world – problems which could only be solved with a general Arab consent. The failure should also be attributed to the unwillingness of the Arab delegates with whom Sasson met to declare in public what they had promised in private. Yet, towards the end of June considerable progress was made even on these questions, not least because of American pressure on the victorious party in the war, an on the whole obstinate Israel, to concede to some of the demands of the defeated, but on the whole realistic Arab countries. It is impossible to know what eventually would have happened, had the Americans sustained their pressure on Israel. But when the second session in Lausanne began in July 1949, American pressure subsided and the Lausanne conference was soon to be pushed aside into the pedestrian sequence of historical events.

Sasson's overtures to individual Arab delegates and the deadlock on the refugee problem led the Americans to ask for a recess in the negotiations at the end of June 1949. On 24 June, just one day before the recess, the Americans tried one more time to revive the Gaza proposal. They did so by suggesting that in return for the annexation of the Gaza Strip to Israel the Jewish state would compensate the Arabs in some other part and would agree to repatriate some of the refugees to Israel proper.[54] This was an interesting combination of the original Gaza proposal, the 'Jessup Principle' and the concept of repatriation. The only concession the Americans made to the Israelis was on a direct Israeli–Egyptian dialogue on this new version. In all likelihood the move was taken in order to counteract Sasson's unofficial negotiations and it annoyed the Israeli policy-makers. Abba Eban accused Washington of abandoning its role of go-between and resorting to what he described as 'Bernadottism', referring to Israel's displeasure in the past with Bernadotte's attempt to propose a solution rather than serve as mediator.[55] Yet it was Eban, then the Israeli ambassador to the UN, who together with Reuven Shiloah advised their government to accept the American proposal. The head of the Foreign Office, Eytan, however, persuaded the government to reject it out of hand as he pointed out that such a move would generate American pressure on Israel to concede part of the Negev and Eilat. He warned: 'The Egyptians will ask for Bernadotte or something much like it. The Americans will say this is too much and will recommend (i.e. insist on) a compromise – viz., that Egypt should content herself with Eilat . . . if we say yes we lose Eilat.'[56]

When the parties reconvened, Syria was to surprise the conference with its own peace initiative: an offer to resettle a considerable number of refugees in return for peace with Israel. Moreover, at the beginning of the second phase, the Israelis for the first time considered making a gesture on repatriation and the Americans turned their eyes to McGhee's 'magic' ideas about a Marshall Plan for the Middle East as the only hope for a solution.

ZAIM'S OFFER (JULY 1949)

On 18 July 1949, after a recess of eighteen days, the delegations returned to Lausanne to resume the negotiations. News had come from Damascus about a new Syrian peace initiative, suggested by Colonel Husni Zaim. Though Zaim did not bring his offer to Lausanne, he none the less affected the course of the conference to some extent and we shall therefore begin our survey of the second phase of Lausanne with an account of his offer. We have already discussed Zaim's unique approach while covering the Israeli–Syrian armistice negotiations. In fact it was towards the end of these negotiations that the Syrian ruler made his rather extraordinary proposal. At the beginning of July Zaim met General Riley, the head of the UN armistice observers in Palestine, and offered to resettle about 300,000 refugees in the al-Jazirah area. This northeastern region of Syria was renowned for its black fertile soil and British experts estimated that one and three quarters of a million acres of fertile land were waiting to be developed there. Earlier on, Zaim had offered that area as a new homeland for the somewhat irridentist Druze community which lived in the south of the country in the area known as Jabel Druze. Although a few days later, in a conversation with the British ambassador to Damascus, Zaim was less generous and limited the number of refugees to about 200,000, it seems that the principle mattered as much, if not more, than the numbers involved.[57]

Like everything else concerning Colonel Zaim, this episode should be treated with caution. His short term in office and the inevitability of his downfall are bound to raise questions about the sincerity and, more important, the viability of his proposal. The American ambassador in Damascus at the time showed considerable confidence in Zaim's peaceful intentions; he wrote to his superiors in Washington that they should not question Zaim's sincerity 'if for no other reason than his awareness that the Palestine problem stands in the way of realizing many of his dreams'.[58] Zaim's principal dream, of course, was no other than being generously supplied with Western money and modern American weapons; a dream that at least as far as the State Department was concerned was to remain such since they regarded the Syrian ruler as an unreliable dictator and suggested to the president not to arm him.[59]

Britain and France were more forthcoming in their response and both governments seemed to have considered Zaim's offer seriously, promising funds if and when Zaim agreed to make a public declaration.[60] But it was not money that Zaim needed in the first place, rather sufficient political support in his own country for his unusual scheme. Failing that support, it would prove impossible for Zaim to stay in power, and in August 1949 he was overthrown by another officer of the Syrian army. His successor showed no interest in adopting Zaim's unique vision. The American press, for one, lamented his downfall and the *New York Times*, which at first had shown a considerable amount of hostility towards the Syrian ruler, commented now that his demise was a setback to the peace process and warned its readers that after Zaim's disappearance the area would regress onto the dangerous path of an inevitable war.[61] Incidentally, the paper attributed the colonel's schemes to his prime minister, Muhsin al-Barazi, who had gone down with his master. *The New York Times'* correspondent in Damascus wrote a few days after Zaim's fall: 'Barazi had gone much further than had generally been realized towards adopting a program of extensive Palestinian refugee resettlement in Syria with international and American financial help.'[62] The paper also reported that it had been Zaim's ambition for Barazi to take the lead in Lausanne and convince the delegates of the Arab countries to include the Syrian scheme in their peace proposals to the conference.[63]

Thus, like many of the other moves in the peace process, this episode had very little effect on future developments. Washington continued to regard the Israelis as the main offenders in obstructing peace. Following Zaim's downfall and the beginning of the second stage of the Lausanne conference, American pressure was resumed therefore and finally resulted in an Israeli response.

AN ISRAELI GESTURE: THE 100,000 OFFER

The PCC members had returned to Lausanne with renewed vigour. They opened the second phase by tabling their own peace plans rather than waiting for the parties to take the initiative. We have already described how the Americans had made a similar attempt at the end of the first session by reviving the Gaza proposal. This unsuccessful attempt probably induced the other two members of the PCC to introduce their own ideas for a territorial settlement. The Turks, who were under strong British influence – as they believed London would pave the way to Turkey's membership of NATO – proposed their own version of the Greater Transjordan concept, defining Arab Palestine as including the West Bank, the Gaza Strip and the Negev.[64] The French, on the other hand, were influenced by their commitment to the Levant states. Thus, they proposed to leave the Negev in Jewish hands – probably for no other reason than to present an antithesis to the British ideas – and recommended the establishment of a trusteeship over the Galilee. The French regarded the delineation of all Israel's borders as open to negotiation and were in particular aware of the need to co-ordinate their policy with the Syrians and the Lebanese.[65]

Whereas the principal American guidelines had been accepted by the Arabs and rejected by the Israelis, the French and Turkish peace proposals were spurned by both sides. While the Americans understood that there was no room for a definite peace plan such as Bernadotte had proposed and confined themselves to general principles for a solution, the two other members left very little room for negotiatons, and so annoyed all parties concerned. But all three member states, by putting forward ideas of their own, had departed from the task of conciliation originally entrusted to them by the General Assembly. The PCC was not meant to be a body for arbitration and when its members turned it into one it was about to face the same intractable problems and difficulties with which Bernadotte had had to cope.

The failure of Turkey and France to advance the negotiations on the territorial framework enabled everyone concerned to focus on the problem of the refugees. The PCC resumed its efforts with added urgency as these refugees, who had gone already through one bitter winter, were about to face another one still living in tents without proper food or medical supplies.

The Americans took the lead once more under the guidance of Paul Porter who replaced Mark Ethridge as head of delegation. Ethridge probably resigned owing to his frequent disagreement with President Truman's political advisers. He was dissatisfied with the low degree of American pressure on Israel, asserting that the administration was too lenient because of the pro-Israeli stance of Truman's aides. The Israelis were obviously relieved at Ethridge's resignation. Eytan could not disguise his somewhat malicious joy at the circumstances in which Ethridge departed: 'Poor Ethridge! I feel really sorry for him, so obviously suffering from sheer frustration and sense of failure – as he himself, incidentally, admitted.'[66] These and other derogatory remarks about Ethridge, leave the impression that the Israelis looked upon Lausanne more as a ground on which personal American ambitions were played out against one another, a kind of hurdle track set up by the State Department in order to test its senior officials, and not (as it was to become), a peace conference whose failure would leave Israel in a state of war with its Arab neighbours.

Ethridge's successor was a lawyer who had held important administrative positions in the American government and was an ardent believer in the Marshall doctrine and its suitability for the Middle East. As we shall see it was Porter together with George McGhee, who would lead the PCC to believe that an economic solution for the refugee problem was the only basis for a comprehensive settlement.[67]

But before this new concept was adopted, Porter, like Ethridge before him, believed that the only way of moving closer to a solution of the problem was by inducing Israel to make a gesture and repatriate a substantial number of Palestinian refugees. The State Department meticulously prepared American public opinion for the renewed American pressure on Israel, as can be inferred from the following report by the first secretary in the Israeli embassy in Washington:

> In the White House, in the State Department, in the American public opinion [*sic*] we have so far failed to put our case across. While the press, and I dare venture also the Department, consider the territorial question as a secondary problem, they consistently say and – maybe – believe that our handling of the refugee problem constitutes the main stumbling block in the present Arab–Israeli negotiation for peace. From justices of the Supreme Court down to the man in the street, most non-Jewish Americans place the onus on Israel.[68]

This report and others similar to it as well as the deep gap which had been disclosed between the United States and Israel on the Gaza proposal had an important effect on Moshe Sharett. The Israeli foreign minister devoted most of the recess to finding ways of pacifying the American wrath. Sharett suggested to his government, on 5 July 1949, that an Israeli gesture on the refugee question could ease the American pressure. He proposed that the Israeli government accept the repatriation of 100,000 refugees. In reality, Sharett offered the return of only 75,000 refugees: 25,000 of the 100,000 had already entered Israel, and 10,000 were refugees whom the Israelis had already consented to include in a project of family reunions.[69]

Only Ben Gurion and one other minister were opposed to the offer; the rest of the ministers supported the initiative. Ben Gurion claimed, and in this he turned out to be right, that the figure of 100,000 would never satisfy the Americans. He was also loyal to his earlier objection to any form of repatriation, based on the argument of the state's security. Ben Gurion succeeded in undermining Sharett's policy by convincing the government that instead of a clear-cut Israeli offer, Israel would first test the waters in the United States to ascertain whether or not this was an acceptable offer.[70] It is not surprising, therefore, to find that the Americans and the PCC members did not, in the final analysis, consider the Israeli offer as a true sign of moderation or as a significant contribution to the peace process.

In fact, the perceptive American officials immediately saw the absurdity of the new Israeli position: in April the Israelis had agreed to annex the Gaza Strip with its 250,000 refugees, in July the Israelis stated that they could not afford to repatriate more than 100,000 refugees.[71] Consequently, the Israelis were told straightaway by the PCC and the Americans that their offer was wholly insufficient.

Needless to say, the Arab delegates rejected the offer, claiming that the Israeli proposal contradicted the UN General Assembly resolution of 11 December 1948. The PCC suggested increasing the number of refugees to be repatriated and resettling the rest in the Arab world. This was, in fact, the American proposition which offered to combine resettlement with repatriation as a logical basis for a solution.[72] The Syrians and the Jordanians indicated to the PCC at the time that they were willing to participate in such a settlement, in other words to resettle all those Palestinian refugees who did not wish to return to Israel.[73] In fact, King Abdullah and Husni Zaim spoke about this solution openly. Zaim's initiative has already been discussed. As for Abdullah, his initiative was soon muffled by Sir Alec Kirkbride, the British representative in Amman, who feared that the resettlement of a considerable number of refugees in Transjordan and the West Bank would lead to the Palestinization of the country.[74] We should not forget that most of the refugees were in Arab Palestine, today's West Bank. Following the American logic, as Abdullah did, would have meant that many of the refugees, even if they did not return to their original residence before the war, would either have been repatriated to Israel or resettled in Arab Palestine – that is in their own *homeland*. This would indeed have formed a rare opportunity to combine resettlement and repatriation, but it was never suggested, neither by Israel nor by the Arab world.

The Israeli reply to the proposals put forward was that it could not absorb more than 100,000 since the Jewish state already had under its jurisdiction 150,000 Arabs. This Arab minority in Israel together with the proposed 100,000 would constitute 28 per cent of the total population and, consequently, any additional number would turn Israel into a binational state.[75] In addition, Israel claimed it could not increase the number of Arabs living under its rule without undermining its effort to absorb the flow of Jewish refugees coming from the Arab countries.

But this Israeli offer pushed Israel into dire straits, since the PCC subsequently asserted that although they did not accept the number offered by the Israelis, they welcomed the acceptance by the Israeli government of the principle of repatriation. When the

Israelis later denied this interpretation in August they would be held up once more as obstructionists and as the main cause for the final failure of the conference. Sharett did not give up. Fearing that the next stage would be the transferral of the Palestine problem from the PCC back to the General Assembly, he asked the Israeli delegation in Lausanne to state more clearly Israel's readiness to discuss the refugee problem before tackling any other issue.[76] He revived his enthusiastic preference for Palestinian autonomy in the West Bank to the annexation of the area to Transjordan, hoping, probably, to convince the PCC of the possibility of finding a solution to the Palestinians outside the territory of Israel.[77]

Ben Gurion was totally opposed to the manoeuvres by Sharett and suggested to the Israeli delegation not to repeat the 100,000 offer. He reflected internal Israeli criticism of Sharett's offer, and would eventually cause Israel to prevaricate even on these limited offers. From now one Ben Gurion was to have more and more impact on the Israeli position in Lausanne as one of his closest confidants would be appointed to head the delegation, Reuven Shiloah.

Shiloah's appointment came in the middle of July 1949 and as Ben Gurion's principal adviser on Arab affairs he reflected more than anyone else the opinions and attitudes of Ben Gurion himself. Like his mentor, he viewed Lausanne not as a peace conference but as a necessary evil.[78]

In contrast, Sharett continued to view Lausanne as a multi-lateral peace conference. At the end of July, after long and exhausting negotiations, Syria and Israel signed an armistice agreement. A day later Sharett told the Israeli Foreign Office staff:

> On the face of it, the new situation [of armistice agreements with all the Arab states] relieves us from the need to sign a formal and written peace agreement with the neighbouring countries, since there is very little difference, as far as territorial integrity is concerned, between the existing armistice agreements and formal peace treaties.

However, he added, 'on the other hand, we shall prejudice the essence of the [Zionist] project, if we imagine that the armistices would solve everything and that we now can duly remove the business of peace making from our national agenda'. The main reason, in Sharett's view, was that for its security Israel depended on regional and international legitimization, without which it would always remain insecure. The practical result of this outlook was that although most of Israel's policy-makers argued that the Jewish state should stay on in Lausanne for 'tactical' reasons alone, Sharett stressed the real value of a multilateral forum from which a permanent peace settlement could emerge. The main risk, in Sharett's eyes, was that if the PCC failed in its task the General Assembly would be called upon to impose a solution.[79] Sharett was wrong on all counts: apart from himself everyone on the Israeli side disregarded the developments in Lausanne, and the UN has never to this day attempted what it dared to offer in 1947 – an imposed solution to the conflict.

THE DEATH THROES OF THE PEACE CONFERENCE
JULY TO SEPTEMBER 1949

Reuven Shiloah's first impressions on his arrival in Lausanne are illuminating. He wrote to Sharett that the main problem was the fact that the Arab delegates were still loyal to the May protocol of 1949. The Turkish member had pointed out to Shiloah that if this state of affairs continued the Arab delegates would reach the scheduled General Assembly session (September 1949) with the backing of the international community. Shiloah promised to do all he could to persuade the Turkish delegate to change his mind. He was satisfied to find that the American and French delegates made no mention of the protocol in their initial discussions with him.[80]

Shiloah's main achievement was in convincing Porter that the continued efforts by Israel to negotiate bilaterally with Egypt, Jordan and Syria, did not actually undermine the work of the PCC. Eliahu Sasson was still in Lausanne meeting often with the Egyptian delegate, Abd al-Mun'im; whereas the Israeli–Jordanian negotiations continued throughout, and through the medium of the Mixed Armistice Committee, Sharett conducted talks with representatives of Syria's ruler, Colonel Husni Zaim.[81]

These bilateral negotiations remained marginal apart from those entered into with Jordan. One feels that the optimistic assessment of the talks with Egypt had more to do with Sasson's imagination than with reality. But as we do not have the Egyptian documentation it is difficult to judge the seriousness of these efforts.

In any case, Sasson reported a most favourable response from both the Egyptian government (led by Ibrahim Abd al-Hadi until August 1949 and then by Husayn Siri) and the palace.[82] British and American documents do not reveal such enthusiasm.

It is our assessment that in actual fact only two peace processes took place: one in Lausanne, and the other between Israel and Jordan, which we treated separately above. Still, many historians believe that a serious chance for a bilateral Israeli–Syrian peace also existed at the time.[83] Since this is a hypothetical question, we shall only provide the reader with the information that the Syrians joined the peace conference at the end of July 1949. The head of the delegation was the Syrian ambassador in Paris, Adnan al-Atasi, the son of a former republican Syrian president. Sasson did not enter into direct negotiations with him, believing that he was unpopular with Husni Zaim, but continued correspondence with Zaim's foreign minister, Muhsin Barazi. The Syrian ruler continued to stipulate two conditions for a bilateral peace with Israel: large-scale international financial aid to Syria and the repatriation of most of the refugees and resettlement of the rest in Syria. Israel declined this offer.[84]

The deadlock on both the bilateral and multilateral fronts signalled the end of the Lausanne conference. One last attempt by the PCC to salvage the conference took place on 15 August 1949. Impressed by its early success on 12 May, the PCC contemplated reconstructing the protocol by inducing the parties to sign yet another joint document. As any knowledgeable negotiator, or for that matter mediator, would agree, it is reasonable, even necessary, at each stage in the negotiations to summarize the points of agreements that have been reached between the conflicting parties in order not to waste time and energy on marginal points. This was exactly what the PCC now attempted to do. It could have been a successful move, had the Israelis not withdrawn their previous concessions. However, the internal situation in Israel itself had changed. The influx of new immigrants from Europe and the relative calmness on the borders as a result of the armistice agreements had stiffened the Israeli position with regard to the refugee problem and to a possible territorial compromise. Moreover, as we stated before, the early Israeli concessions, embodied in the May protocol, had been made merely as a tactical move intended to alleviate American pressure, and not out of any genuine desire to reach a compromise.

The Arab delegates, on the other hand, saw no point in altering their earlier consent to the May protocol and acceptance of the principle of partition provided Israel would, as it had done in May, consent to the principle of repatriation. From a tactical point of view, this was an advantageous position as it undermined Israel's international image.[85]

On 15 August 1949, the PCC presented a memorandum to the heads of delegations in which the commission suggested a joint declaration before the end of the conference. In the proposed declaration, the commission referred to all three aspects involved in a comprehensive peace. Nevertheless, it gave priority, at the request of the Arab delegates, to the refugee problem. The commission suggested the recognition by Israel of the right of return for the Palestinian refugees and for a promise by the Arab states to resettle the rest. Both Israel and the Arab states would be assisted by the international community. The PCC further suggested that a survey group would be sent to the Middle East to explore the particular economic difficulties emerging from repatriation and resettlement of refugees. On the territorial question and the future of Jerusalem the PCC suggested reaffirming the May protocol.[86]

Through this memorandum the PCC indicated its full support for the Arab demand to solve the refugee problem before settling the territorial controversy. It had also given in to the American business-like approach which tended to solve political problems by economic means, an approach which would be highly successful in Europe but was doomed to failure in the Middle East.

That the Americans were behind this protocol is clear from the resemblance between the PCC's new orientation and the ideas McGhee had already put forward in April 1949. The American outlook was based upon the conviction that the refugee problem could be solved by a group of professional experts, that is, people who had dealt successfully in the past with refugee problems. The State Department wanted the team to be composed of American and British experts alone and hoped to induce Britain and other members of the Western bloc to provide financial assistance to those countries willing to share this attempt to find an economic solution to the problem. The new solution incorporated earlier suggestions when it proposed to combine resettlement and repatriation; its novelty lay in the inclusion of this old formula within the framework of a general 'Marshall Plan' for the Middle

East. The focus was thus no longer on the refugee problem but on the economic growth of the Middle East and its political alliance to the West. In American eyes this new plan had the same aims as the original Marshall Plan: political stabilization and the achievement of a higher standard of living as the best guarantees against Communist infiltration and Russian intervention in the region.

With hindsight, it can be seen that this American move soon pushed the Lausanne conference and the PCC into historical oblivion. It proved unrealistic and naïve to assume that the political problems of the Arab–Israeli conflict could be solved by economic means alone. For the Arab world, the refugees symbolized the catastrophe which the creation of the state of Israel had brought upon the Palestinians. It was a question of principle to which, possibly, most of the Arab leaders at the time were committed; even if only ostensibly, they would not dare to desert it. Could a change in this stance be bought by financial aid? The Americans asserted that in the new Third World development was the prime objective which overshadowed, or rather in their minds, should have overshadowed, all other political goals. One still wonders today, whether any of the Third World leaders ever shared this objective or if it was not solely America's prime motive in its policy there. At the time under review, the Arab world was governed by an Ottomanized Arab élite, which certainly did not subscribe to a list of such foreign priorities. Thus, from the very beginning the American approach was doomed to failure.

This historical judgement should be balanced, however, by two additional factors. In our analysis of the Lausanne conference we have tried to show that the Americans were not the only ones who are to be blamed for its failure. Secondly, it should be realized that the American approach was not only guided by their wish to find a way out of the political deadlock, or to align the Middle East to the West. The Americans were the only ones who provided practical aid to the refugees. The refugees, who had been living in tents since the war, were looked after by volunteer aid organizations, mostly American. These organizations were running out of money and good-will and had decided to leave the area at the end of 1948. By April 1949, there were hardly any organizations taking care of the refugees, who had already gone through a very difficult winter but with undiminished hopes for repatriation.[87] Therefore, the financial problem was high on the American list and directly concerned their budget.

The tragic aspect of the American actions during the last days of Lausanne lay not so much in their proposing a new memorandum which shifted the focus to economic solutions, but rather in the fact that the State Department instead of turning the memorandum into another protocol which could reiterate the success of May, was content with eliciting the agreement of Israel and the Arab states for the dispatch of a group of experts to the Middle East, before any conclusions concerning the next stage had been reached.

This course of action enabled the Israelis to accept a new document which *prima facie* seemed harmful to their interests, but which actually marked the end of a very uncomfortable period for Israel. The scheduled General Assembly, which was to discuss a new peace plan for the conflict based on the PCC's finding, was prevented from taking any practical measures until the conclusions of the economic report had been submitted. Israel thereby gained precious time and a break from the American pressure. The Arab and Palestinian delegates on the other hand lost the initiative and were to adopt a rejectionist position for a very long period.

The Arab delegates agreed to the dispatch of an economic survey group, since they also did not wish to risk an open confrontation with the Americans. With the tacit consent of everyone concerned it was now left to economic experts to solve the problem. The end result of this experiment was to be the United Nations Relief and Work Agency (UNRWA), a body which left the refugees stranded in camps, unemployed and without any hope for a solution to their problem.

The cessation of the Lausanne conference meetings until the presentation of the economic survey had in effect ended the conference, which now appears to have been a premature decision. Not so much because of the PCC's own effort, but rather because of American pressure, Lausanne had after all caused a change in the Israeli attitude, brought about a grudging Israeli consent to the principle of repatriation, and elicited an Arab agreement to the partition resolution of November 1947. All these achievements now went by the wayside. It is possible that nothing would have come from a prolonged conference, but it is by now a historical truism to say that the Lausanne avanue to peace was not fully explored.

The PCC tried to induce the parties to join in a concluding declaration about Lausanne before officially declaring the conference ended. The draft declaration suggested an Arab and Israeli consent to tie the problems of resettlement and repatriation to the financial question. In other words, the PCC wanted the two sides to promise a more flexile approach if it succeeded in extracting the necessary funds for projects of resettlement and repatriation. The draft declaration also recorded a consent by Jordan and Syria to resettle all refugees that would not be repatriated to Israel.[88] However, the economic mission went on its way before the signature of such a document was secured – which meant that the Lausanne conference ended without any concluding remarks whatsoever.

The peace efforts had now come to a showdown. American pressure subsided and even those in Israel who, like Sharett and Sasson, had had some faith in multilateral negotiations, adhered now to the idea that peace was possible without external mediation. The intellectual game played by the Americans was in a way the bankruptcy of UN mediation, and every politician in the Middle East watched it unfold with amazement. In September 1949, during the last days of the Lausanne conference, Sasson summarized his arguments against any future Israeli readiness to accept external mediation, and it is possible that at that stage Sharett tended to agree with him: 'The five months of work I spent in Lausanne taught me that any foreign mediation – and be it the best, the most unbiased and the most objective – if it wished, will have to, even with the best intentions, ask us for concessions on the refugee, frontiers and peace questions – something we must absolutely resist.' Foreign mediation, added Sasson, only stiffened the Arab position.[89] Abba Eban supported this analysis, and it seems that after Lausanne so did Sharett and the rest of the Israeli Foreign Office.[90]

The Lausanne conference ended on 14 September, 1949 having made no progress. The PCC resumed its negotiations at Lake Success, New York, the following month. Under American guidance, it now concentrated on two questions: the refugee problem and the future of Jerusalem. The end of the conference also marked the acquiescence of the outside world in the territorial status quo. This recognition was officially granted in the Tripartite Declaration of May 1950. The declaration was mainly a manifestation of Anglo-American co-operation and co-ordination of policy against what was seen as Russian intransigence. The declaration, therefore, had very little impact on the peace process although it was intended to encourage an end to the Arab–Israeli conflict. In June the Israeli foreign minister declared that 'it was a cause of regret that readiness to conclude a lasting peace was not among the conditions set (in the declaration)'.[91] The declaration was a tacit admission of the world's reconciliation with Ben Gurion's *fait accompli* policy, whereby Israel's frontiers after the 1948 war were determined by the position of the armies at the cessation of hostilities, and not through negotiations.

THE FAILURE OF THE CONFERENCE

It is possible to discern two main reasons for the failure of the conference. One stems from the uncompromising Israeli attitude and the other from the equivocal Arab behaviour. One might add to these the way the PCC members went about their task, not always adequately fulfilling the role of conciliators and quite often concerned more with their personal careers than with the advancement of peace.

Prior to the Lausanne conference, the Israeli government had met together to set out the policy it was to present there. The major question was the centrality in the overall context of the Arab–Israeli conflict of the Jewish–Hashemite partition agreement. Most of the Israeli cabinet ministers considered this agreement (which had been built into the armistice accord with Jordan), a more than adequate solution by itself to the protracted Palestine conflict; any other initiative including an international conference of the Lausanne variety, was liable to do only damage. Led by Ben Gurion, these ministers had demanded the continuation of Israeli–Jordanian negotiations alongside the Lausanne talks, without the knowledge of the UN and without the participation of other Arab parties. Such talks, Ben Gurion hoped, would consolidate the armistice accord into a bilateral agreement.[92]

When, at the end of the armistice talks between Israel and Jordan, King Abdullah sought an immediate peace dialogue ignoring the Lausanne conference, Ben Gurion voiced his whole-hearted consent for such a joint policy. Sharett, by contrast, was willing to postpone negotiations with Jordan for as long as the Lausanne talks continued, hoping, so it seems, to keep all options open.[93] Ben Gurion prejudged Lausanne as a waste of time, and was only willing to support bilateral talks with the Arab countries, Jordan in particular. Even before the conference opened, Ben Gurion and Eliahu Sasson, deputy head of the Israeli delegation to

Lausanne and at the same time the chief negotiator with Jordan, agreed that 'the key to peace with the Arab world is our agreement to cede the Arab part of western Palestine to Abdullah'.[94]

The opposing approaches of the two Israeli leaders to the Lausanne conference stemmed from their differing atittudes toward international frameworks in general. Sharett was willing to seek a solution to the Palestine problem within an international forum.[95] Ben Gurion, on the other hand, tended to play down the value of forums such as Lausanne to the point of contempt. His uncompromising attitude towards the UN was shared by many in the Arab world. After all, none of the Arab states had sent a prime minister to the third or the fourth session of the UN General Assembly. As Faris al-Khouri, the Syrian representative at the UN told the Egyptian newspaper, *al-Misri*: 'I am ashamed to appear in the UN.'[96]

Ben Gurion's disparaging attitude towards the Lausanne conference originated in factors other than his attitude to the UN. In the period under discussion the establishment of peace does not appear to have been the prime minister's main concern; his initiatives therefore were fully congruent with Abba Eban's assessment of the Israeli viewpoint: 'There's no need to run after peace. The armistice is enough for us. If we pursue peace, the Arabs will demand a price of us – borders or refugees or both. Let us wait a few years.'[97] The incumbent prime minister instead accorded top priority to improving Israel's economic position and absorbing the flow of immigrants from Eastern Europe and the Arab countries. For Ben Gurion the armistice accord guaranteed Israel a breathing space to enable it to handle these very urgent matters.

To some Israeli contemporaries this position of Ben Gurion seemed absurd. Although not referring to the prime minister by name, Eliahu Sasson said as much in the following report to Moshe Sharett:

> The Jews think they can achieve peace without paying any price, maximal or minimal. They want to achieve: (a) Arab surrender of all areas occupied today by Israel; (b) Arab agreement to absorb all the refugees in the neighbouring countries; (c) Arab agreement to border modification in the centre, in the south and in the Jerusalem area to Israel's exclusive advantage; (d) the relinquishing by the Arabs of their

assets and property in Israel in exchange for compensation which would be evaluated by the Jews alone and which would be paid, if at all, over a number of years after the attainment of peace; (e) de facto and de jure recognition by the Arabs of the state of Israel and its new frontiers; (f) Arab agreement to the immediate establishment of diplomatic and economic relations between their countries and Israel etc. etc.[98]

Nevertheless, Israel felt compelled to attend the Lausanne conference. It was first of all the only way the Jewish state could ensure its admission to the UN. Moreover, since the Americans were the life and soul of the conference. Israel's refusal to participate would have severely damaged its relationship with the United States. One should also not underrate the genuine hope of Sharett and Sasson to advance the peace process at Lausanne. As the conference drew nearer Sharett devised an alternative to the 'Greater Transjordan option', which he hoped to use in negotiations with the Palestinian delegates at Lausanne to establish an independent state on the West Bank. The Israeli foreign minister's support of Israeli–Palestinian negotiations therefore originated in his conscious preference for an Israeli–Palestinian agreement to an Israeli–Jordanian one. By adopting such an attitude, Sharett undermined the Jewish–Hashemite understanding and clashed with Ben Gurion, for whom this understanding formed the cornerstone of Israeli policy.[99]

To this analysis of the Israeli attitude towards Lausanne the impression gained by the head of the American delegation to the talks, Mark Ethridge, adds a further angle:

> If there is to be any assessment of blame for stalemate at Lausanne, Israel must accept primary responsibility. Commission members, particularly the United States representative, have consistently pointed out to the Israeli Prime Minister, Foreign Minister and delegation that the key to peace is some Israeli concession on refugees.[100]

In contrast, we have comments about Ethridge's own part in the failure of the conference from James McDonald, who recalls Ethridge as the most inexperienced of all the commission's members in Middle Eastern affairs. In McDonald's eyes, it was this lack of expertise on Ethridge's part which led to the conference's failure since he lost his patience at a very early stage of the negotiatons.[101]

But Israel's negative attitude was not the only obstacle in the path of peace. In his summary of the conference, for instance, Sasson cast the blame on the member states themselves. He asserted that the representatives of France, Turkey and the USA were attempting to utilize their participation in the conference in order to reinforce their respective countries position in the Arab world.[102] However, since their governments had access to more effective means and opportunities for improving such relations, it seems more likely that those representatives were seeking to further their own personal careers in these negotiations.

On the Arab side, the crux of the matter lies with their representatives' inability or unwillingness to declare publicly what they had promised or even agreed upon privately. This became the stumbling block not only at the multilateral forum but even at the bilateral discussions. Indeed, Mark Ethridge, who in the end was to be so critical of the Israelis, was at first annoyed with this pervasive feature of Arab behaviour. In a letter to Marshall, he noted that while the Arab delegations were privately declaring their intention to resettle the refugees, they refused to do so publicly.[103]

To this we should add the Israeli perceptions of, and dissatisfaction with, the Arab position in Lausanne. The Israelis found it unacceptable that they should concede territory, as demanded by the Egyptians and Jordanians, after the Arabs had waged a war against the Jewish state. In Tel Aviv, these demands together with the Arab insistence on repatriation as a condition for a peace settlement, were tantamount to the absence of a genuine will for peace on the Arab side.

One could argue that what stifled a public Arab declaration was the leaders' apprehension of their 'public opinion'. While the usefulness of this term is questionable, in regimes which were at best quasi-democratic and at worst autocratic monarchies, it is difficult to deny the impact of the Arab press and of mass demonstrations on the Arab politicians of those days. One discerns genuine fear for their own lives in the verbatim reports of the conversations they had with British, American and Israeli officials, not entirely unjustified when one realizes that three Arab leaders were indeed assassinated owing to the unpopularity of their foreign or domestic policies: Riad al-Sulh, King Abdullah and Mahmud Nuqrashi.

It might be expected, therefore, that the appearance of a united Arab front in a multilateral forum would help soothe Arab public resentment resulting from agrements with Israel. This seemed to have been the case in the armistice negotiations at Rhodes. In our opinion, one of the primary reasons for the success of the Rhodes negotiations was the approval it had of the Arab League. In many ways this formula was repeated in Lausanne. The Arab League demanded, and the PCC accepted, that a united Arab delegation would be sent to Lausanne, although as we have seen, each Arab country instructed its own member on the joint delegation to pursue individual interests and policies. These delegates eventually were able to dictate the joint Arab position that was approved in retrospect by the Arab League. This Arab position corresponded to the PCC's perception of Lausanne as a comprehensive peace conference and the Arab delegates did agree to discuss and even made concessions in all the three areas which composed the final settlement in Palestine. For the Arabs it was a conference of *Sulh*, (peace) as *al-Ahram* had put it.[104] The peace conference, however, was too short-lived to fully exhaust the opportunity it opened.

To our mind, the Lausanne conference offered a unique opportunity to resolve the Arab–Israeli conflict, but since it was never fully exploited it is impossible to say whether or not it was, historically, a missed opportunity: to this very day Israeli and Arab delegates have never met again in such a broad forum to discuss such crucial topics as the status of Jerusalem or the fate of the Palestinian refugees, which formed the focus of Lausanne.

10

The Final Quest for Peace

THE PERPETUATION OF THE REFUGEE PROBLEM

On 23 August 1949 the PCC announced the establishment of the Economic Survey Mission (ESM) as a subsidiary body under its authority. Gordon Clapp, the chairman of the board of directors of the Tennessee Valley Authority, was appointed as the mission's chairman, with Sir Desmond Morton of the British Foreign Office as his deputy. They were assisted by Turkish and French officials. The mission was charged with studying the economic situation in the countries affected by the war in Palestine and looking for solutions to the economic dislocations created by the war. Furthermore, it was given the authority to recommend ways of facilitating the repatriation, resettlement and economic and social rehabilitation of the Palestinian refugees and payment of compensation according to the provisions of the UN resolution of December 1948. Finally, the Economic Survey Mission was asked to look for means of promoting economic conditions conducive to the maintenance of peace and stability in the area.

The ESM produced an interim and a final report. These reports did not differ much in substance as the mission arrived at its conclusion after only two months of work. The interim report, published in November 1949, was sufficient to indicate that the economic approach was doomed to fail. It conceded that as long as the political stalemate continued, there was little hope of repatriation or large-scale resettlement. However, this report starts from the premise that all the political hurdles would be somehow overcome, its basic assumption being that the Arab governments were seeking foreign aid in order to carry out large development projects. The report suggested that the Western world should condition future financial assistance upon Arab readiness to include the resettlement of the refugees in their development projects.

It was optimistically assumed in the report that declaring resettlement a 'development project', meant that it would automatically contribute to the rise in the standard of living of the host countries. 'Rise in standard of living' in the 1940s and 1950s was a euphemistic term for the emergence of pro-Western regimes able to resist Communist threats and Russian penetration. This formula, equating economic growth and affluence with pro-Western tendencies and policies, first used by the Americans in their European Recovery Programme after the Second World War, characterized the activities of the Americans until the late 1960s, if not beyond.

The report specified the exact way in which resettlement would be involved in development. The refugees were to be employed in public works such as building the infrastructure for their future villages. Thus engaged in 'productive' work such as reclaiming the land, laying the irrigation systems, expanding the road network, erecting the sanitation layout and so on, they would be building their future homes and at the same time contributing to the welfare of the host country.

But until such an ideal time, and given the fact that the political deadlock was far from having been solved, ESM had some practical advice and suggestions. Aware of the voluntary organizations' disinclination to continue working and collecting funds for the refugees, the mission was looking for a new source of relief and recommended that until the end of 1950 the UN, from its own budget, would finance the relief programmes – after which date the responsibility would fall on the Arab governments. In the meantime the UN would conduct a census in order to determine and withdraw from the payrolls those people, estimated at 200,000, who undeservedly had benefited in the past from the relief funds. Without those 'fictitious' refugees, the Arab governments were supposed to provide for a total of about 750,000 'genuine' refugees.

Moreover, so that the refugees would bring some advantage to their host country, they would be integrated for the time being in the local work-force. Yet, the report admitted that given the limited employment opportunities in the Arab countries, only about 80,000 refugees could be expected to find jobs.[1] In practice, the refugees who were offered jobs in the Arab countries in the early 1950s were used as cheap labour mainly in communication and transport projects, whereas it would have been better to allow them to develop the camps, which now stood in an appalling state.

In all, most of the interim report's suggestions, plans and forecasts remained on paper – the refugees stayed in the camps, and the principal and only operative outcome of the report was its final recommendation for the establishment of UNRWA, the United Nations Relief and Work Agency for the Palestine refugees, an agency that was intended to supervise relief and employment projects and at the same time continue to contemplate resettlement.

In Washington the report disappointed many officials in the State Department, whose experts on Middle Eastern affairs expected trouble. Together with the American diplomats in the area they held a conference in Istanbul at the end of 1949, where the interim report was one of the many issues discussed. Almost everyone displayed dissatisfaction with the report, stating as its main problem that it would be 'handicapped at the start in certain states because of ESM's connection with the PCC and the Palestinian problem'.[2] In the eyes of the American Middle East experts the report failed to extricate the solution of the refugee problem from the context of the Palestine problem; that is, they felt that the heads of the mission had not brought the economic approach to its logical conclusion, and they demanded an even stronger emphasis on a purely economic approach recommending that the pilot development projects be separated – at least in the public's mind – from the refugee problem and the PCC. Needless to say, while their views departed from the terms of reference of the ESM they coincided with the views of George McGhee. However, they were even more mistaken than the report in their perception of the nature of the problem at hand – the refugee problem was above all a political question.

In London, on the other hand, most of the senior diplomats greeted the report with satisfaction. The Foreign Office believed that through a joint effort the British government and the American administration could work out a list of pilot projects which would prove the benefits of resettlement to both the refugees and the host countries. Not everyone on the British side, however, was equally happy with the report. Sir Alec Kirkbride and the pro-Hashemites in the Foreign Office in particular were highly dismayed by it. They claimed that by not offering concrete settlement solutions for the refugees, ESM had left most of the refugees where they were, that is in Jordan (including the West Bank). The risk of the Palestinization of Jordan was a nightmare for Sir Alec Kirkbride and others within the Foreign Office. But these gloomy views were not shared by his superiors in London and, altogether, Morton was commended for his 'excellent' work.[3]

Immediately after the publication of the report the British and American governments conferred on the next step to be taken. The Americans suggested that since Iraq possessed the greatest possibilities, the two powers should press the Baghdad government to resettle the largest possible number of refugees. Though the British in principle agreed with this, they did not wish to alienate one of the few countries still loyal to Britain in an increasingly hostile area. The Foreign Office suggested that Britain should not even discuss the matter with the Iraqis, let alone pressure them.[4] Nevertheless, the office was pleased to note that the Americans were interested in Iraq and not in Jordan. In fact, at those meetings and during the Istanbul conference the Americans for the first time gave their official blessing to the incorporation of Arab Palestine within Transjordan – McGhee told the conference that the incorporation would help to solve both the refugee problem and the conflict itself.[5]

Meanwhile, the ESM members continued to tour the area and conduct discussions with the governments of the Arab states and Israel. After three further months of work they submitted a final report at the end of 1949. In this report the mission spoke in more sober terms and there was no trace of the optimistic mood that had characterized the interim report. It began with an admission of the mission's failure to solve the refugee problem by purely economic methods. 'Economic development cannot by itself make peace' since 'where the political will to peace is lacking', economic solutions had little meaning.[6]

In the final analysis, the report discussed in only academic terms the long-range economic development prospects in the Middle East. It noted in particular that Israel and Egypt could be left out of this effort since Israel had already begun to develop an irrigation system and 'to employ modern agriculture methods, while possessing the scientific infrastructure required for development', and as to Egypt, 'the knowledge and skill available in that country are already on high level'.[7]

As regards other Arab countries, the report had almost nothing new to offer. It excluded the immediate possibility of large projects in Syria, Jordan and Iraq, owing to the scarcity of capital, skills, research facilities, governmental organization, and administrative infrastructure. Instead, for those countries and for Lebanon it recommended limited pilot projects, aimed mainly at the improvement in the exploitation of water resources.

On the technical level, the mission recommended the curtailment of the UN relief operations and transferring responsibility for these to the Arab governments. Those governments willing to take upon themselves relief operations were advised to begin programmes of public works which, it was hoped, would improve the productivity of the area through absorption of unemployed refugees.

As for UNRWA, it was decided that this organization would come into the world on or after 1 April 1950 and would be given full autonomy and decision-making authority, the agency was to operate until the end of June 1951, then to be re-examined by the General Assembly. This, suggested the report, might provide the opportunity to remove 400,000 refugees from the relief payrolls.

ESM's conclusions, as we shall see, were void of any practical relevance – all it did was, first, to enhance the American concept of a purely economic solution for the problem and then to question it without offering any alternative suggestions.

Though the mission itself was welcomed by the countries involved, its report was rejected out of hand and widely condemned both in Israel and the Arab countries. In Israel, the press argued that the report encouraged Arab intransigence as it did not emphasize resettlement. Opposition in the Arab world was particularly strong in those countries which the report had designated as having a potential economic infrastructure for absorbing the refugees. The Arab Palestine press demanded that the Arab world must refuse to endorse the report as it would jeopardize the right of return, and condemned the mission for not placing the responsibility clearly on Israel's shoulders.[8]

The only legacy of the report is UNRWA, which exists to this day. As mentioned, ESM intended it to be a temporary relief agency and yet, until today no one has found a replacement for it: nor did UMRWA itself ever venture to put forward suggestions for resettlement or development programmes that in the first place were to benefit the refugees. The powers whose brain-child UNRWA had been gradually abandoned their responsibility for it and soon lost interest in the agency, although the Americans continued to show a rather keen interest, during the early 1950s, in the financial and practical aspects of the problem – providing most of UNRWA's budget and introducing schemes for resettlement of the refugees.[9] By then, however, the Arab governments were firmly rejecting any initiative related to the refugee problem which did not recommend complete repatriation.

When UNRWA concluded its first year of work, not one refugee had been settled. In fact, the number of destitute refugees had increased. Discussion of resettlement possibilities was cut short early on when Britain and the USA agreed to concentrate on short-term development programmes rather than long-term ones. The experts on both sides no longer mentioned resettlement or repatriation as viable solutions: short-term development programmes meant that the best the refugees could hope for from now on was relief. In the words of the ESM final report: 'The region is not ready for resettlement, and to press forward on such a course is to pursue folly and frustration and thereby delay sound economic growth.'[10] Development projects did ensue eventually in the Arab world, but not because of the ESM report – they became the cornerstone in the policies of the new nationalist leaders who liberated their countries from foreign rule in the 1950s. These development projects, however, did very little to relieve the plight of the Palestinian refugees.

For their part, the refugees refused to partake in the work projects out of fear that participation would prejudice their right and chances of repatriation. Those few who were employed contributed more to their host countries than to themselves. Paradoxically, instead of being made more self-supporting, they became more dependent on the UN, since the organization became their employer as well as their provider. According to UNRWA's working contracts, skilled workers among the refugees who participated in development works were supposed to acquire their host country's nationality. UNRWA's reports of 1951 and 1952 reveal that very few Arab countries complied with this provision. In fact, it seems that only Iraq (apart from Jordan) was prepared to accept a small number of refugees as its citizens.

As the first annual UNRWA report concluded, the UN was held responsible by the refugees for their past and present misfortune, and their inevitably bleak future.[11] By November 1950, when the first report was published, Britain no longer played a leading role in the relief organization. The Americans remained very active throughout the early 1950s. A new terminology – reintegration and rehabilitation were the favourite terms – accompanied the works of the energetic American officials dealing with refugee problems in Washington, but it did very little to ease the misery of the refugees, who after an ESM estimate of 750,000 at the end of 1949, by the end of 1951 had increased to a total of 950,000.[12] Part of the problem was UNRWA's limited budget – apart from the Americans no other country was willing to contribute substantial funds to an organization that needed at least $80 million a year just for the relief work and payrolls.[13]

The UN took some interest in the matter in November 1950, when the Political Committee of the organization discussed the refugee problem. The result was a draft resolution tabled by Britain, the USA, Turkey and France, suggesting the establishment of a UN reintegration fund for the Palestinian refugees with a budget of $50 million. The General Assembly approved this resolution and added to it a Pakistani amendment reiterating the UN commitment to repatriation.[14]

The funds were finally recruited throughout 1951. The American administration passed a new foreign-aid bill providing financial assistance to various projects, including $50 million to the refugees.[15] The quid pro quo was total American control over the UN action for the refugees. The UN, without much hesitation, confirmed this American monopoly in yet another General Assembly resolution of May 1951. The PCC which at least on paper continued to exist until the late 1950s, formed a new Refugee Office for the administration and distribution of the American funds to UNRWA and for other projects.[16]

While money was allocated and UN debates lingered on, the situation in the camps worsened. With prospects for resettlement gone, many refugees who tried to find work and accommodation in towns and villages were driven back to the camps, since only there were they entitled to a relief grant.[17] The obvious increase in the refugee population in the camps was noted by UNRWA's officials in the summer of 1951, and the refugees were assisted in building mud huts which became the symbol and familiar characteristic of the camps – and remain so to the present day.

The year 1952 was marked by the enthusiastic rhetoric of the American head of UNRWA, James Blandford. Blandford tried to revive schemes for resettlement, and Damascus and the Sinai were only two of the many venues he suggested for his ambitious plans, into which he tried to induce the countries concerned by means of bilateral agreements with the USA. President Truman was in favour of these plans (since they could have advanced American penetration in the area), as was the PCC. As none of the plans included Israel, in Tel Aviv and Jerusalem government and Foreign Office officials expressed satisfaction. But no one in the Arab world was any longer prepared to discuss such ideas.[18] The Arab League in response called on the Arab countries to resettle refugees near the border with Israel awaiting the day of return.[19]

In the years that followed, UNRWA tried to introduce other resettlement schemes. For example, in 1953 to 1956 in the Yarmuk valley, where the Jordanians co-operated in transferring some refugees from the West Bank to the hinterland. In 1959 similar resettlement plans were offered, only to meet with Arab rejection, but there was a complete absence of any mention of repatriation. The resultant bitterness and frustration in the camps was the fertile ground from which the PLO would emerge, and with it the revival of Palestinian nationalism.

At the same time as the ESM was trying unsuccessfully, to come forward with possible solutions for the refugee problem, another UN body, the Trusteeship Council, was attempting to introduce a settlement of the Jerusalem question – with similar consequences.

NO PEACE FOR JERUSALEM

The outside world had been persistent in its attitude to Jerusalem's future since the First World War, some would argue even since the Crimean War. A holy city for the three monotheistic religions, Jerusalem was regarded as an international area, one that ought to be excluded from the direct sovereignty of any of the local states. The League of Nations deviated from this approach when it put Jerusalem within the British mandate, but the British themselves and the UN since its foundation in 1945 stressed again the necessity of granting Jerusalem a special status. Hence, it was only natural that the UN partition resolution included a clause calling for the establishment of a Corpus Separatum in Jerusalem.

When the Political Committee of the UN heard of Israel's declaration of independence, it had tried to recruit a majority in the General Assembly for the imposition of a temporary international regime in Jerusalem. This initiative had failed, but the UN had been able to maintain a representative body in the city – the Trusteeship Council, composed of the American, French and Belgian consuls there.[20]

As mediator, Count Folke Bernadotte had attempted a fresh approach in his first proposals when he allocated the city to the Arab Palestinian state. However, this had been resented not only by the Israelis but also by the rest of the world, and in his final report he adhered to the principle of the internationalization of the city. This same approach was adopted by the UN General Assembly in its resolution of 11 December 1948. The General Assembly resolved that: 'The city of Jerusalem ... should be treated separately and should be placed under effective UN control with maximum feasible local autonomy for its Arab and Jewish communities, with full safeguards for the protection of the holy places and sites and free access to them and for religious freedom.'[21]

However, even before this resolution was adopted, the Israelis and the Jordanians had taken irreversible steps. Already in August 1948 they had divided the city between themselves and consolidated this partition later in the armistice accord in April 1949. Hence, when the Lausanne conference was convened, there existed already an official Israeli–Jordanian agreement determining the future of the city. The Americans, as ever, directed the Lausanne participants to seek solutions regardless of the *faits accomplis* and the actual situation they were confronted with. The American team persuaded the Conciliation Commission to devise its own solution for the future of the city.

In fact, it is possible to say that the PCC adhered to the principles set by the UN partition resolution of November 1947. In that, the commission enjoyed the full support of most of the UN member states. The Arab states, apart from Jordan, joined the others in giving their backing to internationalization. The historian Arif al-Arif explains that this was done out of fear that otherwise the city would fall into Jewish hands; nor did the Arab states wish to see a Hashemite rule over the third holiest city for Islam.[22] This wide consensus threatened the Israeli–Jordanian accord.

The PCC's main problem was thus a joint Israeli–Jordanian front against the internationalization of the city. Both Israel and Jordan used much the same arguments to justify their control over their part of the city. Both claimed that without partition one of the two parties would inevitably have tried to occupy the whole of the city, forcing the other to give in on a highly emotional issue and a national asset.[23]

Unofficially, but in very strong terms, the Jordanian opposition to internationalization was supported by the British government. This did not help the Israelis in their attempt to present a similar position, since the Americans regarded them and not the Jordanians as the stumbling block on the way to internationalization, an allegation that left Israel quite isolated *vis-à-vis* a world consensus – a situation incurred by all successive Israeli governments who refused to give in on this point. Since Jerusalem's future was a matter of considerarble moral and ideological importance to the Jewish people, the Israelis were and are willing to bear the global condemnation and have more than once defied international opinion by words and deeds. The American position, for instance, was greatly affected by Israel's immediate response to the UN decision on internationalization, which they decided to counter by turning Jerusalem into the official seat of the government and later into Israel's capital. Only Sharett felt this immediate reaction was unwarranted and as long as he was foreign minister, the Foreign Office remained in Tel Aviv. He and some other officials were even willing to consent to some form of internationalization in order to appease world public opinion. Keeping the Foreign Office in Tel Aviv was also a tactical move which eased matters for the foreign diplomats whose governments did not recognize Israel's sovereignty over Jerusalem.[24] But the official line was strong opposition to the idea of internationalization, a line which to this day feeds the Israeli consensus on the future of the city.

In order to confront the Israeli policy the officials in Washington entrusted the task of devising a plan of internationalization to the PCC. The commission discussed the issue from April until September 1949 and published a plan in which it suggested handing the administrative and municipal responsibilities over to the Jordanians and the Israelis in their respective parts, but leaving the city itself under international sovereignty. An international body, which was not described by the PCC in name, was to represent the UN as the sovereign of the city.[25]

The Israelis reacted swiftly by declaring their part of the city the capital of Israel whereas, by contrast, the Jordanians refrained from issuing any public declarations and confined their activity to an attempt to persuade London to do its utmost to postpone the implementation of, or even repudiate, the PCC plan.[26] In this the

Jordanians turned out to be quite successful as the British government convinced the Americans to delay the submission of this plan to the United Nations General Assembly. The British were supported by the American Defense Department which noted that the establishment of an international enclave in Jerusalem would require the formation of an international force. Such a force, warned the military men in the American administration, might include Russian troops which in turn would be 'prejudicial to our national security'.[27] However, Britain's associates in the Commonwealth, the Australians, decided to act independently and submitted a draft resolution to the Political Committee of the UN calling for the creation of a Corpus Separatum in the city of Jerusalem.[28]

The Political Committee decided to refer the problem to the Trusteeship Council which it instructed to prepare a detailed plan along the lines of the PCC suggestions.[29] The General Assembly granted its blessing to the new arbitrators in its resolution from 9 December 1949. All delegations voted in favour of the resolution apart from three conspicuous delegations who opposed it: the British, the Americans and the Israelis. The Jordanians would probably have joined them had they been members of the organization, but fortunately for them they did not have to appear in a vote against the general Arab and, in this case, world public opinion.[30]

It might be useful to point out that by all accounts the discussion was not a heated one – Jerusalem was not a topic high on the agenda of the international community and the UN Secretariat hoped that at least on this score it would be possible to reach a consensus. In his memoirs Ben Gurion reveals that a genuine effort was made by some UN members in order to elicit a more favourable Israeli position. According to his version, the Lebanese representative in the UN together with his Russian colleague had suggested amendments to the resolution in order to moderate the Israeli opposition. The Lebanese declared this intention in a speech in front of the General Assembly. However, as Ben Gurion put it: for Israel to accept any form of internationalization would have been the betrayal of the very essence of Zionism.[31]

The Trusteeship Council held its discussions in Geneva at the beginning of 1950. The President of the Council, the Frenchman Roger Garreau, drafted a plan based on the PCC suggestions and which proposed once more the transformation of the Jerusalem area into a Corpus Separatum. The plan was supported by the Political Committee of the UN.[32]

However, the Garreau plan, like the schemes before it and the plans and resolutions that were to follow it in the 1950s, was doomed to fail, owing to the Israeli and Jordanian, and to some extent the British, opposition which made UN implementation impossible. No less important was the American reluctance to provide troops for an international force whose formation was a prerequisite for the success of any plan for the internationalization of Jerusalem.

The ineffectiveness of the UN action induced the Jordanians and the Israelis to try again to reach a more substantial understanding over the future of post-mandatory Palestine, and in the years 1950 to 1951 a final attempt was made. Its failure and that of the PCC marked the end of the peace efforts in the wake of the 1948 war.

ONE-MAN'S AMBITION: THE ISRAELI–JORDANIAN PEACE NEGOTIATIONS

The Israeli–Jordanian armistice agreement marked the end of major military operations between the two countries. The agreement provided both sides with two possible channels for direct negotiations: the Mixed Armistice Committee, formed with the aim of supervising the implementation of the agreement, and the special committee on Jerusalem intended to formulate plans regarding freedom of access to the city and its holy places.

In those two committees the future of Jerusalem was the main topic discussed throughout 1949. The Israelis urged the Jordanians to implement the commitment they had given in the armistice agreement to allow freedom of access to Mount Scopus and the Jewish quarter in the Old City, such Jordanian co-operation would have indicated that Abdullah was sincere in his desire to reach a bilateral peace agreement. However, it seems that by the end of 1949 Abdullah's ability to pursue his own policy had considerably weakened. His government showed its displeasure with the armistice agreement by laying obstacles on the king's way to peace with Israel. Since their representatives, and not Abdullah's envoys, were conducting the talks in the armistice committees, the ministers were doing their utmost to slow down the implementation of the armistice agreement. There was little Abdullah could do

– the committee meetings were public and it would have been dangerous and unwise to openly confront his ministers, especially with the rest of the Arab world closely watching him and eagerly awaiting his downfall.[33]

There was only one way out of the deadlock, and this was the resumption of unofficial secret negotiations with Israel. After five months of useless and futile negotiations in the committees, Abdullah approached the Israelis in October 1949, offering them another round of direct contacts with his personal envoys. Abdullah's message was clear: it was not the administrative problems of Jerusalem which had bothered him – these were tactical questions that would easily be solved; what was needed now was an understanding in principle about the future of post-mandatory Palestine. The Jordanian king seemed to be possessed with a fear that unless official Israeli consent for the annexation of the West Bank was given, his newly acquired kingdom now containing both banks was in grave danger. Moreover, Abdullah regarded an agreement with Israel as a *sine qua non* for the success of his plans to unify both banks of the river under his rule. Very few in Jordan viewed matters in the same manner. Sir Alec Kirkbride and Prime Minister Tawfiq Abu al-Huda saw no point in resuming direct contacts with the Israelis before the completion of the formal union. They warned the king that another round of talks with the Israelis would be a political blunder that could only complicate the process of unification and even render it virtually impossible. Kirkbride in particular apprehended that the king's policy would arouse the indignation of the Palestinian population already infuriated by the loss of the Little Triangle. The Palestinians, owing to Abdullah's own policy of ostensible democratization, were represented, since July 1949, in the Jordanian government by three ministers, who had been appointed to strengthen Abdullah's claim to represent the Palestinian people and their cause. Kirkbride and Abu al-Huda asserted that the ministers' co-operation would not go beyond the acceptance of the armistice agreement. In short, Abdullah found himself alone more than ever in his attempt to overcome the deadlock in the negotiations. But, since peace with Israel in his eyes was essential for the survival of his Greater Jordan, he was willing to confront both the domestic and the Arab opposition he was facing.

In order to circumvent his obstinate prime minister, the king appointed Samir al-Rifa'i as special minister to the palace, giving him a status equal to that of his prime minister. Al-Rifa'i, unlike Abu al-Huda, was more inclined to carry out the king's plans and wishes without pursuing his own policy. As a sign of protest Abu al-Huda left the kingdom for two months, thereby playing into the king's hands as this allowed Abdullah to operate unhindered.[34]

Abdullah's eagerness, however, was not reciprocated by the Israelis. As stressed before, the priorities of the state of Israel had changed during the course of 1949. The armistice agreements had brought relative calm to the borders and establishing formal peace was no longer a first priority. The government was now preoccupied with absorbing new immigrants and trying to overcome economic difficulties. It seems that Israeli policy-makers were more or less satisfied with the *modus vivendi* that had been reached in the relationship with their Arab neighbours.

Nevertheless, contacts continued, and the Israelis engaged in the negotiations were highly impressed by the king's commitment to the peace process. They conveyed to their government the impression that Abdullah was prepared and would know how to overcome both domestic and foreign opposition to his policy.[35]

In the negotiations of December 1949, the discussion between the two sides evolved around Jordan's request for a land corridor to the Mediterranean through Israeli territory. After a few days, on 15 December, the parties signed a document entitled 'Political Questions and Territorial Changes' in which Israel granted its formal consent to such a corridor, which was to connect Hebron in the West Bank with the Gaza Strip. This was certainly not a marginal issue as its implemention called for a peaceful and cordial relationship between the two countries.[36]

However, when Samir al-Rifa'i brought the document to the Jordanian government in January 1950 for ratification, he discovered that he was the only one, among the ministers, who supported the sovereign's policies *vis-à-vis* Israel. The rest of the ministers, despite Abdullah's autocratic rule, were quite vociferous in their opposition to the attempt to reach a separate peace with Israel. Owing to his secret manoeuvres Abdullah had completely lost the confidence and co-operation of his ministers. While the government was fully behind him on the question of the union, it did not back him in his negotiations with Israel.[37]

Sir Alec Kirkbride found himself in between the two centres of power in the kingdom. He was driven into these straits not only because of his influential position in Amman but also owing to his own desire to hold the balance of power in the monarchy he had helped to create back in 1920. This was a very delicate position. It has created the impression among some writers that Kirkbride was bitterly opposed to the direct negotiations and that he was the main reason for their failure. All he did, in fact, was to side with the ministers in their attempt to check Abdullah's tendency to be over-anxious to go it alone and conclude a peace treaty with Israel, but he did not share their absolute opposition to such an agreement. Kirkbride advocated cautious progress towards peace, the practical outcome of which was that the king lost the counsel and blessing of his most important adviser in Jordan.[38]

After the Jordanian government refused to ratify the paper, the Israelis began to display growing signs of impatience. Shiloah, Ben Gurion's principal emissary to the talks, sent a letter to the king warning him that Israel would abandon the negotiations unless the Jordanian government approved the December 1949 document. The Israeli government wanted to move on with the negotiations and discuss a final agreement over the future of Jerusalem, so as to be able to consolidate the partition of the city before the UN completed its discussions on internationalization.[39]

Israeli anxiety about a possible change in Jerusalem's international status matched that of Abdullah. The Jordanian ruler, no less than the Israelis, was convinced of the necessity of reaching a bilateral understanding before the UN completed its discussions. In order to advance the negotiations, the king suggested at the beginning of January 1950 that Ben Gurion and al-Rifa'i should meet personally, hoping that the seniority of these two men would facilitate a rapid agreement. However, Ben Gurion, as he had done since 1947, left the negotiations with Abdullah to his aides, a tactic which shows something of the premier's disparaging attitude towards the king and also indicates the low priority he attached to peace at the time.[40]

The contact was nevertheless resumed in January 1950 in the winter palace in Shuneh. In the first meeting, the Israelis proposed that the two parties should form an anti-internationalization front in the UN against the attempt to exclude Jerusalem from the sovereignty of both countries. The Jordanian ministers who were present in the meeting rejected that proposal but consented to propose concrete and practical arrangements that would consolidate the *de facto* partition of the city.[41]

In February, the Israelis retreated from their earlier consent to a corridor and suggested that instead they would build a highway on which Jordanians would be allowed to pass freely. They also demanded, in return, that the Jordanians fulfil their obligation in the armistice agreement to concede Mount Scopus and the Jewish quarter in the Old City to Israel. While the king accepted both conditions, his ministers saw no reason for giving in to Israel's demands. They resented the king's submission and unanimously passed a formal resolution in the Amman cabinet refusing categorically to hand over to Israel any part of the Old City.[42]

The steadfastness of the Jordanian ministers was a reflection of their satisfaction with the smoothness of the annexation process. During 1949 important steps were taken to lift the barriers and remove the frontiers between the two banks of the river Jordan. In fact, short of a formal annexation, which would be declared only in April 1950, the West Bank to all intents and purposes was part of Jordan.[43] The Arab League, notwithstanding its strong verbal protestations, did very little to obstruct Jordan's efforts to absorb this part of Palestine. The ministers therefore saw no reason for continuing the rapprochement with Israel. Abdullah, on the other hand, was less troubled by the Arab world's reaction and more concerned lest Israel should retract from its earlier consent to Greater Transjordan. As we have seen, for Abdullah the only way of avoiding such an unfavourable development was by eliciting an official Israeli blessing for the annexation. The official union and the relatively mute Arab reaction did not change his view on this matter. This dispute between the king and his government was not motivated only by a difference in strategic thinking. It seems that the ministers used the negotiations with Israel as a tool in their struggle to gain more authority and power in a country hitherto ruled predominantly, or rather solely, by the Hashemite dynasty.

The Israelis, aware of Abdullah's difficulties with his government, proposed resorting to the former (clandestine and direct) way of negotiating with the king. This Abdullah gladly accepted and on 17 February 1950 he met Shiloah at Shuneh. He surprised his visitor by handing him a draft for a peace treaty with Israel. There were seven points in this plan: it included a suggestion for a five-year non-aggression pact; a proposal for free Israeli access to Scopus in return for Jordanian movement on the Bethlehem–Jerusalem road; it offered compensation to those citizens in Jerusalem whose property remained under the control of the other party; it asked in the vaguest terms, for an Israeli agreement to initiate a process of liquidating Arab property in Israel and Jewish property in the West Bank and, finally, it called for free trade between the two countries.[44]

The Israeli representatives, pleased with the draft agreement, gave their approval in principle, pending their government's consent. A jubilant Abdullah told Shiloah that he would replace his cabinet if it should oppose the agreement. One week later, representatives of both sides met to initial a draft treaty. It was probably owing to al-Rifa'i's influence that this draft treaty was accepted by the Jordanian government. Jordan's ministers accepted it with one reservation: the omission of the clause which called for the initiation of trade relations between the two countries.[45]

Abu al-Huda, however, decided to fight it with all his might. The Jordanian prime minister had the support of most of his ministers, who regretted their earlier consent, and had also succeeded in enlisting Kirkbride's backing. With the British representative behind him it was easy for Abu al-Huda to persuade the government to postpone the ratification of the agreement until after the official union of the two banks of the River Jordan. To Abdullah's great dismay, even his loyal ally Samir al-Rifa'i now deserted him, reversed his attitude and accepted Abu al-Huda's conditions. Al-Rifa'i must have realized that the king was quite alone on this issue, with both the British representative and all the Jordanian ministers against him.

Abu al-Huda's suggestion was very wisely devised. In 1949 Abdullah had already decided that the formal union of the two banks would be accompanied by general elections for the Lower House of the Jordanian Parliament – the House of Representatives – and by the selection of new senators to the Upper House – the Senate. The elections and the selection were to be carried out on a parity basis, i.e., equal representation to the West and East Banks. It was to be the first election in which the dramatic demographic changes that had taken place in Jordan were clearly reflected. The parity principle discriminated against the Palestinians in the West Bank, since they constituted two-thirds of the eligible voters. But even as an equal force to the East Bankers they were a significant voice in the kingdom, as long as the quasi-democratic features were intact (they would be totally abolished by King Husayn in 1957). The armistice agreement with Israel which allocated more

Palestinian territory and population to Israel was executed in June 1949. It led most Palestinians in the West Bank to vehemently oppose any agreement with Israel. Abu al-Huda knew, therefore, he could rely after the election on a parliament which would be even more anti-Israel in its attitude.[46] Thus it was decided, contrary to the king's wishes, to suspend the talks until after the elections.

The Israelis were told about the suspension and reluctantly agreed to wait until after the Jordanian elections. The Israeli government pleaded with the American government for external US financial and economic assistance to the Jordanians, so that Amman could be induced to ratify the agreement. However, the Americans were more interested in the PCC and even President Truman felt that his country should not be involved in this matter.[47] To this we may add that Abdullah's predicament was not financial or economic, it was a political problem.

After the Israeli papers reported the existence of direct Israeli–Jordanian contacts, rumours about the new draft pact began circulating throughout the Arab world. Consequently, Abdullah was exposed to heavy pressure from several Arab leaders. The Syrians warned him that they would close their joint border if Jordan were to continue negotiations with Israel. Ibn Saud threatened that the Arab world would 'build an impenetrable wall around Jordan'. The Arab League met in March 1950 and discussed the Israeli–Jordanian talks. At this conference which lasted until April, Abdullah was bitterly attacked.[48] The Egyptian delegation proposed to expel Jordan from the Arab League if it concluded a treaty with Israel. Owing to this Egyptian pressure, the Jordanian voted in favour of a Lebanese proposal that any member concluding an agreement with Israel should be expelled.[49]

The Arab pressure had an enormous effect on the newly-elected Jordanian government, under the premiership of Sa'id al-Mufti, a Pan-Arabist who had opposed the king's policies in the past. The ministers decided not to ratify the February 1950 agreement, Abdullah, ignoring the growing discontent among his ministers, continued to meet with the Israelis, mainly Shiloah, without his ministers' and, sometimes, without Kirkbride's knowledge.[50]

Three days before the formal union was declared, that is on 27 April 1950, Reuven Shiloah and Moshe Dayan came to Amman. The king evaded his ministers and succeeded in conducting a secret meeting with the two Israeli envoys. He told them that Jordanian public opinion supported his policy and that only the 'politicians' were the stumbling block on the way to a treaty between the two countries. He seemed to his Israeli interlocutors to be unconcerned about the Arab League's decisions against him and his policy. On the contrary, as so often before, he reiterated his determination to leave the League altogether. As for future meetings, he promised to delegate an official representative in the near future.[51] Before attending to further moves on the path to peace, the king first had to complete the annexation of the West Bank.

On 30 April 1950 the unification of the two banks of the River Jordan was duly executed. Only Britain and Yemen granted *de jure* recognition to the enlarged kingdom of Abdullah. Still at this juncture, in Abdullah's eyes general Arab resentment was not the real problem, what was missing was an official Israeli blessing.

Abdullah resumed contacts with the Israelis in May 1950. He was not deterred either by Kirkbride's warnings or by his own government's opposition. Abdullah was not completely candid with the Israelis, however. He presented the British as the main antagonists and obstructors, instead of admitting that he was losing his grip over his ministers. In a note sent to Shiloah in May 1950, the Israeli delegate was told that the British had advised the king 'to go slow' with the negotiations. The king stated, none the less, that he was determined to go ahead without consulting the British any further. By blaming the British, Abdullah could have complicated Anglo-Israeli relations which had considerably improved since the British *de jure* recognition of Israel in January 1950.[52] The king was, therefore, asked by Kirkbride not to extricate himself from the difficulties with the Israelis by telling them that he had been curbed by the British. But it seems that the Israelis, realizing that the king's problems were with his government and not with the British, were in any case disinclined to accept his explanation.[53]

In May 1950, the Israelis made their last attempt to facilitate an agreement by offering a territorial concession in the Little Triangle area in return for a Jordanian consent to call off its claims for the Negev area. By then it seemed that both the Jordanian and the Israeli governments were content with the territorial status quo.[54] The Tripartite Declaration of May 1950, which included *inter alia* the powers' recognition of the existing frontiers, only reinforced this conviction.

After the Tripartite Declaration even those Israelis who hitherto had been as eager as the king to conclude a formal peace treaty, seemed satisfied with the situation as it was. The declaration and the Israeli support for the UN action in Korea had normalized Israel's relations with the West, and concepts such as the 'Jessup Principle' were no longer mentioned. In the second half of 1950, the Israelis could not have asked for more, and peace with Jordan was now clearly perceived as a 'bonus', not a necessity.

Yet, the talks continued owing to Shiloah's personal ambition, which matched that of the king, to conclude a peace treaty of which he would have been the architect. Shiloah staked his reputation on being able to bring about a peace settlement. However, the Israeli government strove only to implement Article 8 of the armistice that would grant the Israelis access to Jerusalem and Mount Scopus.[55]

In July 1950, for the first time, Shiloah suggested to the king that he 'put the whole idea [of negotiations] into cold storage for an indefinite time, owing to the futility of the contact'.[56] However, the first British ambassador to Tel Aviv, Sir Knox Helm, persuaded Shiloah to persist with the negotiations for a while. Helm asserted that now that Britain had excellent relations with both Israel and Jordan a peace settlement could be achieved.[57] Shiloah failed to interest his government and prime minister in this new attempt; and he was now quite alone in the campaign for peace with Jordan.[58]

Meanwhile, the newly-elected Palestinian deputies in the Jordanian House of Representatives voiced their opposition to the continuing talks with Israel. With the government behind them, they created the impression among many outside observers that there was an active anti-Israeli public opinion in the Hashemite kingdom. This impression was accentuated when the results of a fact-finding mission to the West Bank were published. The mission was composed of Palestinian deputies who had convened with West Bank notables in Nablus and Jerusalem and jointly with the latter signed a petition against the negotiations.[59]

At this point the king could have derived some consolation from a dramatic shift in Kirkbride's attitude to the negotiations. Kirkbride had hitherto been very cautious in his approach, but during 1950 he became an ardent supporter of a peace settlement with Israel. He probably felt he had to side with the king, since the alternative in his eyes at least, would have been the Palestinization of Jordan. He was also impressed by the considerable improvement in Anglo-Israeli relations and grew to trust the Jewish state as a pro-Western element in the area. Nevertheless, he still challenged some of the king's tactics *vis-à-vis* Israel. Kirkbride asserted that only under the auspices of the PCC could Jordan hope to achieve its goals in the negotiations with Israel, and more important, this would have been the only form of negotiations to which the Jordanian government, and the Arab world at large, would agree.[60]

The Foreign Office in London accepted Kirkbride's line of thinking. Under Foreign Office pressure, the PCC arrived in Jerusalem in August 1950. For the first time after a long period of shunning any involvement in the peace process, Britain, for a brief moment, once again took the lead. It urged the two governments of Jordan and Israel to co-operate with the PCC in order to advance the chances of peace. The PCC officials were more than happy to act jointly with the experts in London. In a meeting between the British diplomats and the commission's members it was agreed that the only feasible solution was an imposed one. Both the UN officials and their British counterparts estimated that many of the Arab leaders would welcome outside pressure on them as they, the Arab leaders, genuinely sought a peaceful agreement with Israel.[61]

The Jordanian government told the PCC that it was prepared to widen the scope of the negotiations by raising the level of the delgates from junior officials to ministers. This move was welcomed by the Israelis but displeased Abdullah. Kirkbride complained in a letter to Bevin that Abdullah tried to sabotage the commission's links with the Jordanian government.[62] Abdullah's displeasure with the PCC echoed similar Israeli feelings. In the Israeli Foreign Office the new PCC initiative was seen as a 'fresh attempt to defame Israel'.[63] Thus the Israelis were happy to learn that Abdullah had found ways of thwarting the commission's efforts. The king was once more engaged in a trial of strength with his ministers. Consequently, in September 1950 he invited the director-general of the Israeli Foreign Office to come and meet him the following month in Amman. He gave a poor pretext for such a personal meeting to his ministers, referring to an incident between the Legion and some Israeli settlers who had crossed the Jordan river to cultivate a plot near the former Palestine Electricity Plant. The Israelis claimed that on the Rhodes map, that is the armistice map, this area was within their territory.[64] In the past incidents like this – and there were few – had been satisfactorily solved in the Mixed Armistice Committee. In any case, Abdullah still yielded enough authority to invite to his palace anyone he wished, including the Israelis.

The king revealed to his Israeli guest that he intended to remove and replace all those opposing his policy, including the prime minister, Sa'id al-Mufti. After Eytan had left Amman, the king then told Kirkbride he contemplated a reshuffle in the cabinet. The British representative, however, was still convinced that a peace process under the auspices of the PCC would be acceptable to al-Mufti and the other ministers and succeeded in persuading the king to postpone these moves until after the PCC had exhausted its efforts.[65] With no one else on his side, Abdullah had no choice but to accept, as so often in the past, Kirkbride's advice.

Everyone concerned soon discovered, however, that Kirkbride had been over optimistic. The ministers in Amman were in priciple opposed to any negotiations with Israel, be it direct or indirect, and were only willing to act under the auspices of the Arab League. Abdullah, thereupon, decided to persist in his efforts, even at the cost of an outright confrontation with his government.

The internal strife in the kingdom was in many ways a struggle between a conservative king on the one hand and the protagonists of a new political order on the other. The arena was the relations with Israel. But even those ministers who might have wished to preserve the old order – and surely there were some – were not willing to incur public odium by making peace with Israel.

Throughout 1950, notwithstanding the growing opposition in his government, Abdullah continued to meet the Israelis. After the PCC despaired of its efforts and left the area without much to show by way of results, Abdullah carried out his intended reshuffle – al-Rifa'i once more changed his allegiance and agreed to act as the new prime minister. Shiloah, in spite of his early disappointment, was encouraged by al-Rifa'i's appointment and responded eagerly to Abdullah's resumed overtures. Their major achievement was the extension of the co-operation between the two states within the framework of the armistice agreement.[66] Apart from this, the status quo remained.

The contact at the beginning of 1951 was through correspondence between Shiloah, the ailing Israeli President Weizmann, and Abdullah. In the main it concentrated on solving the various border disputes which erupted owing to Palestinian infiltrations into Israel. The correspondence also dealt with the question of peace in general, Shiloah, on his own initiative, suggested the return of the Arab quarters of Jerusalem to Jordan as part of a peace settlement. In January 1951, Shiloah met al-Rifa'i to discuss his offer, but found him unwilling to deviate from the armistice agreement. In fact, at the end of the meeting al-Rifa'i, under strong pressure from the West Bank ministers in the government, declared that this had been their last secret one and that all future contacts would be under the auspices of the Mixed Armistice Committee.[67]

On 20 July 1951 the king was assassinated by a Palestinian in Jerusalem. It is beyond the scope of the present study to attempt an analysis of the reasons for the king's assassination. Suffice it to say that there exists little doubt among historians that the former Mufti, Hajj Amin al-Husayni, was behind the assassination. Abdullah had become his enemy both because of the annexation of the West Bank and because of his direct negotiations with Israel. Thus, directly or indirectly, the king's violent end was connected to his negotiations for peace with Israeli.[68]

The Israeli–Jordanian negotiations, void of any content after April 1950, had been terminated even before the king's death. However, it should be noted that despite a continued cycle of infiltrations from Jordan and Israeli reprisals, the basic understanding reached between the two sides in November 1947 was kept – in fact, one might even say it was kept until 1967.

From April 1950 onwards the Israelis, the Jordanian ministers and the British, satisfied with the status quo, no longer regarded a formal peace between Israel and Jordan as a prerequisite for maintaining the 1947 understanding. Only Abdullah, and to a lesser degree, Shiloah, continued trying to find ways to conclude a formal peace treaty from 1950 to 1951.[69]

THE FINAL ACT: THE PCC – AN EPILOGUE

Despite the Israeli decision to leave the Lausanne conference in the summer of 1949, when the PCC declared (in the summer of 1950), its intention to embark on a new peace initiative in the Middle East, the Israelis were more receptive than the Arabs. One Israeli newspaper remarked that the Arab unwillingness to co-operate with the commission, and in particular Abdullah's categorical rejection of the new initiative, was a 'blow' to the peace process as the new suggestion 'is the only chance of breaking down the political blockade'.[70] Sharett echoed this sentiment by declaring that Israel welcomed any peace initiative by an outside power. Indeed, Sharett was consistent in leaving open as many options as possible. He told the Political Committee of the UN that Israel was prepared to negotiate with the Arab states, either directly or under the auspices of the PCC.[71]

However, the categorical Arab refusal, this time, to co-operate any further with the PCC put an end to this enterprise before it even began. To everyone concerned this failure seemed the final blow to the PCC's efforts. What was supposed to be the final session of the commission was convened in Geneva, and this was followed by the official closure of the PCC's offices there. The event was accompanied by an exchange of notes between the commission and the parties concerned. The Arab governments in their note expressed their willingness to sit down with Israeli representatives provided the Israelis would allow the repatriation of the Palestinian refugees. Otherwise they denounced any readiness to continue the dialogue. The PCC suggested that bilateral negotiations would begin through the Mixed Armistice Commission, that is, through committees composed of military representatives of Israel and the respective Arab country and headed by a UN official. Designated as these committees were to supervise the execution of the armistice agreements, the Arab states refused to see these committees as political bodies.[72]

But the PCC still had some breath of life. The energetic secretary of the PCC, unable to watch this body sink in oblivion, resumed the PCC efforts in August 1950. Once again, the Israelis were most forthcoming. Sources in the Israeli cabinet told the foreign press that this new move was 'regarded in Jerusalem as a tribute to the PCC members' character and persistence'.[73]

A year later, in August 1951, the commission invited the parties to participate in a convention in Paris. The purpose of the new convention was 'to discuss the whole range of the Palestine issue'.[74] The PCC proposed a mutual Arab–Israeli declaration about each country's right to security and immunity from attack, and adherence to an obligation to refrain from warlike or hostile acts.

The Israeli government responded favourably and suggested the conclusion of non-aggression pacts with each Arab country. What caused this sudden twist in Israel's policy? It might be attributed to a genuine shift in Israeli perceptions and objectives in the peace process, or, more likely, it may be explained as stemming from the crystallization of a united Arab rejectionist front against further participation in the UN efforts – the negative Arab attitude in 1951 had rendered any solution or even progress in the peace process impossible and Israel would run no risk therefore by appearing to be forthcoming on the subject of peace. It may also have been that the consistent line that Sharett had adopted was now accepted, even by Ben Gurion, as the best course for Israel's diplomacy. After all, the stiffening of the Arab position enabled Israel to accept tentatively and in principle new UN initiatives, even if only to strengthen its international image without prejudicing its strategic and national interests.

Yet, once more, Sharett appears the more genuine in his efforts to advance the chances of peace. The importance of satisfying some of the grievances of the Palestinians, which had for Sharett always formed a precondition for peace, now directed him along new avenues. He suggested to the PCC the possibility of replacing repatriation with compensation for the refugees.[75] In the following year, when Israel started negotiations with Germany about reparations, Sharrett suggested transferring some of the money to the Palestinian refugees, in order to rectify what has been called the small injustice (the Palestinian tragedy), caused by the more terrible one (the Holocaust).[76] At the end of 1951, Abba Eban repeated this suggestion for separate negotiations and compensation and revived the idea of non-aggression pacts. Eban talked about a comprehensive peace, that is combining the solution of the territorial question with the refugee problem. However, he adopted the American line that the refugee question should be resolved by economic means and should not be treated as a political question.[77]

In the Paris convention of August 1951, as in Lausanne, the American State Department was running the show. Its senior officials hoped that this time they would be able to exert pressure on Israel to moderate its adamant refusal to any form of repatriation. The Americans sought the advice and co-operation of the British in this overture. However, by that time, Whitehall had developed what one Foreign Office official has called 'practical pessimism towards the possibility of success in the peace process'.[78] Without simultaneous British leverage on the Arab states there was very little hope for American pressure on Israel. And, in any case, it would seem that the time was past for a dramatic shift in the entrenched positions of both sides.

In the summer of 1951 the PCC published its conclusive report. It admitted that it had been unable to 'make substantial progress on the task given to it by the General Assembly'. The commission claimed credit for its systematic approach to the conflict. In an academic manner it listed three different stages in the PCC accord. It had tried conciliation in Lausanne, direct negotiations in Geneva, and mediation (i.e., arbitration) in Paris. This admittedly clear pattern does not always correspond to the actual work of the commission, but one may agree that at least it had tried every possible way to bring a peaceful solution to the conflict.

Thus, according to the terms of its own report, in Lausanne, in the spring of 1949, the PCC had tried to render its services in the role of an intermediary between the parties. Failing that, in Geneva, in 1950, the commission opted for bilateral negotiations by stimulating the conflicting parties to embark on direct talks. It had confined its role to the provision of venues and media for negotiations. The principal medium was to be the Mixed Armistice Committees, the military bodies established by the UN at the beginning of 1949 to supervise the armistice agreements. Only in the case of the Israeli–Jordanian accord, and then not because of the PCC's offer but rather due to the parties' own initiative, had the Mixed Armistice Committee been turned into the main channel of communication. This stage in the peace process, however, did not last long and furthermore had failed to produce any significant agreement. After Abdullah's death, in July 1951, the Israeli–Jordanian Mixed Armistice Committee, and its sister committees with Egypt, Syria and Lebanon, were merely tools for devising military arrangements. Finally, the PCC called on the parties to convene in Paris and to discuss the commission's own ideas about peace. This was the mediation stage, in which the UN, as in the days of UNSCOP and Bernadotte, presented its own comprehensive peace plan. It was not a concrete plan but rather a set of guidelines for a future solution that was, as in the past, rejected by both sides.[79]

In reality, the PCC tried to fulfil at one and the same time all three functions mentioned in the concluding report. In particular the report is misleading in creating the impression that the PCC succeeded in convening three different conferences for peace. Only Lausanne was a proper peace conference: the other attempts never reached the stage of practical discussion. This reality emphasizes the importance and uniqueness of the Lausanne conference, despite efforts by some Israeli scholars to underrate its significance.[80]

After the Lausanne conference the quest for peace lost its

momentum and with it the PCC's importance declined. The partial success in Lausanne would not be repeated for a very long time, and in this sense the PCC may be said to form a chapter of failure in the history of the search for peace in the conflict. The writers of the report seem to attribute the failure to a deficiency of all UN mediation bodies – the absence of any sanctional capacity or authority. The PCC was entirely dependent on the warring parties' will and readiness to co-operate; but this will simply did not exist, neither on the Israeli side nor on the Arab side. It is in particular the Israelis who are blamed by the report for their unco-operative attitude. The authors of the report especially regretted the Israeli policy toward the refugee problem. One of the PCC's rare successes was persuading the General Assembly, almost un-animously, to give its blessing to the principle of repatriation. But as the report states 'It is, in particular, the government of Israel which is not prepared to implement Article 11 of the General Assembly Resolution of 11 December 1948.' The Arab side also carried responsibility in the eyes of the PCC for the deadlock in the negotiations because of its refusal to deal with territorial questions; however one discerns a slightly different tone in the way the remarks referring to the Arab position were phrased. 'The Arab governments, on the other hand, are not prepared *fully* to implement article 5 of the said resolution, which called for the final settlement of all questions outstanding between them and Israel' (my italics).[81]

Yet it would be wrong to regard the PCC as a futile exercise in diplomacy. It left an important legacy to future peace-makers – the concept of comprehensive peace in Palestine: 'The commission considers that further efforts towards settling the Palestine question could yet be usefully based on the principles underlying the comprehensive pattern of proposals which the commission sub-mitted to the parties.' In brief, these principles meant that the UN was offering a solution combining territorial settlements, on a bilateral basis, and a political resolution of the refugee problem, which was only workable with multilateral consent. This nexus between the refugees' plight and the territorial disputes was rightly discerned by the PCC in its final report. It warned future generations that 'positive progress in the transition from war to peace in Palestine is impossible if the refugee problem remains unsolved'.[82] The refugee problem has remained unsolved and peace has not been established in Palestine to this very day.

Conclusions

Both the Jewish and the Palestinian communities in Palestine lost 1 per cent of their population in the war of 1948. Israel's day of independence follows a day of national mourning in which Israel's casualties from all the wars are remembered. Among them the number of those killed in the 1948 war is the highest, and of these the great number of promising young men and women who lost their lives in that war is often pointed out. Thus, joy and sadness are interwoven in the collective Israeli memory of the war.

The Palestinian recollection is not mitigated by any happy memories, and the Palestinians mourn more than just their dead, for they also lost a homeland; the tragedy of 1948 has fuelled the fire of their national movement ever since. Palestinian culture, society and politics of today are entirely centred on the trauma of 1948, as are the aspirations and hopes of more than four million Palestinians living in Israel, the Israeli-occupied territories, the refugee camps, and those in the Palestinian diaspora.

The analysis presented in this study stands in sharp contrast to the emotional recollections and myths on both sides. It was argued in the book's opening chapters that the fate of Palestine, and hence that of the Palestinians, had been determined in the session rooms and corridors of the UN, in the meetings of various international inquiry committees and inside the discussion halls of the Arab League long before even one shot had been fired. It was the Jewish success first in building the infrastructure for a state and then in winning the diplomatic campaign that decided the battle long before it started; as it was the inadequacy of the Palestinian leadership and the meandering politics of the Arab League that helped explain the consequences of this war.

The wheels of fortune also played their part, as they so often do when formidable and resolute human beings try to determine history's course. The global situation in the late 1940s led the Soviet Union and the United States to support Jewish statehood in a rare moment of co-operation in the midst of the Cold War. It would be folly to associate the impact of the Holocaust with the decisions concerning Palestine's future wheels of fortune. But along with those scholars before us who succeeded, even temporarily, in separating their historical judgement from the emotions linked to this horrendous tragedy, we agree that it would be equally wrong to deny that the Holocaust at a crucial moment tilted world public opinion entirely in Israel's favour – thereby leaving very little sympathy for or even completely ignoring the aspirations and plight of the Palestinians.

The equal percentage of casualties on both sides reflects the clear parity on the battlefield; a parity, as shown above, not between the Palestinians and the Jews but between the military force employed by the Arab League and that of Israel. Rather than a Palestinian–Jewish confrontation, the war of 1948 was a war between the Arab states and the Jews. The dividing-up of mandatory Palestine between Israel, Egypt and Jordan testifies to this reality more than anything else. The conflict continued to be a regional affair until 1982 when the Israelis decided upon open warfare with Palestinian guerrillas in Lebanon and again in 1987 when, after twenty-one years of occupation, the Palestinians in the West Bank and the Gaza Strip confronted the Israelis, this time all alone, with nothing more than stones, Molotov cocktails, knives, axes and public strikes.

As war had been mainly with the Arab states, so peace was to be concluded between Israel and those Arab states participating in the 1948 war. From the outset Iraq was not interested in concluding even an armistice with Israel. It did not share a border with Palestine, and thus did not need a cease-fire with the Jewish state. But the other Arab states, Syria, Lebanon, Jordan and Egypt, wanted more than a cease-fire. These states were headed by political élites that had not wanted to be dragged into the Palestine fiasco in the first place and, though willing at the end of the fighting to reach an understanding with Israel, demanded a price in the form of territorial concession. The same domestic and perhaps cultural factors that had driven them to side with the Palestinians, now forced them to stipulate an Israeli consent for repatriation as a prerequisite for any serious peace negotiations. As much as their rejection of the partition plan prior to the war seemed unreasonable to the international community, their acceptance of it after the war won UN understanding and support. Unlike Israel, the UN did not recognize punishment as a viable factor in determining peace in Palestine. The Arab refusal to accept the partition plan before the war – which in part was also the cause of the war – did not mean a logical invalidation of the plan after the war. The Americans led the UN to try and persuade Israel to accept the partition plan as a basis for negotiations on peace. However, strengthened by its military successes and already aware of the impotence of the UN and of American reluctance to reach a confrontation, Israel was only willing to negotiate for peace without having to make any gestures on either territories or repatriation.

The Israelis were not alone in this perception of the situation. Britain, for one, had never been enthusiastic about the principle of partition. Like its ally in the area, Transjordan, it advocated the annexation of parts of Palestine to the Hashemite kingdom thus suggesting the division of the holy land between the Jews and the Transjordanians. This was the only peace plan ever seriously considered by Israel after the war. Intensive bilateral negotiations on this matter went on until 1951. That these failed was due both to Israel's inflexibility and, probably primarily, to Abdullah's inability to impose his will on his government, which included Palestinians and Pan-Arabists. These members saw Jordan as an Arab state and not necessarily as the bridgehead for the West in the Middle East that the king wished it to be.

Since 1948, many layers have been added to the edifice of the Arab–Israeli conflict. Israel occupied parts of Syria and Egypt proper in the 1967 war. The Camp David accord meanwhile has shown that bilateral negotiations can form a viable option for a peaceful solution to Israel's struggle with the Arab world. Camp David also proved that these negotiations had very little to do with the settlement of the Palestinian problem. The problem preoccupies the minds and influences the daily lives of hundreds of thousands of people on the West Bank and the Gaza Strip, as well as Palestinians who do not live in those areas but are either refugees, or residents in other countries of the world, some even citizens of Israel. Their aspirations and perceptions of a solution are today still associated strongly with the events and consequences of the war of 1948.

Notes

PREFACE

1 Simha Flapan, *The Birth of Israel; Myths and Realities* (New York, 1987).
2 Edward H. Carr, *What is History?* (London, 1964), p. 21.
3 Quoted in Carr, op. cit., p. 9.

INTRODUCTION

1 Nahum Goldmann, *Memoirs* (London, 1970), p. 284.
2 Israel Zangwill, 'The Return to Palestine', *The New Liberal Review*, 2(1901), p. 627.
3 Eli'ezer Beeri, *Reschit Hasichsuch Israel 'Arav* (The Beginning of the Israeli–Arab Conflict), (Tel Aviv, 1985), pp. 44–7.
4 Ibid., pp. 158–9.
5 Zeine N. Zeine, *The Struggle for Arab Independence* (Beirut, 1960), pp. 107–29.
6 League of Nations Official Journal, The League's Covenant.
7 See Jukka Nevakivi, *Britain, France and the Arab Middle East, 1914–1920* (New York, 1969), pp. 153–4.
8 Readers are advised to consider Ernest C. Dawn, *From Ottomanism to Arabism* (Illinois, 1973), Chapters 1 and 4.
9 Elie Kedourie, *The Chatham House Version and other Middle Eastern Studies* (New York, 1984), pp. 351–95; see also Elizabeth Monroe, *Britain's Moment in the Middle East, 1914–1971* (London, 1981), pp. 71–95.
10 Mary C. Wilson, *King Abdullah, Britain and the Making of Jordan* (Cambridge, 1987), p. 44.
11 Ibid., pp. 44, 46.
12 Kirkbride's reaction is described in Ilan Pappé, 'Sir Alec Kirkbride and the Making of Greater Transjordan', in *Asian and African Studies*, 23/1(March 1989), pp. 43–70.
13 Uriel Dann, *Studies in the History of Transjordan, 1920–1949, The Making of State* (Boulder, 1987); Wilson, *Abdullah* and Elie Kedourie, *England and the Middle East* (London, 1987) do not mention the will to prevent the emergence of an Arab–Jewish conflict as one of the motives lying behind Churchill's policy. The only one who hints at this possibility is Aaron S. Klieman, *Foundations of British Policy in the Arab World: The Cairo Conference 1921* (Baltimore, 1978).

14   Michael J. Cohen, *Palestine and the Great Powers, 1945–1948* (Princeton, 1982), p. 110.
15   Two of them have left written personal accounts which shed light on its proceedings, and the subject was also treated in three recent books: Amikam Nachmani, *Great Power Discord in Palestine: The Anglo–American Committee of Inquiry into the Problem of European Jewry and Palestine, 1945–46* (London, 1986); Ritchie Ovendale, *Britain, the United States, and the End of the Palestine Mandate, 1942–1948* (London, 1989) and Martin Jones, *Failure in Palestine: British and United States Policy after the Second World War* (London, 1986), pp. 39–143.
16   Cohen, *Palestine*, p. 102.
17   Ibid., p. 108.
18   Richard Crossman, *Palestine Mission: A Personal Record* (London, 1947).
19   See Nachmani, op. cit., passim.
20   Cohen, *Palestine*, p. 45.
21   Menachem Kaufman, 'Demut Hamedina Hayehudit be'eney Hava'ad Hayehudi Haamerikani, 1947–1948' (The State of Israel as Conceived by the American Jewish Committee, 1947–1948), *Yahadut Zemanenu*, 3(1986), pp. 171–85.
22   Cohen, *Palestine*, pp. 292–3.
23   Ibid., pp. 116–134.
24   CP(47), 6 February, 1947, CAB 129/16.
25   Avi Shlaim, *Collusion Across the Jordan* (Oxford, 1988), p. 85.
26   William Roger Louis, *The British Empire in the Middle East 1945–1951; Arab Nationalism, the United States and Post War Imperialism* (Oxford, 1985), pp. 474–5.
27   See for example Amizur Ilan, *America, Britanya ve-Eretz Israel* (The USA, Britain and Palestine), (Jerusalem, 1979), p. 267; for the British decision see Elizabeth Monroe, 'Mr. Bevin's Arab Policy' in *St. Antony's Papers*, 11, p. 32.
28   Gabriel Cohen, however, sees the withdrawal as a gradual process that was began in 1943 and continued by Bevin who did not wish, or at least found it very hard, to alter it. See Gebriel Cohen, 'Mediniyut Britaniya 'Erev Milhemet Haazma'ut' (British Policy on the Eve of the War of Independence) in Y. Wallach, *Hayinu Keholmim* (We Were Like Dreamers), (Tel Aviv, 1985), pp. 13–77. Miriam J. Haron, on the other hand, attributes it to Bevin's era and the foreign secretary's personality and policies. See Miriam J. Haron, 'The British Decision to Give the Palestinian Question to the UN', *Middle Eastern Studies*, 17/2(April 1981), pp. 241–8.
29   Bruce Hoffman, *The Failure of the British Military Strategy with Palestine, 1939–1947* (Tel Aviv, 1983).

CHAPTER 1

1   Aviva Halamish, 'Emdat Artzot Habrit be-Parashat Oniyat Ham'apilim "Exodus 1947"' (The United States' Position in the Exodus Affair), *Yahadut Zemanenu*, 3(1986), pp. 209–27; Cohen, *Palestine*, p. 260.

2   FO to British Delegation in the UN, 21 March 1947, FO 371/61769, E1786.
3   Jorge Garcia-Granados, *The Birth of Israel* (New York, 1948), pp. 6–7.
4   Ibid., p. 5.
5   Silvero Ferari, 'Hakes Hakadosh ve-Be'ayat Eretz Israel Aharey Milhemet Ha'olam Hashniya; binum Yerushalayim ve-Haganat Hamekomot Hakedoshim' (The Holy Seal and the Internationalization of Jerusalem), *Yahadut Zemanenu*, 3(1986), pp. 187–209.
6   Granados, *Birth*, p. 4.
7   UNSCOP Report to the General Assembly, vol. 1, pp. 59–64, UN Official Records of the General Assembly, 2nd Session, vol. 1.
8   Granados, *Birth*, p. 26.
9   Cohen, *Palestine*, p. 260.
10 First Committee on the Establishment of UNSCOP, in the UN Official Records of the General Assembly, vol. 1, doc. A/307, pp. 126–7.
11 Cohen, *Palestine*, p. 261.
12 Aaron Krammer, *The Forgotten Friendship* (Illinois, 1974), pp. 17–19. Krammer also quotes the Arab press at the time and describes the dismay and frustration which characterized the Arab reaction.
13 Ya'acov Ro'i also accepts the American explanation that it was an attempt on the part of the Soviets to try and satisfy everyone concerned and stall for time. See Ya'acov Ro'i, 'Soviet–Israeli Relations 1947–1954', in Michael Confino and Shimon Shamir, (eds) *The USSR and the Middle East* (Tel Aviv, 1974), pp. 123–46.
14 Yehosua Arieli, 'Azmaut Israel Beprespectiva Historit' (The Independence of Israel in a Historical Perspective), *Betefuzot Ha-Gola*, 18(1981/2).
15 See Benny Morris, *1948 and After* (Oxford, 1990), pp. 1–34; Zachary Lockman, 'Original Sin', *Middle East Report*, May–June 1988.
16 Arieli, op. cit.
17 Krammer, op. cit., p. 17.
18 David Ben Gurion, *Medinat Israel Hamehudeshet* (The Restored State of Israel), (Tel Aviv, 1969), p. 73.
19 FO Minute, 25 April 1947, FO 371/61805.
20 Ilan Pappé, 'From Open Confrontation to a Tacit Alliance', *Middle Eastern Studies*, 26/4(October 1990), pp. 561–82. For years after 1948 Bevin's effigies were burned at various feasts.
21 Robert A. Divine, *American Immigration Policy, 1942–1952* (New York, 1969), pp. 110–29.
22 *Foreign Relations of the US 1947*, vol. 5, Truman's Declaration, 5 June 1947, p. 1101 (hence *FRUS 1947*) and see *Manchester Guardian*, 24 April 1949.
23 Granados, *Birth*, p. 39.
24 Ibid.
25 Akram Zu'aytar, *Al-Qadiyya Al-Filastinyya* (The Palestine Problem), (Cairo, 1965), p. 190; Taysir Jabara, *Dirasat fi Tarikh Filastin Al-Hadith* (Studies in the Modern History of Palestine), (Jerusalem, 1987), p. 150.

26 Granados, *Birth*, p. 40.
27 Jewish Agency Executive Meeting in New York, 13 May 1947, CZA Z5/2362.
28 Mathieson Review, 16 July 1947, CO 537/2338.
29 Ibid.
30 Christopher Sykes, *Crossroads to Israel* (Indiana, 1965), p. 321.
31 See both Falah Khaled Ali, *Al-Harb al-'Arabiyya al-Isra'iliyya, 1948–9, wa Taasis Isra'il* (The Arab–Israeli War, 1948–9 and the Foundation of Israel), (Cairo, 1982), p. 13; and Yehosua Freundlich, 'Hamediniyut HaZiyonit Likrat Hakamat Hamedina, August 1946–May 1948' (Zionist Policy towards the Establishment of the State of Israel, August 1946–May 1948), (Ph.D. Thesis, Hebrew University of Jerusalem, 1986), pp. 117–29.
32 Halamish, *Exodus*, pp. 209–27.
33 The two sergeants were kidnapped by IZL on 12 July 1947 and executed on 29 July. Their bodies were booby-trapped.
34 Epstein to Meirson, 2 August 1947, CZA S25/1697.
35 Meir Pa'il, 'Hafqa'at Haribonut Hamedinit shel Filastin miyedei Hafalestinim' (The Expropriation of the Sovereignty of the State of Palestine from the Palestinians), *Ziyonut*, 3(1973), pp. 438–45.
36 Yusuf Ibish (ed.), *Mudhakirat al-Amir Adil Arslan* (The Memoirs of the Amir Adil Arslan), (Beirut, 1983), 16–24 July 1947, pp. 687–8.
37 Ibid.
38 Baghdad to FO, 24 July 1947, FO 371/61876, E6730.
39 Ibish, *Arslan*, p. 687–8.
40 Shlaim, *Collusion*, pp. 91–5.
41 Granados, *Birth*, p. 227.
42 Sharett to Linton and Goldberg, 21 June 1947, S25/1694 CZA; Refael (who was one of the delegates) to Sharett, 14 July 1947, ISA 65/1. See also the minutes of the meeting of the representative of the central committee of the 'Liberated Jews' in S25/5456 CZA. And compare to subcommittee 3, 2nd report, 20 August 1947 in the UN Official Records of the General Assembly, Ibid.
43 Granados, *Birth*, p. 246.
44 The British official was MacGillivary of the Colonial Office.
45 Crossman, *Mission*, p. 57.
46 Granados, *Birth*, p. 233.
47 UNSCOP Verbatim Report of 46th meeting (private), Box 2, United Nations Archives, 27 August 1947.
48 Granados, *Birth*, p. 238.
49 Freundlich, *Hamediniyut*, p. 118.
50 Henry Cattan, who was the first Palestinian to appear before the committee, would try years later (in 1973), to dispute the legal basis of this Zionist argumentation but, at the time, the lack of Palestine co-operation left the arena to the legal reasoning of the Jews. Henry Cattan, *Palestine and International Law: The Legal Aspects of the Arab–Israeli Conflict* (London, 1973), pp. 7–13.
51 Eliahu Elath, *Hama'avak 'al Hameidna* (The Struggle for Statehood) (Tel Aviv, 1982), vol. 2, pp. 194–5.

52   Ibid., pp. 193–5 and see UNSCOP Verbatim Report, op. cit. See also
     MacGillivary (Geneva) to FO, 21 August 1947, FO 371/61786,
     E7852.
53   Granados, *Birth*, pp. 236–7.
54   Ibid., pp. 238–9.
55   'Palestine: A Study of Palestine (A British document) April 1947', in
     ISA 72/17 and Coupland to Sharett, 3 December 1947, ISA 2268/21.
     Both are discussed also in Yoram Nimrod. 'Defusim Beyahsei
     Yehudim-'Aravim' (Patterns of Israeli–Arab Relations, The Forma-
     tive Years, 1947–1950), (Ph.D. Thesis Jerusalem 1985), vol. 1, p. 5.
56   Freundlich, *Hamediniyut*, p. 125.
57   The UNSCOP Report, op. cit.
58   Hurewitz Memo, 18 August 1947, ISA 2270/1.
59   Majority and Minority Report of UNSCOP in the UN Official
     Records, 2nd Session, op. cit.
60   *FRUS 1947*, vol. 5, Marshall to Austin, 13 June 1947, pp. 1088–96;
     Uri Milstein, *Milhemet Ha'azmaut* (The War of Independence), (Tel
     Aviv, 1989), vol. 1, pp. 249–52. See the elaborated discussion in
     Louis, *Empire*, pp. 478–80.
61   UNSCOP Verbatim Report, 41st Meeting, 28 July 1947.
62   FO to Bevin, 14 April 1947 FO371/61722, E3092 and CP(47)40,
     28 April 1947, CAB 129/18.
63   Freundlich, *Hamediniyut*, p. 141.
64   The archive of Hajj Amin al-Husayni quoted in Khaled Ali, *Al-Harb*,
     p. 16 note 3.
65   UN General Committee, Summary Records, 35th meeting,
     17 September 1947, UN Official Records, op. cit.
66   British delegation in the UN to FO, 20 September 1947, FO 371/
     61789, E8917; and Cabinet Minute 27 September 1947, CAB 128/10.
67   Alan Bullock, *Ernest Bevin, Foreign Secretary, 1945–1951* (London, 1983),
     p. 476 and Louis, *Empire*, pp. 470–5.
68   Bullock, op. cit., p. 476, note 2.
69   Cohen, *Palestine*, p. 277.
70   Freundlich, *Hamediniyut*, p. 143.
71   Louis, *Empire*, p. 473.
72   Ibid., pp. 474–5.
73   David Ben Gurion, *Behilahem Israel* (When Israel Fought in Battle),
     (Tel Aviv, 1975), vol. 2, pp. 42–3; see also Louis, *Empire*, p. 481.
74   Louis, *Empire*, pp. 478–9.
75   Freundlich, *Hamediniyut*, p. 147.
76   In the words of Roger Louis: 'Though cynics then and later find it
     hard to believe, the element of impartiality played an important part
     in American attitude towards Palestine in the winter of 1947–8.'
     Louis, op. cit., p. 484.
77   Ad hoc Committee on the Palestine Question, 19th meeting,
     21 October 1947, UN Official Records, op. cit., pp. 127–37.
78   Moshe Sharett, *Besha'ar Haumot* (At the Gate of the Nations), (Tel
     Aviv, 1958), p. 150.
79   Ad hoc Committee on Palestine, op. cit., p. 137.

80 Ibid., Annex 25, pp. 270–300.
81 Freundlich, *Hamediniyut*, p. 155.
82 Cohen, *Palestine*, p. 289.
83 FO to Washington, 12 November 1947, FO 371/61794, E 10538.
84 Chaim Weizmann, *Trial and Error* (London, 1949), pp. 458–9.
85 Sharett, *Besha'ar*, p. 147; Zvi Ganin, *Truman, American Jewry and Israel, 1945–1948* (New York, 1979), pp. 138–41. Walid Khalidi reminds us that 'in the proposed Jewish state the Jews would possess 1.67 million dunamms out of 15 million dunamms'. In 'The Arab Perspective' in William Roger Louis and Robert S. Stookey (eds), *The End of the Palestine Mandate* (London, 1986), p. 121.
86 UNSCOP Report to the GA, UN Official Records, op. cit.
87 Freundlich, *Hamediniyut*, pp. 168–9.
88 Ibid., p. 167.
89 Ferari, op. cit.
90 Cohen, *Palestine*, p. 290.
91 Given the position of some of the Americans, I would join those who suspect the State Department. Yet, no one has so far unearthed solid evidence to prove this supposition. See Milstein, *Milhemet*, p. 269 and FO Memo. 25 November 1947, FO 371/61890, E1129; meeting of American Department in the Jewish Agency, 26 October 1947, CZA Z5/2375.
92 Milstein, *Milhemet*, p. 269.
93 Cohen, *Palestine*, p. 295.
94 Elath, *Hama'avak*, vol. 2, pp. 430–3.
95 Plenary Meetings of the General Assembly, 126th meeting, 28 November 1947, UN Official Record, op. cit., vol. 2, pp. 1390–1400.
96 Baghdad to FO, 17 November 1947, FO 371/61888; *FRUS 1948*, vol. 5, PSS statement, 19 January 1948, p. 548.
97 Freundlich, *Hamediniyut*, p. 207 note 202. Kamil Sham'un called the Assembly to postpone the voting and consider a new proposal but his initiative was rejected; see Isam Sakhnini, *Filastin al-Dawla* (Palestine – the State), (Acre, 1986), p. 198.
98 Sharett, *Besha'ar*, pp. 147–50.
99 Menachem Kaufman, 'Hanemanut ma he? Tochnit Hanemanut shel Artzot Habrit le-Pitron Be'ayat Eretz Israel, 1948' (The American Trusteeship Proposal), *Yahadut Zemanenu*, 1(1984), pp. 249–73.
100 Flapan, *Birth*, pp. 13–54.
101 The popular portrayal of the war has become an endless source for national myths as well as part of the indoctrination in schools and the Israeli army; see Nethanel Lorch, 'Hahistoriographia shel Milhemet Ha'azmaut' (The Historiography of the War of Independence), *Cathedra*, vol. 1, p. 65.

CHAPTER 2

1 Yehuda Slutzky, *Sefer Toldot Hahagana* (The History of the Hagana) vol. 1, (Tel Aviv, 1972), p. 12.
2 David Ben Gurion, 'From the Vision of a State to the War of

Independence', an introduction to IDF, General Staff History Branch, *Toldot Milhemet Hakomemiyut* (History of the War of Independence), (Tel Aviv, 1967), pp. 21–2.

3 Milstein, *Milhemet*, vol. 2, p. 13.
4 Benny Morris, *The Birth of the Palestinian Refugee Problem, 1947–1949* (Cambridge, 1988), p. 8.
5 The Political History of Palestine under the British Administration, a memo presented by HMG to UNSCOP, July 1947, FO 371/61932.
6 Yigal Eilam, *Hahagana: Haderech Haziyonit Lakoah* (The Hagana: The Zionist Way to Power), (Tel Aviv, 1979), pp. 331–49.
7 Slutzky, *Sefer*, vol. 9, pp. 1457–85.
8 Ibid.
9 Ibid.
10 Ibid, vol. 6, pp. 979–89.
11 Ibid, vol. 11, pp. 1249–55.
12 Ben Gurion, *Behilahem*, vol. 5, p. 211.
13 Meir Avizohar and Avi Bareli, *Achshav o L'olam Lo* (Now or Never: Proceedings of Mapai in the Closing Year of the British Mandate, Introductions and Documents), (Beit Berl, 1989), vol. 2, p. 363.
14 Ibid., pp. 369–404.
15 Morris, *Birth*, p. 62.
16 Ibid.
17 Gershon Rivlin and Elhanan Orren (eds), *Yoman Hamilhama-Tashah, 1948–1949* (David Ben Gurion's War Diary), (Tel Aviv, 1982), 21 March 1948, p. 315.
18 Ibid., 13 January 1948, p. 141.
19 Ibid., 30 March 1948, p. 326.
20 Ibid., 10 January 1948, p. 132.
21 Ibid., 14 December 1947, p. 46.
22 Alexander Schölch, *Palestina in Umbruch, 1882–1956* (Stuttgart, 1986), pp. 161–78.
23 Ibid., p. 161.
24 Alexander Schölch, 'Was There a Feudal System in Ottoman Lebanon and Palestine', in David Kushner, *Palestine in the Late Ottoman Period: Political, Social and Economic Transformation* (Jerusalem, 1986), pp. 134, 141.
25 Ibid., pp. 134, 141.
26 Ibid.
27 Ibid., p. 141.
28 *Waqf* is the Islamic religious endowment.
29 Alexander Schölch, 'European Penetration and the Economic Development of Palestine, 1856–1882', in Roger Owen (ed.), *Studies in the Social and Economic History of Palestine in the 19th and 20th Centuries* (London, 1982), pp. 10–87.
30 On the rise of the Husaynis see Butrus Abu-Manneh, 'The Husaynis: The Rise of a Notable Family in 18th Century Palestine', in Kushner, *Palestine*, pp. 93–108. For their rise to power in the mandatory period see Yehosua Porath, *Zemihat Hatenu'a Ha'aravit Hafalestinait, 1918–1929*

(The Emergence of the Palestinian National Movement, 1918–1929), (Tel Aviv, 1971), pp. 149–69.

31 Salim Tamari, 'Factionalism and Class Formation in Recent Palestinian History' in Owen, *op. cit.*, pp. 177–203. See also Bayan al-Hout, 'The Palestinian Political Elite during the Mandatory Period', *Journal of Palestine Studies*, 9/1(1979), pp. 85–111. Al-Hout asserts that it is impossible to talk about a recognized Palestinian national leadership before 1945 and argues that the new Arab Higher Committee was highly respectable.

32 See Humphrey Bowman, *A Middle East Window* (London, 1942).

33 Joseph Nevo, 'Hahitpathut Hapolitit shel Hatnu'a Haleumit Ha'aravit Hafalestinait, 1939–1945' (The Political Development of the National Arab Palestinian Movement, 1939–1945), (Ph.D. Thesis, Tel Aviv University, 1977), p. 138.

34 Joseph Nevo, 'Hafalestinayim ve Hamedina Hayehudit' (The Palestinians and the Jewish State, 1947–1948), in Wallach, *Keholmim*, p. 295.

35 Ahmad al-Alami, *Al-Harb 1948* (The War of 1948), (Acre, 1989), p. 183.

36 Nevo, 'Hafalestinayim', p. 296.

37 Arif al-Arif, *Al-Nakba*, (The Catastrophe), (Beirut 1988), vol. 1, pp. 44–5.

38 Joseph Nevo, 'The Arabs of Palestine 1947–48: Military and Political Activity', *Middle Eastern Studies*, 23/1(January 1987), p. 4.

39 Nevo, 'Hafalestinayim', p. 297.

40 Notable of these local commanders was Abd al-Qader al-Husayni the son of Musa Qazem al-Husayni, the chairman of the Arab Higher Committee in 1934. For the inability to organize a military force see Nevo, 'The Arabs', pp. 11–12.

41 Muhammad Nimr Al-Hawari, *Sir al-Nakba*, (The Secret of the Defeat), (Nazareth, 1955), p. 128; an interview with the former Mufti in *Aakhar Sa'a*, 13 June 1973.

42 Flapan, *Birth*, pp. 73–5, 94–5.

43 *Aakhar Sa'a*, 20 June 1973.

44 For an estimate of the Jewish forces see Rivlin and Orren, *Yoman*, editorial notes, p. 1016; Arab forces see al-Arif, *Al-Nakba*, vol. 1, p. 128 and Nevo 'The Arabs', pp. 16–17 and 23–4; a British estimation see in Henry Gureny, 'A Short History of the Last Days of the Mandate', Private Papers, the Middle East Centre, St. Antony's College, Oxford, 4 April 1948, p. 34.

45 Khaled Ali, *Al-Harb*, p. 70.

46 The letter appears in Khaled Ali, op. cit., appendix 9.

47 Morris, *Birth*, p. 77.

48 Nevo, 'The Arabs', pp. 15–16.

49 Ibid.

50 *Aakhar Sa'a*, 4 July 1973.

51 Khalil Sakakini, *Kadha Ana, Ya Dunya* (This is me, Oh World) (The Diaries of Khalil Sakakini), (Jerusalem, 1959), p. 384.

52 Hawari, *Sir*, pp. 186–7.

53 A telephone conversation intercepted by the Jewish intelligence in Rivlin and Orren, *Yoman*, 4 January 1948, pp. 112–14.

54 Samih S. Shakib, 'Shakhziyat al-Mufti wa Nashtatiha' (The Personality of the Mufti and its Activity) a review article on Husni Adham Jarar, *Al-Hajj Amin al-Husayni: Ra'id Jihad wa Batl al-Qadiyya al-Filastiniyya* (Hajj Amin al-Husayni, the Commander of the Struggle and the Hero of the Palestine Question), (Amman, 1987) in *Shu'un Filastiniyya*, 186(September 1988), pp. 87–90.

55 Muhammad Khalil, *The Arab States and the Arab League* (Beirut, 1962), vol. 1, pp. 55–6.

56 Nevo, 'The Arabs', p. 9.

57 Muhammad Izat Darwaza, *Hawla al-Haraka al-'Arabiyya al-Haditha* (About the Modern Arab Movement), (Sidon, 1959), vol. 2, pp. 55–60.

58 Nevo, 'Hafalestinayim', p. 334.

59 Al-Arif, *Al-Nakba*, vol. 1, p. 41.

60 Shmuel Segev, *Meahorei Hapargod*, (Behind the Curtain: Hebrew Translation of the Proceeding of the Iraqi Parliamentary Committee on the War in Palestine), (Tel Aviv, 1954), pp. 100–2.

61 The letter from 7 January 1948 is quoted in Al-Arif, op. cit., vol. 1, p. 22.

62 Yaacov Shimoni, 'Ha'aravim likrat Milhemet Israel 'Arav, 1945–1948' (The Arabs on the Eve of the Arab–Israeli War, 1945–1948), *Hamizrah Hehadash*, 12(1962), p. 208.

63 Al-Arif, *Al-Nakba*, pp. 45–7.

64 Nevo, 'Hafalestinayim', pp. 311–12.

65 Muhammad Amin Al-Husayni, *Haqai'q an Filastin* (The Truth on Palestine), (Cairo, 1956), pp. 22–3.

66 Al-Arif, *Al-Nakba*.

67 Al-Husayni, *Haqai'q*.

68 *Al-Difa'a* (Jerusalem), *Filastin* (Jaffa), 10 December 1947.

69 Ahmad Salama, *Al-Kifah 'an Filastin 'Arabiyya* (The Struggle for Arab Palestine), (Acre, 1988), p. 8.

70 Al-Arif, *Al-Nakba*, vol. 3, p. 703.

71 A conversation between Farid Sa'ad, the manager of the Arab Bank in Haifa and Husayn Khalidi, intercepted by the Jewish intelligence, in Rivlin and Orren, *Yoman*, 12 January 1948, pp. 134–5.

72 Salima Awdeh, *Misr wa al-Qadiyya al-Filastiniyya* (Egypt and the Palestinian Problem), (Cairo, 1986), p. 184.

73 *Hapargod*, p. 59.

74 Ihsan al-Nimr, *Tarich Jabal Nablus wa al-Balqa* (The History of Mount Nablus and al-Balqa), (Nablus, 1975), p. 54.

75 Ilan Pappé, *Britain and the Arab–Israeli Conflict, 1948–1951* (London, 1988), pp. 74–84 and Meir Pa'il, *Hafqa'at*, p. 441.

76 Izhak Levi, *Tish'a Qabin* (Jerusalem in the War of Independence), (Jerusalem, 1986), pp. 337–41.

77 Intelligence Report, 6 December 1947, CO 537/2294.

78 Al-Alami, *Al-Harb*, p. 16.

79 Rivlin and Orren, *Yoman*, 1 January 1948, p. 99.

80 Ibid.
81 Avizohar and Bareli, *Achshav*, pp. 302–39.
82 Milstein, *Milhemet*, vol. 2, p. 47.
83 Avizohar and Bareli, op. cit., pp. 310–15.
84 Ibid.
85 Rivlin and Orren, *Yoman*, 2 January 1948, p. 105. Uri Bar-Joseph asserts that Abdullah prepared a 'limited war' against the Jewish State, Uri Bar-Joseph, *The Best of Enemies, Israel and Transjordan in the War of 1948* (London, 1987), pp. 155–92.
86 A conversation intercepted by the Jewish intelligence quoted in Rivlin and Orren, *Yoman*, 4 January 1948, pp. 113–14.
87 High Commissioner in Jerusalem to the Secretary of State for the Colonies, 26 April 1948 and 3 May 1948 CO 537/3875. See there also the War Office's report to the Private Secretary of the Foreign Secretary titled 'Middle East Special Situation Report', 29 April 1948.
88 Milstein, op. cit., vol. 2, p. 47.
89 Ben Gurion's Diary, 5 January 1948, Ben Gurion Archives (BGA) in Sdeh Boker.
90 Milstein, op. cit., vol. 2, p. 78.
91 Ibid., pp. 79–81.
92 Marriot in Haifa to Bevin in London, 26 April 1948, FO 371/68505.
93 Rivlin and Orren, *Yoman*, 1 January 1948, p. 98.
94 Ibid., 11 December 1947, p. 37.
95 Ibid., 1 January 1948, p. 97.
96 Ibid., 19 February 1948, p. 255.
97 Report by Peel, 12 April 1948, War Office 75/48.
98 Summary of April–May 1948, E7808, FO 371/68808; Pappé, *Britain*, pp. 4–5.
99 Pappé, op. cit., pp. 14–15.
100 For the Jewish intelligence point of view see Rivlin and Orren, *Yoman*, 28 January 1948, p. 187.
101 Fritz Ben Eshet in Ben Gurion's Diary, 14 December 1947, BGA.
102 Yehuda Slutzky, *Kizur Sefer Toldot Hahagana* (The Abridged Book of the Hagana), (Tel Aviv, 1978), pp. 486–7.
103 Ibid.
104 Nevo, 'Hafalestinayim', pp. 317–318.
105 On the link between nationalistic ideology and deeds such as Deir Yassin see Yosef Heller, 'Bein Meshichiut le Realism Politi – Lohamei Herut Israel ve-Hashelah Ha'aravit, 1940–1947' (Between Messianism and Realpolitik – the Stern Gang and the Arab Question, 1940–1947), *Yahadut Zemanenu*, 1(1983), pp. 223–48.
106 Rivlin and Orren, *Yoman*, editorial note, pp. 332–3.

CHAPTER 3

1 Flapan, *Birth*, p. 87.
2 Morris, *Birth*, p. 30.
3 Shabtai Teveth, 'The Palestinian Refugee Problem and its Origins' (review article), *Middle Eastern Studies*, 26/2 (April 1990), pp. 214–49.

4   Quoted in Ibid.
5   Walid Khalidi, 'Plan Dalet: Master Plan for the Conquest of Palestine', *Journal of Palestine Studies*, 18/69 (Autumn 1988), p. 4–20.
6   Ibid. See there appendix E, the Spectator Correspondence between Erskine Childers, Jon Kimche and Hedley Cook from August 1961. For Morris's view see *Birth*, p. 63.
7   Morris, *Birth*, p. 90.
8   Ibid., pp. 62–3.
9   Ibid.
10 Khalidi, 'Dalet', p. 8.
11 Ibid. Yigal Eilam in *Memalei Hapekudot* (The Obeyers of Orders), (Jerusalem, 1990), pp. 31–52, relates the expulsion of the Arabs to the Zionist ideology as it developed in the 1920s.
12 Slutzky, *Sefer*, vol. 3, appendix 48, pp. 1955–9.
13 Ibid.
14 Morris claims that since so many fled before its implementation, Plan D is an insignificant document.
15 Meeting in the prime minister's office on the problem of Arab refugees, 18 August 1948, ISA 2444/19.
16 Benny Morris, 'Yosef Weitz and the Transfer Committees, 1948–1949', *Middle Eastern Studies*, 22/4 (October 1986), pp. 522–61.
17 Ibid.
18 Morris, *1948 and After*, pp. 173–90.
19 Ibid.
20 Ibid.
21 Heller, op. cit.
22 Morris, *Birth*, pp. 61–132.
23 Final Report of the Economic Survey Mission, 28 December 1949.
24 Benny Morris, 'Operation Dani and the Palestinian Exodus from Lydda and Ramleh in 1948', *The Middle East Journal*, 40/1 (Winter 1986), pp. 286–7.
25 Ibid and compare with Nethanel Lorch, *The Edge of the Sword: Israel's War of Independence, 1947–1949* (New York, 1968), pp. 286–7.
26 Morris, *Birth*, p. 229.
27 Ibid., pp. 225–7.
28 Ibid., pp. 233–9.
29 Charles S. Kamen, 'After the Catastrophe II, The Arabs in Israel, 1948–1951', *Middle Eastern Studies*, 24/1 (January 1988), p. 68.
30 Morris, 'Weitz', p. 534.
31 Meeting in prime minister's office in ISA 2444/19, Ibid.
32 Kamen, op. cit.
33 Morris, 'Weitz', p. 522.
34 High Commissioner in Jerusalem to the Secretary of State for the Colonies, 5 February 1948, FO 371/68366, E 1785.
35 Michael Cohen, 'The Birth of Israel – Diplomatic Failure, Military Success', *Jerusalem Quarterly*, 17 (Autumn 1980), p. 33.
36 New York to FO, 31 January 1948, FO 371/68531, E1388.

37 Pappé, *Britain*, pp. 6–8.

CHAPTER 4

1 Al-Arif, *Al-Nakba*, vol. 1, p. 15–16.
2 Ibid, pp. 20–21; Ahmad al-Shuqayri, who would become the first chairman of the PLO, claimed that even Safwat's recommendations were too optimistic in his *'Arab'in 'Aam fil Hayat al-'Arabiyya wa al-Duwaliyya* (Forty Years in the Arab and International History), (Beirut, 1960), p. 310.
3 Kirkbride to London, October 1947, FO 371/61530, E9551.
4 *al-Mawsw'at al-Filastiniyya*, (The Palestinian Encyclopedia), (Beirut, 1986), vol. 4, p. 30. For the best analysis of what happened in Aleh see Walid Khalidi, 'The Arab', pp. 117–19.
5 Al-Alami, *Al-Harb*, p. 10.
6 *Hapargod*, pp. 60–7.
7 FO Minute, October 1947, FO 371/61893, E12064. See also Mamduh al-Rusan, *Al-'Iraq wa Qadayya al-Sharq al-'Arabi al-Qawmi* (Iraq and Pan Arabist Problems), (Beirut, 1979), pp. 249–50. This book claims that Iraq played the leading role in the meeting, pressuring the other Arab countries to intervene in Palestine.
8 FO Minute, 17 February 1948, FO 371/68381, E2518.
9 Rada Hilal, 'Al-Siyasa al-Misriyya wa al-Masala al-Filastiniyya, 1922–1948' (Egyptian Politics and the Question of Palestine), *Shu'un Filastiniyya*, 190(January 1989), pp. 29–60; Abd al-Rahman al-Salihi, 'Harb al-'Aam 1948: Ru'uwiyya 'Arabiyya wa-'Alamiyya' (The War of 1948, an Arab and an International Viewpoint), *Shu'un Filastiniyya*, 191(February 1989), p. 21.
10 Thomas Meyer, 'The Military Force of Islam, the Society of the Muslim Brotherhood and the Palestine Question, 1945–1948', in Eli Kedourie and Sylvia Haim (eds), *Zionism and Arabism and Israel* (London, 1981); Kamil Isma'il al-Sharif, *Al-Ikhwan al-Muslimun fi Harb Filastin* (TheMuslim Brethren in the Palestine War), (Cairo, no date), pp. 43–4.
11 Anis al-Sayigh, *Al-Hashimyun wa Qadiyat Filastin*, (The Hashemites and the Problem of Palestine), (Beirut, 1966), pp. 197–8.
12 Ahmad Rashidi, 'Al-Jami'a al-'Arabiyya wa Qadiyat Filastin' (The Arab League and the Problem of Palestine), *Shu'un 'Arabiyya*, 19(September 1982), p. 181–2.
13 Quoted in Muhammad Fa'iz al-Qasri, *Harb Filastin al-'Aam 1948* (The Palestine War 1948), (Cairo, 1961), pp. 155–6.
14 Pappé, *Britain*, pp. 51–4.
15 Monroe, *Britain*, p. 169.
16 New York to FO, 31 January 1948, FO 371/68531, E1388.
17 Rif'at Sayd Ahmad, *Watha'iq Harb Filastin: al-Millafat al-Siriyya lil Generaliyat al-'Arab* (The Documents of the War of Palestine 1948: the Secret Files of the Arab Armies), (Cairo, 1988), p. 122.
18 Chiefs of Staff paper COS (48), 23 April 1948, DEFE 4/2.
19 Ben Gurion, *Hamehudeshet*, vol. 1, pp. 69–71.

20   Ahmad, *Watha'iq*, p. 121.
21   Thomas Meyer, 'Medinot 'Arav ve Shelat Eretz Israel Bashanim 1945–1948' (The Arab States and the Question of Palestine, 1945–1948), in Wallach, *Keholmim*, p. 349.
22   Slutzky, *Kizur*, p. 467.
23   Pappé, *Britain*, pp. 4–6.
24   Ibrahim Shakib, *Harb Filastin 1948: Ru'uwiyya Misriyya* (The War of Palestine 1948: The Egyptian Side), (Cairo, 1988), p. 199, note 2 and 3; *Watha'iq*, pp. 122–3.
25   Slutzky, *Kizur*, p. 517.
26   Ahmad *Watha'iq*, p. 79. In this source the estimation for the Egyptian forces is on pp. 147–52 and for the rest of the Arab armies on pp. 509–12.
27   Rivlin and Orren, *Yoman*, pp. 1018–19; and entries for 7 May 1948 and 21 July 1948, pp. 397 and 614. For the numbers of the Arab side see also note 24.
28   Milstein, *Milhemet*, vol. 1, p. 201.
29   Al-Arif, *Al-Nakba*, vol. 1, p. 47.
30   Israeli historians have later claimed that even greater sums could have, and should have, been allocated to the military effort, but even these figures are impressive compared with the declared, though unattained, Arab goal of recruiting 1 million dollars. Notable of these historians is Uri Milstein in *Milhemet*, vol. 1, pp. 213–36; see also Rivlin and Orren, *Yoman*, editorial note, p. 1010.
31   Shakib's evaluation of the Jewish forces is accurate; see Shakib, *Al-Harb*, pp. 185–94.
32   FO Minute, Pyman, 27 April 1948, FO 371/68361, E7.
33   See for instance the report from Cairo to London, 12 May 1948, FO 371/68372, E6176.
34   George Antonius, *The Arab Awakening* (New York, 1979), pp. 276–325.
35   Dann, *Studies*, pp. 52–3.
36   Yehosua Porath, 'The Palestinians and the Negotiations for the British–Hejazi Treaty', *Asian and African Studies*, 8/1(1972), pp. 20–49.
37   Avi Shlaim who has written the most comprehensive, thorough and updated account of Abdullah's relationship with the Jews in Palestine, addresses these questions in the opening chapter of *Collusion Across the Jordan*, op. cit. See also Bar-Joseph, *Best of Enemies*.
38   Shlaim, *Collusion*, pp. 42–3.
39   Ibid., p. 45.
40   Ibid., pp. 46–7.
41   Keneth Stein, *The Land Question of Palestine, 1917–1939* (North Carolina, 1984), pp. 192–9.
42   Shlaim, *Collusion*, pp. 59–62.
43   Ibid., p. 83.
44   Ibid., p. 76.
45   Damascus to London, 12 January 1948, FO 371/68403, E300.
46   Eliahu Sasson, *Baderech el Hashalom* (On the Road to Peace), (Tel Aviv, 1978), p. 364–6.
47   Yoav Gelber, 'Maga'im Diplomatim Terem Hitnagshut Zevait –

Hamasa Umatan Bein Hasochnut Hayehudit Lemizrayim ve Yarden, 1946–1948' (The Negotiations of the Jewish Agency with Egypt and Transjordan, 1946–1948), *Cathedra*, 35(April 1985), p. 131.

48 *Filastin*, (Jaffa), 2 February 1936.

49 Hyder H. Abidi, *Jordan: A Political Study, 1948–1957*, (New York, 1965), pp. 26–7.

50 See minute from 26 January 1948, S25/9038, CZA.

51 FO Minute, 11 February 1948, FO 371/68637, E1980; Pappé, *Britain*, pp. 9–15.

52 Brief for Bevin's meeting with Tawfiq Abu al-Huda, 6 February 1948, FO 371/68818, E1901; for detailed description of the meeting see Shlaim, *Collusion*, pp. 132–9.

53 Pappé, *Britain*, pp. 9–15.

54 Abidi, op. cit., pp. 26–7.

55 Taha al-Hashimi, *Mudhakirat al-Harb* (War Memoirs), (Beirut, 1978), vol. 2, pp. 190–5.

56 Alec Kirkbride, *From the Wings* (London, 1976), pp. 22–4; John B. Glubb, *A Soldier with the Arabs* (London, 1957), pp. 82–5.

57 Wilson, *Abdullah*, p. 165.

58 Amman to FO, 25 April 1948, FO 816/118.

59 Pappé, *Britain*, p. 25.

60 Muhammad Hassanein Heikal, 'Reflections on a Nation in Crisis, 1948', *Journal of Palestine Studies*, 69/1 (Autumn 1988), p. 117.

61 Al-Salihi, op. cit.

62 Muhammad Hassanein Heikal, *Mudhakirat al-Siyasa al-Misriyya* (Recollections on Egyptian Politics), (Cairo, 1978), vol. 3, p. 25.

63 Hasan Nafi'a, *Misr wa al-Sira'a al-'Arabi al-Isra'ili* (Egypt and the Arab–Israeli Conflict), (Beirut, 1984), pp. 15–19.

64 An interview by Fastin Ahmad Fuad with General (Liwa) Ahmad Muhammad Mawawi in *al-Difa'a*, (Cairo), no. 22, May 1988, p. 41.

65 Shlaim, *Collusion*, p. 226.

66 Pappé, *Britain*, p. 25.

67 Bevin's Minute in CM(48)12, 5 February 1948, CAB 128/12.

68 Pappé, *Britain*, p. 26.

69 Al-Arif, *Al-Nakba*, vol. 1, pp. 284–9.

70 Shlaim, *Collusion*, p. 227.

71 Wahid al-Daly, *Asrar al-Jami'a al-'Arabiyya wa-'Abd al-Rahman 'Azzam*, (The Secrets of the Arab League and Abd al-Rahman Azzam), (Cairo, 1978), p. 234–5.

72 See note 56.

73 Memo by Glubb, March 1948, FO 371/69369, E3371.

74 Memo by Sasson, March 1948, S25/9383, CZA.

75 Sasson to Abdullah's Chamber, 2 March 1948, S25/1704, CZA.

76 Ben Gurion's File, 27 May 1947, Hagana Archives.

77 Ben Gurion's Diary, 27 April 1948, BGA.

78 Kirkbride to Burrows, 15 April 1948, FO 371/68552, E5087.

79 Glubb, *Soldier*, p. 107; Shlaim, *Collusion*, pp. 180–5.

80 Kirkbride to Bevin, 13 May 1948, in Foreign Secretary Private Files, FO 800/477, 48/7.

81 Ibid.
82 See note 79.
83 See note 80.
84 Meyrson Report, Israel State Archives, *Haprotocolim shel Minhelet Ha'am*, (The Protocols of the People's Directorship), (Tel Aviv, 1979).
85 Abidi, *Jordan*, p. 27.
86 Clifford Papers, Box 13, ORE7–48, Truman Library.
87 Rivlin and Orren, *Yoman*, 1 May 1948, p. 382.
88 Kirkbride to Bevin, 22 May 1948, FO 816/120.
89 Amman to London, 14 February 1948, FO 371/68367, E2163.
90 Kirkbride to Bevin, op. cit.

CHAPTER 5

1 Doc. S/801 in UN Official Records of the General Assembly, 3rd Session.
2 Sharett, *Besha'ar*, p. 242.
3 *New York Times*, 26 May 1948.
4 Israel State Archives, *Te'udot Lemediniyut Hahutz shel Medinat Israel, 14 May–30 September 1948* (Documents on the Foreign Policy of Israel 14 May–30 September 1948), (Jerusalem, 1981), ed. Yehoshua Freundlich, vol. 1, Doc. 95, Sharett to Eban, 27 May, 1948 (Hence *Documents*, vol. 1).
5 Levi, *Tisha' Qabin*, pp. 225–7.
6 Ibid., p. 226.
7 *Documents*, vol. 1, doc. 48, Report by Herzog, 21 May, 1948, pp. 42–8.
8 Levi, op. cit., pp. 225–7.
9 *Documents*, vol. 1, doc. 17, UN Resolutions 186, 14 May, 1948.
10 Rivlin and Orren, *Yoman*, vol. 2, Introduction, p. 421.
11 *Documents*, vol. 1, doc. 27, Eban to Locker, 18 May 1948 is one of many examples.
12 Pappé, *Britain*, pp. 34–6.
13 293rd meeting of the Security Council, 17 May 1948, UN Official Records of the General Assembly, 3rd Session.
14 Shakib, *Al-Harb*, pp. 239–41.
15 Ibid., p. 243.
16 311th meeting of the Security Council, 2 June 1948, UN Official Records of the General Assembly, 3rd Session.
17 Ben Gurion's Diary, 24 May 1948, BGA.
18 Rivlin and Orren, *Yoman*, 29 May 1948, p. 466.
19 For a detailed description see Shlaim, *Collusion*, pp. 250–5.
20 Rivlin and Orren, *Yoman*, 30 May 1948 and 6 June 1948, pp. 470, 488–90. See also Folke Bernadotte, *To Jerusalem* (London, 1951), pp. 112–13.
21 *Foreign Relations of the US 1948*, vol. 5, Memo by Lovett, 24 May 1948, p. 1036–7 (hence *FRUS 1948*).
22 Rivlin and Orren *Yoman*, 29 May 1948, p. 467.
23 *FRUS 1948*, vol. 5, ASoS to Douglass, 28 May 1948, pp. 1070–1.
24 *Documents*, vol. 1, doc. 154, Sharett to Eban, 7 June 1948; doc. 156, Bernadotte to Sharett, 8 June 1948.

25 Bernadotte's first proposals can be found in various sources: 27 June 1948, ISA 2424/40 and Bernadotte, *Jerusalem*, p. 128; Sune Person, *Mediation and Assassination: Count Bernadotte's Mission to Palestine, 1948* (London, 1979), p. 145.

26 Report by Kirkbride to Stabler, 3 June 1948, American National Archives 501BB/6–348.

27 *FRUS 1948*, vol. 5, Memo by McLintock, 23 June 1948, pp. 1134–5; SoS to Douglass, 25 June 1948, p. 1148.

28 Shlaim, *Collusion*, pp. 259–61; Rivlin and Orren, *Yoman*, editorial notes, p. 509.

29 *FRUS 1948* Vol. 5, Jessup to SoS, 30 June 1948, p. 1164.

30 *Haaretz*, 18 May 1948 and see Zvi Elpeleg, *Hamufti Hagadol* (The Grand Mufti), (Tel Aviv, 1989), p. 97.

31 *FRUS 1948*, vol. 5, Jessup to Austin, 21 June 1948, pp. 1088–9.

32 Consult note 26.

33 *FRUS 1948*, vol. 5, Memo conversation Beeley-Near Eastern Affairs Staff, 6 June 1948, p. 1100.

34 Pappé, *Britain*, pp. 38–42.

35 *FRUS 1948*, vol. 5, memo by Henderson, 6 June 1948, pp. 1099–1100; see also Louis, *Empire*, pp. 537–8.

36 Consult note 26.

37 Beeley's Minute, 2 July 1948, FO 371/68569, E9031.

38 Quoted in Louis, *Empire*, p. 543 note 32.

39 Mahdi Abd al-Hadi, *Al-Masala al-Filastiniyya wa Mashar'i al-Hulul al-Siyasiyya* (The Palestine Question and the Plans for its Political Solutions), (Beirut, 1975), p. 127.

40 Sulayman Musa and Munib al-Madi, *Tarikh al-Urdun fi'l-Qarn al-'Ashrin* (The History of Jordan in the Twentieth Century), (Amman, 1959).

41 Shlaim, *Collusion*, p. 260 and Sharett, *Besha'ar*, Report to the State Council, 15 July 1948, pp. 249–50.

42 Louis, *Empire*, p. 541.

43 Sharett to Bernadotte, 6 August 1948, Box 5, Peace in the Middle East, Dayan Centre, Tel Aviv University.

44 Sharett, *Besha'ar*, pp. 249–50.

45 Ben Gurion, *Hamehudeshet*, pp. 166–7.

46 Sharett to Shitrit, 8 August 1948, ISA 65/4.

47 Ben Gurion, *Hamehudeshet*, pp. 166–7.

48 Minutes of cabinet meeting concerning Bernadotte's plan, 4 July 1948, in ISA, 2424/10.

49 Ben Gurion, *Hamehudeshet*, pp. 163–6.

50 Ibid., p. 167.

51 *Documents*, vol. 1, doc. 381, Foreign Ministry Memo, 27 July 1948.

52 ISA 65/4, Ibid.

53 *FRUS 1948*, vol. 5, Jessup to SoS, 30 June 1948, p. 1161.

54 *FRUS 1948*, vol. 5, Douglass to SoS, 6 July 1948, p. 1192.

55 *Documents*, vol. 1, doc. 291, Sharett to T. Lie, 8 July 1948.

56 *FRUS 1948*, vol. 5, Report by the CIA, 27 July 1948, p. 1243.

57 Shakib, *Harb*, p. 256; Rivlin and Orren, *Yoman*, editorial note, p. 513.
58 Shlaim, *Collusion*, p. 264.
59 Pappé, *Britain*, pp. 49–50.
60 Morris, *Birth*, p. 206.
61 For the development of Bernadotte's view see his book *To Jerusalem*, pp. 163–4.
62 Telegram from the Egyptian CiC to his Operational Officer, 12 July 1948 in Shakib, *Al-Harb*, p. 279.
63 Sami Hakim, *Tariq al-Nakba* (The Road to Catastrophe), (Cairo, 1969), p. 90.
64 Interview of General Shakib with General Sa'ad al-Din Sabur, 27 February 1980, in Shakib, *Al-Harb*, p. 273.
65 Shakib, op. cit., p. 281.
66 Rivlin and Orren, *Yoman*, 11 July 1948, pp. 581–2.
67 Pappé, *Britain*, pp. 49–57.
68 Sharett, *Besha'ar*, p. 289.
69 Morris, *Birth*, pp. 143–9; in Khalidi, 'Dalet', the reader can find in appendix D a map and list of the villages concerned.
70 *FRUS 1948*, vol. 5, McDonald to SoS, 27 June 1948, p. 1151; Jessup to SoS, 27 July 1948, p. 1248.
71 Ibid.
72 Final report can be found in doc. A/638, 18 September 1948 in the UN Official Records of the General Assembly, 3rd Session and in Joseph Zasloff, 'Great Britain and Palestine: A Study of the Problem before the UN', (D.Phil. Thesis submitted to l'Université de Genève, 1952), p. 154.
73 Note in particular, Person, *Mediation*, pp. 297–313; Howard Sachar, *Europe Leaves the Middle East* (New York, 1972), p. 524 and Jon and David Kimchie, *Both Sides of the Hill* (London, 1960), p. 198.
74 *FRUS 1948*, vol. 5, Douglass to SoS, 1 September 1948, p. 1363.
75 Louis, *Empire*, p. 548
76 Pappé, *Britain*, pp. 79, 86, 91, 98–100, 114, 174.
77 *FRUS 1948*, vol. 5, Douglass to SoS, 1 September 1948, p. 1363.
78 *FRUS 1948*, vol. 5, Griffith (Cairo) to SoS, 15 September 1948, p. 1398.
79 *New York Times*, 17 October 1948.
80 See various references in Bernadotte, *Jerusalem*.
81 Consult note 74.
82 Ibid.
83 Louis, *Empire*, p. 548.
84 FO Minute, Burrows, 18 August 1948, FO371/68582.
85 See Chapter 8.
86 Ben Gurion's speech in front of the People's Council in Rivlin and Orren, *Yorman*, vol. 2, p. 617.
87 Age Lundström, *Death of a Mediator* (Washington, 1968), p. 17.
88 Ibid., pp. 7–20.
89 Rivlin and Orren, *Yoman*, vol. 2, p. 698, note 7.
90 For the way the Israelis pursued the investigation see Yosef Heller, 'Failure of a Mission: Bernadotte and Palestine 1948', *Journal of*

Contemporary History, 14/3(January 1979), p. 519 and Cary David Stanger, 'A Haunting Legacy: The Assassination of Bernadotte', *Middle East Journal*, 42(1988), pp. 260–370.

CHAPTER 6

1 Pappé, *Britain*, pp. 14–15, 54–5.
2 Part of the Negev to Egypt and part of the Hula Valley to Syria.
3 Kirkbride to FO, 8 September 1948, FO371/68861, E11809.
4 Document S/801, UN Official Records of the General Assembly, 3rd Session.
5 *FRUS 1948*, vol. 5, Douglass to SD, 10 September 1948, p. 1388. This entry shows that even before the murder Britain had tried to persuade the Americans that a prior acquiescence to the plan by the two sides should not be a precondition for its implementation.
6 *Hansard*, vol. 456, Col. 899–900, 22 September 1948.
7 Ibid.
8 *FRUS 1948*, vol. 5, memo of conversation Clifford and Lovett, 29 September 1948, p. 1430.
9 Ibid. For Clifford's role in the American Palestine policy see Louis, *Empire*, pp. 424–9.
10 Rivlin and Orren, *Yoman*, 8 September 1948, p. 676.
11 Sharett, *Besha'ar*, pp. 291–2.
12 Ibid., pp. 291–6; Ben Gurion, *Hamehudeshet*, pp. 291–5.
13 See Ilan Pappé, 'Moshe Sharett, David Ben Gurion and the "Palestinian Option", 1948–1956', *Studies in Zionism*, 7/1, (1986), pp. 77–97.
14 Ben Gurion, op. cit., p. 294.
15 Ibid.
16 Israeli Defence Forces, *Toldot Milhemet Hakomemiyut* (The War of Independence), (Tel Aviv, 1959), pp. 229–79.
17 *FRUS 1948*, vol. 5, SoS to ASoS, 13 October 1948, p. 1470.
18 *FRUS 1948*, vol. 5, Douglass to SD, 13 October 1948, p. 1469.
19 *FRUS 1948*, vol. 5, ASoS to McDonald, 13 October 1948, p. 1473.
20 *FRUS 1948*, vol. 5, memo by McClintock to Lovett, 6 October 1948, p. 1459.
21 *FRUS 1948*, vol. 5, memo by ASoS to the President, 21 October 1948, pp. 1494–5.
22 *FRUS 1948*, vol. 5, ASoS to SoS, 23 October 1948, p. 1507; Clifford to Truman, 23 October 1948, p. 1509.
23 Harry S. Truman, *Years of Trial and Hope*; *Memoirs by Harry S. Truman* (New York, 1965), vol. 2, p. 198.
24 Pappé, *Britain*, p. 191.
25 *FRUS 1948*, vol. 5, ASoS to SoS, 21 October 1948, p. 1502; and 31 October 1948, p. 1534.
26 *FRUS 1948*, vol. 5, SoS to ASoS, 21 October 1948, p. 1502, the mediation efforts in the Greek civil war had met up to that point with utter failure, see Bullock, *Bevin*, p. 630.
27 *FRUS 1948*, vol. 5, ASoS to SoS, 22 October 1948, p. 1505.

28 *FRUS 1948*, vol. 5, Dean Rusk to ASoS, 23 October 1948, p. 1511.
29 Ibid.
30 First Committee, Summary Records, meetings of 21 September 1948 to 9 December 1948, UN Official Records of the General Assembly, 3rd Session.
31 Ben Gurion, *Hamehudeshet*, p. 302.
32 See Chapter 6.
33 *Documents*, vol. 1, doc. 547, Comay to the Israeli mission to the UN Session in Paris, 27 September 1948.
34 Avi Shlaim argues, convincingly, that Ben Gurion was acting upon pressure from the army and did not make an effort to persuade the government to accept the plan. Yet, Ben Gurion later argued that this was a 'missed opportunity' to occupy the West Bank. Shlaim, *Collusion*, pp. 306–10.
35 The Egyptians were caught in Suweidan Menshiyeh and in Faluja. See Pappé, *Britain*, pp. 58–62.
36 Shakib, *Al-Harb*, p. 324.
37 The story of the besieged garrison is vividly portrayed in the War Museum in the Qla'a in Cairo.
39 Rivlin and Orren, *Yoman*, 22 October 1948, p. 760.
39 Monitoring Service of the IDF: conversation between the head of the 4th Brigade of the Legion and Major Crocker, the British officer commanding the Legion units in the Hebron area. In Rivlin and Orren, *Yoman*, 23 October 1948, p. 766.
40 Ibid., 31 October 1948, p. 790.
41 Shakib, *Al-Harb*, pp. 352–3.
42 See Pappé, 'Alliance', pp. 561–81.

CHAPTER 7

1 Israel State Archives, *Te'udot Lemediniyut Hahutz shel Medinat Israel, Sihot Shvitat-Haneshek 'im Medinot 'Arav, December 1948–July 1949* (Documents of the Foreign Policy of Israel, December 1948–July 1949), ed. Yemima Rosenthal, (Jerusalem, 1983) vol. 3, (hence *Documents*, vol. 3) doc. 56, Eytan to Sharett, 28 Janaury 1949; doc. 67, Eytan to Sharett, 29 January 1949; Pappé, *Britain*, p. 178.
2 *Documents*, vol. 3, introduction, p. 14.
3 *Documents*, vol. 3, doc. 37, Eytan to Ben Gurion, 21 January 1949; doc. 41, Elath to Shrett, 23 January 1949.
4 *Documents*, vol. 3, doc. 54, Eytan to Sharett, 27 January 1949; doc. 56, Eytan to Sharett, 28 January 1949.
5 *Documents*, vol. 3, introduction, pp. 15–17.
6 *Documents*, vol. 3, doc. 4, meeting of Israeli delegation with Dr Bunche, 12 January 1949.
7 *Documents*, vol. 3, doc. 30, Sharett to Eytan, 19 January 1949; doc. 32, Eytan to Sharett, 19 January 1949.
8 Shlaim, *Collusion*, p. 390, note 6.
9 Shlaim, op. cit., p. 390.
10 Rivlin and Orren, *Yoman*, 8 October 1948, pp. 739–40; see also Avi

Shlaim, 'The Rise and Fall of the All-Palestine Government in Gaza', *Journal of Palestinian Studies*, 20/1, no. 77(1990), pp. 37–53.
11 *Documents*, vol. 3, doc. 76, Eytan to Sharett, 30 January 1949; doc. 78, meeting of Israeli delegation with Dr Bunche, 31 January 1949.
12 Taha al-Hashimi, *Mudhakirat*, vol. 2, p. 262.
13 Shlaim, *Collusion*, p. 391, note 7.
14 See note 13.
15 L. Khon to Ben Gurion, 19 May 1948, CZA S/25.
16 *FRUS 1948*, vol. 5, Jerusalem to SoS, 8 June 1948, p. 1105.
17 On Kirkbride's view see Pappé, 'Kirkbride'.
18 Ibid.
19 Pappé, *Britain*, p. 196; Shlaim, *Collusion*, pp. 294–5.
20 Pappé, *Britain*, p. 166.
21 Abbas Murad, *The Political Role of the Jordanian Army* (Beirut, 1973), p. 60; Abdullah al-Tal, *Karithat Filastin* (The Palestine Disaster), (Cairo, 1959), pp. 420–1.
22 Shlaim, *Collusion*, p. 360–70.
23 Brief for the SoS for the Defence Committee Meeting, 5 January 1949, FO 371/75045, E367.
24 FO to Baghdad, 10 February 1949, FO 371/75331, E1692; Baghdad to FO, 16 March 1949, FO 371/75836, E510.
25 Shlaim, op. cit., pp. 306–11, 406–7, 460.
26 Pappé, *Britain*, p. 168.
27 Ibid., p. 173.
28 Amman to FO, 9 December 1948, FO 371/68862, E15724.
29 Bevin to Kirkbride, 16 December 1948, FO 816/42; Wright to Kirkbride, 3 December 1948, FO 371/68822, E15531.
30 Avi Shlaim, *The Politics of Partition: King Abdullah, the Zionists, and Palestine 1921–1951* (Oxford, 1990), abridged and revised edition of *Collusion Across the Jordan*, pp. 26–272.
31 Pappé, *Britain*, pp. 171–3.
32 Kirkbride to Bevin, 17 December 1948, FO 816/142.
33 Pappé, *Britain*, pp. 174–6.
34 Ibid.
35 Shlaim, *Collusion*, pp. 401–4.
36 See section of this chapter on the armistice talks with Egypt.
37 FO Minute, January 1949, FO 371/75336.
38 Abdullah to Bevin, 19 January 1949, FO 371/75330, E1105.
39 *Foreign Relations of the US, 1949*, vol. 6, Stabler to SoS, 1 February 1949, p. 716 (hence *FRUS 1949*).
40 See note 3.
41 *FRUS 1949*, vol. 6, Stabler to SoS, 24 February 1949, p. 767.
42 Al-Tal, *Karithat*, p. 493.
43 Pappé, *Britain*, pp. 180–1.
44 Ibid.
45 *FRUS 1949*, vol. 6, memo Satterthwaite, 18 March 1949, p. 845.
46 Pappé, *Britain*, pp. 180–3.
47 Kirkbride to Bevin, 24 March 1949, FO 371/75836, E3844.
48 Al-Tal, *Karithat*, p. 521.

49 The ceremony and the signature in Rhodes is vividly described in Shlaim, *Collusion*, pp. 425–33.

50 See Pappé, *Britain*, pp. 100–06.

51 Shlaim, *Collusion*, p. 391, note 7.

52 Ben Gurion's Diary, 1 March 1949, BGA.

53 Kamal S. Salibi, *The Modern History of Lebanon* (London, 1965), pp. 185–7.

54 Avi Shlaim, 'Husni Zaim and the Plan to Resettle Palestinian Refugees in Syria', *Middle East Focus*, Fall 1986, pp. 26–31; and Arieh Shalev, *Shituf Pe'ula bezel 'Imut* (Co-operation under the Shadow of Conflict), (Tel Aviv, 1989), pp. 49–65.

55 Zaim's peace offer became another topic in the historiographical debate in the 1980s when the question of missed opportunity was raised by various scholars in two conferences in Israel. It is indeed difficult to determine whether or not Zaim seriously sought a peace treaty with Israel, although Shlaim for instance does not hesitate to state that 'one of Zaim's top priorities was to make peace with Israel'. See Shlaim, *Collusion*, p. 427.

56 For the official policy see *Documents*, vol. 3, introduction p. 30 and editorial note 11 attached to doc. 36 on p. 69.

57 *Documents*, vol. 3, introduction, pp. 29–31.

58 Ibid.

59 *Documents*, vol. 3, doc. 4, Bunche's meeting with the Israeli delegation, 12 January 1949.

60 *Documents*, vol. 3, doc. 37, Eytan to Ben Gurion, 21 January 1949. See also Hasan Sabri Al-Khuly, *Siyasat al-Isti'imar wa al-Sahayuniyya tijja Filastin* (The Imperialist and Zionist Policy towards Palestine), (Cairo, 1973), vol. 1, pp. 784–6.

61 Sadia Touval, *The Peace Brokers* (Princeton, 1982), p. 57.

62 Ibish, *Arslan*, vol. 2, 18 March 1949, p. 799.

CHAPTER 8

1   Sharett, *Besha'ar*, p. 335.

2   Ben Gurion, *Hamehudeshet*, pp. 320–7.

3   *FRUS 1948*, vol. 5, SoS to ASoS, 16 October 1948, p. 1481.

4   Ibid.

5   Doc. A/318 UN Official Records of the General Assembly, 3rd Session.

6   *FRUS 1948*, vol. 5, SoS to ASoS, 16 October 1948, p. 1481.

7   *FRUS 1948*, vol. 5, ASoS to SoS(Paris), 19 October 1948, p. 1496.

8   James G. McDonald, *My Mission to Israel* (New York, 1951), p. 177.

9   David P. Forsythe, *UN Peacemaking: The Conciliation Commission for Palestine* (Baltimore, 1972), p. 27.

10 Khaled Ali, *Al-Harb*, p. 255, note 1.

11 Israel State Archives, *Te'udot Lemediniyut Hahutz shel Medinat Israel, May–December 1949* (Documents on the Foreign Policy of Israel, May–December 1949), ed. Yemima Rosenthal, (Jerusalem, 1986), vol. 4, document 1, G. Avner to Sharret, 1 May 1949 (hence *Documents*, vol. 4).

12 *Documents*, vol. 3, doc. 7, Eytan to Sharett, 13 January 1949.
13 McDonald, *My Mission*, p. 177.
14 Pablo de Azcarate, *Mission in Palestine* (Washington, 1966), pp. 140–6.
15 *FRUS 1949*, vol. 6, Burdet (Amman) to SoS, 2 March 1949, p. 786.
16 *Documents*, vol. 3, doc. 32, Eytan to Sharett, 19 January 1949.
17 Sasson to Eytan, 9 March 1949, ISA 2441/1.
18 On al-Hashimi's quality see Yehoshua Porath, 'On the Writing of Arab History by Israeli Scholars', *The Jerusalem Quarterly*, 32(Summer 1984), p. 34.
19 Al-Hashimi, *Mudhakirat*, p. 259.
20 *Al-Ahram*, daily reports on the PCC throughout the month of February 1949.
21 *Al-Hayat*, 22 March 1949.
22 In the summer of 1949 Transjordan became officially the Hashemite Kingdom of Jordan.
23 *Al-Difa'a*, 26 March 1949 and *Filastin*, 26 March 1949.
24 Ibid.
25 Azcarate, *Mission*, pp. 142–4.
26 Apart from Iraq, FO 371/75371, the whole file; Forsythe, *PCC*, pp. 45–7; Azcarate, *Mission*, pp. 148–9.

CHAPTER 9

1 FO 371/75350 and ISA 2442/3; on al-Shuqayri see Ibish, *Arslan*, 20 July 1949, p. 860.
2 Eytan's declaration on 30 April 1949, in Box 5, Peace in the Middle East, Dayan Centre.
3 Israel's refusal to negotiate with the Syrians in Lausanne before the two countries completed the armistice accord was ignored as the PCC did not refuse to include the Syrians in Lausanne; see Ibish, *Arslan*, 14 May 1949, p. 831.
4 *Davar* and *Haaretz*, 22 April 1949.
5 *Al-Ahram*, 22 April 1949.
6 *Documents*, vol. 4, doc. 4, Eytan to Sharett, 3 May 1949.
7 *Documents*, vol. 4, doc. 13, Eytan to Sharett, 9 May 1949.
8 *Documents*, vol. 4, doc. 14, Elath to Sharett, 9 May 1949.
9 *Documents*, vol. 4, doc. 17, Elath to Sharett, 10 May 1949; see also Ibish, *Arslan*, 14 May 1949, pp. 831–2.
10 *Documents*, vol. 4, Editorial Note, p. 50.
11 The 1947 partition map appeared only in the annex to his proposals since at the time he had intentionally not defined the boundaries, leaving the issue open for future negotiations.
12 al-Khuli, *Siyasat*, p. 792, note 1.
13 The quotations from Arslan's diary, ibid, 13 July 1949, p. 858; for the explanation on the decision making process also there on 20 July 1949, p. 832.
14 *Documents*, vol. 4, doc. 26, Eytan to Sharett, 14 May 1949.
15 *FRUS 1948*, vol. 5, Cairo to ASoS, 13 October 1948, p. 1471.

16 Milner's Report to the Commission's Secretariat, 11 November 1949, ISA 2447/8; *al-Sha'ab*, 17 November 1949. See also Forsythe, *PCC*, p. 51.
17 Pappé, *Britain*, pp. 120–3 for explanation of why Britain did not join the PCC.
18 *FRUS 1948*, vol. 5, SoS to ASoS, 16 October 1948, p. 1481.
19 *FRUS 1948*, vol. 5, Moscow to ASoS, 15 October 1948, p. 1480 and First Committee's summary of meetings, 21 September 1948–9 – December 1948, UN Official Records of the General Assembly, 3rd Session.
20 *Documents*, vol. 4, doc. 26, Eytan to Sharett, 14 May 1949.
21 *Al-Ahram*, 11 April 1949.
22 *Documents*, vol. 4, doc. 74, Eytan to Sharett, 13 June 1949, p. 124.
23 Foreign Office Minute, 18 March 1949, ISA 36/10.
24 Comay to Jessup, 24 July 1949, ISA 73/4.
25 Varda Schiffer, 'The 1949 Israeli Offer to Repatriate 100,000 Palestinian Refugees', *Middle East Focus*, vol. 9/2 (Fall 1986), pp. 14–15.
26 Sharett in the Knesset in June 1949, in *Besha'ar*, pp. 370–1.
27 Report on the possible settlement of the refugee problem, undated, ISA 2445/3.
28 *FRUS 1948*, vol. 6, Ethridge to SoS, 8 June 1949, p. 1096.
29 *Documents*, vol. 4, Editorial Note, p. 10.
30 Ibid.
31 *FRUS 1949*, vol. 6, Memo of conversation between Elath and McGhee, 25 May 1949.
32 On the Gaza government, see Shlaim, 'All-Palestine'.
33 *Documents*, vol. 4, Eytan to Sharett, 3 May 1949.
34 *FRUS 1949*, vol. 6, Hildring to SoS, 25 July 1949, p. 1249. See also in *Documents*, vol. 4, doc. 41, President Truman's letter to Ben Gurion of 29 May 1949.
35 *Documents*, vol. 4, McDonald to Ben Gurion, 29 May 1949, p. 75. Israeli prime ministers have been receiving similar notes and warnings from 1948 to this very day. At times, for example during the negotiatons on the disengagement agreements with Syria and Egypt in the 1970s, these warnings would indeed effect a shift in Israeli policy. But since the Americans would not implement most of them, they seldom seriously affected Israeli policy.
36 Louis, *Empire*, p. 596.
37 Shlaim, *Collusion*, p. 472.
38 *Documents*, vol. 4, doc. 4, Eytan to Sharett, 3 May 1948, editorial note 20, p. 13.
39 *FRUS 1949*, vol. 6, Rockwell to SoS, 11 August 1949, p. 1286.
40 Morris, *Birth*, pp. 163–4, 171, 176–7, 191–2. See also Tom Segev, *1949, The First Israelis* (New York, 1986), pp. 43–67.
41 *FRUS 1949*, vol. 6, McGhee to SoS, 19 July 1949, p. 1237.
42 *Documents*, vol. 4, doc. 45, Eytan to Barco, 31 May 1949. As for the Arab position see al-Arif, *Al-Nakba*, vol. 2, p. 492.
43 *Documents*, vol. 4, doc. 62, Sasson to Sharett, 8 June 1949.
44 *Documents*, vol. 4, doc. 48, Sasson to Sharett, 1 June 1949.

45 *Documents*, vol. 4, doc. 91, Eytan to Sharett, 21 June 1949.

46 *Documents*, vol. 4, pp. 87–9, 94, 99, 101.

47 In fact, as we shall see, the permanent residents at least in Jordan hindered Abdullah's effort to reach a separate peace treaty with Israel.

48 *Documents*, vol. 4, doc. 4, Eytan to Sharett, 3 May 1949, editorial note 11, p. 12.

49 *Documents*, vol. 4, doc. 12, Sasson to Sharett, 8 May 1949.

50 *Documents*, vol. 4, doc. 52, Sasson to Sharett, 2 June 1949. Tom Segev explains that those supporting the 'Hashemite Option' asserted that it would increase Jordan's dependence on Israel. Segev, op. cit., pp. 38–9.

51 *Documents*, vol. 4, doc. 56, Sasson to Sharett, 5 June 1949.

52 *Documents*, vol. 4, doc. 13, Eytan to Sharett, 9 May 1949, editorial note 2, p. 29.

53 Pappé, 'Sharett'.

54 *Documents*, vol. 4, doc. 107, Sasson to Sharett, 26 June 1949.

55 *Documents*, vol. 4, doc. 63, Eban to Eytan, 8 June 1949.

56 *Documents*, vol. 4, doc. 111, Eytan to Sharett, 30 June 1949.

57 Shlaim, 'Zaim'.

58 *FRUS 1949*, vol. 6, Damascus to SoS, 14 July 1949, p. 1226.

59 Ibid.

60 Conference on the Middle East, 22 July 1949, FO 371/75072, E9044.

61 *New York Times*, 26 July 1949.

62 Ibid., 19 August 1949.

63 Ibid., 26 July 1949, 19 August 1949. This impression is also gained from Arslan's diary who at the time was demoted to the post of ambassador to Ankara.

64 Schiffer, op. cit.

65 *FRUS 1949*, vol. 6, SoS to US Embassy in London, 13 July 1949, p. 1223; Porter to SoS, 5 August 1949.

66 *Documents*, vol. 4, doc. 74, Eytan to Sharett, 13 June 1949.

67 *FRUS 1949*, vol. 6, it seems that Porter was behind the shift in American policy after he had replaced Ethridge, see pp. 1312–20.

68 *Documents*, vol. 4, doc. 115, Heyd to Herlitz, 1 July 1949.

69 *Documents*, vol. 4, Editorial Note, p. 206.

70 Ibid.

71 *Documents*, vol. 4, doc. 160, Elath to Sharett, 28 July 1949.

72 A/3922 PCC progress report (9 June–15 September 1949), UN Official Records of the General Assembly, 3rd session.

73 *FRUS 1949*, vol. 6, memo by Dean Rusk, 28 July 1949, p. 1262.

74 FO Minute, Morton, 16 September 1949, FO 371/75439, E11376; and see Kirkbride's position in Kirkbride to Bevin, 2 August 1949, FO 371/82706, ET1017/2.

75 On 15 May 1948, there were 650,000 Jews in Israel, Government of Israel, *Facts about Israel* (Jerusalem, 1958).

76 *Documents*, vol. 4, doc. 146, Sharett: Guidelines for Israel Missions Abroad, 25 July 1949, p. 239.

77 Ibid., p. 246.

78 *Documents*, vol. 4, doc. 136, Consultation at the Ministry of Foreign Affairs, 13 July 1949.
79 *Documents*, vol. 4, doc. 146, Ibid.
80 *Documents*, vol. 4, doc. 162, Shiloah to Sharett, 29 July 1949.
81 *Documents*, vol. 4, doc. 171, Shiloah to Sharett, 2 August 1949.
82 *Documents*, vol. 4, doc. 167, Sasson to Sharett, 1 August 1949; doc. 178, Sasson to Sharett, 4 August 1949.
83 See Preface.
84 *Documents*, vol. 4, doc. 188, Sasson to Sharett, 8 August 1949.
85 Following Flapan's explanation for Israel's acceptance of the 1947 resolution, one might suggest that the Arabs accepted the PCC move since it was clear the Israelis would reject it. The absence of adequate archival material does not allow a clear-cut judgement on this episode. The important feature which emerges is that the pattern in Lausanne was a receptive Arab response to UN peace initiative and a stubborn Israeli position. A pattern which would recur in the 1980s.
86 *Documents*, vol. 4, doc. 213, Sasson to Sharett, 15 August 1949.
87 Ilan Pappé, 'Britain and the Palestinian Refugees, 1948–1950', *Middle East Focus* 9/2(Fall 1986), pp. 19–25.
88 *Documents*, vol. 4, doc. 265, Sasson to Sharett, 5 September 1949.
89 *Documents*, vol. 4, doc. 310, Sasson to Sharett, 28 September 1949.
90 Sharett to Sasson, 24 September 1949, ISA 2412/26.
91 Bipartite discussions, May 1950, FO 371/81908; *Jewish Agency Digest*, 30 June 1950.
92 Comay to Sharett, 10 May 1949, ISA 38/9.
93 Pappé, 'Sharett'.
94 Ibid., and see Rivlin and Orren, *Yoman*, 14 July 1949, p. 993.
95 Pappé, 'Sharett'.
96 *Al-Misri*, 2 October 1949.
97 Rivlin and Orren, *Yoman*, 2 January 1949, p. 921.
98 Sasson to Z. Divon, quoted in Shlaim, 'Zaim', pp. 29–30
99 Pappé, 'Sharett', pp. 84–5.
100 *FRUS 1949*, vol. 6, Ethridge to SoS, 14 July 1949, p. 1124.
101 McDonald, *My Mission*, p. 177–9.
102 Sasson to Divon, Ibid.
103 *FRUS 1949*, vol. 6, Ethridge to SoS, 9 May 1949, p. 988.
104 *Al-Ahram*, 11 April 1949.

CHAPTER 10

1 UN Resolution 302(IV), a copy appears in 10 November 1949, FO 371/75446, E13588. See also Troutbeck to FO, 12 November 1949, FO 371/75446, E13701.
2 The agreed conclusions of the Istanbul conference, 26–29 November 1949, *FRUS 1949*, vol. 6, p. 173 and see George McGhee, *Envoy to the Middle World* (New York, 1983), pp. 80–7.
3 It has to be remembered that Abdullah, unlike Kirkbride was willing to resettle as many refugees as possible in his territory. See McGhee, op. cit., p. 40 and Pappé, 'Kirkbride', pp. 43–70.

4 Morton to FO, 10 October 1949, FO 371/75442.
5 The Istanbul conference, Ibid.
6 Final Report of ESM, 28 December 1949, part 1, p. 2.
7 Ibid.
8 Palestine Affairs Survey for December 1949, FO 371/75329, E12423; G. Rafael to W. Eytan, 16 February 1950, Israel State Archives, *Te'udot Lemediniyut Hahutz shel Medinat Israel 1950*, (Documents on the Israeli Foreign Policy 1950), ed. Yehosua Freundlich, vol. 5, (Jerusalem, 1988), doc. 96 (hence *Documents*, vol. 5).
9 Such as the Blandford Scheme of the summer of 1951.
10 Final Report of ESM, Ibid.
11 UNRWA's First Report, pp. 11–12.
12 Ibid.
13 Ibid.
14 Resolution accepted on 7 November 1950 in the Ad-Hoc Political Committee, Official Records of the UN General Assembly, 5th Session.
15 Washington to FO, 22 May 1951, FO 371/91185, E1024/23.
16 The office was established on 22 May 1951 see FO 371/91367, E1071/69.
17 Burrows to Bowker, 22 May 1951, FO 371/91185, E1024/24.
18 Rapp to FO(Evans), 9 June 1951, FO 371/91217, E1345/20; see also *The New York Times*, 21 June 1951, *al-Ahram*, 13 December 1951, *Filastin*, 22 December 1951 and *al-Nahar*, 1 January 1952. See also Edmond Buehrig, *The UN and the Palestine Refugees* (New York, 1971), pp. 18–21.
19 Avi Plascov, 'The Palestinians on Jordan's Borders', in R. Owen, op. cit., p. 225.
20 We first heard about this body when we discussed the war in Jerusalem at the beginning of the fighting. It assisted the UN in supervising first the implementation of the UN partition resolution, and after its demise, the various truce arrangements.
21 UN Resolution, 194[III], 11 December 1949.
22 Al-Arif, *Al-Nakba*, vol. 2, p. 492.
23 Glubb, *Soldier*, pp. 291–2.
24 Gabriel Shefer, 'Pitron Kolel mul Mitun Hasichsuch Haisraeli Ha'aravi; Behina Mehudeshet shel Hahitnagshut bein Moshe Sharett ve David Ben Gurion' (A Comprehensive Solution *vis-à-vis* Conflict Management of the Arab–Israeli Conflict: A Reappraisal of the Confrontation between Moshe Sharett and David Ben Gurion), in Shmuel Etinger, *Haziyonut ve Hasheela Ha'aravit* (Zionism and the Arab Question), (Jerusalem, 1979), p. 146. See also *FRUS 1949*, vol. 6, Conversation between Burrows and Rockwell, 3 January 1949, p. 783.
25 The plan was drafted as 'Instrument Establishing a Permanent International Regime for the Jerusalem Area', in the Official Records of the UN General Assembly, 4th Session, the proceedings of the Ad-Hoc Political Committee, vol. 1, p. 10.
26 Jerusalem to FO, 13 September 1949, FO 371/75351, E11112.
27 *FRUS 1948*, vol. 5, Memo of the Joint Chiefs of Staff to Forrestal, 23 October 1948, p. 1527.

28 *FRUS 1949*, vol. 6, Greenhill (British Embassy in Washington) conversation with Wilkins of the Office of Near Eastern Affairs, 14 October 1949, p. 1426.
29 United Nations' Delegation to FO, 2 December 1949, FO 371/75344, E14491.
30 Plenary Meeting of the UN General Assembly 4th Session, pp. 35–7; Resolution 303(IV) adopted in this session.
31 Ben Gurion, *Hamehudeshet*, vol. 1, p. 401.
32 *The Times*, 30 January 1950; *New York Times*, 12 February 1950.
33 For reports on this see Amman to FO, 8 June 1949, FO 371/75338, E7042.
34 Monthly Report of July 1949, FO 371/75273, E10169.
35 Shlaim, *Collusion*, pp. 522–7.
36 Amman to FO, 15 December 1949, FO 371/75277, E14906.
37 Pappé, *Britain*, pp. 190–3; *New York Times* 23 January 1950.
38 Amman to FO, 30 January 1950, FO 371/82715, E151/7; see also Pappé, 'Kirkbride', pp. 43–70.
39 Amman to FO, 16 January 1950, FO 371/82177, E1015/7.
40 Ben Gurion's Diary, entries for April 1950, BGA.
41 Amman to FO, 24 January 1950, FO 371/82177, E1015/10; *Documents*, vol. 5, Dayan and Shiloah's meeting with Fawzi al-Mulki, Jordan Defence Minister, doc. 40, 24 January 1950.
42 Amman to FO, 13 February 1950, FO 371/82171, E1015/22.
43 Amman to FO, 18 February 1950, FO 371/82177, E1015/22; Shlaim, *Collusion*, p. 540.
44 Jordanian draft in Amman to FO, 22 February 1950, FO 371/82178, E1015/33; and in Shlaim, *Collusion*, Appendix 4; Israeli draft in ISA 2453/3, 24 February 1950 and in *Documents*, vol. 5, doc. 105.
45 Amman to FO, 6 March 1950, FO 371/82715, E1015/18.
46 *Foreign Relations of the US 1950*, vol. 6, Memo by Hare, 8 March 1950, p. 787 (hence *FRUS 1950*); *Documents*, vol. 5, Drafts of a Non-Aggression Agreement between Israel and Jordan, doc. 112, 28 February 1950.
47 McDonald, *My Mission*, pp. 195–6.
48 *Bourse Egyptienne*, 30 March 1950, 15 April 1950; Shlaim, *Collusion*, pp. 550–60.
49 Annual Report for 1950, Jordan, FO 371/91705. The irony of course is that on the basis of this clause Egypt itself was expelled from the League for concluding a separate peace agreement with Israel.
50 Helm in Tel Aviv was more updated than Kirkbride, see Helm's Brief for Bevin, 14 March 1950, FO 371/82715, E1015/12.
51 *Documents*, vol. 5, Meeting Shiloah and Dayan with King Abdullah in Amman, doc. 213, 27 April 1950.
52 Pappé, 'Alliance'.
53 Brief for Bevin, 14 March 1950, FO 371/82715, E1015/12.
54 Amman to FO, 27 May 1950, FO 371/82178, E1015/61.
55 See *Documents*, vol. 5, M. Sasson to E. Sasson, doc. 292, 27 June 1950; for the other Israeli point of view see Divon to Sharett, doc. 282, 16 June 1950. See also Tel Aviv to FO, 23 June 1950, FO 371/82178.

56 Tel Aviv to FO, 7 July 1950, FO 371/82178, E1015/70.
57 Tel Aviv to FO, 11 July 1950, FO 371/82178, E1015/74.
58 Ibid.
59 Monthly Report for July 1959, FO 371/82704, E1015/79.
60 *FRUS 1950*, vol. 5, Douglas reporting a conversation with Kirkbride to Secretary of State, 19 May 1950, p. 902; similar PCC impression in *Documents*, vol. 5, Eytan to Sharett, doc. 342, 17 August 1950.
61 Meeting with PCC, 8 July 1950, FO 371/82719, E1015/80.
62 Kirkbride to Bevin, 2 August 1950, FO 371/82179, E1015/82.
63 *Documents*, vol. 5, Biran to Sharett, doc. 345, 21 August 1951.
64 Annual Report for Israel, 1950, FO 371/91705.
65 Kirkbride to Bevin, 20 October 1950, FO 371/82179, E1015/117.
66 Shlaim, *Collusion*, pp. 575–82.
67 Kirkbride to FO, 15 January 1951, FO 371/91364, E1041/8.
68 Pappé, *Britain*, pp. 205–6.
69 Final stages of the negotiations see Shlaim, *Collusion*, pp. 583–612.
70 *Haaretz*, 27 June 1950.
71 Box 5 in the Dayan Center Library, Arab–Israeli Conflict, p. 25.
72 *Jewish Agency Digest* (Hence JAD), 21 July 1950.
73 *JAD*, 11 August 1950.
74 Ibid., 1 August 1951.
75 Dayan Center, Box 5, p. 25.
76 Ya'acov Talom, *Be'idan Haalimut*, (In the Age of Violence), (Tel Aviv, 1974), p. 315.
77 *JAD*, 11 December 1952.
78 Memo by Vogel, 4 September 1950, FO 371/82196, E1052/15.
79 Itamar Rabinovich and Jehuda Reinharz, *Israel in the Middle East* (New York, 1984), doc. 14.
80 This is manifested in the introduction by Yemima Rosenthal to *Documents*, vol. 4.
81 Rabinovich and Reinharz, op. cit.
82 Ibid.

Bibliography

1. UNPUBLISHED PRIMARY SOURCES

Britain

Public Record Office:
Cabinet Papers (CAB 128–9)
Colonial Office (CO 537, CO 733)
Foreign Office (FO 371, FO 800, FO 816)
Prime Minister's Office (PREM 8)

Middle East Centre, St. Antony's College, Oxford:
Alan Cunningham's Private Papers
Henry Gurney's Private Papers

USA

Independence, Missouri:
Clark M. Clifford Papers
Harry S. Truman's Private Papers
UN Official Records

National Archives, Washington:
State Department Files (867N, 501.BB Palestine)

Israel

Central Zionist Archives, Jerusalem:
Political Department, Jewish Agency (S 25)
Records of the People's Directorship

Israel State Archives, Jerusalem:
Foreign Office Files

Ben Gurion Archives, Sdeh Boker:
Ben Gurion's Diary

2. PUBLISHED PRIMARY SOURCES

The Arab World

Ahmad, Rif'at Sayd, *Watha'iq Harb Filastin*: *al-Millafat al-Siriyya lil Generaliyat al-'Arab* (The Documents of the War of Palestine 1948: the Secret Files of the Arab Armies), (Cairo, 1988).
Al-Hashimi, Taha, *Mudhakirat al-Harb* (War Memoirs), (Beirut, 1978), 2 Vols.
Ibish, Yusuf, *Mudhakirat al-Amir Adil Arslan* (The Memoirs of the Amir Adil Arslan), (Beirut, 1983).
Sakakini, Khalil, *Kadha Ana, Ya Dunya* (This is me, Oh World) (The Diaries of Khalil Sakakini), (Jerusalem, 1959).
Shakib, Ibrahim, *Al-Harb Filastin 1948*: *Ru'uwiyya Misriyya* (The War of Palestine 1948: The Egyptian Side), (Cairo, 1988).

Britain

Hansard

Israel

Avizohar, Meir and Bareli, Avi, (eds), *Achshav o L'olam Lo* (Now or Never: Proceedings of Mapai in the Closing Year of the British Mandate, Introductions and Documents), (Beit Berl, 1989), 2 vols.
Israel Defence Forces, *Toldot Milhemet Hakomemiyut* (The War of Independence), (Tel Aviv, 1959).
Israel State Archives, *Haprotocolim shel Minhelet Ha'am* (The Protocols of the People's Directorship), (Tel Aviv, 1979).
Israel State Archives, *Te'udot Lemediniyut Hahutz shel Medinat Israel, 14 May–30 September 1948* (Documents on the Foreign Policy of Israel 14 May–30 September 1948), ed. Yehoushua Freundlich, vol 1 (Jerusalem, 1981).
Israel State Archives, *Te'udot Lemediniyut Hahutz shel Medinat Israel, Sihot Shvitat-Haneshek 'im Medinot 'Arav, December 1948–July 1949* (Documents on the Foreign Policy of Israel, December 1948–July 1949), ed. Yemima Rosenthal, vol. 3 (Jerusalem, 1983).
Israel State Archives, *Te'udot Lemediniyut Hahutz shel Medinat Israel, May–December 1949* (Documents on the Foreign Policy of Israel, May–December 1949), ed. Yemima Rosenthal, vol. 4 (Jerusalem, 1986).

Israel State Archives, *Te'udot Lemediniyut Hahutz shel Medinat Israel 1950* (Documents on the Foreign Policy of Israel, 1950), ed. Yehosua Freundlich, vol. 5 (Jerusalem, 1988).

Rivlin, Gershon and Orren, Elhanan, (eds), *Yoman Hamilhama-Tashah, 1948–1949* (David Ben Gurion's War Diary), (Tel Aviv, 1982), 3 vols.

Sharett Moshe, *Besha'ar Haumot*, (At the Gate of the Nations), (Tel Aviv, 1958).

Shmuel Segev (trans.), *Meahorei Hapargod* (Behind the Curtain: Hebrew Translation of the Proceeding of the Iraqi Parliamentary Committee on the War in Palestine), (Tel Aviv, 1954).

Slutzky, Yehuda, *Sefer Toldot Hahagana* (The History of the Hagana), (Tel Aviv, 1972) 3 vols. (Co-editors Shaul Avigur, Yitzhak Ben Zvi, Elazar Galilili, Ben Zion Dinur and Gershon Rivlin).

— *Kizur Sefer Toldot Hahagana* (The Abridged Book of the Hagana), (Tel Aviv, 1978).

USA

Foreign Relations of the US 1948, vol. 5.
Foreign Relations of the US 1949, vol. 6.
Foreign Relations of the US 1950, vol. 6.

3. NEWSPAPERS AND PERIODICALS

Al-Ahram (Cairo)
Aakhar Sa'a (Beirut)
Bourse Egyptienne (Cairo)
Al-Difa'a (Cairo)
Al-Difa'a (Jerusalem)
Filastin (Jaffa and Jerusalem)
Haaretz (Tel Aviv)
Al-Hayat (Beirut)
Manchester Guardian
Al-Misri (Cairo)
Al-Nahar (Beirut)
The New York Times
The Times (London)

4. SECONDARY SOURCES (ENGLISH)

Abidi, Hyder A., *Jordan: A Political Study, 1948–1957* (New York, 1965).

Abu-Manneh, Butrus, 'The Husaynis: The Rise of a Notable Family in 18th-Century Palestine', in David Kushner (ed.), *Palestine in the Late Ottoman Period; Political, Social and Economic Transformation* (Jerusalem, 1986), pp. 93–108.

Antonius, George, *The Arab Awakening* (New York, 1979).

Bar-Joseph, Uri, *The Best of Enemies, Israel and Transjordan in the War of 1948* (London, 1987).
Bernadotte, Folke, *To Jerusalem* (London, 1951).
Bowman, Humphrey, *A Middle East Window* (London, 1942).
Buehrig, Edmond, *The UN and the Palestine Refugees* (New York, 1971).
Bullock, Alan, *Ernest Bevin, Foreign Secretary, 1945–1951*, (London, 1983).
Cattan, Henry, *Palestine and International Law: The Legal Aspects of the Arab–Israeli Conflict* (London, 1973).
Cohen, Michael J., *Palestine and the Great Powers, 1945–1948* (Princeton, 1982).
—— 'The Birth of Israel – Diplomatic Failure, Military Success', *Jerusalem Quarterly*, 17(Autumn).
Crossman, Richard, *Palestine Mission: A Personal Record* (London, 1947).
Dann, Uriel, *Studies in the History of Transjordan, 1920–1949, The Making of State* (Boulder, 1987).
Dawn, Ernest C., *From Ottomanism to Arabism* (Illinois, 1973).
de Azcarate, Pablo, *Mission in Palestine* (Washington, 1966).
Divine, Robert A., *American Immigration Policy, 1942–1952* (New York, 1969).
Flapan Simha, *The Birth of Israel; Myths and Realities* (New York, 1987).
Forsythe, David P., *UN Peacemaking: The Conciliation Commission for Palestine* (Balitmore, 1972).
Ganin, Zvi, *Truman, American Jewry and Israel, 1945–1948* (New York, 1979).
Garcia-Granados, Jorge, *The Birth of Israel* (New York, 1948).
Glubb, John B., *A Soldier with the Arabs* (London, 1957).
Goldmann, Nahum, *Memoirs* (London, 1970).
Haron, Miriam J., 'The British Decision to Give the Palestinian Question to the UN', *Middle Eastern Studies*, 17/2(April 1981), pp. 241–8.
Heikal, Muhammad Hassanein, 'Reflections on a Nation in Crisis, 1948', *Journal of Palestine Studies*, 69/1(Autumn 1988).
Heller, Yosef, 'Failure of a Mission: Bernadotte and Palestine 1948', *Journal of Contemporary History*, 14/3(January 1979).
Hoffman, Bruce, *The Failure of the British Military Strategy with Palestine, 1939–1947* (Tel Aviv, 1983).
Al-Hout, Bayan, 'The Palestinian Political Elite During the Mandatory Period', *Journal of Palestine Studies*, 9/1(1979), pp. 85–111.
Jones, Martin, *Failure in Palestine: British and United States Policy after the Second World War* (London, 1986).
Kamen, Charles S., 'After the Catastrophe II, the Arabs in Israel, 1948–1951', *Middle Eastern Studies*, 24/1(January 1988), pp. 68–109.
Kedourie, Eli, *England and the Middle East* (London, 1987).
—— *The Chatham House Version and other Middle Eastern Studies* (New York, 1984).
Khalidi, Walid, 'Plan Dalet: Master Plan for the Conquest of Palestine', *Journal of Palestine Studies*, 18/69(Autumn 1988), pp. 4–20.
—— 'The Arab Perspective', in William Roger Louis and Robert S. Stookey (eds), *The End of the Palestine Mandate* (London, 1986).
Khalil Muhammad, *The Arab States and the Arab League* (Beirut, 1962), 2 vols.
Kimche, Jon and David, *Both Sides of the Hill* (London, 1960).

Kirkbride, Alec, *From the Wings* (London, 1976).
Klieman, Aaron S., *Foundations of British Policy in the Arab World: The Cairo Conference 1921* (Baltimore, 1978).
Krammer, Aaron, *The Forgotten Friendship* (Illinois, 1974).
Kushner, David (ed.), *Palestine in the Late Ottoman Period: Political, Social and Economic Transformation* (Jerusalem, 1986).
Lockman, Zachary, 'Original Sin', *Middle East Report*, May–June 1988.
Lorch, Nethanel, *The Edge of the Sword: Israel's War of Independence, 1947-1949* (New York, 1968).
Louis, William Roger, *The British Empire in the Middle East 1945-1951; Arab Nationalism, the United States and Post War Imperialism* (Oxford, 1985).
Lundström, Age, *Death of a Mediator* (Washington, 1968).
McDonald, James, G., *My Mission to Israel* (New York, 1951).
McGhee, George, *Envoy to the Middle World* (New York, 1983).
Meyer, Thomas, 'The Military Force of Islam, the Society of the Muslim Brotherhood and the Palestine Question, 1945-1948' in Eli Kedourie and Slyvia Haim (eds), *Zionism and Arabism and Israel* (London, 1981).
Monroe, Elizabeth, *Britain's Moment in the Middle East, 1914-1971* (London, 1981).
—— 'Mr. Bevin's Arab Policy' in *St. Antony's Papers*, 11.
Morris, Benny, *1948 and After* (Oxford, 1990).
—— *The Birth of the Palestinian Refugee Problem, 1947-1949* (Cambridge, 1988).
—— 'Operation Dani and the Palestinian Exodus from Lydda and Ramleh in 1948', *The Middle East Journal*, 40/1(Winter 1986), pp. 82–109.
—— 'Yosef Weitz and the Transfer Committees, 1948-1949', *Middle East Studies*, 22/4(October 1986), pp. 522–61.
Murad, Abbas, *The Political Role of the Jordanian Army* (Beirut, 1973).
Nachmani, Amikam, *Great Power Discord in Palestine: The Anglo-American Committee of Inquiry into the Problem of European Jewry and Palestine, 1945-46* (London, 1986).
Nevakivi, Jukka, *Britain, France and the Arab Middle East, 1914-1920* (New York, 1969).
Nevo, Joseph, 'The Arabs of Palestine 1947-48: Military and Political Activity', *Middle Eastern Studies*, 23/1(January 1987), pp. 3–38.
Ovendale, Ritchie, *Britain, the United States, and the End of the Palestine Mandate, 1942-1948* (London, 1989).
Owen, Roger (ed.) *Studies in the Social and Economic History of Palestine in the 19th and 20th Centuries* (London, 1982).
Pappé, Ilan, *Britain and the Arab-Israeli Conflict, 1948-1951* (London, 1988).
—— 'Britain and the Palestinian Refugees, 1948-1950', *Middle East Focus*, 9/2(Fall 1986), pp. 43–67.
—— 'From Open Confrontation to a Tacit Alliance', *Middle Eastern Studies*, 26/4(October 1990), pp. 561–82.
—— 'Moshe Sharett, David Ben Gurion and the "Palestinian Option", 1948-1956', *Studies in Zionism*, 7/1(1986), pp. 77–97.
—— 'Sir Alec Kirkbride and the Making of Greater Transjordan', in *Asian and African Studies*, 23/1(March 1989), pp. 43–70.

Person, Sune, *Mediation and Assassination: Count Bernadotte's Mission to Palestine, 1948* (London, 1979).

Plascov, Avi, 'The Palestinians on Jordan's Borders', in R. Owen (ed.) *Studies in the Social and Economic History of Palestine in the 19th and 20th Centuries* (London, 1982), pp. 204–26.

Porath, Yehoshua, 'On the Writing of Arab History by Israeli Scholars', *The Jerusalem Quarterly*, 32(Summer 1984).

—— 'The Palestinians and the Negotiations for the British–Hejazi Treaty', *Asian and African Studies*, 8/1(1972), pp. 20–49.

Rabinowitz, Itamr and Reinharz, Yehuda, *Israel in the Middle East* (New York, 1984).

Ro'i, Ya'acov, 'Soviet–Israeli Relations 1947–1954', in Michael Confino and Shimon Shamir, (eds) *The USSR and the Middle East* (Tel Aviv, 1974), pp. 123–46.

Sachar, Howard, *Europe Leaves the Middle East* (New York, 1972).

Salibi, Kamal S., *The Modern History of Lebanon* (London, 1965).

Schiffer, Varda, 'The 1949 Israeli Offer to Repatriate 100,000 Palestinian Refugees', *Middle East Focus*, 9/2(Fall 1986), pp. 14–20.

Schölch, Alexander, *Palestina in Umbruch, 1882–1956* (Stuttgart, 1986).

—— 'European Penetration and the Economic Development of Palestine, 1856–1882', in Roger Owen (ed.), *Studies in the Social and Economic History of Palestine in the 19th and 20th Centuries* (London, 1982), pp. 10–87.

—— 'Was There a Feudal System in Ottoman Lebanon and Palestine', in David Kushner, (ed.), *Palestine in the Late Ottoman Period: Political, Social and Economic Transformation* (Jerusalem, 1986), pp. 130–145.

Segev, Tom, *1949, The First Israelis* (New York, 1986).

Shlaim, Avi, *Collusion Across the Jordan* (Oxford, 1988).

—— 'Husni Zaim and the Plan to Resettle Palestinian Refugees in Syria', *Middle East Focus*, Fall 1986, pp. 26–31.

—— *The Politics of Partition: King Abdullah, the Zionists, and Palestine 1921–1951* (Oxford, 1990).

—— 'The Rise and Fall of the All-Palestine Government in Gaza', *Journal of Palestinian Studies*, 20/1, no. 77(1990), pp. 37–53.

Stanger, Cary David, 'A Haunting Legacy: the Assassination of Bernadotte', *The Middle East Journal*, 42(1988), pp. 260–370.

Stein, Keneth, *The Land Question of Palestine, 1917–1939* (North Carolina, 1984).

Sykes, Christopher, *Crossroads to Israel* (Indiana, 1965).

Tamari, Salim, 'Factionalism and Class Formation in Recent Palestinian History', in Roger Owen (ed.), *Studies in the Social and Economic History of Palestine in the 19th and 20th Centuries* (London, 1982), pp. 177–203.

Teveth, Shabtai, 'The Palestinian Refugee Problem and its Origins', *Middle Eastern Studies*, 26/2(April 1990), pp. 214–49.

Touval, Sadia, *The Peace Brokers* (Princeton, 1982).

Truman, Harry S., *Years of Trial and Hope: Memoirs by Harry S. Truman* (New York, 1965).

Weizmann, Chaim, *Trial and Error* (London, 1949).

Wilson, Mary C., *King Abdullah, Britain and the Making of Jordan* (Cambridge, 1987).

Zangwill, Israel, 'The Return to Palestine', *The New Liberal Review*, 2(1901).

Zasloff, 'Great Britain and Palestine: A Study of the Problem before the UN', (D.Phil Thesis submitted to l'Université de Geneve, 1952).

Zeine, Zeine N., *The Struggle for Arab Independence* (Beirut, 1960).

5. SECONDARY SOURCES (ARABIC)

Abd al-Hadi, Mahdi, *Al-Masala al-Filastiniyya wa Mashar'i al-Hulul al-Siyasiyya* (The Palestine Question and the Plans for its Political Solutions), (Beirut, 1975).

Al-Alami, Ahmad, *Al-Harb 1948* (The War of 1948), (Acre, 1989).

Al-Arif, Arif, *Al-Nakba*, (The Catastrophe), (Beirut, 1988), 3 vols.

Awdeh, Salima, *Misr wa al-Qadiyya al-Filastiniyya* (Egypt and the Palestinian Problem), (Cairo, 1986).

Al-Daly, Wahid, *Asrar al-Jami'a al-'Arabiyya wa-Abd al-Rahman Azzam* (The Secrets of the Arab League and Abd al-Rahman Azzam), (Cairo, 1978).

Darwaza, Muhammad Izat, *Hawla al-Haraka al-'Arabiyya al-Haditha* (About the Modern Arab Movement), (Sidon, 1959), 2 vols.

Hakim, Sami, *Tariq al-Nakba*, (The Road to Catatrophe), (Cairo, 1969).

Al-Hawari, Muhammad Nimr, *Sir al-Nakba* (The Secret of the Defeat), (Nazareth, 1955).

Heikal, Muhammad Hassanein, *'Mudhakirat al-Siyasa al-Misriyya* (Recollections on Egyptian Politics), (Cairo, 1978).

Hilal, Rada, 'Al-Siyasa al-Misriyya wa al-Masala al-Filastiniyya, 1922–1948' (Egyptian Politics and the Question of Palestine), *Shu'un Filastiniyya*, 190(January 1989), pp. 29–60.

Al-Husayni, Muhammad Amin, *Haqai'q 'an Filastin* (The Truth on Palestine), (Cairo, 1956).

Jabara, Taysir, *Dirasat fi Tarikh Filastin Al-Hadith* (Studies in the Modern History of Palestine), (Jerusalem, 1987).

Jarar, Husni Adham, *Al-Hajj Amin al-Husayni: Ra'id Jihad wa Batl al-Qaidyya al-Filastiniyya* (Hajj Amin al-Husayni, the Commander of the Struggle and the Hero of the Palestine Question), (Amman, 1987).

Khaled Ali, Falah, *Al-Harb al-'Arabiyya al-Isra'iliyya, 1984–1949, wa Taasis Isra'il* (The Arab–Israeli War, 1948–9 and the Foundation of Israel), (Cairo, 1982).

Al-Khuly, Hasan Sabri, *Siyasat al-Isti'imar wa al-Sahayuniyya tijja Filastin* (The Imperialist and Zionist Policy towards Palestine), (Cairo, 1973), 2 vols.

Musa, Sulayman and al-Madi, Munib, *Tarikh al-Urdun fi'l-Qarn al-'Ashrin* (The History of Jordan in the Twentieth Century), (Amman, 1959).

Nafi'a, Hasan, *Misr wa al-Sira'a al-'Arabi al-Isra'ili* (Egypt and the Arab–Israeli Conflict), (Beirut, 1984).

Al-Nimr, Ihsan, *Tarich Jabal Nablus wa al-Balqa* (The History of Mount Nablus and al-Balqa), (Nablus, 1975).

Al-Qasri, Muhammad Fa'iz, *Harb Filastin al-'Aam 1948* (The Palestine War 1948), (Cairo, 1961).

Rashidi, Ahmad, 'Al-Jami'a al-'Arabiyya wa Qadiyat Filastin' (The Arab League and the Problem of Palestine), *Shu'un 'Arabiyya*, 19 (September 1982), pp. 180–5.

Al-Rusan, Mamduh, *Al-Iraq wa Qadayya al-Sharq al-'Arabi al-Qawmi* (Iraq and Pan Arabist Problems), (Beirut, 1979).

Sakhnini, Isam, *Filastin al-Dawla* (Palestine – the State), (Acre, 1986).

Salama, Ahmad, *Al-Kifah 'an Filastin 'Arabiyya* (The Struggle for Arab Palestine), (Acre, 1988).

Al-Salihi, Abd al-Rahamn, 'Harb al-'Aam 1948: Ru'uwiyya 'Arabiyya wa-'Alamiyya' (The War of 1948, an Arab and an International Viewpoint), *Shu'un Filastiniyya*, 191(February 1989).

Al-Sayigh, Anis, *Al-Hashimiyun wa Qadiyat Filastin* (The Hashemites and the Problem of Palestine), (Beirut, 1966).

Shakib, Samih S., 'Shakhziyat al-Mufti wa Nashtatiha' (The Personality of the Mufti and its Activity), *Shu'un Filastinyya*, 186(September 1988), pp. 87–90.

Al-Sharif, Kamal Isma'il, *Al-Ikhwan al-Muslimun fi Harb Filastin* (The Muslim Brethren in the Palestine War), (Cairo, n.d.).

Al-Shuqayri, Ahmad, *'Arba'in 'Aam fil Hayat al-'Arabiyya wa al-Duwaliyya* (Forty Years in the Arab and International History), (Beirut, 1960).

Al-Tal, Abdullah, *Karithat Filastin* (The Palestine Disaster), (Cairo, 1959).

Zu'aytar, Akram, *Al-Qadiyya Al-Filastinyya* (The Palestine Problem), (Cairo, 1965).

6. SECONDARY SOURCES (HEBREW)

Arieli, Yehosua, 'Azmaut Israel Beprespectiva Historit' (The Independence of Israel in a Historical Perspective), *Betefuzot Ha-Gola*, 18(1981/2).

Beeri, Eli'ezer, *Reschit Hasichsuch Israel 'Arav* (The Beginning of the Israeli–Arab Conflict), (Tel Aviv, 1985).

Ben Gurion, David, *Behilahem Israel* (When Israel Fought in Battle), (Tel Aviv, 1975), 2 vols.

—— *Medinat Israel Hamehudeshet* (The Restored State of Israel), (Tel Aviv, 1969).

—— *Toldot Milhemet Hakomemiyut* (History of the War of Independence), (Tel Aviv, 1967).

Cohen, Gabriel, 'Mediniyut Britaniya 'Erev Milhemet Haazma'ut' (British Policy on the Eve of the War of Independence) in Y. Wallach, *Hayinu Keholmim* (We were like Dreamers), (Tel Aviv, 1985), pp. 13–77.

Eilam Yigal, *Hahagana: Haderech Haziyonit Lakoah* (The Hagana: the Zionist Way to Power), (Tel Aviv, 1979).

—— *Memalei Hapekudot* (The Obeyers of Orders), (Jerusalem, 1990).

Elath, Eliahu, *Hama'avak 'al Hameidna* (The Struggle for Statehood) (Tel Aviv, 1982), 2 vols.

Elpeleg, Zvi, *Hamufti Hagadol* (The Grand Mufti), (Tel Aviv, 1989).

Ferari, Silvero, 'Hakes Hakadosh ve-Be'ayat Eretz Israel aharey Milhemet

Ha'olam Hashniya; binum Yerushalayim ve-Haganat Hamekomot Hakedoshim' (The Holy Seal and the Internationalization of Jerusalem'), *Yahadut Zemanenu*, 3(1986), pp. 187–209.

Freundlich, Yehosua, 'Hamediniyut HaZiyonit likrat Hakamat Hamedina, August 1946–May 1948' (Zionist Policy towards the Establishment of the State of Israel, August 1946–May 1948), (Ph.D. Thesis, Hebrew University of Jerusalem, 1986).

Gelber, Yoav, 'Maga'im Diplomatim Terem Hitnagshut Zevait – Hamasa Umatan Bein Hasochnut Hayehudit Lemizrayim ve Yarden, 1946–1948' (The Negotiations of the Jewish Agency with Egypt and Transjordan, 1946–1948), *Cathedra*, 35(April 1985).

Halamish, Aviva, 'Emdat Artzot Habrit be-Parashat Oniyat Ham'apilim "Exodus 1947"' (The United States' Position in the Exodus Affair) *Yahadut Zemanenu*, 3 (1986), pp. 209–27.

Heller, Yosef, 'Bein Meshichiut le Realism Politi – Lohamei Herut Israel ve-Hashelah Ha'arvit, 1940–1947' (Between Messianism and Realpolitik – the Stern Gang and the Arab Question, 1940–1947), *Yahadut Zemanenu*, 1(1983), pp. 223–48.

Ilan, Amizur, *America, Britanya ve-Eretz Israel* (The USA, Britain and Palestine), (Jerusalem, 1979).

Kaufman, Menachem, 'Hanemanut ma he? Tochnit Hanemanut shel Artzot Habrit le-Pitron Be'ayat Eretz Israel, 1948' (The American Trusteeship Proposal), *Yahadut Zemanenu*, 1(1984), pp. 249–73.

—— 'Demut Hamdina Hayehudit be'eney Hava'ad Hayehudi Haamerikani, 1947–1948' (The State of Israel as Conceived by the American Jewish Committee, 1947–1948), *Yahadut Zemanenu*, 3(1986), pp. 171–85.

Levi, Izhak, *Tish'a Qabin* (Jerusalem in the War of Independence), (Jerusalem, 1986).

Lorch, Nethanel, 'Hahistoriographia shel Milhemet Ha'azmaut' (The Historiography of the War of Independence), *Cathedra*, vol. 1.

Meyer, Thomas, 'Medinot 'Arab ve Shelat Eretz Israel Bashanim 1945–1948' (The Arab States and the Question of Palestine, 1945–1948), in Y. Wallach, *Hayinu Keholmim* (We Were Like Dreamers), (Tel Aviv, 1985).

Milstein, Uri, *Milhemet Ha'azmaut* (The War of Independence), (Tel Aviv, 1989), 3 vols.

Nevo, Joseph, 'Hafalestinayim ve Hamedina Hayehudit' (The Palestinians and the Jewish State, 1947–1948), in Y. Wallach.

—— 'Hahitpathut Hapolitit shel Hatnu'a Haleumit Ha'aravit Hafalestinait, 1939–1945' (The Political Development of the National Arab Palestinian Movement, 1939–1945), (Ph.D. thesis, Tel Aviv University, 1977).

Nimrod, Yoram, 'Defusim Beyahsei Yehudim-'Aravim', (Patterns of Israeli–Arab Relations, The Formative Years, 1947–1950), (Ph.D. Thesis, Jerusalem 1985), 2 vols.

Pa'il, Meir, 'Hafqa'at Haribonut Hamedinit shel Filastin miyedei Hafalestinim' (The Expropriation of the Sovereignty of the State of Palestine from the Palestinians), *Ziyonut*, 3(1973), pp. 438–45.

Porath, Yehosuha, *Zemihat Hatnu'a Ha'aravit Hafalestinait, 1918–1929* (The

Emergence of the Palestinian National Movement, 1918–1929), (Tel Aviv, 1971).

Sasson, Eliahu, *Baderech el Hashalom* (On the Road to Peace), (Tel Aviv, 1978).

Shalev, Arieh, *Shituf Pe'ula bezel 'Imut* (Co-operation under the Shadow of Conflict), (Tel Aviv, 1989).

Shefer, Gabriel, 'Pitron Kolel mul Mitum Hasichsuch Haisraeli Ha'aravi; Behina Mehudeshet shel Hahitnagshut bein Moshe Sharett ve David Ben Gurion' (A Comprehensive Solution *vis-à-vis* Conflict Management of the Arab–Israeli Confict: A Reappraisal of the Confrontation between Moshe Sharett and David Ben Gurion) in Shmuel Ettinger, *Haziyonut ve Hashela Ha'aravit* (Zionism and the Arab Question), (Jerusalem, 1979).

Shimoni, Ya'acov, 'Ha'aravim likrat Milhemet Israel 'Arav, 1945–1948' (The Arabs on the eve of the Arab–Israeli war, 1945–1948), *Hamizrah Hehadash*, 12(1962).

Talmon, Ya'acov, *Be'idan Haalimut* (In the Age of Violence), (Tel Aviv, 1974).

Wallach, Y., *Hayinu Keholmim* (We Were Like Dreamers), (Tel Aviv, 1985).

Map 1 The Jewish Settlement in Palestine (1945)

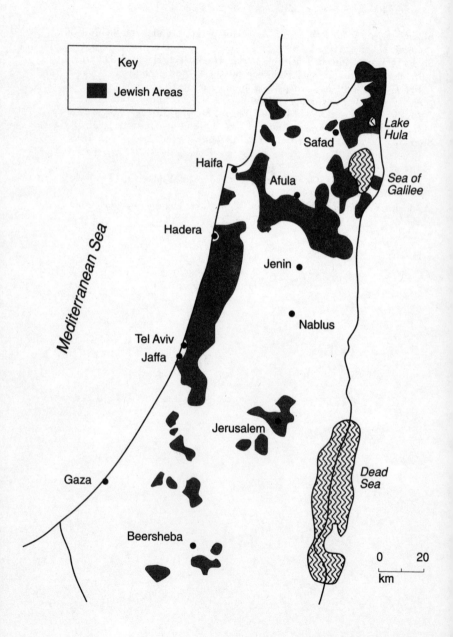

Key

Jewish Areas

Lake
Hula

Safad

Haifa

Afula

Sea of
Galilee

Mediterranean Sea

Hadera

Jenin

Nablus

Tel Aviv

Jaffa

Jerusalem

Gaza

Dead
Sea

Beersheba

0   20
km

Map 2 The UN Partition Resolution

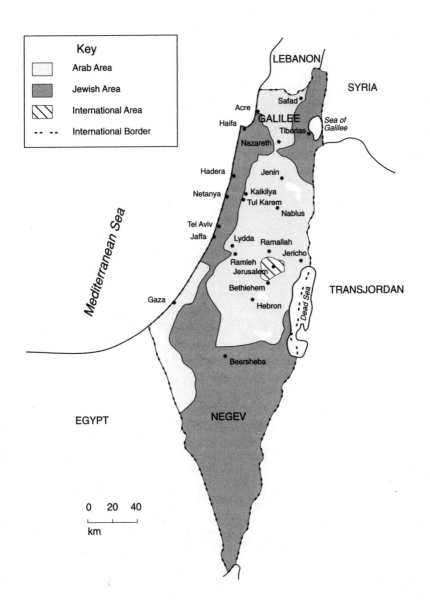

Key

- Arab Area
- Jewish Area
- International Area
- International Border

LEBANON

SYRIA

Acre

Safad

Haifa

GALILEE

Sea of Galilee

Tiberias

Nazareth

Hadera

Jenin

Netanya

Kalkilya

Tul Karem

Nablus

Tel Aviv

Jaffa

Lydda

Ramallah

Jericho

Ramleh

Jerusalem

Bethlehem

Gaza

Dead Sea

TRANSJORDAN

Hebron

Beersheba

EGYPT

NEGEV

Mediterranean Sea

0   20   40

km

Map 3 Israel 1949

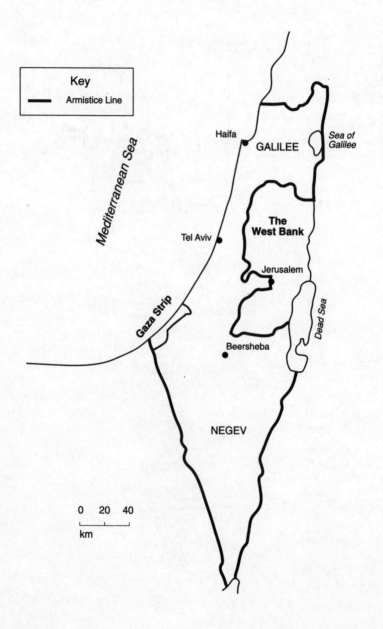

Key

Armistice Line

Mediterranean Sea

Haifa

GALILEE

Sea of Galilee

Tel Aviv

The West Bank

Jerusalem

Dead Sea

Gaza Strip

Beersheba

NEGEV

0 20 40

km

Index